THEOLOGIES OF WAR AND PEACE AMONG JEWS, CHRISTIANS AND MUSLIMS

Albert B. Randall

Toronto Studies in Theology
Volume 77

The Edwin Mellen Press
Lewiston•Queenston•Lampeter

Library of Congress Cataloging-in-Publication Data

Randall, Albert B.
    Theologies of war and peace among Jews, Christians, and Muslims /
Albert B. Randall.
        p. cm.-- (Toronto studies in theology ; v. 77)
    Includes bibliographical references and index.
    ISBN 0-7734-8254-7 (hc.)
    1. War--Religious aspects--Judaism. 2. Peace--Religious aspects-
-Judaism. 3. War--Religious aspects--Christianity. 4. Peace-
-Religious aspects--Christianity. 5. War--Religious aspects--Islam.
6. Peace--Religious aspects--Islam. I. Title. II. Series.
BM538.P3R36 1998
291.1' .7873--dc21   98-40015
                                                                    CIP

This is volume 77 in the continuing series
Toronto Studies in Theology
Volume 77 ISBN 0-7734-8254-7
TST Series ISBN 0-88946-975-X

A CIP catalog record for this book is available from the British Library.

The Edwin Mellen Press   The Edwin Mellen Press
Box 450   Box 67
Lewiston, New York   Queenston, Ontario
USA 14092-0450   CANADA L0S 1L0

The Edwin Mellen Press, Ltd.
Lampeter, Ceredigion, Wales
UNITED KINGDOM SA48 8LT

Printed in the United States of America

TO: Albert, Jaimie and Alicia

For my father Albert, who now in God's presence eternally knows the peace of spirit he so richly deserved but never found in his incarnate existence;

For my daughters Jaimie and Alicia, memories of your childhoods continually fill me with joy and wonder, and your love gives my heart and soul peace.

ACKNOWLEDGMENTS

The twentieth century philosopher Gabriel Marcel reminds us that only fools claim to be self-made. The best in each of us always comes as gifts of knowledge and love from other human beings. The great physicist Isaac Newton recognized his debt to earlier thinkers when he remarked that if he had accomplished great things in his life it was because he stood on the shoulders of giants. The explorations of war and peace that comprise this study have been possible only because of the gifts of others, and it is appropriate that they are recognized.

I am indebted to Dr. John Duke Anthony, the National Council on US-Arab Relations and the Joseph J. Malone Foundation for the opportunity to visit Kuwait and Syria during the summer of 1992 and Yemen in the summer of 1995. These journeys opened my eyes to many stereotypes about Islam and the Middle East and helped create a passion for further study of and travel in this astounding part of the world. Further, I am deeply grateful to ACOR (The American Center for Oriental Research in Amman) for a grant to spend two months in Jordan during the winter of 1994-95. Much of the material that forms the basis for this study was uncovered in their excellent library and in trips to Israel also funded by the grant.

I am also indebted to Austin Peay State University for the following support of my research. (1) Faculty Development grants for travel to Kuwait and Syria in 1992 and Yemen in 1995; (2) two Tower Fund grants--one for travel to the libraries at Louisville Theological Presbyterian Seminary and Ohio State University to complete the research began in Amman and one grant to help with manuscript preparation; (3) one Professional Faculty Development Leave of a semester for writing the first draft of the manuscript. Since a University is really an abstraction, it is two academic administrators who supported my research and activities that must be thanked: Dr. John Butler, past Vice-President for Academic Affairs and Dr. D'Ann Campbell, past Dean of the College of Arts and Sciences. Without their professional concern for scholarship and their warm human support, this project would not have been possible.

Several colleagues also contributed their time, encouragement and expertise: Mr. Joseph Wesley Jarrett, a graduate student at APSU, for his editing the first draft; Dr. William P. Frost of Dayton University for his decade long encouragement and support of my scholarly efforts and the superb **Preface** he wrote for the published manuscript; Dr. Bill Cooney of Briar Cliff College, a co-Marcellean, who edited the final manuscript and provided a review for the Mellen Press; and Dr. Royce Jones of Illinois College, a philosophical soul mate since graduate school in the 1960s, for his pre-publication review.

I should also thank my two philosophical colleagues, Dr. Mark Michael and Dr. Ann Edwards, for their willingness to cover many of my responsibilities during my semester leave and Dr. Kip Muir, the chair of my Department, for his enthusiastic support of professional development and scholarship.

While I appreciate the kindness of several publishing firms for their permissions to cite from other works, the generosity of two publishers stands out. Excerpts from **The Jerusalem Bible**, copyright (c) 1966 by Darton, Longman and Todd, Ltd. and Doubleday are reprinted by permission of Bantam Doubleday Dell Publishing Group. The extensive citations from A. Yusuf Ali's translation, **The Holy Qur'an**, and excerpts from his informative exigetical notes are reprinted by permission of Tahrike Tarsde Qur'an, Inc. Without permission to use both of these translations, this study would have been seriously compromised.

I am grateful for the artistic talents of two colleagues. Given the photographic limitations of her human subject, Ms. Toril Starmer of **The Leaf-**

Chronicle graciously provided the author's picture on the back cover, and the **Leaf-Chronicle**, for whom I write a weekly column on religion, granted permission to use the photograph. Dr. Bruce Childs, Professor of Art at Austin Peay State University, began with my amateurish cover design and created a visual delight for the front cover.

Finally, at the heart of my life are three women whose love and encouragement are the sources of my own search for spiritual peace and hope: my wife Jeanie and my daughters Jaimie and Alicia. The best of what is in me comes as gifts from them. Without them my life would be a spiritual desert.

TABLE OF CONTENTS

PREFACE

The Near East is a hotbed of political divisions rooted in ancient traditions which have great stakes in their territories, flags and symbols marking who is what. Each camp has its own beliefs and private lines with the God of revelation. History records battles of enormous intensity between forces in their claim for superiority and the right for dominance. In the process lines are drawn which provide some degree of stability. But the issues are not settled and the tensions remain explosive.

The irony is that the competing strongholds are all "Children of Abraham." This is really the core of Albert Randall's journey in diagnosing the divisions so that they can be placed in wider perspective which has unifying energies. The danger is that the analysis may be so simplistic that it may become an easy bone of contention. Then the fires may flair up again in new rounds of assaults.

Bert Randall is not a journalist or a political analyst. He is not out there to get a story. Bert is truly moved by the enormous sufferings caused by unnecessary divisions. As a theologian rooted in Biblical spirituality, he knows that the beliefs which separate Jews, Christians and Muslims are far less significant than the faith in life and God's creation which characterizes the Biblical roots.

Much can be learned from political debates on talk shows. After a while one recognizes the different players. Not just their faces but also their positions become familiar. Almost never do participants of such public debates learn from each other. Insights are presented by stating one's views, defending them, and trying to convince the audience that these views are superior. The exchanges are battles for dominance.

Randall approaches the agony of the Near East not as a talk-show host. On the contrary, he becomes a listener and student of the enormity at play. But he is also a professional. First and foremost, Randall is a minister of people. He aborted a promising career as a mathematician to dedicate himself explicitly to churching people who gather in the name of God's Spirit Who breaks down divisive walls and creates celebrations of life. Randall's ministry is enriched and permeated by falling in love with his wife. Together they formed their family, the home of two daughters. Randall is a lover, husband, and father.

In his great care for the integrity of the human spirit, Randall became a dedicated student of the Christian tradition. In the process he earned a Master's degree in theology and a Ph.D. in Philosophy, which qualified him for teaching at Austin Peay State University. His colleagues respect him for his telling integrity and twice elected him as the President of their Faculty Senate.

These personal notes are important for understanding the true nature of Randall's voluminous book, **Theologies of War and Peace Among Jews, Christians and Muslims**. Neurophysiology and its study of people's mentalities recognizes that sane and healthy people demonstrate an inner peace. This shows itself in terms of a mature involvement in species preservative activities. In the biographical sketches of Randall, one finds someone who makes himself available again and again for people as people. Beliefs and systems are only means by which the promises of life can be activated.

Randall identifies himself with Gabriel Marcel, known for his philosophy of co-existentialism. Key insights of co-existentialism are found in the basic idea that people are not individualistic islands but exist together in communities of persons. The life of co-existence is rooted in the energy of making oneself available to others. Randall regards this as a significant appropriation of the Biblical faith.

Marcel's philosophy can be regarded religious insofar as it bespeaks a transcendental awareness of meaning. Randall personifies such a religious awareness when he personally traveled to the Near East at different times to experience for himself the panoramas of these historically conditioned divisions of Abraham's children. His heart aches seeing that so much of the cultural richness of these traditions is also the breeding ground of the deadly wars and destructive tearing down of each other. But his heart delights in sensing a longing for peace among the partisans. It means, they all recognize that there must be something greater than their present predicament. For Randall, the greatest frustration of all is that their common faith contains all the promises of reaching this new land of peace. If they just would see, hear, and let their hearts resound the immense depth of human compassion and quality care for one's neighbors, then these promises can become reality.

How can one explain such an irony, that the common ground of faith is not energizing the healing of divisions? Perhaps, appealing to the spirituality of the Biblical faith is not enough? There is a psychological dimension which needs to be considered in the assessment of the complexity of it all. Such information can be gleaned from recent studies in neurophysiology about the religious experience.

In his "Psychological and physiological responses to stress," (*Acta Physiologica Scandinavica,* Vol. 161, Supplementum 640, November 1997, 10-25) James P. Henry offers an physiological and psychological appreciation of why some people have a need for an explicit concentration of a "Higher Power." It involves a loss of the brain's right hemisphere function, which provides an inner sense of proportion. Much is learned from studies of alcoholics who join the AA program. Henry reports:

> There are many who participate in AA but continue to suffer from the PTSD related inability to sense an "inner life force" will maintain and enhance health and welfare without the intervention of deliberate reasoned effort. This disability may relate to a deficiency of communication across the cerebral commisures, i.e., they continue to be denied the resources of the right brain and are confined to using the left hemisphere system. For those who lack "inner guidance," the

AA system uses the solution employed by religious groups seeking to deal with the distress that comes to those suffering from the loss of the sense of a Higher Power. Those lacking this gift are urged to put their trust in the social group, i.e., in the congregation and the confessional. For the time being the victims must rely on the outside social world for guidance. If fortunate, they eventually recover the capacity to experience healthy inner control and feedback. (21)

Henry refers to evidence that the process of meditation and the practice of yoga during an intensive three-month course leads to an increase in corticoids. This suggests that the intrinsic or personal religious experience of the AA's Higher Power results in an integration and return of sensitivity to brain systems that are dissociated during highly stressful social interaction. Moreover, Henry holds that religious coping is a powerful variable predicting lower rates of depression. This religious coping is independent from the level of education, mental status, or severity of one's predicament.

This reference to Henry allows for the following diagnosis. Perhaps the different groups, i.e., Jews, Christians, and Muslims, are locked into their identity groups which have their own connection with the Higher Power. This connection is needed for providing them with some coping energy in highly stressful social condition. The irony is that the stress is produced by this need to be connected with this particular form of Higher Power worship. This is a vicious circle from which there seems no escape.

With Randall, one may hope that the different groups may "eventually recover the capacity to experience healthy inner control and feedback." Randall substantiates that the Biblical faith itself is about an inner spirit of heart and mind. As an eminent scholar, Randall offers a voluminous documentation of Biblical research and theological studies concerning **War and Peace Among Jews, Christians and Muslims**. It is not a sermon book spiced with nice sounding spiritual admonitions. It purports a quality theology rooted in quality research for the sake of a most compelling issue of the human heart, PEACE in God's land. Bible scholars and theologians, may they be Jew, Christian or Muslim, will benefit greatly from this enormously rich study of the problems, the sociopolitical environments, and the promises for peace as found in the faith the children of Abraham share with each other. Randall's account is also a significant contribution to comparative religious studies.

William P. Frost
The University of Dayton

PROLOGUE
LIGHTS OF HOPE FOR PEACE IN BETHLEHEM

On December 23, 1994, feeling lonely for my wife and daughters celebrating Christmas in Texas with other family members, I left Amman, Jordan for Bethlehem, Israel, controversially located in the explosive Palestinian West Bank. The sixty-mile trip from Amman to Jerusalem required more than four hours because of the many security checks, passport examinations, and transportation changes. Arriving in Jerusalem around noon, I spent four hours touring the Old City before hailing a cab to travel the final eight miles to Bethlehem.

Christmas in Bethlehem: It seemed like a dream? Arriving near dusk, I checked into the Star Hotel, one of only half a dozen hotels in Bethlehem, and moved into a room overlooking Manger Square, the Lutheran Christmas Church, the Greek Orthodox Church, the Syrian Orthodox Church, Saint Catherine's Church (Roman Catholic), the Church of the Nativity that is supposedly built over the birth manger and the Mosque of Omar. As the sun set, a dazzling display of lights brightened Manger Square. According to the **Jerusalem Times** (12/23/94), these lights were new:

> In an unprecedented move, a Bethlehem merchant has donated more than $50,000 to decorate the town. Nicola Cavatini said that his gesture was because of the peace process [between Israel and the PLO]. . . . Mr. Cavatini went on to say that the town's residents are

very satisfied with the outcome of the peace talks, and they are hoping more will be accomplished. He said he saw peace in the eyes of the town's children.

The Muslim Arab population of the city was filled with anticipation over the future return of Bethlehem to Palestinian control. As a result of the Oslo Peace Accords, Christmas 1996 would find the Palestinian Authority responsible for the city; consequently, there were hundreds of pictures of Arafat throughout Manger Square. There were also thousands of crosses, rosaries and Creches ready for the influx of Christian tourists arriving hourly.

As the City of David, now a city whose population is predominantly Palestinian-Muslim with a small Arab Christian presence, prepared to celebrate Christmas Eve, in spite of the problems of poverty, unemployment and frustration in the West Bank and the ever-present commercialism, for Christians who came (many from Jordan for the first time in decades), Christmas Eve 1994 seemed a season for hope and peace and a glorious opportunity to celebrate both at the birthplace of the man called the Prince of Peace. With these thoughts I retired for the evening eagerly awaiting the rising of the sun on Christmas Eve.

Shortly before sunrise on Christmas Eve 1994, the first call to prayer musically filling the air from the Mosque of Omar in Manger Square was followed several minutes later by church bells ringing in the dawn. Alone at the top floor of the Star Hotel as I watched the sun rise over Manger Square and the Church of the Nativity, the moon was still bright overhead, and just below the moon and above the horizon was a brilliant star (actually the planet Venus) which seemed to shine over the place of the Baby's birth as it did almost 2000 years ago. It was the most beautiful, spiritual moment I experienced in Bethlehem--a moment that ended much too quickly.

Less than ten minutes later as I was looking east at the newness of dawn, the brilliance of the moon and Venus, the wonder of the Church of the Nativity, and absorbing the joy of being in Bethlehem, I suddenly became aware of the frailty of human endeavors and hopes for peace when a dozen members of the Israeli military took command for security reasons of the top floor of the Star Hotel as well as all rooftops overlooking Manger Square. There was considerable concern that one of the fanatical terrorist groups, such as Hamas, might again attempt to sabotage the peace process this first Christmas after the signing of the Peace Accords at Oslo. Indeed, the very next day, Christmas day 1994, a Hamas bomb killed several Israelis at the bus station in Jerusalem. As a result the trip back to Amman required over seven hours because of new security measures. Throughout all the activities of Christmas Eve, the presence of the Israeli military was a conspicuous fact. Entrance into Manger Square was allowed only by passing through the kind of security measures that Americans experience in international airports. The mixture of Christians from around the world and local Palestinians was both exciting and fascinating as well as potentially explosive and a golden opportunity for those opposed to the peace process on both sides to engage in fanatical activities. Consequently, metal detectors, military on every rooftop, flak-jackets and automatic rifles surrounding the Manger of Peace were among the many **incongruities** of the day.

As I reflect upon those amazing hours spent in Bethlehem, the term that comes most often to mind is: INCONGRUITY! In the midst of lights for peace, celebrations of the joy and wonder of birth, religious services of ancient beauty and mystery and great hopes for the future, there were constant reminders of anger, fears of violence and the frustrations of poverty. Seen from a larger historical perspective, this ancient land holy to Jews, Christians, and Muslims is above all a land of incongruities. The city of Jerusalem, which means the City of Peace in Hebrew, is among the most war torn cities in the history of the Middle East. Not only is this land the birthplace of three of the West's great monotheisms, it is the birthplace of prophets who dreamed of peace and preached justice as well as prophesied violence and justified holy wars. Such are the subjects of this study: **Theologies of War and Peace Among Jews, Christians and Muslims**.

From Oslo (1993) to Netanyahu and the Likud (1996)

While this holy land is geologically a land of mountains and valleys, it is a spiritual land-mine of exhilarating, desperate hopes for peace and terrifying despairs of violence: in this holy land of sacred prophets, the mountain top of euphoria can quickly turn into the valley of fear and desperation. From the signing date of the Oslo Accords in September 1993 to the lights of hope for peace in Bethlehem in December 1994, not even the fact that those committed to destroying the peace process had taken the lives of 312 innocent human beings--116 Israelis killed by Palestinians and 196 Palestinians killed by Israelis--by January 1995 (Associated Press report, early January 1995) could derail the efforts of those truly committed to a **JUST**[1] peace. Tragically, as we enter fall 1998, realistic hopes for peace are at their lowest ebb since Oslo. So confrontational was the situation in the summer of 1996, that on the last Friday of August, Arafat called on the Muslims of Israel for a Palestinian equivalent of Farrakhan's "Million Man March" of Black Americans on Washington, D.C.: that is, Arafat called for 100,000 Muslims to pray at the Dome of the Rock Mosque and the Mosque of Aqsa as a show of political strength and solidarity as well as a protest of the Israeli decision to build 2000 more homes in the West Bank. According to Knight-Ridder News (8/31/96), Arafat's call initiated a strong and unwise Israeli response: "In the hours before the midday prayers, Israel rushed police reinforcements into the city, doubling the normal deployment to 2000

---

[1]

The nature of and necessary need for a just peace occupies considerable space in the explorations of this study. Either explicitly or implicitly, few issues examined do not have significant implications for a just peace. It is interesting, perhaps illustrative, that there are many philosophical and theological works concerning a just war, but few that explore a just peace. Yet, an examination of history indicates that there have been many examples of forcing an unjust peace on conquered peoples and that a just peace is a necessary (unfortunately not sufficient) condition for any lasting peace among past combatants. It is also of more than passing interest that the phrase most used in the political and media fields today when peace is discussed for the Middle East is "peace with security"; seldom does the phrase "peace with justice" occur. This is troublesome and is addressed in chapters that follow.

troops. Mounted police patrolled the streets outside the crenelated walls of the Old City while hundreds of soldiers, armed with rifles and clubs, crowded through the arched gates into the narrow market streets." This intimidation reduced the crowd of Muslims to less than the usual Friday participation in prayer but also intensified the rhetoric and the potential for violence. Consider, for example, the message that the Palestinian Authority directed all teachers to deliver on the opening day of school, Saturday, August 31: "Israel does not want peace, and the uprising will be born again...." AP (9/1/96)[2] Given the continuing deterioration of the Peace Process, Palestinian children are likely to hear the same message as they begin the 1998-99 school year.

From the Christmas lights of December 1994 to the message delivered to kindergarten students on the fall opening of Palestinian schools in 1996, what had brought about this tragic state of affairs? It is not the purpose of this study to examine the many events which led from September 1993 to the present day. However for later sections, there are four events during this time which deserve brief description because of the role religious belief has in their occurrences or in the responses to them: Goldstein's massacre of several dozen Muslims praying at a mosque in Hebron, the 3000th celebration of David's conquering of Jerusalem, the assassination of Yitzhak Rabin, and the May 29, 1996 election of Benjamin Netanyahu. While it is true for believers that religious beliefs transcend historical circumstances, it is also true that beliefs can never be divorced from history because

---

[2]

While the agreement to withdraw Israeli troops from parts of Hebron is a healthy sign of progress along the lines of Oslo, most of the major explosive issues remain unresolved, including the establishment of a Palestinian state, the status of the 100 plus Israeli settlements in rural West Bank and the final status of Jerusalem. Any of these could reduce the peace process to violence. Further, the continuing divisions in Israel now pose serious threats of violence as those who are committed to the re-establishment of the Biblical Israel, reject Netanyahu as a traitor. The redeployment of the Hebron troops offered a light of peace, but one later negated by beginning the construction of Jewish homes at Har Homa.

they arise in historical circumstance, are interpreted and reinterpreted in specific historical circumstances, and provide bases for believers' interpretations of historical events. Consequently, while the events just mentioned are occurrences of considerable political, social, economic and psychological import, it is their religious dimensions that are the primary concern of this study.

On February 27, 1994 an event occurred at the Ibrahimi Mosque in Hebron that shocked Americans because we receive little world coverage in our news media, and most news stories which concern the Middle East for the past fifty years have tended to demonized Muslims and canonized Israelis. A Zionist extremist[3] named Baruch Goldstein massacred more than two dozen Muslims engaged in prayer. He was killed before he could escape the Mosque. The violence of this atrocity led many Americans to think of Goldstein as mentally deranged, and thus, to consider his actions as isolated and demented. Certainly Goldstein is not representative of stable mental health, but to dismiss his actions as only the consequences of mental illness ignores a major danger which appears and reappears in Western thinking: religious extremism and the kind of distorted values and beliefs it espouses--beliefs and values that have been used religiously to justify even genocide. While responses to Goldstein's actions were varied, one is of particular significance for the subject of this study. A small but intensely devoted cult has been building around Goldstein. For example, almost a year later, the **Jordan Times** (12/27/94) reported that there are more than a dozen residents who "go to his grave and recite prayers; they gather in each other's homes and tell stories about Goldstein." While this is a small number who will probably have little influence on peace in the Middle East, it is a serious mistake to underestimate the kind of religious thinking that supports such pseudo-

---

[3] There is a significant difference between religious fundamentalism and religious extremism, an issue which is examined later in the Prologue. There is also a difference between political extremism (radicalism) and conservatism; an issue that is also examined later in the Prologue. (See pages 17-19.)

martyrs. There are far too many such martyrs (*Mujihads*, Holy Warriors) in Muslim countries, but they have been a part of Western religious traditions long before the emergence of monotheism. Chapters Two, Three, and Four examine this kind of religious thinking as it develops in each of the three monotheisms. Of these three chapters, it is Chapter Two which is of most significance because it explores the first occurrences in Judaism of such Holy Warriors (*Shopet-im*, Judges) long before the religious beliefs of the Hebrews evolved into a major monotheism.

Two events occurred in the fall of 1995 which evidenced the continuing plague of such religious thinking. On September 9, a day of major historical and religious significance not only for Israelis but Jews throughout the world, the AP issued the following release:

> Israel began celebrating the 3000th anniversary of King David's conquest of Jerusalem on Monday, amid accusations the festivities are an attempt to deny Palestinian claims to the city.
>
> . . . .
>
> In a ceremony at Parliament, Prime Minister Yitzhak Rabin stressed the Jewish claims to the city. "There is no state of Israel without Jerusalem, and no peace without Jerusalem united," he said.
>
> . . . .
>
> Dozens of riot police lined rooftops to prevent unrest as Rabin and 200 guests kicked off the celebrations on the slopes below the walled Old City.
>
> Rabin emphasized the central role of Jerusalem in Jewish history. "Jerusalem is the celebration of the Jewish nation, from the day the Jewish people were created in God's image," Rabin said.

Concerning the future for a stable and just peace in the Middle East, it is important to remember Rabin's words which passionately bound peace, the state of Israel, and a united Jerusalem. As one explores the kind of religious thinking which buttresses holy war theologies, it is important to remember Rabin's words concerning God's image: note that any recognition that Palestinians are also created in the image of God is missing. This idea is not unusual in the history of Western theologies of war, especially holy war.

The second event of fall 1995, a tragedy whose consequences have been seriously damaging, if not fatally destructive, to the peace process, was the assassination of Yitzhak Rabin. While his death had and will continue to have many political-social overtones and consequences, it is important to note the religious justifications offered by his assassin, Yigal Amir. The AP released the following statement on November 15:

Yitzhak Rabin's assassination by a Jewish extremist has trained the spotlight on rabbis who preach that it is Israel's sacred duty to control the West Bank and label a traitor anyone willing to give it up.

Speaking to a blindly devoted following, extremist rabbis play a dangerous game when they mix religion with politics, say their mainstream colleagues.

"It is easy to slide down that slippery slope that you know the divine agenda, that you are the 'God Squad,'" David Rosen, former chief rabbi of Ireland, said Tuesday.

In the eyes of Rabin's assassin, Yigal Amir, religion justified the most extreme political act.

"According to Jewish law, you can kill the enemy. My whole life I have learned Jewish law," the 25-year-old Amir told magistrates two days after shooting the prime minister.

Asked if he acted alone, Amir said: "It was God."

Police have said they were investigating whether Amir, a graduate of two Jewish seminaries and a law student at religious Bar Ilan University, had sought a rabbi's blessing before pulling the trigger.

As with Goldstein, to dismiss this tragic murder as simply the consequence of mental derangement is not only inadequate but dangerous. Like Goldstein, Amir should not be the poster boy for stable mental health, but supporting his distorted thinking and justifying his actions is a type of religious thinking that is much too common in the monotheisms of the West. Powerful psychological and theological connections among chosenness, promised-sacred land, and holy war have Western religious origins that are at least pre-exhilic (prior to the Babylonian captivity of the Jews during the sixth century B.C.E.). Significant parts of Chapters Two, Three, and Four explore this connectedness as well as the transmission of these ideas from Judaism to Christianity and Islam.

Before turning to the fourth event, the election of May 29, 1996, it is illustrative of the danger of ignoring the religious dimensions in these events by recalling a phrase the media used to describe the psychological state of Israel after the assassination: Israelis suffered a "loss of innocence." It is not insignificant that the media used the same phrase to describe America after the Oklahoma City bombing. However, what was lost was not innocence; the term is badly used in these contexts. What was lost was ignorance; an ignorance that was and continues to be cultivated by many Americans and Israelis. For those who did not wish to hide their heads in the sand, that is, those who seek the courage to overcome the bliss and safety of ignorance, it has been apparent for many years that there are dangerous divisions in America and that Israel is a fragile, fractured society struggling with the violent passions of religious extremism, realistic fears of daily terrorism, desperate hopes for safety and peace, and guilt concerning the plight of millions of Palestinians. Indeed, the election revealed with considerable clarity this fractured fragility and opened the door for an American style campaign of fear which brought to power an uneasy coalition of the Likud and half a dozen extremist religious parties whose thinking is not far removed from the violence of Amir and Goldstein. As the AP indicated in a wire release on June 2 from Jerusalem, the election of Benjamin Netanyahu was more than a victory for the more extreme religious parties in Israel, it may have also been a win for Hamas:

> Ironically, one of the biggest winners in the election may have been the militant Palestinian group Hamas, which has sought for two years to destroy the peace process with a campaign of bombings.

> Four attacks this winter left 63 people dead and robbed Peres of a commanding lead in the polls. The bombings sent a shudder through Israeli society, which Netanyahu's security-oriented campaign adeptly tapped. And it did not sit well with voters that much of Peres' support came from Arab-Israelis.

> Israeli Jews who, after building their Zionist state for nearly half a century on strife with Arab neighbors, watched in anger as exit polls reported a turnout of 400,000 Arab voters--enough they feared could override a Jewish majority. More than three-quarters of Arab voters went to the polls and an estimated 95 percent voted for Peres.

Even more so than in recent American elections, the passionate activities of various religious groups, both Jewish and Muslim, significantly influenced the outcome of Israel's recent election. From Oslo to the election of 1996, the activities of several extremist Muslim groups, especially Hamas and Hizbollah, have concentrated on creating an atmosphere of violence and terror in order to destroy the peace process. As most Western journalists recognized, the increase in terrorist activities was a direct result of the initial successes of the peace process. The analyses of the *jihad* in Chapter Four clearly shows that these fanatical acts of violence violate and distort the true *jihad* that is at the center of the **Qur'an**. Partly as a result of religious extremism but also as consequences of continuing poverty, massive unemployment, daily fears of violence, loss of confidence in political leaders, old ethnic prejudices, remembered injustices and despair of the peace process, two new elements of violence have entered the situation: Israelis engaging in physical conflict with other Israelis and Palestinians with other Palestinians. Interwoven throughout these conflicts are religious values and beliefs concerning chosenness, promised-sacred land, and holy war. For this reason, the City of Peace (Jerusalem) is not only an overwhelming issue that lies at the heart of any possible peace but is also a microcosm of the Middle East, its history, conflicts and hopes.

A December 18, 1995 article titled "God's City" in **U.S. News and World Report** began with three revealing quotes: "Of the 10 measures of beauty that came down to the world, Jerusalem took nine." **(The Talmud)** "No people blessed as thine, no city like Jerusalem." (**Christian Hymn**) "One prayer in Jerusalem is worth 40,000 elsewhere." **(Islamic Saying)** As a microcosm of both the hopes and conflicts in the area, while it may be a bad pun, it is more than just a geographical fact that the Dome of the Rock Mosque, the third most sacred place in the world for Muslims, is but a stones throw away from the Wailing Wall and only a little further from the Church of the Holy Sepulchre, which is one of the claimed locations for the empty tomb. Perhaps it would not be inaccurate to state that: "As Jerusalem goes so goes the peace process." Once again notice the religious power of sacred land. Karen Armstrong recently published an excellent comprehensive study of Jerusalem's evolution as a holy city: **Jerusalem: One City, Three Faiths**. In a recent review of Armstrong's book in **Time**, June 3, 1996, Johanna McGeary concluded with a summary of Armstrong's religious sensitivities, sensitivities which are shared by this study and provide a value perspective concerning the apology for peace in the final chapter and the Epilogue:

> In the end, Armstrong suggests, claims to Jerusalem cannot be settled by who was there first or who identifies most deeply with its spirituality. All the monotheistic religions have to understand that Jerusalem was and is legitimately sacred to others. Its long and mutable history shows that sovereignty by itself is less important than how well the possessors live up to their faiths ideals of peace, harmony, tolerance and charity, how successfully they encourage inclusion and coexistence. That, says Armstrong, "must be the way to celebrate Jerusalem's sanctity today." But as she sadly notes, never

in history has true holiness triumphed in the Holy City.

If Karen Armstrong is correct, a just peace cannot ignore the wisdom of the United Nations when it established Jerusalem and its environs as a "corpus separatism," that is, as an international city belonging to no one nation or religion, in the partition approval of Palestine into an Arab state and a Jewish state on December 29, 1947. Any just and lasting peace cannot ignore the value concerns which are at the heart of U.N. Resolution # 242 affirmed on November 22, 1967 and reaffirmed as Security Council Resolution #338 in October 1973:

The Security Council

Expresses its continuing concern with the grave situation in the Middle East,

Emphasizing the inadmissibility of the acquisition of territory by war and the need to work for a just and lasting peace in which every State in the area can live in security,

Emphasizing further that all Member States in the acceptance of the Charter of the United Nations have undertaken a commitment to act in accordance with Article 2 of the Charter:

1.   Affirm that the fulfillment of Charter principles requires the establishment of a just and lasting peace in the Middle East which should include the application of both the following principles:

(i)   Withdraw of Israeli armed forces from territories occupied in the recent conflict;

(ii)   Termination of all claims or states of belligerency and respect for and acknowledgment of the sovereignty, territorial integrity, and political independence of every state in the area and their right to live by peace within secure and recognized boundaries free from the threat or act of force;

2.   Affirms further the necessity

    (a)   For guaranteeing freedom of navigation through international waterways in the area;

    (b)   For achieving a just settlement of the refugee problem;

    (c)   For guaranteeing the inviolability and political independence of every State in the area through measures including the establishment of demilitarized zones. . . .

While these resolutions identify many items of controversy and compromise, they clearly reveal the two most difficult issues that must be solved in reaching a peace that is both just and lasting: the status of Jerusalem and the refugee problem. For most Americans the phrase "the refugee problem" is little more than a media phrase, but for Palestinians, Israelis, and Jordanians the refugee problem is an intimidating reality involving several million human beings. Considering only their social, political and economic dimensions, Jerusalem and the Palestinian refugees represent an overwhelming challenge to those committed to a just peace. Add the religious dimension, and the task of peacemaking becomes even more difficult.

Fundamental Principles

One of the purposes of this study is to examine the scriptural basis and theology of this religious dimension. It is a dimension that has been overshadowed by the ascendancy of the economic, political, and social approaches to human relations since the advent of modern humanism. Certainly the social sciences have much to contribute to our understanding of the human condition and to the problems facing efforts to create peace in the Middle East, but the religious dimension is also important. It is hoped that the study which follows will contribute to a better and more tolerant understanding among all those embattled in the Middle East and especially among Americans who continue to practice a chosen, provincial ignorance concerning anything outside the U.S.. Because there is a purpose beyond scriptural-theological analysis in the material that follows, there are three tasks required before turning to the first chapter: (1) a statement of the epistemological, belief and value principles which influence the analyses, interpretations, and evaluations of the study (as ideally as it seems, there is no such thing as a presuppositionless analysis or study of any subject; my moral and philosophical responsibility is to be as honest and clear about these principles as possible); (2) a brief description of the issues that are to be explored; and (3) an description of the structure and content of the study.

The fundamental principles which provide a foundation for exploring the views of war and peace can be described as follows:

(1)　　 Jews, Christians, and Muslims worship the same God. The **Hebrew Bible** (and by extension the **Talmud**), the Christian **New Testament**, and the Muslim **Qur'an** (and the **Hadiths**) are viable sources of revelation, inspiration, and truth. Chapters One and Five and the Epilogue build on this belief and value principle.[4]

---

[4]

In the pages that follow the terms *belief* and *value* are understood in the following manner. Beliefs are idea-actions concerning transcendent realities or truths. In this sense, the affirmation that God is a spirit of love and compassion is a belief as are the Muslim affirmation of Paradise and the Christian hope for Heaven. Values are idea-actions concerning human relationships. Thus, the Christian affirmation that one is to love his or her enemies as well as the Jewish law to leave one-tenth of a field unharvested for the support of the poor are both values. Unquestionably, in religion, beliefs are intimately connected with values. For example, to believe in a God of love and compassion clearly implies that love and compassion should be values practiced in human relationships. As the recent musical made from Hugo's great novel states: "To love another person is to see the face of God." The connection between beliefs and values is why the great prophets preached a message of righteousness (beliefs about the relationship between God and human beings) and justice (values concerning human relationships). As Chapter One makes clear, Jews, Christians, and Muslims share a common base of both beliefs and values.

The term *idea-actions* is used to stress the fact that true beliefs and values must be more than just intellectual ideas or affirmations in the believer's life. For example, as a philosopher, if requested by another, I could probably give half a dozen definitions of justice, but intellectually understanding justice is not the same as practicing justice. Humans have a strong tendency to reduce both beliefs and values

(2)   In addition to affirming ONE God, Jews, Christians, and Muslims share a common base of beliefs and values, mostly because both Christianity and Islam build on the great prophetic movement of the Hebrew prophets whose appearance in the eighth century B.C.E. marks a major evolution toward monotheism in the West. This is not to deny that there are substantive differences among these three children of Abraham. However, if Jews, Christians, and Muslims can find the courage and compassion to look beyond their own chauvinisms, the beliefs and values they share offer golden opportunities for conversation rather than conflict.

(3)   Any healthy effort to move beyond conflict and confrontation must engage in trialogue, a conversation among Jews, Muslims and Christians. The present and future status of Jerusalem illustrates a poignant and passionate need for trialogue. Just efforts at peacemaking must reject self-glorifying monologues, exclusive dialogues between only two of the three children of Abraham and those reductive stereotypes created by historical ignorance, national chauvinisms and the superficial analyses of the mass media. For the Christian West this means that Christians must honestly struggle against two kinds of anti-Semitism: Jewish anti-Semitism, prejudice against Jews, and Arab anti-Semitism, prejudice against Arabs and Muslims. Because the former is so well known and critiqued, I turn to the latter, which is aptly described by Rami G. Khouri in a editorial in the **Jordan Times** (December 6, 1994):

> It is increasingly common in the United States, for example, to hear and read about "Muslim holy warriors," referring to assorted activist groups such as Hamas, Islamic Jihad, the FIS in Algeria and Hizbollah in Lebanon. A controversial documentary called "Jihad in America" aired on public television in the United States last week and

---

to intellectual abstractions, while the truth is that actual values must be concretely a part of day to day decisions. In other words, if what I intellectually claim as my values are inconsistent with my decisions and actions, then I am guilty of self-deception. Thus the need for characterizing beliefs and values as idea-actions.

repeatedly referred to Islamicists as "holy warriors." The image is, of course, chilling; it aims to paint Islamicists as violent, maniacal killers bent on spilling the blood of Jews and Christians. It aptly captures the increasingly confrontational, even martial, context in which Western and Arab/Islamic cultures interact with one another.

This racist, distorted depiction of Islamic culture is mirrored on the other side by Middle Easterners who view American culture as immoral, excessively materialistic, even satanic. Israel is seen as the outpost of Western values, a dangerous cultural toehold in the Middle East from where promiscuous western ways will attack and conquer the Arabs and Muslims of our region. This is perceived as a cultural, rather than an economic or political, threat by many in the Middle East who fear normalization with Israel because of the possible cultural . . . consequences. Therefore, Middle Easterners react by trying to defend their culture, religion, and identity, but this self-defensive self-assertion is seen by the West as a threat. The circle of fear is thus completed, the cycle of antagonism propelled forward.

In order to overcome this vicious "cycle of antagonism," Israelis must honestly and courageously face their forms of Arab anti-Semitism and their injustices against the Palestinians in an effort to construct something more than a peace with security but one with justice. Peace as conceived by the Likud and Netanyahu is little more than a humiliating surrender for the Palestinians, that is, a peace without justice. Muslims, especially Palestinians, must courageously face their forms of Jewish anti-Semitism and find the faith to reject and condemn the violence of Muslim extremists and extend the hand of friendship to Israelis. Further, in their moral claims for returning land occupied in the 1967 War, they must commit themselves to that part of U.N. Resolution 242 which declares the right of Israelis "to live by peace within secure and recognized boundaries free from the threat of act of force."[5] Perhaps, a first step toward creating the trialogue that is needed to overcome these stereotypes and chauvinisms is a tolerant exploration of the views of war and peace in the three great books which circumscribe the lives of believers. Such an approach is asking much of Jews, Christians, and Muslims because it requires a willingness to find the truth of God in more than one revelation and the courage to struggle with the historical, theological, and ethical strengths and limitations of these revelations. As Chapters Two, Three, Four, and Five explore the theologies of war and peace, they do so in the spirit of this principle.

(4)   As there is a difference in politics between conservatism and radicalism which can be found on both the liberal and conservative sides, there is a significant difference between religious fundamentalism and religious extremism. This is as true of Christianity and Judaism as it is of Islam. Unfortunately, for most Americans, the failure to recognize this distinction has consistently reinforced the stereotypes of Muslims that Khouri laments in his editorial. Religious fundamentalism, if it does not deteriorate into religious extremism, can be a healthy critique of current values

---

[5]   For all parties in the peace process--especially the Israelis, Palestinians, Jordanians, and Syrians-- a just peace requires the returning of land which was taken by violence. The terms that are used in regard to this strategy of the peace process are themselves revealing: the *trading* of land for peace. Ethically, a more appropriate term would be the *returning* of land for peace. Such a return has been affirmed by dozens of U.N. resolutions. However, in returning land for peace, the Arab states must also compromise; thus, a peace that is both just and secure may not return to exactly the pre-1967 borders. Whatever the political and economic aspects of the peace process, unquestionably land and sacred land lie at its center. Land is more than power and wealth, psychologically and religiously land is identity, or to use a term recently popularized in the U.S., land is ROOTS! While the psychological power of land for human identity is exceedingly powerful, when land acquires the attributes of holiness and sacredness, as it does for all three great monotheisms, land becomes even more crucial in influencing either war or peace among peoples in the Middle East. Recognizing this places the status of Jerusalem at the very heart of any lasting peace, that is, a peace which provides both security and justice for all parties.

and beliefs as well as a valuable effort at reform in a religion.

Basically, fundamentalism represents an effort on the part of a people to retain their essential roots and traditional values and beliefs which provide identity and purpose for individuals as well as communities. Understood in this sense, fundamentalism is not an escape from the realities of the present into a static past, but a positive search for meaning, value and purpose as well as a critique of the unhealthy aspects of modernity. Thus, there are movements of cultural, social, political, and religious fundamentalism occurring throughout the United States as well as the rest of the world. Native Americans and African Americans seek identity, purpose and dignity as they search for their fundamental roots: roots which have been unjustly ignored in American society. While this kind of fundamentalism can become distorted into racial and ethnic bigotry--Afrocentrism for example--it need not fall into the trap of racist extremism. Much of the "newly discovered" concern about family values (a concern that is centuries old) is a form of both social and political fundamentalism. Most of the movements of Christian fundamentalism are efforts to return to or rediscover the fundamental values and beliefs of Christianity-- such as love, justice, honesty and kindness--as well as rejections of the modern day social club--comfortable pew church. This has always been the case in religion: for example, Jainism and Buddhism both represent fundamentalist movements that originated in a critique of Brahaministic Hinduism and the effort to rediscover the religious insights in the Upanishads. The Protestant Reformation as well as the Catholic Counter Reformation were both fundamentalist movements. Religious fundamentalist movements occur throughout the Islamic world as Muslims struggle with both the good and evil of modern secularism. Many Muslim commentators claim that the most significant ideological conflict occurring in the Middle East is not between Islam and the other monotheisms, but between Islam and McDonalds. In other words, between the values and beliefs of Islam and the ever encroaching values of a fast food, acquisition oriented society. Understood in this way, many Muslim fundamentalist movements are not significantly different than those American movements seeking to recover family values and traditional roots.

As diverse movements, fundamentalism has much to offer for the development of healthy, responsible personalities and stable, responsive communities. These movements are conservative in the sense that they reach into the past to find foundations for coping with the problems of the present, but in their healthiest forms they are also reflective movements in the sense that they represent analyses and critiques of present maladies, and they provide strategies and hope for change. Unfortunately, like all movements--conservative or liberal--they can become distorted into extremism: cultural fundamentalism can deteriorate into ethnic extremism, that is racism; socio-political fundamentalism can deteriorate into archaic, stagnant responses to current problems (the conservative deterioration) or into political correctness (the liberal form of extremism which represents a considerable threat to freedom of both thought and speech in the U.S.); and religious fundamentalism can deteriorate into charismatic and millennial escapism. When this happens, fundamentalism is only one step away from extremism which is only a half-step from fanaticism, that is, terrorism.

The essential difference between religious fundamentalism, which can be individually and socially healthy, and extremism, which is both individually and socially unhealthy, is found in reflection. Fundamentalism in its healthiest forms is a thinking--questioning--open-eyed searching; extremism is a blind--closed minded--emotional condemnation of the present and escape into the past; and terrorism is a fanatical extremism which is committed to violence regardless of the costs or consequences. While most Americans badly confuse fundamentalism in all its various forms with extremism, nowhere is this more evident and more inaccurate than Muslim fundamentalism. The explorations in Chapters Two, Three and Four should suffice to show that fundamentalism is not only consistent with but also founded on the deeper spiritual dimensions of the three great revelations of Judaism, Christianity, and Islam. On the other hand, religious extremism represents a distortion of these revelations that borders on a kind of idolatry.

(5)   Finally the approach used in exploring the **Hebrew Bible**, the **New Testament**, and the **Qur'an** integrates what has come to be known as higher (geographical, historical and theological studies) and lower (linguistic and textual studies) criticism in Biblical studies. This strategy rejects two radically opposing approaches to scriptural study and affirms another. First, it rejects inerrancy and literalism. Not only does the Critical Apparatus[6] of the Masoretic Text of the **Hebrew Bible** and the Greek **New Testament** clearly indicate the folly of inerrancy, since literalism logically depends on inerrancy, it follows that literalism is not an intelligible position. Further, literalism is a human impossibility even when only one language is involved.[7] As most Jews and Christians now read their scriptures in

---

6

The Critical Apparatus, which occurs at the bottom of every page in the Hebrew text of the **Hebrew Bible** and every page of the Greek text of the **New Testament**, is the product of centuries of faithful, devoted and loving scholarship on these scriptures in their original languages. The original of no single book in either of these revelations is extant, that is, still physically exits. In many instances the oldest copy of a particular book that is extant may be one copied hundreds of years after the original book took its final form. The Critical Apparatus summarizes in abbreviated form the major extant tests which include all or most of the designated page in them and a summary of their most important differences. In other words, the Critical Apparatus clearly shows that there is no perfect (inerrant) copy of the Hebrew text of the **Hebrew Bible** or Greek text of the **New Testament**. Consequently, the position of scriptural inerrancy that has been so controversial in recent Protestantism is a Red Herring; no inerrant text exists. The situation concerning the **Qur'an** is different than the other two revelations since tradition claims that the teachings of Muhammad were originally written on treated palm leaves. After these were codified into the canonized **Qur'an** during the reign of Uthman, approximately 25 years after the death of Muhammad, all of the palm leaves were intentionally burned so that there would be no controversy about the authority of the **Qur'an**. Issues concerning the inerrancy of the **Qur'an** are examined in Chapter Four.

7

Since the meanings of both words and ideas are products of their larger contexts--for a word the language in which it occurs, and for an idea the mental frame of reference of the thinker as well as the state of knowledge at the time he lives--three important consequences follow: (1) literal translations are impossible;

translation, the position of literalism is more than just impossible, it is irrational. The rejection of literalism and inerrancy for the Jewish and Christian scriptures represents less of a problem for Jews and Christians than a similar rejection regarding the **Qur'an** for Muslims. Very few Jews believe that God spoke Hebrew; rather they believe that God inspired the prophets who framed their messages in Hebrew. Most Christians know that Jesus spoke Aramaic, that his teachings were later translated from oral Aramaic into written Greek and that Christians read translations in their native languages. Thus, rejecting inerrancy and literalism is less problematic for Jews and Christians than rejecting these positions is for most Muslims. Because it is important that similar principles be applied to the study of all three revelations and because the rejection of inerrancy and literalism poses problems for the **Qur'an** that are more difficult than for the **Hebrew Bible** and the **New Testament**, Chapter Four examines this issue in more depth. At this point it should be sufficient to state that the approach to all three scriptures accepts them as inspired forms of revelation, albeit revelations which cannot be taken literally, and therefore requires the mature and responsible believer to use the tools of higher and lower criticism and to employ that capacity which separates humans from the beasts of the fields: the ability to think!

Second, the approach used in this study rejects what can be described as radical revisionist approaches to these scriptures. In general radical revisionist approaches are the opposite of the literalist approach. Such approaches can be put into several categories: atheistic--agnostic approaches, deconstructionist approaches,

---

(2) since no two human minds are exactly the same, neither the meaning of a word nor an idea can ever literally mean the same thing to two different persons; and (3) since the epistemological state of knowledge is always changing, interpretations of scriptural texts never remain static. While this means that contemporary students of these scriptures can never adequately recover the past meanings of these beliefs and ideas, this does not excuse serious students from the responsibility to engage in the scholarly efforts to recover as much of those past meanings as possible in order to escape the scholarly irresponsibility of deconstructionism (see the following page).

and political agenda approaches. The atheistic--agnostic revisionist usually takes one of two positions on the three revelations: (1) while scholarly study of these three Holy Books may yield limited information concerning past conceptions of reality, they have little utility for those who wish to live in the real world; or (2) the study of these revelations is merely the study of past mythologies and a waste of time. In other words, the atheistic--agnostic revisionist denies any truth value to the revelations of Judaism, Christianity, and Islam. The deconstructionist revisionist, sometimes unintentionally, also reduces the truth value of these revelations for a different reason: he reduces these revelations to little more than literature and their meanings to mere individual subjectivity. This interpretation is not only lazy scholarship--if it can be called scholarship at all--but also emotively dangerous. From the deconstructionist approach, all interpretations are of equal merit. Such views clearly play into the hands of those who would distort their scriptures for personal and political agendas as is done by all religious extremists. Finally, the political agenda revisionists are so busy trying to find textual support for their social, sexual, or racial agendas that they ignore the principles that distinguish scholarship from propaganda. In their own way they are guilty of the same scholarly irresponsibility as the deconstructionists.

The approach used in this study can be characterized as follows: (a) these revelations are sources of truth, meaning, value, purpose, and hope for believers; (b) they begin and develop in specific historical circumstances that the thinking believer has a responsibility to study even though realizing it is impossible to ever adequately recover their past meaning and value; (c) they are understood (interpreted) according to the metaphysical, epistemological, and ethical limitations of specific historical circumstances and consequently interpretations never remain static; (d) not all interpretations are equal, for some do more violence to the historical circumstances or textual contexts of these great revelations than others; (e) translations are never adequate and thus cannot be taken literally; (f) applying the scholarly tools of higher and lower criticism does not destroy the faith of believers but helps it mature and encourages the growth of religious humility and toleration; and (g) an apologetic approach that seeks a common ground of beliefs and values as providing the best foundation for creating a spirit of peace among these quarrelsome children of Abraham.

Dimensions of War and Peace

Having stated the basic principles that provide the tools and boundaries of this study, it is now appropriate to describe the dimensions of war and peace which are the subjects of the analyses in chapters Two, Three and Four as well as the apology for peace in the concluding chapter. As the title of the book indicates, the study is essentially scriptural and theological; however, such a study cannot ignore the historical, psychological, social and moral aspects of war and peace. While there are a multitude of works examining both subjects, war and peace, few attempt to explore the views of both war and peace in all three revelations. There are several reasons for this, but the two major ones are the language challenges involved (Hebrew, Greek, and Arabic) and the mammoth size of the task. Considering the technicalities and precisions of scholarship, such a project is best done by a minimum of three scholars: one in Hebrew and the Jewish studies, one in Greek and Christian studies, and one in Arabic and Islamic studies. Such a joint effort is badly needed today and would make major contributions to understanding the Middle East. On the other hand, there is value in a project written by one person whose audience is students of these three religions and whose purpose is to promote mutual understanding, respect and peace. I hope that the analyses and judgments in the following pages are useful to graduate students and technical scholars in the field. I also hope this study is written so that its message of toleration based on knowledge is useful to undergraduate students and persons outside the realms of academia. After all, it is mostly in the "real" (the public) world that we must learn to live together in peace rather than the academic one.[8]

With these limitations in mind, let us turn to the dimensions of war and peace that are explored in the written texts of the **Hebrew Bible,**[9] the **New Testament,** and the **Qur'an**. The analyses of war in these revelations concentrates on three dimensions: political, spiritual, and eschatological. The first (political) is probably the best known use of the term *war*, that is, as a term for conflict between peoples. All three revelations present views of political war although much more attention is given to this kind of war in the **Hebrew Bible** and the **Qur'an** than in the **New Testament** (see Appendices A, C and E). The reasons for this are examined in Chapters Two, Three and Four. By the term *spiritual war* is meant conflict that occurs internally and destroys peace of spirit. All three revelations develop theologies of such conflict and find their sources in unrighteousness and injustice, that is, essentially in sin. Chapters Two, Three and Four examine these theologies.

---

[8]

As a teacher in a state university, and thus an academician, I have been in many university situations that more accurately resemble a state of war than one of peace. Additionally I often become aware of an academic mentality that denies the value of spirituality without understanding it and that is increasingly falling prey to political agendas which pose a threat to the growth of knowledge either because of close-mindedness, acquiescence, provincialism or escapism. Universities can be most comfortable retreats from the problems and dangers of society.

[9]

Note that the term **Old Testament** is not used, nor will it ever be used except when referring to the Christian Bible. While the 39 books that comprise the Christian **Old Testament** are essentially the same as those that are the **Hebrew Bible**, there is a big difference in meaning and interpretation. The moment the term *old* is applied to these books by Christians their meaning, value, and purpose has undergone considerable change. For practicing Jews, these books are not an **Old Covenant** (the term *testament* means *covenant*). Indeed, they are a living covenant. Consequently this study purposively ignores any Christian interpretation of the **Hebrew Bible** until such an interpretation is needed in Chapter Three which examines Christianity. Further, in order to remove a Christian bias from the dating system implemented by the Medieval Church, dates are listed as either B.C.E. (Before the Common Era) or C.E. (Common Era). For any reader unfamiliar with this less chauvinistic dating system B.C.E. translates into B.C. and C.E. into A.D..

Finally, the term *eschatological war* refers to either future historical wars or to a cosmic conflict between the forces of good and evil that involves mostly supernatural beings but can include human agents. From Jewish beliefs after the Babylonian Captivity (6th century B.C.E.) to the advent of Islam (7th century C.E.) there is a discernable pattern in these Western monotheisms: an increase in theologies of cosmic-eschatological war. Chapters Two, Three and Four examine the importance of this kind of war in each of the three faiths.

Before turning to the dimensions of peace, a brief statement is needed about the place of holy war in the preceding scheme because it overlaps all three dimensions, political, spiritual, and cosmic-eschatological. During those times that a religious group has a national identity and can put an armed force in the field against their enemies, there is usually the incursion of holy war into the realm of political war. At times when there is no such national identity or actual military, the holy war rises to the heavens and becomes a part of the cosmic-eschatological war. Finally, as both Chapters Three and Four show, all three faiths but especially Christianity and Islam often internalize the holy war and understand it as the struggle against sin. Indeed, one of the most common misunderstandings of most non-Muslims is the reduction of the *jihad* to the political war. The message of the **Qur'an**, however, is quite different and is examined in Chapter Four.

Although not surprising, it is disturbing that a computer generated bibliographical search of the topics war and peace generates almost five times as many references for war as for peace. Using the same three dimensions of political, spiritual, and eschatological for the analysis of peace, the scriptures of Judaism, Christianity and Islam give, appropriately, more attention to spiritual peace than the other two dimensions and more to eschatological peace than political peace. Of the three, the **Qur'an** places more emphasis on political peace than the other two Holy Books. While these revelations do not ignore political peace, which can be described briefly as the absence of conflict between peoples, they all argue a theology that political peace must be based on the foundations of righteousness and justice which result from the spiritual peace that comes as a gift from God. Although each understands spiritual peace in generally similar but specifically difference ways--for example, the Hebrew *shalom* and the Greek *eirene* convey different understandings of peace--all three share the conviction that the source of spiritual peace is to be found in God. All three also share the belief that the world was created for peace, has fallen into a state of war and is predestined through apocalyptic events of violence to culminate in a state of eternal peace. In this sense, each of the three presents a view of human immortality and an end of time moving toward the salvation of peace. However even in those passages where the revelations speak of a cosmic-eschatological peace they, especially Christianity and Islam, indicate that eternal peace can be partly glimpsed in the experience of spiritual peace. Thus, before turning to a brief outline of the structure of the study, it is helpful to examine in more detail the nature of spiritual peace.

Spiritual peace, what many philosophies call peace of mind, is not only a desirable state but a most elusive one. Many philosophies, psychologies and most religions explore and offer paths (strategies) for finding spiritual peace. On the existential level, most of us experience times when we seem to have glimpsed the summit of spiritual peace only to remember a past hurt, fear, anger, lust, failure, lie, etc.. Indeed, thousands of pages in both philosophy and religion have been written about the nature and struggle for peace of mind. While most philosophies and several Eastern religions have stressed self-discipline as the path to spiritual peace, the three monotheisms of the West, who share common understandings about those things which destroy peace of mind, have taken different paths than most philosophies and Eastern religions for achieving such peace. The understanding that is shared by most philosophies and religions can be stated in this way: it is only the person who is at "one" with himself who is capable of knowing spiritual peace. In other words, the person who is at war with himself (that is, experiencing internal conflict--modern philosophy and psychology have shown a fondness for the term *alienation* to describe this internal state of war) cannot be a peace with either himself or another person. Many of the causes of this internal conflict are well known and in Western religion often characterized by some formulation of the traditional Seven Deadly Sins: pride, greed, lust, anger, envy, gluttony and sloth. Most religions and philosophies also agree that these internal states of war (conflict) set the internal stage for those externalized actions that create conflicts among human beings: for example, rape, murder and theft.

In contrast to philosophy or a religion such as Buddhism, while agreeing with the need for oneness or wholeness, the West's monotheisms add a transcendent dimension to peace: oneness (wholeness) with oneself cannot be entirely a matter of self-actualization. John Macquarrie, in his insightful book, **The Concept of Peace**, identifies three fundamental, transcendent elements of spiritual peace common to all three Western revelations. His first point is that spiritual peace is a metaphysical mystery:

> By a metaphysical concept, I mean one the boundaries of which cannot be precisely determined, not because we lack information but because the concept itself [also the experience itself] turns out to have such depth and inexhaustability that the more we explore it, the more we see that something further remains to be explored. The more we grasp it, the more we become aware that its grasp extends beyond our reach. Those who have an implacable hostility to the metaphysical might find it easier to speak of peace as a mystery. For a mystery is not something that cannot be understood, but something that, the more clearly it is understood, reveals a breadth or a height or a depth that stretches beyond the limits of understanding. (63)

It should be clear from this statement that spiritual peace cannot be adequately accomplished by some human technique or act of self-realization. Since the experience of spiritual peace lies beyond mere human attainment, Macquarrie's next point is fundamental to all three religions:

> Peace implies not just the application of techniques on a vast

complex scale, not just the remaking of social and political structures, but a profound change in the depths of man himself. There must be a reordering of priorities and a transvaluation of values. (65)

The question then becomes: Is it possible for human beings to reorder their lives, their priorities? Pessimists say "No" because humans are essentially selfish, hostile and aggressive. However, if our true natures are more adequately described by Locke than Hobbes, that is, our true nature is wholeness rather than brokenness, cooperation rather than aggression, empathy rather than envy, self-giving rather than selfishness, then, perhaps, we can reorder our lives. For Macquarrie, this requires awareness that spiritual peace is a gift:

> This is the reason for both religious and [some] secular writers describing peace as somehow a gift, to be accepted or absorbed, for it means in this sense accepting ourselves, accepting what is most fundamentally *given* in our humanity, although in actual life this given is distorted and covered up by the innumerable sins into which men fall. In the pursuit of peace we are summoned to engage in many active enterprises, but within them all and beyond them all we are asked to accept what man truly is. We are being asked to give free course to a wholeness that is already part of the gift of being. (65-66)

Using terminology common to Jewish and Christian theologies, actualizing the spiritual purpose and meaning of our creation requires us to allow the image of God within each of us to grow and bloom. Such growth requires the awareness that spiritual peace comes from God, an honest confession of our brokenness and a willingness to receive the mysterious gift of peace. An often quoted passage from the **Qur'an** recognizes the necessity of this open willingness in affirming that God will not change a man until he is willing to change himself. From this awareness, confession and willingness, how then does one open himself to receive such a spiritual gift? The usual response is through faith, but Macquarrie, quoting Berger, provides a deeper insight when he characterizes the step that humans must make in terms of trust:

> Sociologist Peter Berger gives an illustration of what I have in mind. He pictures a child, waking up in the dark. There are no familiar objects visible, 'the contours of trusted reality are blurred', as Berger expresses it. The child cries out. The mother comes to comfort him. She will probably say something like, 'Don't be afraid, everything is in order, everything is all right.' Berger points out that trivial though such an incident may seem, it has far reaching implications. To say 'everything is in order' is to make a metaphysical assertion. Let me quote his words. 'The formula can, without in any way violating it, be translated into a statement of cosmic scope--"Have trust in being!"' He concludes: 'At the very center of the process of becoming fully human, and the core of *humanitas*, we find an experience of trust in the order of reality.' (67)

Judaism, Christianity, and Islam clearly affirm that "To have trust in God" is necessary to experience spiritual peace. Chapters Two, Three, and Four examine in more detail this shared theology of peace as well as indicate differences among the three.

Chapter Outline and Summaries

Before turning to the first chapter only two brief tasks remain: an outline-summary of the chapters of the book and a statement concerning the purposes and functions of the extensive footnotes in each chapter.

CHAPTER ONE
THE CHILDREN OF ABRAHAM

This chapter explores the traditions of belief and value shared by Judaism, Christianity and Islam. Emphasis is given to the role of Abraham, the theological significance of the Divine Name(?), the nature of and oneness of God, the role of the

30

prophets, and the fundamental significance of the Holy Books. While examining differences in these three great religions, the chapter concentrates on issues of commonality as a basis for respect, dialogue, and peace and provides a perspective for the distinct studies of each religions' theologies of war and peace in the following three chapters.

CHAPTER TWO

FROM YAHWEH THE WARRIOR TO ELOH-IM THE CREATOR

This chapter examines the understandings of both war and peace (in all three dimensions) in the **Hebrew Bible** and the religious traditions which are incorporated in this great revelation of 24 books as they develop through three major periods: the pre-monarchial period (before 1000 B.C.E.), the monarchial period (1000-586 B.C.E.) and the Exile and post-exhilic period (after 586 B.C.E.) that had major influences on Christianity and Islam. This chapter also examines the religious movements from pre-monarchial polytheism to post-exhilic monotheism as evidenced in the **Hebrew Bible**. Throughout the analysis attention is focused on the connections among chosenness, promised-sacred land, and holy war.

CHAPTER THREE

A MESSIANIC ESCHATOLOGICAL PRINCE OF PEACE

This chapter explores the emergence of Christian views of war and peace from their Jewish eschatological roots and ways in which the universalism of Christianity significantly changes the ideas of chosenness, sacred land, and holy war. Attention is given to the **New Testament** theology of war and peace as essentially spiritual and cosmic-eschatological in contrast to the Hebrew view of political war.

CHAPTER FOUR

ISLAM AND THE PEACE OF SUBMISSION

This chapter identifies and concentrates on those passages in the **Qur'an** which speak either (or both) of war or peace. It begins the analyses of war by examining the nature of Arabic warfare during the time of Muhammad, then concentrates on the various theologies of war as developed in the **Qur'an** and the **Hadiths** with emphasis on the spiritual *jihad* as the true *jihad* that is at the center of Muslim theology, and concludes with the **Qur'an**'s considerable theology of peace (a topic unfamiliar to most Americans who wrongly think of the **Qur'an** as little more than a Holy War Manual).

CHAPTER FIVE

REFLECTIONS ON THE TRUE SPIRITUAL JIHAD:

AN APOLOGY FOR PEACE AMONG JEWS, CHRISTIANS AND MUSLIMS

The chapter reflects on the nature of religion and unholy wars. It then explores the sacredness of peace. Finally, it concludes with reflections on the true spiritual *jihad* and the righteous nature of chosenness as chosenness **TO BE** rather than chosenness **TO HAVE**.

EPILOGUE

MANY VOICES BUT ONE HEART

The epilogue presents both a meditation and a hope: a meditation on the ONENESS of God and a hope for the religious ONENESS of humanity! As such it encourages a faith in the providence of God and based on this providence a hope that the dimming lights for peace in Bethlehem will again shine brightly throughout the world!

One final note is required. Identification of sources uses in-text-documentation. Footnotes are used for the following: (1) to clarify or define key terms in the main text; (2) to call attention to other related parts of the study--this is also done in the main text at times; (3) to relate issues in the text to current situations in the Middle East; (4) to call attention to other sources which include important information concerning the subject under examination; (5) to elaborate on an issue in the main text; and (6) occasionally to express a personal judgment on the part of the author.

CHAPTER ONE
THE CHILDREN OF ABRAHAM

On a fall day in 1978 in a seminary bookstore in Bangor, Maine I purchased my first complete copy of the Masoretic Text of the **Hebrew Bible**. As I tenderly carried it from the bookstore, my joy and excitement increased with each step, for in my hands I was holding nearly three thousand years of a peoples' struggle to understand their relationship with God and possibly carrying the most influential book written in the history of the West. Both claims require explanation. First, within those 24 books (see footnote #2 on page 35) that comprise the **Hebrew Bible** were incorporated an oral tradition that quite possibly predates the fifteenth century B.C.E.[1] and a writing period of at least eight hundred years (approximately 1000 to 200 B.C.E.). This was followed by a millennium during which these manuscripts were copied and illuminated with loving care and devotion, and the scholarly, faithful Masorites added vowels to the consonantal texts and began the series of commentaries that form the massive **Talmud** of Medieval Judaism. Altogether,

---

[1]
      There is a considerable and on-going debate among archaeologists concerning the elements of the Patriarchal stories in Genesis 12-50. Some argue for their origins in the Middle Bronze period (c.2200-2000 B.C.E.), others in the Middle Bronze II period (c.2000-1750 B.C.E.), and others in the Late Bronze period (c.1550-1200 B.C.E.). Whatever the outcome of this debate, if it is ever adequately resolved, it seems reasonable to date some of the oral traditions of Genesis to the fifteenth century if not earlier.

then, the **Hebrew Bible** reveals the theological history and faith of one of the most amazing and resilient peoples in the history of the West for a period approaching three millennia. Second, the claim that the **Hebrew Bible** is possibly the most influential book written in the West requires explanation since there are fewer than 14 million Jews in today's world, not all practicing religious Jews. According to recent statistics printed in **Parade Magazine** (August 4, 1996, p.9) the relative populations of the world's major religions are: ". . . about 1.06 billion Roman Catholics, 1.03 billion Muslims, 764 million Hindus, 391 Protestants, 339 million Buddhists and 13.5 million Jews in the world. . . ." While such religious statistics usually have larger margins of error than most population statistics, these figures are reasonably consistent with most sources. If it is correct to claim that both Christianity and Islam developed from the great prophetic movement of the eighth century B.C.E. Jews, as this study argues, then the influence of the **Hebrew Bible** which transmits the preachings and teachings of these prophets has been and continues to be an influence on almost 2.5 billion human beings spread throughout the world. Religiously, this makes it a candidate for the most influential religious work in Western history. As is the case with most works of spiritual greatness, it has inspired courageous acts of sacrifice and spiritual insight, encouraged the growth of compassion, fostered the development of social justice and, unfortunately, been used to justify horrible acts of intolerance and destruction. One of the purposes of this study is to examine the sacred texts in all three monotheisms to better understand their interpretative potentials for inspiring both human creativity and human destructiveness. As a foundation for exploring each revelation individually in the next three chapters, it is important to first examine their connectedness.

The study of the connections among Judaism, Christianity, and Islam which follows is not meant to duplicate the scholarly work of F.E. Peters in **The Children of Abraham** and his impressive three volume **Judaism, Christianity, and Islam** nor the excellent studies of Karen Armstrong in her two superb studies titled **A History of God** and **Holy War: The Crusades and Their Impact on Today's World**.

Rather the purpose of this chapter is to set a common foundation for the study of peace and war in the belief that if we begin by understanding and respecting what we share as Jews, Christians, and Muslims this sets the stage for conversation (trialogue) rather than the conflict which inevitably results from angry, intolerant arguments that focus on whose beliefs represent "THE TRUTH." Consequently, in a spirit of religious humility and toleration, four foundational issues common to all three religions are examined: the theological traditions of Abraham, that is, for what reasons do each religion claim to be the child of Abraham; the theological significance of the Oneness of a God who has no name (or whose name is never to be uttered); the traditions and teachings of the great prophets (eighth century B.C.E. to seventh century C.E.); and, the centrality of the three revelations, the **Hebrew Bible**, the **New Testament** and the **Qur'an**.[2]

2

For purposes of consistency and respect for the quality of translation all cited texts from the **Hebrew Bible** and **The New Testament** are from **The Jerusalem Bible** published by Doubleday & Company, Inc., Garden City, New York. All cited texts from the **Qur'an** are from A.Yusuf Ali's translation, **The Holy Qur'an**, published originally by Amana Corporation and today by Tahrike Tarsde Qur'an, Inc.. While **The Jerusalem Bible** includes translations of additional books accepted by the Jews of the Dispersion (the **Septuagint**) but excluded from the canon accepted by first century C.E. Palestinian Jews, that is, those books usually referred to as apocryphal, for purposes of this study only those included in the Masoretic Text (the Palestinian revelation) are examined. Finally, the 39 books in the Christian **Old Testament,** which follow the organization and titles of the **Septuagint,** are essentially the same as those that comprise the 24 books of the Masoretic Text (M.T.) of the **Hebrew Bible**. The differences in number, 24 or 39, are due largely to organization and combining. Briefly the two organizations are as follows:

The Masoretic Text

The *Torah*: *Bereshith* (Beginnings), *Shemoth* (Names), *Wayiqra* (And he called), *Bemidbar* (In the wilderness), and *Debar-im* (Words);

Nebi-im (Prophets):

Former: *Yehoshua* (Joshua), *Shopet-im* (Judges), *Shemuel* (I & II Samuel), *Melak-im* (I & II Kings);

Latter: *Yeshayahu* (Isaiah), *Yermevahu* (Jeremiah), *Yehezqel* (Ezekiel), *Tere Asar* (Book of the Twelve);

Ketub-im (Writings): *Tehill-im* (Psalms), *Iyyob* (Job), *Mishle* (Proverbs),

The Traditions of the Children of Abraham

Americans who occasionally pay attention to news releases from the Middle East are generally acquainted with the controversy over Hebron. From the pragmatic American perspective, the solution to Hebron seems simple. Since the tension is created because there is a small group of Jews (approximately 450) living in a hostile sea of thousands of Palestinians for whom Hebron is home, the solution is clear: move the 450 Jews. The inconvenience of 450 people is little enough a price to pay for progress in the peace process, especially since the U.N. partition and the 1967 War have more than inconvenienced hundreds of thousands of Palestinians. For those who share a sympathy for this American viewpoint (as I do), it is important, however, to be aware of the reasons for the passion of this small number of Jews. In addition to the courage it requires to live in such circumstances, it requires a powerful passion. While many of the 450 live in Hebron because of their political passion for territory in the occupied lands and passionate commitment to the state of Israel, undergirding this political passion thrives a religious commitment. Religiously, Hebron is second in sacredness to only a few places within the walled Old City of Jerusalem for many Jews: it is the traditional location of the Tombs of the Patriarchs. Hebron, then, is not just any piece of real estate, but sacred land for

---

Ruth Shir Hashirim (Song of Solomon), *Qohelet* (Ecclesiastes), *Ekah* (Lamentations), *Ester* (Esther), *Dan'el* (Daniel), *Ezra'-Nehemya* (Ezra-Nehemiah), *Dibre Hayami-im* (I & II Chronicles).

The Christian Old Testament (**Septuagint**)

The Pentateuch: Genesis, Exodus, Leviticus, Numbers and Deuteronomy;

Historical Books: Joshua, Judges, Ruth, I & II Samuel, I & II Kings, I & II Chronicles, Ezra, Nehemiah, and Ester;

Poetry and Wisdom: Job, Psalms, Proverbs, Ecclesiastes, Song of Solomon;

Prophetic Books: Isaiah, Jeremiah, Lamentations, Ezekiel, Daniel, Hosea, Joel, Amos, Obadiah, Jonah, Micah, Nahum, Habakkuk, Zephaniah, Haggai, Zechariah and Malachi.

both Jews and Muslims and even for Christians. The reason is Abraham.

Abraham, under the name Abram first appears in the **Hebrew Bible** in Genesis 11:27 which describes the journey his father Terah made from Ur to Haran (from lower Mesopotamia to northwest Mesopotamia). From that introduction to the present day, Abraham occupies a seminal place in the religious traditions of all three monotheisms but especially Judaism and Islam. Before examining the religious tradition of Abraham in all three, it is important to describe the historical and archeological issues concerning the person of Abraham and the ethnic origins of both Jews (Hebrews) and Arabs. While these issues still generate considerable controversy, one thing is clear: the religious traditions of Judaism and Islam both claim Abraham as their Father and through Paul, Christianity claims to be the true spiritual child of Abraham.

While it may be uncomfortable for many monotheists to acknowledge, there is no known reference to Abraham outside the religious traditions of Judaism, Islam, and Christianity. For serious scholars this creates many difficult issues. Some view him as a later construction of post-exhilic Jews while others identify the Abraham narratives in Genesis and the **Qur'an** as legend.[3] Understood as legend, three

---

[3]

    It is important to note that such an identification as legend does not deny truth value or historical status to the person of Abraham. One of the scholarly benefits of applying the tools of higher and lower criticism to scriptural studies is the use of literary categories to these revelations. Among the four narrative types found in these scriptures are myth, legend, saga, and fable. None of these categories denies truth value to the narratives, but clarifies the kind of truth associated with each. Myths are narratives whose major agents are supernatural beings or super heroes who are something more than human. Using this classification, then, much of the first eleven chapters of Genesis is myth. Such an identification does not deny that the God of Genesis Chapter One created the universe, only that the chapter cannot be taken literally, and the truths revealed there are of a different kind than those of science. Understood in this manner, the believer in God as a creator does not need to be afraid of evolution, for the truths in Genesis concern the meaning of existence not how it was done. Legends are narratives whose major actors are human persons whose actions take place in time and space, that is, in history. However the category

consequences follow: (1) Since there are no non-scriptural references to Abraham (references outside the religious traditions incorporated in the **Hebrew Bible** and **Qur'an)**, we must be careful about historical claims concerning the life of Abraham. This does not deny his historical existence but warns about a naive acceptance of legend as fact. (2) For the same reasons, we also know very little about the religious beliefs of Abraham. (3) Finally, combined with the historical difficulties of adequately identifying the origins of (the ancestors of) both Jews and Arabs, it is almost impossible to determine the relationship of Abraham to these two groups with any historical accuracy. None of these consequences denies historical truth to the religious traditions, but they do warn against uncritical, emotional acceptance of legend as fact. However, because it is true that their religious traditions have inspired believers in all three religions, it is important to examine the scriptural traditions themselves after a brief description of the problems inherent in identifying the historical ancestors of the Jews and Arabs.

Stated simply, the greatest difficulty, apart from those created by the religious traditions, in identifying the actual ancestors of these two Semitic peoples is the paucity of written records in the third and second millenniums B.C.E..

---

of legend indicates that while there may be considerable historical facts in such narratives, their transmission through generations embellish the actual history involved. Most Americans are aware of this in terms of the legend of George Washington and the cherry tree. Major historical figures, especially political and religious heroes, tend to become more than human through the passage of time. Thus, the identification of the Abraham narratives as legends does not deny the historicity of an individual Abraham, but it does point to the fact that the accounts have undergone considerable embellishment. One of the scriptural scholar's responsibilities is the struggle to recover the actual history from the legend. Briefly, sagas are narratives whose major actors are usually tribes or groups of people, and fables are narratives whose agents are animals or plants. The **Hebrew Bible**, unlike much religious literature, makes little use of fables. Some scriptural scholars argue that the Abraham narratives are more appropriately sagas than legends; that is, they should be understood as describing the movements of a tribal group from Mesopotamia to Palestine rather than understood as stories of an individual. There are merits to both interpretations.

However, before examining the archeological evidence, another issue deserves notice: the problem of identifying to whom the terms *Jew* and *Arab* can be reasonably applied. Even today, much less historically, it is difficult to know how to apply both terms. First, historically or currently, the unfortunately common view that there are groups of people whose ethnicity is monolithic enough to be identified as either Jews or Arabs is simply naive.[4]   In his book, **The Arabs**, Maxime Rodinson aptly examines the near impossibility of finding any single criterion that can be used to identify adequately that group to whom the term *Arab* appropriately applies. In his first chapter, "Who Are the Arabs?," he tries ethnic criteria, geographical criteria, linguistic criteria, cultural criteria, religious criteria, and finally even the idea that one is an Arab if they believe that they are an Arab. None of these kinds of criteria are adequate. He eventually settles on the "Arab ethnos" as the most adequate noun to which the term *Arab* is useful. As such, this use of the term incorporates most of the preceding sets of criteria. His point is important: there is no simple identification of an Arab. The same is true of the term *Jew*. Aware of the difficulties in the uses of these two terms, it is now appropriate to turn to the historical and archeological issues involved.

In addition to the problems of distinguishing the historical Abraham from the religious Abraham of legend and the difficulties of cogently applying the terms *Jew* and *Arab* to peoples, there is the historical problem of written uses of the terms *Hebrew*[5] and *Arab* and a textual problem in Genesis Chapter 14. Let us consider the

---

4

This same point applies to most ethnic identity efforts, especially those that are used to encourage bigotry. If it were not for the horrible human costs of ethnic bigotry, the stereotype of ethnic purity which bigotry assumes would be laughable. There are no pure Africans, Germans, Japanese, Americans, Jews, or Arabs, etc.. In a biological sense, we are all hybrids. Ethnic bigotry, then, is a red herring.

5

For purposes of this study, excluding the following chapter, the terms *Hebrew, Israeli* and *Jew* are used interchangeably. This terminology is in keeping with a common Western tradition that identifies living Jews with the Biblical

textual problem first. Chapter 14:13 contains the most important biblical reference which identifies Abraham as a Hebrew: "a survivor came to tell Abram the Hebrew, who was living at the Oak of the Amorite Mamre . . ." about the capture of his nephew Lot. For the non-critical reader this single statement suffices to prove that Abraham was a Hebrew. But there is a problem with the source of this text as well as the contextual meaning of the term *Hebrew*. Gerhard von Rad in his excellent commentary, **Genesis,** succinctly states the issue:

> As the whole narrative now stands, in view of the many traces of an artificially archaisizing erudition, one must consider it a rather late literary product, in spite of the antiquity of isolated traditional elements. One such artificial element is the designation of Abraham as a "Hebrew." "Hebrew" in ancient times was not a national designation, but rather a frequent designation in the second millennium in many lands for a lower class of society. In the Old Testament the expression is used by non-Israelites or Israelites for foreigners. It is used as a general designation for a people only here and in a likewise literarily late document (Jonah 1:9). (p.174)

In other words, the uses of the term *Hebrew* in the **Hebrew Bible** do not historically

---

Hebrews or Israelites. As pointed out in the preceding paragraph such identifications are both problematic and questionable. Regarding Chapter Two, there is such a considerable difference between the religious beliefs of the Jewish (Hebrew) people before and after the Babylonian Exile that the term *Hebrew* is used to indicate pre-exhilic peoples and beliefs while *Jew* (or *Jewish*) are used to indicate post-exhilic peoples and beliefs. The term *Israeli also* poses considerable problems which can be stated in terms of several questions: Is it applicable to pre-Davidic biblical people? Is it applicable to all Hebrews only during the reigns of David and Solomon? Is it applicable to the Hebrew people of the north after the civil war at Solomon's death but not to those in the south who lived in Judah? It can and has been used in all three ways. Even today, many American Jews would claim to be Israelis, but should this term be limited to only citizens of the state of Israel? In this study the term Israeli will be used, unless otherwise noted, in reference to a political identity rather than a religious or ethnic one.

substantiate an ethnic relation between the Israelites and Abraham. Its pre-exhilic use by both Israelites and non-Israelites was somewhat derogatory, that is, a term for referring to people from the "wrong side of the tracks." Consequentially, the Hebrew text of Genesis 14 offers no substantive help in determining the ethnic identity of Abraham.

The other problematic issue regarding the identity of the Hebrews concerns the relative lateness of written uses of the term compared with traditional dates for the period of the Patriarchs which was between 2000-1700 B.C.E.. While there are revisionists who argue that there were no distinct people called Israelites (Hebrews) until after the Babylonian Captivity, many Biblical scholars argue for a possible identity between the Habiru of the eighteenth-seventeenth centuries B.C.E. and the Hebrews; however, this identification is anything but certain. It is not unreasonable to infer that the Habiru were the Hebrew who would become known as the Israelis (or Israelites), but it is far from certain. What is more certain is that there was an identifiable people known as Israelites by at least the thirteenth century B.C.E.. In a recent interview with archeologist William Dever in **Biblical Archeology Review** (July/August 1996) reference is made to the Merneptah Stele:

> "ISRAEL IS LAID WASTE, his seed is not" declares the Merneptah Stele--somewhat prematurely. The reference to Israel, the oldest known mention of the people outside the Bible, appears on the Stele's second to last line . . . . The 7.5-foot-high monument was erected in the funerary temple in Thebes of Pharaoh Merneptah, who ruled from 1213 to 1203 B.C.. William Dever states in the accompanying interview that this reference presents persuasive evidence against those minimalists who argue that there was no distinct people called Israelites until after the Babylonian Exile. If the pharaoh of Egypt knew them by the name Israelites and felt that a victory against them was worth boasting about, the people must

> have had an . . . identity by at least the end of the 13th century B.C.
> (p.36)

Dever's argument is persuasive for identifying people as Israelites but does not settle the historical issue of the relation between Abraham and the Hebrews (Israelites, Jews).

There is a similar problem in identifying the origins of the Arabs. Rodinson briefly states the archeological problem in the following passage:

> Did the tribes of ancient Arabia that spoke Arabic or proto-Arabic see themselves as having a common identity? Did they call themselves "Arabs"? All we are certain of is that early in the first millennium B.C. their neighbors to the north applied this term to a group of tribes in the northern portion of the Arabian peninsula. In Akkadian the name was Aribi, Arabi, Arubu, Urbu; in Hebrew it was 'Arab. It made its earliest appearance in a [written] text of the Assyrian king Shalamaneser III. In 853 B.C. at Qarqar in Syria he defeated a coalition of Syrian and Israelite kings with 1000 cameleers "from Gindibu in the Arabi country." (13)

To summarize, either within the Biblical texts or from external archeological evidence there is no historically conclusive way to link together Abraham and the Jews or Arabs. However, what is unquestionably certain is that the religious traditions of Judaism, Christianity, and Islam make definite claims about Abraham's children. We now turn to the scriptural claims.

In the **Hebrew Bible** Abram (Abraham) is introduced near the end of Chapter 11 and his death is described in Chapter 25. As told in these fourteen chapters, the legend of Abraham incorporates many narratives and several textual sources, but there are four scriptural passages that are fundamental for the tradition that makes him the father of the Jews, indeed, in Aramaic Abraham may mean "the father is exalted":

> Yahweh said to Abram, 'Leave your country, your family and

your father's house, for the land I will show you. I will make you a great nation; I will bless you and make your name so famous that it will be used as a blessing.

I will bless those who bless you: I will curse those who slight you. All the tribes of the earth shall bless themselves by you.

So Abram went as *Yahweh* told him, and Lot with him. . . . They set off for the land of Canaan, and arrived there.

Abram passed through the land as far as Shechem's holy place, the Oak of Moreh. At that time the Canaanites were in the land. *Yahweh* appeared to Abram and said, 'It is to your descendants that I will give this land'. So Abram built there an altar for *Yahweh* who had appeared to him. (12:1-7)

When Abram was ninety-nine years old *Yahweh* appeared to him and said, 'I am El Shaddai. Bear yourself blameless in my presence, and I will make a Covenant between myself and you, and increase your numbers greatly.

Abram bowed to the ground and God said this to him, 'Hear now is my Covenant with you: you shall become the father of a multitude of nations. You shall no longer be called Abram; your name shall be Abraham, for I make you father of a multitude of nations. I will make you most fruitful. I will make you into nations, and your issue shall be kings. I will establish my Covenant between myself and you, and your descendants after you, generation after generation, a Covenant in perpetuity, to be your God and the God of your descendants after you. I will give to you and your descendants after you the land you are living in, the whole land of Canaan, to own in perpetuity, and I will be your God.'

God said to Abraham, 'You on your part shall maintain my Covenant, yourself and your descendants after you, generation after generation. Now this is my Covenant which you are to maintain between myself and you, and your descendants after you: all your males must be circumcised. (17:1-10)

Yahweh dealt kindly with Sarah as he had said, and did what he had promised her. So Sarah conceived and bore a son to Abraham in his old age, at the time God had promised. Abraham named the son born to him Isaac, the son to whom Sarah had given birth.[6] Abraham circumcised his son Isaac when he was eight days old, as God had commanded him. . . .

The child grew and was weaned, and Abraham gave a great banquet on the day Isaac was weaned. Now Sarah watched the son that Hagar the Egyptian had born to Abraham [Ishmael], playing with her son Isaac. 'Drive away that slave girl and her son,' she said to Abraham; 'this slave-girl's son is not to share the inheritance of my son Isaac.' This greatly distressed Abraham because of his son, but God said to him, 'Do not distress yourself on account of the boy and your slave-girl. Grant Sarah all she asks of you, for it is through Isaac that your name will be carried on. (21:1-12)

The number of years Abraham lived was a hundred and seventy-five. Then Abraham breathed his last, dying at a ripe old age, an old man who had lived his full span of years; and he was gathered to his people. His sons Isaac and Ishmael buried him in the cave of Machpelah opposite Mamre, in the field of Ephron the Hittite, son of Zohar. [Chapter 23 identifies this sight as Hebron.] This was the field that Abraham had bought from the sons of Heth, and Abraham and his

---

[6]

As all Jews, Christians, and Muslims know, Isaac was the second son born to Abraham. The birth of Ishmael is examined in the Muslim tradition of Abraham's children.

wife Sarah were buried there. After Abraham's death God blessed his son Isaac, and Isaac lived near the well of Lahai Roi. (25:7-11)

Setting aside the scholarly problems of separating the historical Abraham from the legendary one and the immense difficulty of identifying a people to whom the designation Hebrew, Israelite, or Jew applies prior to the fifteenth century B.C.E., these four scriptural passages connect the elements that have become passionately central to claims on the part of Jews, Christians, and Muslims: chosenness and promised-sacred land. More specifically for Jews, these are the passages which express those beliefs that have formed their religious and ethnic identity for millennia: they are the **Chosen** children of Abraham through the favored son Isaac, and as the Chosen Ones the sign of their chosenness is male circumcision, and the most important physical benefit of their chosenness is the **Promised Land**. Other aspects and benefits of being the Chosen People of God emerge in two other covenants: the Mosaic--Sinai Covenant which reaffirms chosenness, promised land and something new and of major significance, the gift of God's Law **and** the Davidic-Zion Covenant which affirms past covenant elements and also adds a most important new one: the sacredness of Jerusalem. Christians and Muslims, however, offer different interpretations of these covenant elements. In considering their views, although it is out of chronological order, it is best to examine the Muslim view before the Christian one.

While there are over twenty *suras* (chapters) and more than 100 *ayats* (verses) in the **Qur'an** which mention Abraham, the identification of Arabs as children of Abraham first originates in the religious traditions of the Jews and is incorporated in several key passages in Genesis; the two most important are:

Abram's wife Sarai [Sarah] had borne him no child, but she had a maidservant named Hagar. So Sarai said to Abram, 'Listen, now! Since *Yahweh* has kept me from having children, go to my slave-girl. Perhaps I shall get children through her. Abram agreed to what Sarai had said.

Thus after Abram had lived in the land of Canaan for ten years Sarai took Hagar her Egyptian slave-girl and gave her to Abram as his wife. He went to Hagar and she conceived. . . .

[There follows an account of Sarai's jealousy and mistreatment of Hagar who flees into the desert to escape her tormentor. An angel of *Yahweh* appears to Hagar informing her to return to her mistress with a familiar promise.]

The angel of *Yahweh* said to her, 'I will make your descendants too numerous to be counted'. Then the angel of *Yahweh* said to her: 'Now you have conceived, and you will bear a son, and you shall name him *Ishma-el*, for *Yahweh* has heard your cries of distress. A wild-ass of a man he will be, against every man, and every man against him, setting himself to defy all his brothers.

. . . .

Hagar bore Abram a son, and Abram gave to the son that Hagar bore the name Ishmael. Abram was eighty-six years old when Hagar bore him Ishmael. (16:1-16)

. . . . [Following God's command to Abraham to send Hagar and Ishmael away and the declaration that it is through Isaac that Abraham's "name will be carried on," the text of Genesis 21 continues.] 'But the slave-girl's son I will also make into a nation, for he is your child too'. Rising early next morning Abraham took some bread and a skin of water and, giving them to Hagar, he put the child on her shoulder and sent her away.

She wandered of into the wilderness of Beersheba. When the skin of water was finished she abandoned the child under a bush. Then she went and sat down at a distance . . . saying to herself, 'I cannot see the child die'. So she sat at a distance; and the child wailed and wept.

But God heard the boy wailing, and the angel of God called to Hagar from heaven, 'What is wrong, Hagar?' he asked. 'Do not be afraid, for God has heard the boy's cry from where he lies. Come, pick up the boy and hold him safe, for I will make him into a great nation'. Then God opened Hagar's eyes and she saw a well, so she went and filled the skin with water and gave the boy a drink.

God was with the boy. He grew up and made his home in the wilderness, and he became a bowman. (21:13-20)

While the Hebrew scriptures affirm that God was with Ishmael, it is not in the same way that God is with Isaac; in other words, the relationship of the sons of Isaac (the Chosen Ones) with God is a covenant one including promised land, but the relationship with the sons of Ishmael (the unchosen ones) has no covenant aspect in the **Hebrew Bible** and all that such a covenant signifies.

The **Qur'an**, however, develops quite a different theology of chosenness. First it elaborates on God's protection of Hagar and Ishmael and interprets this as a sign of Ishmael's own chosenness. A key *sura* is the second one:[7]

---

[7]

The translation of Ali which is used in this study attempts to maintain the form of poetry by a vertical separation of each *ayat* as is common to English poetry rather than the horizontal form of prose. Because this requires considerable space on a page, this study compresses each *ayat* into paragraph form, but in order to indicate the vertical structure of Ali's translation, each line in the compressed paragraph retains the capital letter as in his poetic form and is separated by a slash, "/". Doing this does not compromise the content of the *ayat* although it does betray the visual form of the poetry. The same procedure is used with lengthy citations of poetry from the **Hebrew Bible**. The **Qur'an** is written in the form of Arabic poetry from beginning to end. Unfortunately, while something is always lost in translating from one language to another, more is lost when translating poetry than any other form of literature. Will Durant's analogy is most descriptive when he writes that translating poetry is like translating a song without the musical score. So beautiful are the poetic revelations of the **Qur'an** that it is not unusual to see grown men weep as it is recited by an *Imam*. The music that is lost in translation is also the reason that many Christians find translations of the **Qur'an** tedious and repetitive. Nothing could be less true for Muslims.

And remember that Abraham / Was tried by his Lord / With certain Commands,/ Which he fulfilled: He said: / "I will make thee / An Imam to the Nations." / He pleaded: "And also / (Imams) from my offspring!" / He answered: "But my Promise / Is not within the reach / Of evil-doers."

Remember We made the House [the Ka'ba] / A place of assembly for men / And a place of safety; / And take ye the Station / Of Abraham as a place / Of prayer; and We covenanted / With Abraham and Isma'il, / That they should sanctify / My House for those who / Compass it round, or use it / As a retreat, or bow, or / Prostrate themselves (therein In prayer).

And remember Abraham said: / "My Lord, make this a City / Of Peace, and feed its People / With fruits--such as them / As believe in God and the Last Day." / He said: "(Yea), and such as Reject Faith-- / for a while Will I grant them their pleasure, / But will soon drive them / To the torment of Fire,-- / An evil destination (indeed)!"

And remember Abraham / And Isma'il raised / The foundations of the House / (With this prayer): "Our Lord! / Accept (this service) from us: / For Thou art the All-Hearing, / The All-Knowing.

. . . .

And this was the legacy / That Abraham left to his sons, / And so did Jacob; / "Oh my sons! God hath chosen / The Faith for you; then die not / Except in the Faith of Islam."

Were ye witnesses / When Death appeared before Jacob? / Behold, he said to his sons: / "What will ye worship after me?" / They said: "We shall worship / Thy God and the God of thy fathers,-- / Of Abraham, Isma'il, and Isaac,-- / The One (True) God: / To Him we bow (in Islam)." (*ayats* 124-133)

In the citations from both Genesis and the second *sura*, the religious traditions of both Jews and Muslims identify the Arabs as the children of God, however, with one critical difference: the issue of chosenness. The **Hebrew Bible** identifies those children of Abraham through Isaac as the Chosen Children, that is, those who received the covenant and covenant promises from God, while the **Qur'an** recognizes a covenant relationship through Isma'il as well as Isaac: ". . . We covenanted / With Abraham and Isma'il . . . ." and later in response to the approaching death of Jacob, ". . . We shall worship / Thy God and the God of thy fathers,-- / Of Abraham, Isma'il, and Isaac,--The One (True) God: / To Him we bow (in Islam)." While accepting that the Jews have a covenant relationship with God, the **Qur'an** does claim that it is one they have misunderstood and abused, but it never denies a special relationship for the Jews nor for the Christians with the God of Abraham, Isaac, Isma'il, and Jacob. Whatever the actual historical facts, the religious traditions of both Jews and Muslims identify Abraham as their Father. While the same may be said for Christianity, the reasons are quite different.

While originally the teachings of Jesus were confined to a small collection of Jews mostly in the vicinity of Jerusalem within two decades after the crucifixion, these teaching had begun to spread not only beyond Palestine but beyond the Jewish community. The missionary whose activities were largely responsible for this astounding growth was also the theologian whose struggles with the relationship between Judaism and Christianity would eventually result in the claim that it is Christians who are the "spiritual children of Abraham": Paul. Paul's missionary successes among the Gentiles not only helped spread the Christian message around the Mediterranean, but they also created the first major crisis for the young faith that would initially be called Christian as a mark of derision: must Gentile Christians be circumcised before they are baptized? While this question seems strange to contemporary Christians, it was crucial for the future of Christianity as a missionary religion and for the developing of Christian theology. The crisis over circumcism concerned one fundamental question: what is the relationship between God's actions through Jesus and God's covenant with the Jews? The fact that there were no written scriptures for Christians at this time made the issue even more difficult to decide. Consequently, what has been called the Jerusalem Council[8] met to decide the issue. Historically we know very little about this meeting other than that a moderate decision was made: Christians are to respect the covenant that God made with the Jews, a covenant mostly understood in terms of the Laws of God, but they are not confined by this covenant and its resulting laws. In other words, for Christians, God has offered in the incarnate Christ a new covenant that, while built upon the one with the Jews, cannot be confined to the old covenant. One eventual consequence of this decision is readily seen in the Christian Bible, for it contains an Old Testament (Old Covenant) and a New Testament (New Covenant). Although the Jerusalem Council set the stage for the two testaments, it was the theological struggles of Paul, especially those struggles communicated in his letter to the Christians in Rome, that became the fundamental Christian theological interpretation of the old covenant. Paul's interpretative theology on this relationship is developed along many lines, but the two most important are his theologies of the two Adams (Romans Chapter 5) and of the true children of Abraham (Romans Chapter 4).

In Romans Chapter 4 Paul writes:[9]

---

[8]

What little is known about this pivotal meeting during the very early history of Christianity is recorded in Acts Chapter 15. The chapter provides a frustrating scarcity of information other than the position advanced by James that is characterized in this paragraph as the moderate position.

[9]

In his various letters Paul's references to scripture usually referred to writings that were sacred to the Pharisees, the more liberal of the Jewish schools of religion. The majority of the Greek texts which eventually comprised the Christian **New Testament** were composed approximately between 40-100 C.E. and were 99 percent completed by the middle of the second century C.E.; thus, Paul's references to scripture were references largely to the Pentateuch and the teachings of the great prophets. The Masoretic Text of the **Hebrew Bible**, while informally canonized, that is, accepted as religiously authoritative by most Palestinian Jews, was not formally

Apply this to Abraham, the ancestor from whom we are all descended. If Abraham was justified as a reward for doing something, he would really have something to boast about, though not in God's sight because scripture says: *Abraham put his faith in God, and this faith was considered as justifying him....* Is . . . happiness meant only for the circumcised, or is it meant for others as well? Think of Abraham again: *his faith*, we say, *was considered as justifying him*, but when was this done? When he was circumcised or before he had been circumcised? It was before he had been circumcised, not after; and when he was *circumcised* later it was only *as a sign* and a guarantee that the faith he had before his circumcism justified him. In this way Abraham became the ancestor of all uncircumcised believers, so that they too might be considered righteous; and ancestor, also, of those who through circumcised do not rely on that fact alone, but follow our ancestor Abraham along the path of faith he trod before he had been circumcised.

The promise of inheriting the world was not made to Abraham and his descendants on account of any law but on account of the righteousness which consists in faith. . . . That is why what fulfills the promise depends on faith, so that it may be a free gift and available to all of Abraham's descendants, not only those who belong to the Law but also those who belong to the faith of Abraham who is the father of us all. As scripture says: *I have made you the ancestor of many nations*--Abraham is our father in the eyes of God, in whom he put his faith, and who brings the dead to life and calls into being what does not exist. . . .

canonized and closed until 90 C.E., approximately 30 years after Paul's death and after the majority of the writings that comprise the 27 books of the **New Testament** were written.

Though it seemed Abraham's hope could not be fulfilled, he hoped and he believed, and through doing so he did become *the father of many nations* exactly as he had been promised: *Your descendants will be as many as the stars. . . .* This is the faith that was '*considered as justifying him*'. Scripture does not refer only to him but to us as well when it says that his faith was thus 'considered'; our faith too will be 'considered' if we put our faith in him who raised Jesus our Lord from the dead, Jesus who was *put to death for our sins* and raised to life to justify us. (1-25)

While Paul does not deny the Jews as covenant children of Abraham, he does suggest in this passage that there must be more than just circumcism, Paul's symbol for keeping the Law, to be a true child of Abraham: there must be faith. Since faith is the key to belonging to the covenant children of Abraham, for Paul, faith makes Christians truly the children of Abraham. There is no Jewish anti-Semitism in Paul's theological position, for he does not deny the covenant relationship between God and the Jews, but unfortunately and tragically, encouraged by the crusader fever of the later Medieval ages (after the 10th century C.E.), Paul's theology was twisted into a view that still creates conflict between Christians and Jews today. The conflict historically occurs when Christians argue that Jews are damned because they have denied the divinity of Christ, and , thus, they have violated their covenant with God. Such distorted interpretative theologies plague the history of Christianity from late Medieval times into the present and have been used to religiously justify a litany of atrocities against the Jews. This issue is further examined in the chapter on Christianity. Suffice it to conclude this section of the present chapter with the following observation: independent of the actual historical facts, which are largely unknown, and apart from arguments about the identity of the "true chosen ones," Jews, Christians, and Muslims all claim to be the Children of Abraham. While it is true that so often family conflicts are more bitter than those outside the family, it is also true that to identify a collection of people as a family means that there must be something which binds them together. It is an assumption, perhaps hope is a more accurate term, of this study that if we begin with what binds us together rather than what separates us, there is a greater possibility for trialogue than conflict. Proceeding on this hope, let us turn to those common beliefs which bind these three children: The Name (?) of God, the Oneness of God, the Tradition of the Prophets, and the Holy Books.

The Name (?) of God

Even in today's secular world, an orthodox rabbi when reading from the **Hebrew Bible** at worship in the synagogue cannot verbally utter the most sacred and ineffable term in the whole of Judaism: the Tetragrammaton (Greek for "four written letters"), *YHWH*. This tradition has a long, controversial history and a religious significance that is easy to underestimate. Consider for example, the following response from Francis Landry in the journal **Theology** (May 1981) to a previous article by David Clines which claimed that Jews as a whole did not object to Christian use of the Divine Name (*YHWH*):

> When David Clines claims that Jews on the whole would not be offended by the Christian use of the Divine Name, he is utterly mistaken. It is we who preserve Hebrew as a sacred language in which the Divine Name participates, even in its absence. One has only to hear the intimacy and affection with which the orthodox Jew says '*Hashem*' (i.e., 'The Name'). We are not allowed, however, nor has it been given to us, to say it, for we are in exile, and the loss of the Divine Name is one of the most poignant symbols of that exile.
> (164)

However, the Divine Name *YHWH* for Jews throughout the world is much more than a recognition of the ineffability of God but also a continuing reminder of the special covenant relationship that exists with God, that is, a reminder of their chosenesss. In other words, in the giving of the Divine Name to Moses, the covenant with

54

Abraham is reaffirmed and deepened and Moses is blessed beyond the Patriarchs:[10]

> God spoke to Moses and said to him, 'I am *Yahweh*. To
> Abraham and Isaac and Jacob I appeared as *El Shaddai*; I did not
> make myself known to them by my name *Yahweh*. Also, I made my
> covenant with them to give them the land of Canaan, the land they
> lived in as strangers. . . . Say this, then, to the sons of Israel, "I am
> *Yahweh*. . . . I will deliver you. I will adopt you as my own people,
> and I will be your God. Then you will know that it is I, *Yahweh* your
> God, who have freed you. . . . I will bring you to the land I swore that
> I would give to Abraham, and Isaac, and Jacob and will give it to you
> for your own; I, *Yahweh*, will do this!"' (Exodus 6:2-9)

For most Jews, then, the Divine Name has not only religious (covenant) significance
but also existential (emotional) and political--geographical (promised land) import.
In order to understand this, there are several issues that must be examined concerning
this Name that is, in certain respects, not a name: the importance of names in the

---

[10]
    One of the theological advantages of **The Jerusalem Bible** is its refusal to
translate the term *YHWH*. The Tetragrammaton has always created difficult
problems of translation. Many English translations followed the King James'
practice, which followed the LXX (**The Septuagint**) practice of translating *YHWH*
into *Kurios* (Greek for "Lord"), others have even used the less acceptable "Jehovah."
There is an excellent article in **The Bible Translator**, October 1992, pp.403-06
which describes the concerns of and conclusions reached by the UBS Triennial
Translation Workshop in Victoria Falls, Zimbabwe, May 1991, concerning
translating the Divine Name. Briefly, because translations in any language are
always misleading, especially those of names, and because Jewish sensitivities
concerning *YHWH* should be respected, they recommend the transliteration *YHWH*
or *Yahweh* rather than any translation (see footnote # 21, page 63). Except for the
terms "Israel," "Islam" and "Muslim," which are transliterations rather than
translations of Arabic terms, all other key terms which are transliterations from
Hebrew, Greek or Arabic are italicized to remind the reader that they are not
translations. Since the terms "Israel," "Islam" and "Muslim" are so extensively used,
and there are sections in Chapters Two and Four which explain their rich religious
meanings, they are not italicized.

ancient world, the transmitted history of the name (?) *YHWH*, the religious significance of *YHWH*, and the influence of the Jewish tradition concerning the name of God on Christianity and Islam.

From the moment that language emerged from human consciousness, which must have been millennia before the advent of written languages, nouns probably had a significance beyond all other parts of speech. While some nouns served to provide categories for the ordering of experience,[11] another kind of noun went beyond the mere categorizing of experience: names. In the ancient world names were invested with mana, that is with power and mystery: to know the name was to have a kind of power through knowing the true essence of that which has a name. In many primal tribes each individual had an all-purpose public name (not their true name) by which they could be addressed, but their true name was known by only a few persons, usually the tribal shaman and the parents. The reason was the power of names: to know the name was to exercise a kind of power, especially in speaking the name. There is a sense in the ancient world in which words in general (names in particular) had a kind of life (mana)[12] In the terrible power of blessings and curses an excellent

---

[11]

There are several ways that the human mind orders the varied experiences of life, in more colloquial terms, makes sense out of what happens. Two of the most important are: the creation of words, that is, language, and the correlating of events as cause and effect. Anyone who has the wonderful opportunity to watch a child grow becomes aware of the organizing power of words, especially nouns. As an infant learns such words as Mommy, Daddy, dog, horse, cow, etc., these terms are providing categories for their ordering of experience. Essentially this is what is done in a biological typology, for it is a collection of nouns which are used as organizing tools to correlate similarities and differences among various animals and plants. While such nouns (grammatically identified as improper nouns) are indispensable for making sense out of the world, there is a special class of nouns which have a psychological and religious significance far different in nature: names, that is, proper nouns.

[12]

Mana is the term that has come to be used by most ancient historians, archaeologists, and anthropologists to describe a kind of non-individual power or

example of this living power of words is found throughout all three sacred revelations, but especially the Jewish one. Modern readers are familiar with numerous passages which speak of one individual "blessing" or "cursing" another. Few passages are more misunderstood today, mostly because the power of words that functions in the ancient world has been lost. A quick look at Levitical law indicates the power of words when it declares that the punishment for cursing one's mother or father is death. The strength of the punishment reveals the seriousness of the crime. From the ancient perspective, words possessed much more than an emotional status, but a metaphysical power, that is, certain words could heal or harm, perhaps even kill. This connection resulted in a most important relation between words (especially names) and the oldest known religious practices, magic.[13]

---

life-force that resides in those things that possess life or power. For those who think that the modern world suffers from over population, the ancient world was overwhelmed with all kinds of powerful forces and beings, some having empathetic sensitivities toward human beings and others more inclined to cause harm than good. While mana was itself an undifferentiated power, the beings and forces in which it resided could be named, and, thus, humans could exercise some power in their relationships with them. One of the crucial tools for the using of this power was the speaking of the name.

[13]

Today the term *magic* is misused and misunderstood. As used by historians, philosophers, theologians, archaeologists, anthropologists and sociologists it, has nothing to do with "pulling rabbits out of hats," that is, with performing illusions. Rather, magic is a collection of beliefs and practices whose origins coincide with (or predate) those of religion. In order to understand this, it is necessary to comment briefly on a modern distinction that is absent from the ancient world: the distinction between the natural and the supernatural. In the ancient past this metaphysical distinction was unknown. The world was overpopulated with all kinds of forces and beings, many of whom today would be identified as supernatural--gods, angels, demons, animas (spirits), jinn, mana, etc.. In such a world, humans needed reassurance that they could exercise at least some control over events. The result was the development of magic which may be defined as "the belief that there are things human beings can do to influence the various forces which have a causal role in the occurrence of events." One of the most important works on the importance of magical beliefs and rites in the ancient world is that of Sir. J.G. Frazer, his multi-volume **The Golden Bough**. Although his thesis that magic precedes and develops

While magical rites which were also religious rituals, involved such elements as sacrifices (grain, animal, blood, etc.), physical postures (drama or dance), instruments (drums for example), and patterns (shooting flaming arrows into the air to imitate lightening as part of the rain ceremony), they also required the use of powerful sacred words, most especially names. Samuel Cohon aptly describes the metaphysical power of names in his article, "The Name of God, A Study in Rabbinic Theology," **Hebrew Union College Annual**[14]:

> Divine names embody the conceptions of God of a particular religion. Coming down from a distant past their meanings often are obscure. The personal name of a deity thus represents an epithet the meaning of which has been forgotten. The epithet generally derived from some function, characteristic or relation of the deity to the tribe, its members or surroundings. Acquiring the distinction of a personal name, it is identified with the deity and invested with *mana*, i.e., with power and mystery. Being sacred it is guarded by taboos against profane use and is reserved for magic rites and tribal mysteries by medicine men or priests. For ordinary relations new epithets are created denoting the relation of the deity to the life and destiny of the people and to nature. These newer appellations, expressed in more transparent language, in turn become the titles by which the deity is invoked, sometimes independently and often in combination with the original personal name.

---

into religion has received considerable criticism, his identification of the fundamental patterns of magic, his phrase is *Sympathetic Magic*, is a distinction widely accepted and used in the analysis of primal magic.

14

Cohon's article is a concise, clear, and superbly developed study of the power of names, the significance of and the history of the Divine *Name YHWH* in Jewish tradition and rabbinic literature. It is, in my judgment, one of the best available on the historical and theological issues that relate to the Divine Name.

. . . .

> As in magic so in ancient religion, knowledge of the name of a spirit or deity was believed to give one power over him and the means of securing his help. However, improper mention of his name might spell disaster. Hence caution was required in its employment. (vol.XXIII, part 23, 579-85)

After examining the power and danger of divine names in ancient religions, Cohon continues by describing a polarity in the Jewish religious experience of the Divine Name, an experience that differs from the use of such names in polytheism. The pantheons of ancient polytheisms require names to differentiate one divinity from another. However, monotheism has no such need for a name; thus, the issue of divine names takes another focus. Because the pre-exhilic Jews were not yet monotheists,[15] the Jewish search for the name of God exhibited a twofold trend, in Cohon's words:

> Though God is shrouded in mystery, the questing spirit strives to draw near to Him, to behold His graciousness and to perceive something of His relation to man and the world. The whole endeavor of religion may be said to consist in bridging the gap between the finite and the infinite and thus to endow human life with sanctity and spiritual purpose.

---

[15] Whoever were the ancestors of the Jews, it is reasonable to judge that they were polytheists since no other form of religion is evidenced in the Middle East prior to the second millennium. However, during the time between Moses (13th century B.C.E.) and the Babylonian Captivity (6th century B.C.E.) the Jewish religion was slowly progressing from polytheism to monotheism (see Chapter Two). Many scholars use the term *monolatry* to describe this transitional stage between the two forms of religion. In Chapter Two the term *henotheism* is used instead of monalotry. Reasons for this usage and an analysis of the developments of such religious beliefs as chosenness, promised land, and holy war as they relate to both henotheism and monotheism are examined in this chapter.

In view of this polarity of the religious experience, the development of the Jewish idea of God exhibits a twofold trend. On the one hand, Judaism strove to discover the essential being and nature of God, which in the idiom of the ancients, meant to find His true name. Accordingly it persisted in ascertaining the significance of the divine names in general and the Tetragrammaton in particular. On the other hand, in its steady spiritual advance it sought to divest itself of the thought that the Divine Name may be named as men or objects are named. Popular society clung to the first. Advanced theological thought tended toward the other position. (581)

Especially in Jewish and Muslim popular religion, and too a much lesser extent in Christian society, the former impulse resulted in the traditions of the 70 direct names of God and the infinite number of indirect names of God in the Jewish Midrash and the 99 names of God in Islam.[16] On the more sophisticated theological level, the latter impulse became a constant theme among Medieval theologians of all three monotheisms in their struggles to eliminate the distortions and dangers of anthropomorphism in our conceptions of God. Fearing the dangers inherent in conceiving of God in human terms, many such theologians reject the very idea that God has a name.

It is important not to dismiss these historical and theological concerns about the name of God as superstitious or gratuitously mythological because it was, and is, the religious significance of *YHWH* that began to separate the pre-exhilic Jews from most of their neighbors and prepared them for religious greatness, a greatness inherited by both Christianity and Islam. In other words, in the Jewish search for the meaning of and nature of *YHWH* are found those religious insights that led them

---

16

On an even more popular, almost superstitious level, the tradition developed in Islam of a 100th name of God know only to the camel, who used this name while praying, that is, kneeling to allow the rider to mount.

from the magical rites of polytheism to the prayerful worship of monotheism. The religious greatness that separated the Jews from their neighbors was their struggles with and covenant relationship with a deity who either "Had No Name" or "Had A Name Never To Be Uttered." Christianity and Islam inherit this same religious understanding, an understanding which rejects magic and depends on prayer.[17] The best way to understand this is twofold: to examine the most important tradition concerning the revelation of *YHWH* and explore the theological problems inherent in its translation. Then we can examine the spiritual significance of *YHWH* and the continuation of this in the **New Testament** and the **Qur'an**.

As well known by Christians, Muslims and Jews, the story of the Burning Bush illustrates the tradition of the revelation of the Divine Name to Moses and becomes one of the best known stories in the **Hebrew Bible**. The narrative begins as Moses is looking after his father-in-law's flocks when

> . . . the angel of *Yahweh* appeared to him in the shape of a flame of fire, coming from the middle of a bush. . . . [The story continues as Moses converses with a voice from the bush and culminates in the following revelation].
>
> Then Moses said to God, 'I am to go, then, to the sons of Israel and say to them, "The God of your fathers has sent me to you". But if they ask me what his name is, what am I to tell them?' And God said to Moses, 'I Am who I Am'. This he added 'is what you must say to the sons of Israel: "I Am has sent me to you".' And God

---

[17]

As stated in footnote #13, magic is basically the belief that humans have ways to influence supernatural beings and forces. Put crudely, magic is the belief that through the use of such things as sacrifices and names, humans can manipulate the gods. While there are many kinds of prayer, at its deepest spiritual level, prayer is the opposite of magic. In other words, fundamental to prayer is the human being offering himself to the influence of the deity. The prayer in Gethesemane is the paradigm: God take this cup away, **but nevertheless it is your will that must be done.**

also said to Moses, 'You are to say to the sons of Israel: *"Yahweh, the God of your fathers, the God of Abraham, the God of Isaac, and the God of Jacob, has sent me to you".* This is my name for all time; by this name I shall be invoked for all generations to come.' (Exodus 3:1-15)

In the **Qur'an** there are four *suras*[18] which describe the encounter of Moses and the "fire." Considering the revelation of the Divine Name, it is *suras* XXVII and XXVIII that are most important. In each the account begins as Moses sees a "fire" and leaves his family to investigate. The conversation which occurs is similar to that of Exodus as it moves toward a revelation to Moses of the divinity who speaks to him from the fire:

> But when he came / To the (Fire), a voice / Was heard from the right bank / Of the valley, from a tree / In hallowed ground: "O Moses! / Verily I am God [*Al-Lah*], the / Lord Of the Worlds . . . . (XXVIII:30)

> But when he came / To the (Fire), a voice / Was heard: "Blessed are those / In the Fire and those around: / And Glory to God, / The Lord of the Worlds.

> "O Moses! / Verily, I am God [*Al-Lah*], the Exalted / In Might, the Wise! . . . (XXVII:8-9)

Such are the revealed accounts of the burning bush. What is of paramount importance in these accounts is the nature and meaning of that which is revealed in

---

18

While there are differences between the Exodus account and those in *suras* XIX, XX, XXVII, and XXVIII concerning the encounter with the burning bush, the most important one is that the accounts in the **Qur'an** do not indicate the singular identification of God's chosen children as the Hebrews. Instead of stressing, as does Exodus, that Moses is being sent to Pharaoh to free his children, the sons of Israel, the **Qur'an** indicates that Moses is sent because Pharaoh and his Chiefs are "a people rebellious and wicked."

the statements: "I Am who I Am [Hebrew, *YHWH*]" and "I am God." In other words, what is the religious significance of the Divine Name (?)? Before exploring this central question, it is advantageous to examine the issues of translation that have been so problematic.

Concisely, *YHWH* is first person singular, imperfect tense, causative mood of the verb "to be." This accounts for one of the two most common translations of *YHWH* as "I AM."[19] While this translation is more desirable than other options that have been used, it is still inadequate for two reasons: it fails to take note of the problem of translating imperfect verb tenses and the causative mood. Hebrew verbs are organized according to a different principle than time, which is the case with Indo-European languages such as English. Because English verbs are organized according to time, there are three fundamental tenses: past, present and future. Hebrew verbs, however, are organized according to action; thus, there are only two fundamental tenses: either the action is complete (Hebrew perfect tense, English past tense) or the action is incomplete (Hebrew imperfect tense, English present or future tenses). Consequently, the translation could just as well be "I Will Be" as "I Am." However, neither takes into account the causative mood. Considering all the aspects of the verb form *YHWH*, the best translation is one of the following: "I Cause To Be" or "I Will Cause To Be."[20]   Because of these translation problems and the

---

[19]

The other most common translation has already been referenced; the translation of the King James which follows the Septuagint rendering of *YHWH* as *Kurios*, in English "Lord." Other than the use of Jehovah, Lord is one of the least desirable translations for reasons examined later.

[20]

Whatever the meaning of these enigmatic words, they do express a fundamental belief shared by all three monotheisms concerning the relationship between God and the created world: that God, whether he is addressed as I AM, Lord, Father or *Al-Lah*, is the ground of being, the cause of all that exists and all that will exist. The **Qur'an** especially captures this "Cause To Be" motif in such passages as the following which describes the method of God's actions in the world:
She [Mary] said: O my Lord! / How shall I have a son / When no

recognition that translating names always distorts, some translations of the Bible simply transliterate rather than translate the Hebrew verb *YHWH* as "*Yahweh*."[21] Since the vowels "a" and "e" were added centuries after the original use of the term *YHWH*, it is impossible to know with any accuracy the correct pronunciation of this word. Further, the later prohibition that developed concerning its verbal utterance makes the pronunciation moot for those who accept the prohibition. Fortunately, neither the problems of translation or pronunciation are crucial to the major issue: what is the religious meaning of this revelation, one which separated the beliefs of the Jews from the beliefs of their neighbors in the ancient world? This question cannot be divorced from another: Is *YHWH* truly the Divine Name which is never to be uttered or is *YHWH* not really a name?

Let us return to the burning bush and the response: *YHWH*. What is Moses being told? There are at least two ways to interpret the theological significance of this Divine Name(?), and both have been argued for centuries. One interpretation is that *YHWH* is truly the Divine Name, but a name that is never to be uttered. This interpretation is the most common one. However, there are two problems that must be addressed: (1) if it is truly a name, then why does the historical evidence point

---

man hath touched me?" / He said: "Even so: God createth / What He willith: /When He hath decreed / A Plan, He but saith / To it, 'Be,' and it is! (III:47)

21

Briefly, translations are concerned with the meanings of words, that is, translating a word from one language into another involves the effort to find a term in the latter that is as close to the meaning in the former as is humanly possible. Literal translations are humanly impossible. Even good translations change the meaning of a word. Transliterations involve the substituting of alphabetical characters from one language's alphabet into that of another's alphabet. The purpose of transliterating is for purposes of pronunciation, for example: "*Yahweh*" (or "*YHWH*") is the transliteration of the Divine Name (?) and "I Cause To Be" is the translation of the same term. As indicated in footnote #10, page 54, except for the terms "Israel,""Islam" and "Muslim," all English transliterations of significant Hebrew, Greek and Arabic terms are italicized in the text to emphasize that they are transliterations rather than translations.

to the prohibition against uttering it as most likely post-exhilic[22]; and (2) from Philo Judaeus to the present, why have so many excellent Jewish scholars on the **Hebrew Bible** claimed that it is not a name, that the name of God is unknown? Concerning this last position consider, the following statements from Philo (first century C.E.) and Cohon (twentieth century):

> It follows that not even a proper name can be given to the Truly Existent [God]. Observe that when the prophet inquires what he must answer to those who ask about his name, He says, "I am He that is" (Exodus 3:14), which is equivalent to "My nature is to be, not to be spoken." But that mankind should not be in complete want of a designation for the Supremely Good, He allows them to use analogically, as though it were His proper name. . . .
>
> This is also shown by an oracle revealed as from the mouth of the Ruler of the universe that no proper name of him has been disclosed to anyone. "I appeared," He says, "to Abraham, Isaac, and Jacob, being their God, and My name of 'Lord' I did not reveal to them" (Exodus 6:3). For if the order of the words is changed back to the normal grammatical sequence, the meaning would be as follows: "My proper name I did not reveal to them," but only the one for analogical use. . . . So ineffable indeed is the Existent that not even the ministering powers tell us a proper name. . . .
>
> Do not then be thoroughly perplexed if you find the highest of all things to be ineffable, when His Word too, cannot be expressed

---

[22]

See Michael Sales article, "Who Can Utter the Name of God?--From the Holiness of His Name to the Seriousness of All Words," **Communio (International Catholic Review)**, vol.XX, No.1, spring 1993, pp.26-48. See also the section on "Pre-Monarchial Theologies of War" in Chapter Two which provide textual evidence that pre-monarchial Hebrew warriors shouted the Divine Name *Yahweh* as a battle cry to terrorize their enemies.

by us through His own name. And indeed, if He is ineffable, He is also inconceivable and incomprehensible. (From Philo's "On the Changing of Names, 7-15, in Peter's **Judaism, Christianity, and Islam**, vol.3, 272-3)

God is essentially nameless, transcending any designation that man can apply to Him. Within this limitation, however, names of God are spiritual necessities. They stem from human habits of thought and speech. An emotion, experience or idea is incommunicable unless it is verbalized. Only when expressed in a fitting word or name does it acquire power. Names of God have retained their place in advanced Jewish monotheism not merely as survivals of earlier and less developed religious views but also as indispensable designations of the . . . attributes of His nature. Instead of being proper names of God, in the customary sense of the word, they simply point to His reality and to His effects. They awaken the devout and searching mind to the awesome mystery and meaningfulness which environ the soul.

. . . .

To the Jewish mind they [names] conveyed provisional and figurative but nonetheless real presentations of the deepest truths of religion, of God's being, His transcendence and His nearness, His baffling mysteriousness and His clear light and accessibility. The conviction was firm--though not philosophically demonstrated--that while God is one and unique, nameless and inscrutable, He acts outward on the universe, revealing attitudes and ways to which names may be given. But these are human creations and consequently apply to God only provisionally. (Cohon, 582-3 and 603)

YHWH (*Yahweh*): is it the Divine Name or a human creation which is not a name? The debate continues and most likely will continue as long as there are practicing

Jews, Christians and Muslims. Fortunately, whether *YHWH* is the unutterable Divine Name or not a name, the theological significance remains the same, and it is a significance which provides an introduction to the next section of this chapter, "The Traditions of the Prophets."

To understand this, we must return to the distinction between magic and prayer and especially the importance of names in magic. In contrast to their neighbors, there developed a special religious class among the Jews in the eighth century B.C.E. that differed from the magicians, shamans, and seers that controlled most ancient religious practice and belief. Magic involved the belief that those human beings who possessed the sacred gnosis could use such secret knowledge, knowledge that required knowing the god's proper names, in order to influence events in the world. In this sense, magic represents a combination of a kind of pre-science (knowledge of the universe) and technology (applications of that knowledge) in the ancient world before the advent of science and philosophy which began the separation of causality from divine beings and other supernatural powers. In contrast, then, to neighboring religions who had gods with names and shamans and seers who could manipulate these gods through magic and the knowledge of divine names, the Jews developed a belief in a God with no name (or one whose name was never to be uttered) and prophets. This difference is religiously immense, both historically and theologically. Gods with names have graven images and can be influenced by human actions. *YHWH*, on the other hand, has no graven image and cannot be manipulated by human beings. Thus, this pivotal understanding of the Divine Name(?) led to the rejection of magic and replaced the seer with the prophet.

While it is true that the Hebrew prophet exercised a capacity that resembled that of the seer, the one who through magical rites could see into the future, their eschatological teachings (prophecies about the future) were secondary to and depended upon the two central foci of their teachings: righteousness and justice.[23] The message of the prophets was clear, it was not for humans to influence God; rather, the proper relationship with God, righteousness, was found by listening and obeying. This understanding replaced magic with prayer. For although one may present supplications to God, it is clear to Jews, Muslims, and Christians that these petitions do not manipulate God; they are only requests that should always involve the commitment, "Nevertheless it is Your will that must be done."

A God with no name (or one whose name cannot be uttered) is a God who cannot be influenced by magic but can only known in what He chooses to reveal through prophets (those who speak forth) and approached only through prayer (worship). What made the Jews religiously great was their worshiping a God with no name(?), a God of prophets. While there are other appellations used in the **Hebrew Bible** to refer to *YHWH* such as *Eloh-im* (a noun which means "God"[24]) and *El Shaddai* (which means "God of the Heights"), none of them are proper names; they indicate only attributes.

Both Christianity and Islam, partly because they develop from the great prophetic movement of Judaism, inherit a God with no proper Divine Name. In other words, they both worship a God whose relationship with humans is communicated through prophets rather than seers and personally actuated through prayer rather than

---

23

While the emerging prophets of eighth century B.C.E. Judaism resembled the seers of many other religions, there were significant differences, and these are examined in the next section on "The Traditions of the Prophets." Briefly, they preached a three-fold message: (1) eschatology, that is, prophecies of the future whose fundamental purpose was to provide hope in times of great danger and despair; (2) righteousness, that is, messages of the *right* relationship with God; and (3) justice, that is, messages concerning human relationships. In general, the prophets also assumed that the foundation for justice was righteousness.

24

It is interesting to note that grammatically the Hebrew term *eloh-im* is plural in form; thus, a root translation would be: gods. This shows the foolishness of literalism.

magic. There is no proper name for God in the **New Testament**. The two most common appellations used by Christians for the Transcendent Power that became incarnate in the Christ are: *Theos* (a Greek noun which means "God," a noun but not a proper name) and *Pater* (a noun whose meaning is "Father," a relational noun but not a proper name). The same is true of the **Qur'an**, which has many names of God in its hundreds of *ayats*--but these so-called names are actually attributes such as Merciful, Compassionate, Wise, Eternal, etc.. One noun, however, dominates all others: *Al-Lah*. In Arabic, *Al-Lah* means "The God." As with Judaism and Christianity, *Al-Lah* is a noun but not a proper name, and the religious lesson is the same: the relationship between God and human beings is one of listening first, then obeying through worship and prayer. Herein lies the religious greatness of these monotheisms, a greatness that unfortunately is often distorted.

The Traditions of the Prophets

In the "Introduction" to his magnificent study of the prophets, Abraham Heschel refers to them as "some of the most disturbing people who ever lived: the men whose inspiration brought the Bible into being--the men whose image is our refuge in distress, and whose voice and vision sustain our faith." **(The Prophets**, ix) From the time that the term *nebi* (plural, *nebi-im*) appeared among the Hebrews and eventually became the title designation for the second part of the Masoretic Text of the **Hebrew Bible**, the *Nebi-im* (the Prophets), these men and occasionally women have indeed disturbed the consciences of millions of human beings. The term itself, *nebi*, which has etymological affinities with the term *seer*, that is "one who sees," mostly likely entered Hebrew in the ninth century B.C.E. in reference to mystical bands of "seers." However, these roving bands had little influence on the developing Jewish faith; rather, it was in the historical disasters of the eighth century B.C.E. Assyrian devastations when the great prophetic movement began. It has been suggested by more than one Biblical commentator that the parents of the great prophets were destruction and despair, and the midwife was hope. From the eighth century B.C.E. to the twentieth century C.E. they have indeed been "some of the most disturbing people who ever lived."

Had their impact remained only within Judaism their influence on Western culture would be limited, but they began a tradition that inspired Christianity and Islam. Not only did Jesus often quote the great prophets, the writers of the **New Testament** and the leaders of Christianity both theologically and historically grounded their beliefs and values in the teachings and prophecies (eschatology) of the Hebrew prophets. The three-fold message of the great prophets as described earlier--eschatology, righteousness, and justice--adequately described the foci of the teachings of Jesus. The teachings of Muhammad and the **Qur'an** continued to expound, re-interpret, and add to the traditions of the prophets. According to the Muslim Holy Book, since the creation of Adam, *Al-Lah* has sent thousands of prophets to teach His truths, and of the twenty-eight named in the **Qur'an**, twenty-six are found in the Christian Bible. Of these twenty-six, six stand above all the others: Adam, the Chosen of *Al-Lah*; Noah, the Preacher of *Al-Lah*; Abraham, the Friend of *Al-Lah*; Moses, the Speaker of *Al-Lah*[25]; Jesus, the Word of *Al-Lah*; and, Muhammad, the Prophet of *Al-Lah*.

Who were these distressing "Speakers for God"? In order to explore this question there are several tasks: (1) to clarify the approach that is used in this study; (2) to identify how they differed from seers and magicians; and (3) to briefly describe their three-fold message. This provides a foundation for the last two sections of this chapter: the Oneness of God and the Holy Books.

First, because they are such distressing personalities with often disturbing messages, the approaches to studying both them and their words have varied between two extremes already noted: a non-reflective literalism which fails to take note of the

---

[25]

    I have often wondered if there is not a subtle sense of humor at play in this ascription to Moses given his excuse as being "clumsy of tongue," a claim the **Qur'an** notes along with Exodus.

historical circumstances and the personalities of (that is, the personal strengths, weakness, and eccentricities of) the individual prophet[26] and the dry, overly rationalistically reflective study of the prophets that occupies the academic disciplines and completely ignores the revelatory context of the prophets and their words. Heschel uses the terms "pan-theology" and "pan-psychology" to describe such studies. These studies make the mistake of believing that an impartial, rational analysis is capable of both understanding and uncovering the message of the prophets. The worst of such studies reduce the messages of the prophets to historical superstitions and the prophets themselves to mentally deranged individuals. While such studies may gain a professor tenure or academic status, they fail to miss what lies at the heart of the prophetic message, and why these individuals still speak to millions of human beings throughout the world. Heschel provides a clear description of the "spiritual bankruptcy" of such approaches when he writes:

> What drove me to study the prophets?
>
> In the academic environment in which I spent my student years philosophy had become an isolated, self-subsisting, self-indulgent entity . . . encouraging suspicion instead of love of wisdom. The answers offered were unrelated to the problems, indifferent to the travail of a person who became aware of man's suspended sensitivity in the face of stupendous challenge, indifferent to a situation in which good and evil became irrelevant, in which man became increasingly callous to catastrophe and ready to suspend the principle of truth. I was slowly led to the realization that some of the terms, motivations,

---

26

The relationship of the Prophet Muhammad to the teachings in the **Qur'an** is somewhat different than that of the Hebrew prophets to the books of prophecy in the **Hebrew Bible** and the teachings of Jesus in the **New Testament**. This difference is mostly the result of Muslim beliefs about the nature of *Al-Lah*'s transmission of the *ayats* of the **Qur'an** to Muhammad and the belief that the **Qur'an** is eternal. This issue is addressed in the fourth chapter which examines Islam.

and concerns which dominate our thinking may prove destructive of the roots of human responsibility and treasonable to the ultimate ground of human solidarity. The challenge we are all exposed to, and the dreadful shame that shatters our capacity for inner peace, defy the ways and patterns of our thinking. One is forced to admit that some of the causes and motives of our thinking have led our existence astray, that speculative prosperity is no answer to spiritual bankruptcy. It was the realization that the right coins were not available in the common currency that drove me to study the thoughts of the prophets. (xiv-xv)

In keeping with Heschel's warning, the approach to the prophets in this study seeks to understand the messages of the prophets as revealed truths, but truths grounded in the historical circumstances and personalities of the prophets. Additionally, this study approaches both Christianity and Islam as movements that grow from the prophetic movement that began among the Jews in the eighth century B.C.E.

Second, who were these disturbing personalities? How did they differ from other religious functionaries who "seemed" to resemble them? These questions must be considered together. That the prophets shared at least one function in common with seers is evidenced in the etymology of the Hebrew term for prophet, *nabi,* which is from the verb "to see." Unfortunately, it has been this "seeing," that is, their eschatologies, which has struck the popular imagination; so much so that their other two foci are often placed in the background. While it is true that their prophecies of the future offered hope during times which counselled despair, the major religious significance of the prophets, the function which separated them from magicians and seers, was their "speaking forth" the message of God, a message centered on two foci: righteousness and justice. However, in struggling to hear and understand this dual message, it is just as important to realize that the prophet was also a part of his message, and the great teachings of the prophets cannot be divorced from their times and lives, and this is, ultimately, what has been so disturbing and charismatically appealing about them to Jews, Christians, and Muslims throughout the centuries. In his characterization of the prophets, Heschel provides a privileged glimpse of their power in Western monotheism:

> The significance of Israel's prophets lies not only in what they said but also in what they were. We cannot fully understand what they meant to say to us unless we have some degree of awareness of what happened to them. . . .
>
> My aim therefore is to attain an understanding of the prophet through an analysis and description of his *consciousness*, to relate what came to pass in his life--facing man, being faced by God--as reflected and affirmed in his mind. By consciousness . . . I mean here not only the perception of particular moments of inspiration, but also the totality of impressions, thoughts, and feelings which make up the prophet's being.
>
> . . . .
>
> The prophet is a person, not a microphone. [27] He is endowed with a mission, with the power of a word not his own that accounts for his greatness--but also with temperament, concern, character, and individuality. As there was no resisting the impact of divine inspiration. so at times there was no resisting the vortex of his own temperament. . . .
>
> The prophet's task is to convey a divine view, yet as a person he is a point of view. He speaks from the perspective of God as

---

27

See footnote 26 regarding the special relationship between Muhammad and the *ayats* of the **Qur'an**. In traditional Muslim thought, there is a sense in which Muhammad is understood as a "microphone." This may account for the popularity of the **Hadiths** among many Muslims, for in these traditions of the Prophet his personality emerges. Chapter Four examines these issues in more depth.

perceived from the perspective of his own situation. . . . . [28]

. . . .

The prophet is not only a prophet. He is also a poet, preacher, patriot, statesman, social critic, moralist. There has been a tendency to see the essence and chief significance of prophecy in the display of one or another of these aspects. Yet this is a misapprehension of the intrinsic nature of prophecy.

. . . .

For them to be alive and present to us we must think, not *about*, but *in* the prophets, with their concern and their heart. Their existence involves us. Unless their concern strikes us, pains us, exalts us, we do not really sense it. Such involvement requires accord, receptivity, hearing, sheer surrender to their impact. . . .

. . . .

The prophet was a man who said No to his society, condemning its habits and assumptions, its complacency, waywardness, and syncretism. He was often compelled to proclaim the very opposite of what his heart expected. His fundamental objective was to reconcile man and God. Why do the two need

---

28

Heschel's insight here is pivotal for this study. "Perceived from his own perspective" means perceived through, and thus limited by, his own particular historical circumstances, his understandings of the nature of God and the cosmos, and his personality. As examined in the next three chapters, but especially the second one, it is a judgment of this study that as the Jewish faith developed through time there was a corresponding spiritual growth on the part of Jews concerning the nature of God. The most important aspect of this spiritual growth was the understanding that led from the tribal deity *YHWH* to the belief in *Eloh-im*, that is, from henotheism to monotheism. This growth occupies a major place in the development of the theology of war and peace in Judaism, the topic of the next chapter. It also forms the basis for the apology for peace and recognition of the true spiritual *jihad* that occupies the final chapter.

reconciliation? Perhaps it is due to man's false sense of sovereignty, to his abuse of freedom, to his aggressive, sprawling pride, resenting God's involvement in history. (ix-xv)

This lengthy citation from Heschel has two benefits: it provides a comprehensive understanding of the nature and charismatic power of the traditions of the prophets in Western monotheism as well as a beginning glimpse at their continued significance in the lives of believers today. While he speaks specifically of only the Hebrew prophets, Christians and Muslims accept his views with only one difference. Heschel indicates that the age of prophecy ended before the advent of Christianity, and on this point, Christians and especially Muslims disagree. Without ignoring or underestimating this difference, one of the principles of this study is that the Jewish prophetic tradition continued in Christianity and Islam, and acceptance of this principle of toleration provides a basis for trialogue rather than continued conflict. The best way to defend this principle of interpretation and belief is by briefly examining the three-fold message of the prophets of Judaism, Christianity, and Islam. In agreement with Heschel, the fundamental focus of the prophet is the reconciliation of God and human beings which is righteousness, and realizing that justice cannot be separated from righteousness, I begin with the least important foci of their messages, their eschatologies. This order is also consistent with the view presented earlier that the major religious importance of the prophets is not found in their views of the future but in their speaking forth the messages of reconciliation (righteousness) and justice.[29]

During pre-exhilic times when the prophetic consciousness had not yet understood that *YHWH* was the only God and, as a consequence, the developing

---

[29]

Because of the length of this chapter and because its purpose is providing a foundation for the explorations in the next three chapters, the examination of common themes in the prophetic traditions of all three monotheisms is illustrated by single examples in each of the three dimensions of the prophets' messages. Fully exploring the depth of shared prophetic traditions would require a book or more.

Jewish faith had not yet become a monotheism, the earliest element in their credo was that of providence.[30] As understood by pre-exhilic Hebrews, *YHWH* was a tribal deity who chose the Jews as His people and communicated His will to them through prophets. The other two dimensions of God's activities, creation and eschatology, were slowly added to that of providence in the Jewish faith. In pre-exhilic times, the limited creation story in Genesis 2:4b-ff,[31] was probably the second dimension added and later during the eighth century the prophets added an element of historical eschatology.[32] Post-exhilic Jews added the cosmic dimension to eschatology, and

---

[30]

Theologically the term *providence* refers to God's actions in history. For all three religions, as is examined in the next section of this chapter on the ONENESS of God, God is a God whose will works in and through historical events. The primary methods through which His will is known and actualized are the choosing of peoples and the calling of prophets. However, the God of Jews, Christians and Muslims is more than a God of providence (historical actions) but also a God of creation and a God of eschatology (of future events).

[31]

The creation account in Genesis 2:4b-ff, which differs in many regards from the magnificent account of creation in Genesis 1:1-2:4a, represents one of the earliest Hebrew understandings of the relationship of their god *YHWH* to the existence of the world, at least that part of the world they knew. The best Biblical scholarship argues that the account as described in Genesis Chapter Two was most likely put into written form during the ninth century B.C.E. (possibly during the reign of Solomon) by an unknown figure of great literary talent. Since his identity is unknown, his written account of an older oral tradition is referred to as the Yahwist account because he uses the term *YHWH* in contrast to the writers of Genesis Chapter One who use the more generic term *Eloh-im*. The use of these terms and the issues that relate to then are examined in the next chapter.

[32]

In the pages which follow, there is need to refer to three kinds of eschatology: human, historical, and cosmic. In general, the term *eschato-logy* derives from the Greek terms which mean "words about the last days." However, while this is still the basic meaning of the term, it is also used to refer to God's actions in the future. Human eschatology, then, refers to beliefs about what happens when the human being dies; historical eschatology refers to God's actions in the future prior to the last days; and cosmic eschatology refers to the end of or transformation of the created world. Post-exhilic Jews refer to the "terrible day of *YHWH*," Christians to the II

Christians and Muslims inherited a multitude of eschatological views from post-exhilic Judaism.

As an example of their shared belief in historical eschatology let us turn to the hopeful belief in the *Mesiah* of God, a belief whose origins are found in the Assyrian devastations of the eighth century. During the reigns of David and Solomon, Hebrew immigrants moving into Palestine built a nation and a powerful military force. Although not even the genius of David could conquer important sea-coast lands from the Philistines and the Phoenicians, it was during his reign and that of his son Solomon that Israel lived though her golden days of power and influence. However, even before the death of Solomon, forces were at work that resulted in a civil war at his death, and the once proud and powerful united kingdom was split into a northern state, Israel, and a southern state, Judah. From their capital Nineveh on the Tigris River during the eighth century, the Assyrians ravaged Mesopotamia and Palestine. In their path toward Jerusalem, they destroyed the northern kingdom of Israel (the Ten Lost Tribes) and made Judah into a vassal state, but most importantly Jerusalem and Solomon's temple survived. The eighth century was a terrible time for the Jews and presented them with more than a political and economic crisis in the Assyrian invasion; the Jews experienced a major psychological and religious crisis. Since they were *YHWH*'s chosen people, why did *YHWH* allow these disasters to occur? In response to this crisis, great prophets such as I Isaiah,[33] Amos, Micah, and

---

Coming (Day of Judgment, Millennium, Rapture, etc.) and Muslims to the Day of Judgment (Day of Separation, Day of Accountability, etc.) as the cosmic end of the world as we know it.

[33]

The book of Isaiah contains teachings and prophecies from at least two historical periods, and some Biblical scholars argue for three. With a few exceptions, the first forty chapters include teachings of the eighth century prophet Isaiah. After his death many authorities believe that a school of prophecy (theology) developed around his teachings and continued into the Babylonian Exile. From there, a prophet whose name is unknown offered hope to his exiled people in teachings that have been incorporated into the latter part of the Book of Isaiah, especially chapters 40-55.

Hosea arose to preach a three-fold message of righteousness, justice, and historical eschatology. It is the latter that concerns us at this point.

Remembering that David was anointed as a sign of his selection as *Yahweh's* chosen king and that his reign was a golden age for Israel (at least in the memories of those facing the terrors of the eighth century) and because of his charismatic personality, David became known as the "man after God's own heart." In other words, David became the central personality in the historical eschatologies of the prophets. In the midst of great destruction and despair, the eighth century prophets spoke of a new David, a new Anointed One, who would one day be sent by God to lead Israel to power and justice. Two representative examples of this hope, known as the "Messianic Hope," in Hebrew the term *Mesiah* means the "Anointed One", are evidenced in the teachings of I Isaiah:[34]

> A shoot spring from the stock of Jesse, / a scion thrusts from his roots: / on him the spirit of Yahweh rests, / a spirit of wisdom and insight, / a spirit of knowledge and of the fear of *Yahweh* (11:1-2) For there is a child born for us, / a son given to us / and dominion is laid on his shoulders; / . . . .
>
> . . . .
>
> Wide is his dominion / in a peace that has no end, / for the throne of David / and for his royal power, / which he establishes and makes secure / in justice and integrity. (9:5-7)

While many prophets between the eighth and second centuries nurtured and developed the Messianic Hope, the critical elements in I Isaiah's vision remained:

Because his name is unknown, he is identified in Biblical literature as II Isaiah (Deutero-Isaiah). His teachings of a "Suffering Servant" became central to Christian claims concerning Jesus.

34

As indicated in footnote #7, page 47, in order to conserve space on the page, lengthy citations of poetic passages from the **Hebrew Bible** utilize the slash ("/") between the lines of a stanza as is done with citations of *ayats* from the **Qur'an**.

the long awaited Jewish *Mesiah* would bring about a miraculous return of Jewish exiles scattered throughout the Western world to Jerusalem; he would restore the Davidic line to the resurrected state of Israel; the Temple would be rebuilt; and, the *Mesiah* would create an endless era of world peace and harmony. Religiously and emotionally, these are great visions which significantly influenced both Christianity and Islam.

As the Jews of the Diaspora[35] awaited the coming of the promised *Mesiah*, the Alexandrian Jewish community engaged in an unprecedented event: the translation of the most important Jewish scriptures into Greek. The result was the magnificent and highly influential **Septuagint** (LXX). It is the most important translation of the Jewish scriptures in the history of Judaism. Its influence for Judaism was immense, but even more so for Christianity because the **Septuagint** became the basis for the Christian **Old Testament**. As the translators of the **Septuagint** struggled with their task, they chose to translate the Hebrew term *Mesiah* (the Anointed One) into the Greek term *Christos*. Consequently, as Christianity began to spread beyond the confines of Jerusalem and beyond the Jewish community into the Gentile world, Christians began to identify Jesus, the son born to Mary and Joseph, as the *Christos* (in English, the Christ). While the developing Christian theology of the first century found in the Christian *Christos* (*Mesiah*) a being who was more than just a man and prophet but the incarnate Son of God, they found the historical foundations for their beliefs in the claim that He was the fulfillment of the

---

[35]
      The term *diaspora* refers to the migrations of Jews from Palestine over several centuries. The original impulse for these migrations was to escape the ravages incurred because of the Assyrian, Babylonian and Roman conquests. As a result by the time of the Common Era, there were three major Jewish communities in the Mediterranean world: those centered around Jerusalem, Babylon, and Alexandria. From the third century B.C.E. to the first century C.E., the Alexandrian community became the most intellectually influential because of their scholarly work in theology and philosophy, work which benefited from living in a Hellenistic (a Greek influenced) setting.

Mesiah promised by Jewish prophecy, especially the son of David *Mesiah* of I Isaiah and the Suffering Servant *Mesiah* of II Isaiah. To these two prophetic visions Christians added their theology of a resurrected, cosmic Christ who would return at the end of time establishing a world of justice and peace. While different Christian groups have differed over the nature and location of this new world and intolerantly over who will populate it, all affirm the hope that God will act in the future through His Son the Christ, an eschatology inherited from Judaism.

Within the Muslim tradition, it is the persecuted Shi'ites[36] who most definitively build on the Jewish hope of a *Mesiah* who is to establish a world of justice and peace at some future time of God's choosing. While Sunni Muslims believe that God has a plan for the world He created and is inevitably moving historical events toward the fulfillment of that plan, it is the Shi'ites whose theology most passionately affirms a Future One To Come who is most similar to the Jewish *Mesiah*. The reason is found in a set of experiences shared by both Jews and Shi'ites: the tragic experiences of persecution and destruction.[37] In Islam the One-to-come

---

[36]

As with most large and successful missionary religions, Muslims have divided over political and doctrinal issues. While the divisions in Islam are less extensive than those of Christianity, which is the most diverse religion in human history due in a large part to its tremendous missionary success and complex theology, there are several identifiable divisions in Islam. The most important three are: Sunni Islam (approximately 80% of the Muslim world is Sunni, but there are differences in the Sunni Islam found in Saudi Arabia and that in Jordan, Syria, Kuwait, Egypt, etc.), Shi'ite Islam whose major stronghold is Iran, and Sufi (mystic) Islam.

[37]

Persecuted minorities, and there have been far too many such groups who are often identified as heretics in all three religions, find an emotional and religious significance in eschatology, and often mysticism, that far exceeds their roles in the orthodoxy of the majority. This is not difficult to understand. Times of destruction and persecution confront victims with two difficult challenges: finding the courage to remain faithful and the hope to overcome despair. Beliefs in the triumph of justice and the future coming of One from God provide sources of strength and endurance.

is known as the *Mahdi*[38] (in Arabic, the "Guided One," or "Divinely Guided One"). As in Judaism his lineage is most significant; he must come from the line of the Prophet Muhammad through his only surviving child (a daughter) from Khadijah (his first wife) and Ali (his first cousin and son-in-law). Further, just like the Jewish *Mesiah* he will create a world of perfect justice and peace even if it takes considerable violence to bring about such an accomplishment. There are many **Hadiths** (traditions, that is reported teachings of the Prophet not incorporated in the **Qur'an**) which speak of the Divinely Guided One to come; the following is a typical and important one:

> If there were to remain in the life of the world but one day, God would prolong that day until he sends in it a man from my community and my household. His name will be the same as my name. He will fill the earth with equity and justice as it was filled with oppression and tyranny. (Peters, **Judaism, Christianity, and Islam**, vol.3, 353)

The preceding discussion should suffice to establish that Christian views about the *Christos* and Muslim views about the *Mahdi* build upon the traditions of the Jewish *Mesiah*, that is, the traditions of the prophets. Apart from differences concerning the roles of chosen peoples and violence (especially holy wars) in the coming of the Future One, all agree that He is to create a world of righteousness and justice. Thus, before turning to the Oneness of God, it is instructive to conclude this section on the Traditions of the Prophets by exploring the connection that accounts

---

[38]
Unfortunately, *Mahdi* theology in most of Islam, but especially Shi'ite thought, is integrated into beliefs concerning holy wars. This issue is examined in the fourth chapter. Works in English which explore Shi'ite history and theology are rare. One of the best is the translation by Seyyed Hossein Nasr from the Persian work by Allamah Sayyid Muhammad Husayn Tabataba'i, **Shi'ite Islam**. For those interested in an intellectual survey of Islamic culture from its pre-Muhammadian origins to the middle of the twentieth century, Marshall G.S. Hodgson's three volume masterpiece, **The Venture of Islam**, is highly recommended.

for the prophets influence both within the circles of faith and outside: the relationship between righteousness and justice.

The moral greatness of the prophets, which has influenced believers as well as non-believers, results from their charismatic passion for justice. The religious greatness of the prophets that has touched the lives of countless believers for centuries is found in their recognition that justice depends upon, and thus, cannot be separated from righteousness. Four brief passages from these three revelations easily establish this connection--the thunderous proclamations of Amos, the gentle persuasions of Micah, Jesus' summary of the law and the prophets and a powerful **Hadith** of compassion:

> I hate and despise your feasts, / I take no pleasure in your solemn festivals.
>
> . . . .
>
> But let justice flow like water, / and integrity [righteousness] like an unfailing stream. (Amos 5:21, 24)
>
> What is good has been explained to you, man; / this is what *Yahweh* asks of you: / only this, to act justly, / to love tenderly / and to walk humbly with your God. (Micah 7:8)
>
> But when the Pharisees heard that he had silenced the Sadducees they got together and, to disconcert him, one of them put a question, 'Master, which is the greatest commandment of the Law?' Jesus said, *'You must love the Lord your God with all your heart, with all your soul*, and with all your mind. This is the greatest and the first commandment. The second resembles it: *You must love your neighbor as yourself.* On these two commandments hang the whole Law, and the Prophets also.' (Matthew 22:34-40)
>
> On the authority of Abu Hurayrah (may *Al-Lah* be pleased with him), who said that the Messenger of *Al-Lah* (may the blessing and peace of *Al-Lah* be upon him) said: *Al-Lah* (mighty and sublime

be He) will say on the Day of Resurrection:

O Son of Adam, I fell ill and you visited me not. He will say: O Lord, and how should I visit You when You are the Lord of the worlds? He will say: Did you not know that My servant So-and-so had fallen ill and you visited him not? Did you not know that had you visited him you would have found Me with him? O Son of Adam, I asked you for food and you fed Me not. He will say: O Lord, and how should I feed You when You are the Lord of the worlds? He will say: Did you not know that my servant So-and-so asked you for food and you fed him not? Did you not know that had you fed him you would surely have found that [the reward for doing so] with me? O Son of Adam, I asked you to give me drink and you gave Me not to drink. He will say: O Lord, how should I give You to drink when you are the Lord of the worlds? He will say: My servant So-and-so asked you to give him to drink and you gave him not to drink. Had you given him to drink you would have surely found that [the reward for so doing] with me. (Sacred Hadith 18, trs. by E. Ibrahim and D. Johnson-Davies in **Forty Hadith Qudsi**, 88-90)

Without denying differences of attitude, interpretation, conflicts over chosenness and religious debates over the incarnation of a God-Man (the Christ), the preceding descriptions should suffice to establish that Jews, Christians and Muslims share a common tradition of both moral and spiritual greatness which bases justice upon righteousness. Further, all three religions seek righteousness by affirming the Oneness of God.

The Oneness of God

With the second destruction of the Temple by the Romans in 70 C.E. as punishment for a rebellion, the Jewish religion, which was by this time an unequivocal monotheism, faced several crises. While Jewish worship occurred throughout the Diaspora, the religious heart of the Jew had always turned toward Jerusalem and the Temple, but the Temple no longer existed. Two of the most important consequences of this destruction were the canonization of the twenty-four books of the Masoretic Text at Jabneh in 90 C.E., that is, the approval of an authoritative revelation for Palestinian Jews[39] and the expansion of worship liturgies apart from the Temple, that is, intended for the synagogue. Because of the Diaspora, these liturgies were centuries old, but the destruction of the Temple gave them an added religious importance. Even in today's world where Jews are spread throughout much of the Western world and divided into several different religious theologies and orientations,[40] there are several common elements in the liturgies of the synagogue. Perhaps the most fundamental is the confessional affirmation of the *Shema*: "Hear, O Israel, the Lord our God is one Lord."[41] In any Middle Eastern city with a Muslim population, five times a day the powerful call to prayer from several minarets fills the air, a call affirming the power, majesty, and oneness of God. Translated from the Arabic, the call to prayer is: "God is most great! God is most great! God is most great! [each sentence is repeated three times] I bear witness that there is no God but God. . . . I bear witness that Muhammad is the Prophet of God. . . . Come to prayer . . . Come to fulfillment. . . . God is most great. . . . There is no God but God. . . ." As Muslims begin their worship of prayer, they affirm the *Shahadah* (the short

---

[39]

The Jewish communities in Alexandria and Babylon developed slightly different canons of sacred scripture. The concluding section of this chapter examines the Holy Books themselves and the issues of canonization.

[40]

The three best known divisions within the Jewish faith are Orthodox, Conservative, and Reformed, but there are other divisions as well.

[41]

The scriptural basis for the *Shema* is found in Deuteronomy 6:4-5: "Listen Israel: *Yahweh* our God is the one *Yahweh*. You shall love *Yahweh* your God with all your heart, with all your soul, with all your strength. Let these words I urge on you today be written on your hearts." Jesus' response to the Pharisees in Matthew 22 (see page 81) simply quotes this passage from Deuteronomy.

84

confession, creed): "There is no God but God, and Muhammad is His Prophet."[42] Once post-exhilic Judaism committed itself to monotheism, there have been no questions concerning either Judaism or Islam[43] as monotheisms.

The issue of God's Oneness has been a different matter for Christianity because of the Trinity. While Jews and Muslims have raised difficult questions concerning the logical consistency of this doctrine with monotheism, this issue has even been a major theological conflict among Christians. The teachings of Jesus, at

---

[42]

This often affirmed confession is quoted from *sura* 112 which is titled "Unity." While the first half of the *Shahadah* aligns Muslims with both Jews and Christians, it is the second half which indicates their differences and is, perhaps, the more religiously definitive, for it commits the Muslim to accepting the **Qur'an** as a new revelation from God which came through the Prophet Muhammad. As stated in the Prologue, if Jews, Christians and Muslims would concentrate on beliefs and values they share, perhaps there would be less conflict among them. The final chapter and the Epilogue reinforce this view.

[43]

Of all three monotheisms, the one that has always been most unequivocally monotheistic is Islam. In Muslim theology, there is no greater sin than that of *shirk*, which is attributing partners to God. In other words, the worst sin in Muslim thought is that of polytheism. For this reason, there has often been either religious debate or conflict over the doctrine of the Trinity between Christians and Jews or Muslims and even other Christians at times. There was, however, a most unusual event in the life of Muhammad that for at least a few weeks seemed to compromise the absolute monotheism of his teachings in Mecca. This occurred during a time of both personal and political distress for Muhammad. His wife Khadijah, who was one of the most important stabilizing forces in his life, had died and the political persecution of the small Muslim community was experiencing a new intensity. Sometime between 620-- 622 C.E., Muhammad received a revelation which "seemed " to indicate that Muslims should also remember (worship) three other deities: *Al-Lat*, *Al-Uzza* and *AL-Manat*. This caused a considerable uproar in the small community of Muslims in Mecca. However, several days (weeks?) later a revelation came correcting the first and affirming the absolute monotheism of Islam. The reason for the first revelation was its source: Satan. These are the famous (infamous) Satanic Verses. As strange as this incident seems to the modern reader, it is not all that unusual in Western religious tradition once the character of Satan is introduced in the theologies of Judaism, Christianity, and Islam. With his appearance, Satan's efforts to tempt or confuse God's prophets and divide God's people are attested many times.

least as they were preserved through an oral Aramaic tradition and translated into written koine Greek provide little foundation for affirming or denying the Trinity. The written letters of Paul and John's Gospel promise a *Paraclete* (a Comforter) and several other **New Testament** books offer some textual support for its affirmation. However for the early church, the issue was far from decided. W.T Jones, in the second volume of his history of Western philosophy **The Medieval Mind**, aptly describes the controversy over the Trinity that occupied considerable energy and time in the early church:

> The second major heresy, the Arian, reflects the paradox inherent in the notion of a god who is both three and one. . . . The monotheistic leaders of Christianity had sought to resolve the puzzle about the divinity of Jesus by speaking vaguely of Father and Son. Moreover, a third element, the Holy Spirit, had been introduced, so that--like many others ancient religions--Christianity affirmed a trinitarian godhead. This was no problem, of course, for the Eastern mystery cults, which rested easily in their polytheism; but it was an *embarras de richesse* for monotheistic Christianity. How could three gods be one? Various solutions were offered . . . and . . . were at one time or another defended by scriptural exegesis.
>
> Gradually the debate grew more acrimonious, and finally, shortly after the beginning of the fourth century, the whole matter came to a head. In accordance with the practice based on Irenaeus' theory, a Church council was called. It met in 325 at Nicea. . . . The council's final position, promulgated in a Nicene creed, was reached only after prolonged and heated debate, and the minority refused to accept is defeat. The adherents of the rival view soon took to arms . . . thousands of people lost their lives [in ensuing conflicts]. . . .
>
> What was this view that aroused such passions? Since its principle advocate was Arius, a presbyter of the church in Alexandria,

the heresy has been called by his name. Arius . . . held Christ to be, as the orthodox claimed, the logos of God--but he denied that Christ shares God's nature. Christ, he held, is not like the Father, eternal and perfect. On the contrary, like everything else, he was created by the Father out of nothing, and he subsequently became incarnate in the body of Jesus of Nazareth. (63-4)

Although there are some differences, the position of Arius concerning the logical inconsistency of trinitarian doctrine with monotheism and the reducing of the divine nature of Jesus are not far different than the position taken about Jesus in the **Qur'an** where he is given the ascription, "The Word of God." Even though the Council at Nicea had considerable influence on this controversy for succeeding centuries of Christianity, the Arian heresy continues to be debated among Christians.

Arian or trinitarian, Christian thought has centered on maintaining the monotheism of Christianity, either by rejecting the traditional doctrine of the Trinity or by affirming that the Trinity is a mystery (some use the term *paradox*) which must be accepted on the basis of faith and is consistent with monotheism. Consequentially, it is reasonable to conclude that Jews, Christians and Muslims all worship a God whose Oneness is fundamental to their theologies. While there are many Jews, Christians, and Muslims--perhaps the majority in each religion--who deny that the same God is worshipped in all three religions, it is a conviction of this study that *Yahweh* the God of Jews, the Father God of Christians, and *Al-Lah* are the same divinity. Further, Jews, Christians and Muslims share a stunning similarity of beliefs about the nature of the God Who is One and values about the just treatment of human beings who are created in the image of God. These common beliefs and values should serve as a foundation for trialogue rather than confrontation.

To begin with, all three religions agree concerning the three ways that God acts in history. This theological belief separates them from many other religions, especially Eastern ones, for the God of Jews, Christians and Muslims is a God whose will and actions are immersed in history. In general terms, there are three ways that

God intervenes in history: creation, providence, and eschatology. All three monotheisms accept God as the creator of the universe. While there are some differences in the two creation accounts in Genesis One and Two, and there are arguments in Christianity about the presence of the Christ at the creation of the world, and the creation accounts in the **Qur'an** evidence differences from those in Genesis, one shared belief is beyond dispute: God is the agent of creation. Second, all three affirm that God is a providential God who acts in human history in many ways but primarily two: through choosing peoples and calling prophets. Unfortunately, there have been far too many intolerant conflicts over whom God has chosen and occasionally over who is a prophet of God. Still, beliefs in the ways that God works His will are essentially the same.[44] Finally, all three monotheisms believe in a fulfillment of the created world, that is, a cosmic eschatology. Again while there are differences concerning the signs of the fulfillment, the actions of God which lead to the fulfillment and the identity and responsibilities of the chosen in the fulfillment, all three affirm that history moves inevitably toward a pre-determined divinely ordained end.[45]

---

[44]

The role that wars, especially holy wars, have in the providence of God and their relation to chosen peoples and promised lands occupies a central concern in the chapters which follow.

[45]

The development of cosmic eschatological views do not make their appearance in Judaism until after the Exile although the pre-exhilic prophets do affirm historical eschatology in a most interesting manner: their use of the Prophetic perfect. In passages such as I Isaiah 5:13 and II Isaiah 43:1, the prophets use the perfect (past) tense to describe an event that has not yet occurred in human history. In other words, they use the past tense to describe future events. The meaning of this intriguing verb usage is debated among scholars, but one possible interpretation is that the use of the Prophetic perfect stresses that these future events are pre-determined. Christianity builds on this tradition and develops one of its most interesting and controversial doctrines, predestination. While the Hebrew prophets speak of the predestination of whole peoples, some Christian theologies take this view and reduce it to the individual, whose decisions and eternal destinies are

88

In addition to agreements concerning the basic ways that God works in the world,[46] Jews, Christians and Muslims share an astounding number of beliefs about the divine nature. In Judaism and Islam many of these shared beliefs are characterized as the names of God. As stated earlier, the Mishna develops views about the 70 names of God and Islam about the 99 names of God. However, these are not really names but attributes. While Christians have not indulged in the "naming game," they are basically agree about the essential attributes of God: eternal, omnipotent, omniscient, infinite, compassionate, forgiving, merciful, loving, goodness, transcendent, etc.. Unfortunately, all three religions also affirm several more troubling anthropomorphic attributes such as wrathful, angry, and unforgiving.[47]

---

already predestined. Islam takes this view even further in its doctrine of *Kismet*, a doctrine that comes exceedingly close to fatalism. Particularly as applied to individual human decisions and actions, these doctrines create major problems for theologians of all three monotheisms, especially how to reconcile God's predestination and foreknowledge with human free will.

[46]

The major difference between Christians and both Jews and Muslims on the ways that God works in the world, other than who is chosen, is the claim that God became incarnate and necessarily had to die in order to save human beings. This is no small difference to overcome in any plea for toleration, but given a number of other fundamental Christian beliefs and especially values shared with Jews and Muslims, it should be possible to keep differences over the incarnation from leading to conflict. The last chapter and the Epilogue suggest ways to overcome this stumbling block between Christians and the other two monotheistic groups.

[47]

The problem of anthropomorphism, thinking of God in human terms, has been a theological danger for all three religions, and one that the great theologians have critiqued. On one level, anthropomorphism is unescapable, for as human beings we can only think and understand in human terms. In other words, all human thoughts are anthropomorphic. However, especially in religion, there are certain human traits attributed to the God of Jews, Christians and Muslims that are more harmful than healthy. Consider, for example, the following pairs: loving or angry, forgiving or vengeful, compassionate or wrathful. In evaluating these attributes,

Finally, as discussed in the two previous sections of this chapter, Jews, Christians and Muslims unequivocally affirm that the "right" relationship with God, righteousness, involves three elements: (1) hearing and accepting the word of God as transmitted through the traditions of the prophets; (2) offering one's life to God through worship and prayer; and (3) daily striving to live in a relationship of justice and forgiveness with our fellow human beings for **WE ALL** are the created children of God. Having explored the shared belief in the Oneness of God, only one task remains before turning to examine Jewish theologies of war and peace in the next chapter: a brief discussion of the importance of the three holy scriptures: the **Hebrew Bible**, the **New Testament**, and the **Qur'an**.

The Holy Books

As these three monotheisms, too often in open conflict with one another and almost always intolerantly ignorant of the spiritual strengths of the other two, have circumscribed historical events around the Mediterranean and Persian Gulf areas, so three Holy Books have circumscribed the lives of their believers. In his eloquent manner that nearly turns prose into poetry, Will Durant describes the impact of one of these Holy Books in words that could just as well describe the other two: (in order to hide the identity of the specific book, several key nouns are omitted in the following citation):

> Revered to the edge of idolatry, copied and illuminated with loving skill and care, used as the book from which the . . . [believer] learned to read, and then again as the core and summit of his education, the . . . [Holy Book] has for . . . centuries filled the memory, aroused the imagination, molded the character. . . of hundreds of millions of men. . . . It's message raised the moral and

consider the following question: Who is more needed in our fragmented world, a wrathful, vindictive, angry God or One whose love, compassion, and forgiveness can salvage broken human beings and heal the conflicts that divide us from one another?

cultural level of its followers, promoted social order and unity. . . lessened superstition and cruelty. . . lifted the lowly to dignity and pride, and produced among . . . [believers] a degree of sobriety and temperance unequaled elsewhere in the white man's world. It gave men an uncomplaining acceptance of the hardships and limitations of life, and at the same time stimulated them . . . [to astonishing expansions]. . . . And it defined religion in terms that any. . . [orthodox Jew, Christian or Muslim] might accept:

>"Righteousness is not that ye turn your faces to the East or to the West, but righteousness is this: whosoever believeth in God, and in the Last Day, and the angels, and the Book, and the Prophets; and whosoever, for the love of God, giveth his wealth unto his kindred, unto orphans, and the poor, and the wayfarer, and to the beggar . . . and whoso observeth prayer . . . and, when they have covenanted, fulfill their covenant; and who are patient in adversity and hardship and in times of violence: these are the righteous, these are they who believe in the Lord! (**The Age of Faith**, 181-82)

Which Holy Book does Durant describe? The **Hebrew Bible**? The **New Testament**? The **Qur'an**? While it accurately describes any one of the three, his passage concerns the **Qur'an.**

Since the explorations of theologies of war and peace in the three following chapters concentrates on the Holy Books, it is important to understand the processes by which they were written and accepted as sacred revelation. Essential for understanding these processes are four concepts: oral tradition, writing period, extant manuscript and canonization. The first three are quickly definable, the fourth is a more complex and important issue.

The phrase *oral tradition* is most descriptive. Throughout the world, for religions with written scriptures, there was usually a period of time when the accounts which were written down during specific historical periods were transmitted from one generation to another verbally (orally, hence, oral tradition).[48] Concerning the oral tradition there are two issues which should be noted. First, the oral tradition represents the period of greatest human creativity in the formation of and development of the accounts that eventually receive written form. The writers, some known and some unknown, usually strive to remain true to the accounts as they receive them; however, they must adapt the oral forms of transmission to those more appropriate for written forms and often adapt the content for the historical times in which they live. Second, the longer the oral tradition, then, regrettably but inevitably, the greater the differences in the written account from the original oral content. Consequently the length of the oral tradition is an issue of considerable significance in attempting to determine the original content of many scriptural texts.[49]

The phrase *writing period* descriptively refers to the historical period of time in which the oral tradition takes written form. For the three monotheisms of the West that are the subject of this study, the most common kinds of materials used were: papyrus (an ancient form of paper made from the papyrus plant, although a similar paper can be manufactured from other plants such as canes that have considerable soft fiber in them); parchment (treated animal skins, usually sheep, goats, or camels),

---

[48]

There are exceptions to this process such as Joseph Smith's digging up tablets already in written form, but the usual process is described in the text above. It is also the case that most of the great cultural epics were originally transmitted in an oral tradition before being put into written form: e.g., the Arthurian epic and the Song of Roland.

[49]

It should be stated that although an extensive oral tradition raises difficult issues concerning dates, authorship, content and meaning of written scriptural texts, raising these issues should not be understood as an attack on the truth value of these texts. Rather they reinforce a point made earlier: these sacred texts cannot be taken literally, and, thus, faithful efforts to understand the meaning, value and truth of these Holy Books requires thinking and the use of those skills characterized as higher and lower criticism.

and treated palm leaves. Although there were other materials used such as clay tablets, the three materials mentioned above were the most common during the writing periods of Judaism, Christianity and Islam because of their manufacturing ease and the utility of marking on them with "ink-like" materials and tools. Carving on a clay or stone tablet produced a longer lasting record but required extensive time compared to copying on papyrus or parchment.

Because the written scriptures of all three Holy Books occurred before the knowledge of printing in the West, the only method of reproducing a manuscript was the time consuming, labor intensive, and fallible process of hand copying. A further complication for textual scholars concerns problems of deterioration of the materials used for copying. While papyrus and parchment are moderately durable materials, the inks used tended to fade, and the conditions under which the manuscripts were kept contributed to their physical deterioration.[50] Textual scholars, those who work with hand written copies of scriptures in their original languages, face considerable challenges in their efforts to put together manuscripts of these ancient scriptures that are as close as possible to the original writings, since none of the originals have survived the ages. As if the problems of material deterioration and hand copying fallibility are not difficult enough, in many instances the oldest extant manuscripts textual scholars have to work with may be centuries removed from the first written ones. An *extant* manuscript is one that physically exists in some definite location,

---

[50] As examples consider the present condition of some of the Dead Sea Scrolls and the four oldest copies of the American Declaration of Independence. Concerning the former, in several of the jars uncovered at Qumran, there were no whole manuscripts; instead there were hundreds of small pieces. To use a metaphor, some of the work that has been and is still being done with these scrolls is like working on a jig-saw puzzle with thousands of pieces and no picture to guide their placement. Concerning the latter, the four oldest copies of the Declaration of Independence are now in such fragile condition that they must be maintained at a constant temperature, protected from the ravages of moisture and kept in special light to prevent further fading of the ink.

and the oldest are so valuable that they are carefully guarded and usually available only to a few select scholars.[51]

Finally, the process of canonization is of utmost importance in understanding the scriptural traditions of all three religions. The term *canonization* may originate from the Hebrew word *qaneh* which means "cane reed" or "balance" or most likely from the Greek noun *kanon* which means "cane reed" or "straight stick." Keeping in mind that one of the purposes of a cane reed, straight stick or balance is to measure something else, that is, to provide a standard for evaluating or judging, the use of the phrase *canons of the faith* means the standards by which beliefs and values are judged orthodox or heretical. It is in this sense that the **Hebrew Bible** becomes the fundamental canon of the Jewish faith, the **New Testament** the central canon of the Christian faith and the **Qur'an** the canon of Islam.[52] Recognizing these Holy Books as canons, however, does not answer the important question: how did they achieve the status of canons, that is, standards of the faith. The answer is through the process of canonization, which can be briefly described as follows: canonization is the historical process through which a specific collection of written texts come to be accepted as religiously authoritative by a community of believers. The process may occur in a few years or require many generations. Further, at least in the case of the three monotheisms under study, there is a historical point in time when the canon,

---

[51]

See footnote #6, page 20, on the Critical Apparatus in the Masoretic Text (Hebrew Text) of the **Hebrew Bible** and in the Greek text of the **New Testament**. The problem of the age of extant manuscripts is a considerable one for textual scholars. This is one of the reasons that the Dead Sea Scrolls are so important: the antiquity of several of their scrolls. For example, the gem of the Dead Sea Scrolls is a complete manuscript of the book of Isaiah that is three hundred years older than any other extant manuscript of this pivotal prophetic book.

[52]

Identifying each of these three revelations as the fundamental canon does not deny that there are other canons in each of these three religions, but it does imply that additional canons must be consistent with the basic beliefs and values in these three Holy Books.

that is, the Holy Book, is declared closed.[53] The formal closing of the canon usually has many consequences, but the two most important are: (1) strong religious taboos develop to prevent adding any new material to the Holy Book (see the threat that is stated in the last verse of the book of Revelation); and (2) most written material after the closing is understood as commentaries on the closed canon and usually judged by its consistency with the views in the Holy Book. However, the closing of the canon in Judaism did not prevent the continuing of an informal oral canon of the teachings of Moses and in Islam of the addition of a secondary canon in the Sacred **Hadiths** of Muhammad.

Before moving to the next chapter, an examination of the oral tradition, writing periods and canonization of each of the three Holy Books as holy canons provides a final background for exploring their theologies of war and peace. Since the purpose is only as background for the three following chapters, the descriptions which follow do not analyze the debates and complexities of the immense scholarship on the origins, writers and transmissions of these three Holy Books.

One of the difficulties in determining the oral tradition of the **Hebrew Bible** has already been identified: the problem of the ancestors of the Hebrews. Until recently, most Biblical scholars tended to date the age of the Patriarchs between 2000-1700 B.C.E. (see footnote #1, page 33). Inferences based on these dates results in an oral tradition which at the very least pre-dates Abraham, that is, 2000 B.C.E. However, as noted in a previous section, the historical problems, apart from the religious tradition, of dating Abraham raise serious questions concerning the temporal span and content of the oral tradition of this Holy Book. If it is the case that the first writings that eventually became incorporated into the **Hebrew Bible**

---

[53]

    This formal closing is not always the case, especially in Eastern religions. No such formal closing has taken place in either Hinduism or Buddhism. Such a formal closing of the canon is, however, one of the most definitive and controversial elements in the West's monotheisms.

originating during the early monarchy (between 1000--922 B.C.E., the reigns of David and Solomon), although there is some evidence that a few fragments may have been written during the time of the Judges (1225--1050 B.C.E.), it seems reasonable to speak of an oral tradition at least several hundred years in length if not closer to a millennium. At this point in time, archeological information does not allow for a more definitive period to be designated.

Fortunately, Biblical scholarship is more definitive concerning the writing period. With the exception of a few fragments from the period of the Judges, the victory song of Deborah for example, present evidence points to a writing period of approximately 700 to 800 years (1000-200 B.C.E.) with a multitude of contributors. Compared to both the **New Testament** and the **Qur'an**, the **Hebrew Bible** has a longer oral tradition, a more extensive number of contributors and a longer period of writing. While this poses much more difficult questions and problems for students of the **Hebrew Bible,** it also makes it a richer historical and theological document.

As with the writing period, there is more definitive evidence concerning the canonization of the 24 books that comprise this Holy Book. Remembering that the process of canonization usually goes through a slow informal stage, there is evidence to support the following generally agreed upon dates for the acceptance as canon of the three parts of the **Hebrew Bible**:

(1)   The *Torah* (in Greek, the Pentateuch, the Five Books) by 400 B.C.E.;

(2)   The *Nebi-im* (the books of the prophets) by 200 B.C.E.;

(3)   The *Ketub-im* (the writings) by 100 B.C.E..

In other words, there is evidence to support the judgment that by the first century B.C.E. the Jewish community in Palestine had accepted the 24 books in the present Masoretic Text as an authoritative revelation from God. In 90 C.E. at Jabneh (Greek, Jamnia), most probably because of the Roman destruction of the Temple in 70 C.E. and further dispersion of Jews from Jerusalem, the leaders of the Palestinian community met these crises by declaring an official Holy Canon, the **Hebrew Bible**. However, this declaration did not mean that other writings were not read and

96

informally accepted as canon as well as a continuing oral tradition. Brief comments are needed concerning both of these informal canons.

While the 24 books of the **Hebrew Bible** were accepted as revelation by 100 B.C.E., other works continued to be written approximately between 200 B.C.E. and 200 C.E. Further, there were many other writings that were read and accepted as canonical before the third century B.C.E. that were not included in the Masoretic Text. The majority of these writings have been combined into two collections known as the **Apocrypha**, from the Greek word meaning "hidden, secret,"[54] and the more extensive **Pseudepigrapha**, from the Greek *pseudes* meaning "deceitful, false" and *graphe* meaning "writing."[55] Although much less attention has been given to the **Pseudepigrapha**, recent scholarship recognizes its importance especially in regard to cosmic eschatology. In some ways, the books of I and II Enoch in this collection had more influence on Jewish, and therefore Christian, cosmic eschatology than the books that were accepted in the **Hebrew Bible.**

Before turning to the Greek **New Testament**, two additional items need addressing. First, in addition to the written scriptures there has continued an oral tradition of the teachings of Moses, passed from one generation of rabbis to another from the 13th century B.C.E. to the 20th century C.E., that still influence Jewish

---

54

Several of the books in the **Apocrypha** were included in the **Septuagint**, the canon that was accepted by the Jewish community in Alexandria. The Council of Trent in 1546 C.E., as a part of the Roman Catholic Counter-Reformation, added the **Apocrypha** to the 66 books of the **Vulgate** and declared that they were a secondary canon of scriptures. Several English translations of the Christian Bible now include the books of the **Apocrypha**, either placing them between the two Testaments or after the **New Testament.**

55

Until recently there was little availability to translations of and scholarship on the **Pseudepigrapha** in English. However, in 1983 Doubleday and Company published an excellent two volume translation of and commentary on the books of this important collection of ancient texts. It is edited by James H. Charlesworth of Duke University.

theology. These teachings, while still important within the Jewish religious community, are not included in this study. Finally, while most Jews describe Hebrew as a sacred language, they do so in a manner that is different than a Muslim does when he declares that Arabic is the language of God. Few religious Jews believe that God literally spoke Hebrew; rather, God inspired the prophet who interpretatively communicated his received revelations in the language of the Jewish people. In other words, while based on the revelations of God, prophetic preachings incorporated the personality of the prophet and the historical traditions of the time that he lived. The difference in the Muslim view concerning the sacredness of Arabic is striking.

Compared to the problems of oral tradition, writing period, and contributors **New Testament** issues seem simple, but this is deceptive for two reasons: the issue of canonization is less clear and there is a considerable language difficulty for those parts of the **New Testament** that include the teachings of Jesus. Beginning with the language problem helps clarify the oral tradition.

The generally accepted period for the public teaching and preaching of Jesus is approximately 30-33 C.E.. There is no evidence that Jesus ever wrote anything or that anyone listening to him made notes on his teachings. Further, the audience that could understand his teaching was limited to those who understood Aramaic, the dialect of Hebrew common in Galilee; in other words, his audience consisted of Jews in Palestine. While there is no extant copy, a majority of Christian scholars believe that the earliest effort to save in written form some of the teachings of Jesus occurred approximately 15-20 years after his death and is referred to in Biblical literature as the Q Document. If a two decade delay in putting the teachings of Jesus in some written form seems surprising to contemporary Christians, the reason for this delay may be found in the early Christian community's passion for cosmic eschatology. Several of Paul's letters as well as several of the "little letters" not written by Paul evidence that early Christians were convinced the Second Coming would occur within a generation. Given this belief a written record, especially as there were still "eyewitness" disciples still living, may have seemed superfluous. However, the end did not arrive and those who actually knew and heard Jesus continued to decrease in numbers; consequently, the Q Document may have been written to respond to such an emergency. If this scenario is correct, then the oral tradition concerning the teachings of Jesus is between one and two decades in length.

Regarding the writing period of the 27 books in the **New Testament**, several of the letters of Paul were the first writings eventually incorporated into the **New Testament**. Some of Paul's early correspondence[56] may have predated the Q Document or occurred shortly after it. There is not adequate evidence to know which came first. Although every few decades a controversy arises over the first of the gospel accounts to be written, the issue is usually decided in favor of Mark, and the view that the writers of Matthew and Luke had copies of Mark for the writing of their more developed gospel accounts is essentially unquestioned. Based on this scholarship it seems reasonable to conclude given current information, the basic writing period of the **New Testament** was approximately four decades (40-50 C.E. to 90 C.E.). It is generally accepted that 99 percent of the **New Testament** was in written form by the end of the first century C.E..[57]

The issue of canonization is less certain than those of oral tradition and writing period. Unlike a formal declaration such as occurred at Jabneh, there is no historical document which establishes a formal decision closing the Christian canon

---

[56]

Some of his correspondence is no longer extant. For example there is evidence indicating that Paul may have written at least seven different letters to Corinth, parts of which are incorporated in I and II Corinthians.

[57]

Only a few passages are thought to be added after the end of the first century. One of the most interesting, controversial and sometimes tragic additions may be the last twelve verses of Mark 16. The oldest Greek copies of Mark end with verse 8. It is only later copies which contain verses 9-20, and it is in these verses that references to the handling of serpents has led several small sectarian groups of Christians to liturgical practices which have resulted in tragedies.

to the present 27 books. There is evidence that early Christian communities read scriptures other than these 27, but no clear evidence as to when and who closed the canon. Perhaps such a decision was reached at the Council of Nicea in 325 C.E.. All that is clearly known is that a fourth century Church Father Athanasius, wrote a letter mentioning the 27 books in the currently accepted **New Testament**, listing them in the order they presently take and declaring them a canon for the faithful.

Finally, there is a significant issue concerning language that needs mentioning. Few, if any, Christians think of Greek as a sacred language. Greek is an important religious language because it is the language in which the **New Testament** was written and transmitted until the great Latin translation of Jerome, the **Vulgate** which decreased the sacredness of Greek. The part of the **New Testament** that poses the greatest problems for scholarly study concern the teachings of Jesus. Since he taught in Aramaic, his teachings in written form are already in translation in the Greek **New Testament**. For the Christian student who does not read Greek, an American for example, when he reads what follows the words "Jesus said," he is reading a translation of a translation.[58]

While the areas of oral tradition, writing period, and canonization are less complex for Islam than either Christianity or Judaism, there is a considerable difference in the language issue. It is this language issue that asks more of Muslims in accepting some of the principles of tolerance in this study than is asked of Jews and Christians. Fortunately, however, the **Qur'an** itself provides a position on the Holy Books of Jews and Christians which offers a good foundation for tolerance.

---

[58]

    While knowledge of these translation problems denies the simplistic view created by those "red letter editions" of the **New Testament**, that is, that the words in red are what Jesus "actually" said, it does not deny the transmission of his teachings as sacred revelation. Rather, the problems of translation show the foolishness of any effort at literalism and infer that serious Christians must use their abilities to think and the tools of Biblical scholarship in order to find the truths of revelation in the Holy Book.

The last chapter offers an argument for such toleration in terms of an apology for peace.

In February of 610 C.E., a Meccan merchant by the name of Muhammad was fasting and meditatively searching in a cave when he received a revelation from God. While consisting of only five *ayats*, this revelation confirmed that God had created humans, that God cared for his creations, that humans still need instruction in how to live righteously, and that God would inform them with a new writing.[59] From this night, a night Muslims call the Night of Power and Glory, until his death twenty-two years later (632 C.E.) Muhammad continued to receive revelations from God. At first he was doubtful and reticent, but slowly he began to share them with others beginning with his immediate family. Since he was illiterate,[60] Muhammad could not write his revelations. Further, since those who were willing to listen to his preaching were so few and growth in the size of the Muslim community in Mecca was exceedingly slow, it is reasonable to infer that for the first years of his preaching, no one considered these revelations important enough to write on the most common

---

[59]

    There is still some debate among Muslim scholars as to the first revelation; most accept the following five *ayats* from *sura* 96, titled the "Clot":

> Proclaim! In the name / Of thy Lord and Cherisher, Who created-- / Created man, out of / A (mere) clot / Of congealed blood: Proclaim! / And thy Lord is Most Bountiful,-- / He Who taught / (The use of) the Pen-- taught man that / Which he knew not.

Other Muslim scholars believe that the following seven *ayats* from *sura* 74, titled "One Wrapped Up," were the first revelation:

> O thou wrapped up / (In a mantle)! / Arise and deliver thy warning! / And thy Lord / Do thou magnify! / And thy garments / Keep free from stain! / And all abomination shun! / Nor expect, in giving, / Any increase (for thyself)! / But for they Lord's (Cause), / Be patient and constant!

[60]

    Muhammad's illiteracy is, for Muslims, an unquestioned sign that the **Qur'an** must come from God, for how could an illiterate Arab, no matter how great a man, compose the greatest poetic revelation in the history of the human race!

material available, treated palm leaves. However, as more and more began to accept Muhammad as the Prophet of God, then it is just as reasonable to infer that before his death, perhaps as much as the last ten years of his life, there were efforts on the part of literate Muslims to record his teachings on palm leaves. This suggests an oral tradition of approximately 10-15 years (610--625 C.E.) and a writing period of approximately the same length (620-632 C.E.). Compared to Christianity and especially Judaism, both periods are very short. Additionally, since Muhammad taught in Arabic and the writings were in Arabic, it is possible to be more historically certain about his teaching than those of either the non-writing Hebrew prophets or Jesus. Whatever the exact length of the oral tradition and the writing period, clearly by the time of the third caliph, Uthman (644-656 C.E.), there were hundreds of unorganized palm leaves with the revelations to Muhammad written on them. The great religious accomplishment of Uthman's leadership was the organization of this multitude of writings into the canonized **Qur'an** consisting of 114 *suras* organized poetically. By his death in 656 the **Qur'an** as it is accepted today was in use. Unfortunately in order to eliminate any controversy about the authority of the collated **Qur'an**, Uthman ordered the burning of all the palm leaves.

However, in a manner similar to Judaism, there continued a tradition of revelations outside the **Qur'an**. Collectively they became known as the **Hadiths** or the traditions of the Prophet. By the time of the Medieval ages, there were several thousand individual **Hadiths** spread throughout the Muslim world. One of the most significant accomplishments of Medieval Muslim scholarship was the reducing of the authoritative traditions to several hundred. Although this study concentrates on the **Qur'an**, there are occasions when references to the **Hadiths** are useful. Before turning to the next chapter only one issue needs clarification: the sacredness of Arabic.

As indicated earlier, there is a most significant sense in which Arabic is sacred for the Muslim that is quite different than Jewish views about Hebrew and Christian views about Greek. It has to do with the Muslim understanding of the

102

chain of transmission of the **Qur'an**. According to traditional Islam, that chain is as follows: *Al-Lah* gives the revelation (the *ayats*) to the angel Gabriel in **Arabic**; the angel then **Recites** the revelation to the Prophet Muhammad in **Arabic**; the Prophet then **Recites** the revelation to the Muslim community in **Arabic**. The Arabic term *Qur'an* means "Recitation." From this perspective, forgive the anthropomorphism, each **Arabic** word in the **Qur'an** "literally" came from the mouth of God. For this reason the **Qur'an** is for Muslims, the **Miracle** that God has given to them. There is a tradition that whenever Muhammad was challenged to present a miracle to prove he was the Prophet of God, his response was always: the **Qur'an** is God's miracle. This answer also accounts for the designation of each verse of the **Qur'an** as an *ayat*, from the Arabic term for "miracle." It also the reason for the original prohibition against translating the **Qur'an** into any other language; a prohibition that Islam had to overcome as it spread into many other cultures with different languages. Still today, many translators refuse to translate unless the Arabic text accompanies the translated text. In ways different than for Christians and Jews, the language of the Holy Book, Arabic, is sacred for Muslims.[61]

Examining the rich traditions shared by Jews, Christians and Muslims as a background for serious study of their theologies of war and peace also provides a background for seeking peace among them. The next three chapters examine their theologies individually, and the final chapter returns to shared values and beliefs as a foundation for peace.

---

[61]

The sacredness of Arabic as the language of God also accounts for an interesting phenomena. While orthodox synagogues teach continuing classes in Hebrew, it is the case that most others teach enough Hebrew in order to allow their youth to understand and participate in the worship services. Finding a Christian church that conducts on-going classes in Greek for its worshippers is exceeding rare; however, the overwhelming number of mosques in non-Arabic speaking nations conduct systematic classes in Arabic whose fundamental purpose is preparing believers to read the Arabic **Qur'an** and, thus, to gain a deeper spiritual understanding and richer aesthetic experience.

CHAPTER TWO

JUDAISM--FROM YAHWEH THE WARRIOR GOD
TO ELOH-IM THE CREATOR

As indicated earlier, the ancients considered names as more than mere sounds and social conventions for identifying persons. In the case of the Divine Name (?), there was a power at work such that any misuse, perhaps even any utterance, of this Name could lead to harmful consequences. In the very process of naming, such as the man (*adam*) naming the animals in Genesis 2, there was power. Consequently, the naming of human beings was a serious undertaking, for the name was believed to reveal the nature and character of the person named. When the One bestowing the name upon a human being was God, the name acquired a religious significance far beyond that of parents naming a child. It is not surprising, then, that the name given in Genesis Chapter 32 is second only to the Divine Name (?) in sacredness for Jews:

> That same night he rose, and taking his two wives and his slave-girls and his eleven children he crossed the fork of the Jabbok. He took them and sent them across the stream and sent all his possessions too. And Jacob was left alone.

> And there was one that wrestled with him until daybreak who, seeing that he could not master him, struck him in the socket of his hip, and Jacob's hip was dislocated as he wrestled with him. He said, 'Let me go for day is breaking'. But Jacob answered, 'I will not let

you go unless you bless me'. He then asked, 'What is your name?' 'Jacob', he replied. He said, 'Your name shall no longer be Jacob, but Israel, because you have been strong against God, you shall prevail against men'. Jacob then made this request, 'I beg you, tell me your name', but he replied, 'Why do you ask my name?' And he blessed him there.

Since the Yahwist[1] first put into written form this cherished narrative from the oral

---

[1]

As indicated in the Prologue, the approach taken in this study to the **Hebrew Bible** employs the tools of higher and lower criticism. Although there are still considerable issues of debate among scholars who use these tools, there is general agreement that the *Torah* (the *Pentateuch*, the first five books) are a synthesis of at least four sources from different historical periods. In Biblical studies this position on the authorship and development of the *Torah* is known as the Documentary Hypothesis. It is usually contrasted with the traditional view that Moses was the author of these five books. While the latter view has been of considerable use in establishing the authority of these five books, the difficulties in maintaining Mosaic authorship began to be critiqued even before the beginning of the Common Era. The modern Documentary Hypothesis, abbreviated as JEDP for the four major sources, was initiated by the publication of Julius Wellhausen's **Prolegomena to the History of Israel** in 1885. While Wellhausen's views that these four sources (documents) reflected an evolutionary development in Israel's faith have been critiqued, his sequence is generally accepted. The view that is current among Biblical scholars is that each source reflects an older oral tradition as well as the historical circumstances of the periods they describe and the times in which they were written. Briefly, the four sources are:

(1) The Yahwist tradition (J), which dates from the 10th century B.C.E. and named because *Yahweh* is the primary term for the deity;

(2) The Elohist tradition (E), which was likely written after the death of Solomon from the Northern Kingdom, Israel, and named because *Eloh-im* is the term for the deity;

(3) The Deuteronomic tradition, which dates from the 7th century and receives its name because it is limited to material in the book of Deuteronomy;

(4) The Priestly tradition, which was completed during the late exhilic period, 6th century. While this study does not accept the simple linear evolutionary view of Wellhausen--that is, that E is essentially a more sophisticated development of the earlier source J, it does argue that from the time of Moses to the post-exhilic period major changes and developments occurred in the Jewish religion, especially

tradition, the story of Jacob and his night-time wrestling adversary has captured the imagination of both children and adults within these monotheisms. For this study, the meaning of the name is more important than the intriguing question as to the identity of Jacob's opponent in this drama. The name *Isra-el*, while etymologically meaning "May *El* (God) rule or persevere," is given in the context of the story a different meaning. The name itself is the combining of two Hebrew terms, *sarita* which means "to rule," "to persevere," or "to be strong" and *el* which means "god"; thus, "May God rule or persevere." However, the Yahwist offers a popular etymology that must have originated in the oral tradition: *Isra-el* means "He who has striven against God" or "He who has been strong against God." Even if not precisely correct, it is an etymology which struck the popular imagination of a whole people who came to know themselves as Israelites. In this sense, it would not be incorrect to state that the **Hebrew Bible** is the story of *Isra-el*, that is, the story of a centuries old struggle between a people and their God: a struggle seeking righteousness in their relationship with God and a struggle for justice in their human relationships. It was, and continues to be, both a search and a struggle involving fundamental human needs and passions that are actualized in and through a multitude of controversial beliefs about chosenness, promised land, wars and holy wars, peace, and future eschatologies.

Special Problems and Difficulties

Chapter Two is the first of three chapters whose purpose is exploring the theologies of war and peace in each of the Holy Books of these three Western monotheisms before returning in the final chapter to a plea for both righteousness and justice, that is, an apology for peace. Of these three chapters, the second poses the greatest difficulties and challenges. There are several reasons that deserve mention

---

its movement from a henotheism to a monotheism. These changes become most evident in contrasting the earliest of the sources, J, with the latest P.

before turning to the Masoretic Text of the **Hebrew Bible** and its theologies of war and peace.

First, the age of the oral tradition and its length is problematic. Given that the oral tradition pre-dates the 15th century B.C.E. and could in some instances approach a millennium in length, two consequences follow: (1) while the writings themselves provide information concerning the forms and content of the oral tradition, that tradition is only marginally recoverable; (2) the very process of writing changes the form, content and nature of those accounts in the oral tradition.[2] Second, the writing period was so extensive, several centuries, that the earlier sources were often subjected to "editing procedures," the term used by Biblical scholars is *redactions*, whose purposes were accomplishing such tasks as clarifying earlier texts and reconciling later texts and their views with earlier ones. As a consequence, the ability to reconstruct adequately the views and world of the Yahwist is, while not completely impossible, compromised. Finally, the extensive impact of the Babylonian Exile on the Jewish religion and the writings which came to comprise the **Hebrew Bible** are so important and controversial that hundreds of books, dissertations, and articles still debate these developments. Although a one chapter study can hardly do justice to all these complexities, nonetheless, they can be described in adequate enough detail to provide a basis for exploring the theologies of war and peace in the **Hebrew Bible**.

In order to better understand the study which follows, it is helpful to accomplish three tasks before turning to the texts of the **Hebrew Bible**: clarify a special use of the terms *Hebrew* and *Jew* for purposes of this chapter; summarize in outline form the dimensions of war and peace which dominated specific historical

---

2

As an example of this problem consider the views of one of the most influential writers in the history of the Western world: Plato. He makes it clear in several dialogues that the written word is so inferior to the spoken word that he rejects any effort to communicate his most important truths and ideas in writing. This may also be the reason Socrates never put his thoughts into written form.

periods; and, describe the strategy for examining the theology of war and the theology of peace that occupy the heart of this chapter. First, because of the influence of the Exile, religious beliefs and values that can be reasonably attributed to pre-exhilic times are identified by the term *Hebrew*. Beliefs and values which bear the influence of the Babylonian Exile and post-exhilic influences are identified by the noun *Jew* or the adjective *Jewish*.[3]

Second, because the pre-exhilic period consists of several centuries, it is advantageous to divide it into two periods: pre-monarchial (Moses to Saul, approximately 13th through 11th centuries) and the monarchial period (David to the destruction of Jerusalem and the Temple, 10th through 6th centuries). The result is three historical periods important for the development of views about war and peace: pre-monarchial, monarchial and post-exhilic. A brief summary of the dimensions of both war and peace that dominate in each period helps set a background to explore these periods in more depth. As stated in the Prologue, the dimensions of war are: political war, spiritual war, and eschatological war. Concerning the latter, there are two categories: historical eschatological war (future political war) and cosmic eschatological war (end of time conflict). The dimensions of peace are: political, spiritual, and cosmic eschatological. While these dimensions are not exclusive of one another, there are clear patterns of dominance in each historical period because of the special circumstances of the Jewish people in those periods. In summary form, views of war are as follows:

(1)   Pre-Monarchial Period (Moses to Saul): political war (understood mostly as holy war) dominates, beliefs about cosmic eschatological war are non-existent, and little attention is given to spiritual war;

3

    As stated earlier, for other chapters, the terms *Hebrew*, *Jew*, and *Israelite* (or *Israeli*) can be understood as synonyms. Because this chapter must address the historical developments of several centuries, it is helpful to have terms for referring to both pre-exhilic and post-exhilic periods, beliefs, and values.

(2)   Monarchial Period (David to the Exile): again political war dominates, but a concern for non-holy wars receives attention, and there is a slow developing concern over spiritual war and the first glimpses of eschatological war, especially historical eschatological war;

(3)   Post-exhilic Period (From 6th century B.C.E. to last writings in the **Hebrew Bible**): the emphasis turns almost exclusively to cosmic eschatological war with some attention directed to historical eschatological war and added attention given to spiritual war.

Views of peace in these periods can be summarized as:

(1)   Pre-monarchial Period: less attention is given to all dimensions of peace than of war, views of eschatological peace are absent and only slight attention given to spiritual peace;

(2)   Monarchial Period: attention is given to political peace, the importance of spiritual peace receives its first emphasis in the preachings of the 8th century prophets, and views concerning eschatological peace slowly begin to appear;

(3)   Post-Exhilic Period: there is a continued emphasis on spiritual peace but a major development of eschatological peace, especially its cosmic dimensions.

        Exploring the dimensions of war and peace in each of the historical periods follows a strategy which is described by the following outline:

(1)   A description of the movement of the Hebrew faith from its henotheistic period to the development of Jewish monotheism after the Exile;

(2)   An examination of the theologies of war in the **Hebrew Bible** which includes a word study (Appendix A provides a listing of the most significant passages in the **Hebrew Bible** that concern the various dimensions of war) and a description of war in all its dimensions in each of the three historical periods;

(3)   An examination of peace following the pattern described for war (Appendix B provides a listing of the most significant passages concerning peace).

Completion of the third goal, theologies of peace, then, provides both the historical and theological foundations for examining **New Testament** views of both war and peace in the third chapter.

From the Warrior Yahweh to the Creator Eloh-im

As indicated in previous passages, this section could just as well be titled "From Pre-Exhilic Henotheism to Post-Exhilic Monotheism." Before a more precise statement of the differences between henotheism[4] and monotheism is given, contrast the views of the deity in the following brief excerpts from the two creation accounts in Genesis Chapters One and Two:

> *Yahweh* God fashioned man of dust from the soil. Then he breathed into his nostrils a breath of life, and thus man became a living being.
>
> . . . .
>
> *Yahweh* God said, 'It is not good that the man should be alone. I will make him a helpmate.' So from the soil *Yahweh* God fashioned all the wild beasts and   all the birds of the heavens. These he brought to the man to see what he would name call them; each was to bear the name the man would give it. . . . So *Yahweh* God made the man to fall into a deep sleep. And while he slept, he took one of his ribs and enclosed it in flesh. *Yahweh* God built the rib he had taken from

---

[4]
The term *henotheism* is used in this study rather than the more common term *monolatry*. Both originate from Greek roots and are used to describe beliefs about the nature of the divine (supernatural). The term *monolatry* derives from the Greek roots *monos*, which means "alone" (usually translated as "one," a translation that is usually adequate except for religion) and *lateria* which means "worship," hence "the worship of one." I find the term unfortunate for two reasons: first, negative connotations because of the more commonly known term *idolatry*; and, second, the Greek term *henos* actually means "one" while *monos* means "alone" or better "only one." As the discussion in this part of the chapter establishes, there is considerable difference between the religious claim for "one god" (henotheism) and the claim that there is "only one God" (monotheism). For this reason I find the term *henotheism* to be preferable in exploring the nature of religious claims about the nature of the divine. In this study the term *henotheism* is synonymous with the term *monolatry* as used by most scholars.

the man into a woman and brought her to the man. . . .

. . . .

The man and his wife heard the sound of *Yahweh* God walking in the garden in the cool of the day, and they hid from *Yahweh* God among the trees of the garden. But *Yahweh* God called to the man. 'Where are you?' he asked. 'I heard the sound of you in the garden;' he replied 'I was afraid because I was naked, so I hid.' (Genesis 2-3, selected verses)

In the beginning God [*Eloh-im*] created the heavens and the earth. Now the earth was a formless void [emptiness], there was darkness over the deep, and God's spirit hovered over the water.

God said, 'Let there be light', and there was light. God saw that the light was good, and God divided light from the darkness. God called light 'day', and darkness he called 'night'. Evening came and morning came: the first day.

God said, 'Let there be a vault in the waters to divide the waters in two'. An so it was. . . . God called the vault 'heaven'. Evening came and morning came: the second day. (Genesis 1, selected verses)

Even a cursory reading of these two magnificent creation accounts indicates a considerable difference in their views of the deity. In the Yahwist account (Genesis 2, a pre-exhilic one) the *Yahweh* God of creation is most anthropomorphic. His method of creation for most life forms resembles a potter at work molding clay, and he walks in the garden enjoying the cool of the day. Contrasted with the Priestly account (Genesis 1, exhilic or post-exhilic) written approximately 400 years after the Yahwist one, *Eloh-im* is a de-anthropomorphized spirit of immense power who can create simply by saying: "BE," that is, simply by the power of His Word. While 400 years of Jewish growth in understanding the nature of God, humans, and the universe account of many of the differences in these two narratives, fundamental to their differences is that the Yahwist was a henotheist and the writers of the Priestly account were monotheists or at least so close to monotheism that they can be considered monotheists for purposes of this study.

In exploring the development of the Hebrews' religious understanding of God from their entrance into Canaan in the 13th century B.C.E. to their return to Jerusalem from exile in the 6th century, there are three terms that need defining: *polytheism, henotheism* and *monotheism*. Each consists of the Greek root *theos*, which means "god," and the suffix *ism*, which means "a position or belief." The prefixes, however, indicate quite different religious views. A polytheism is the belief that there are many gods and, usually, goddesses. The dividing of the supernatural into sexual categories indicates the process that lies at the heart of a polytheism: anthropomorphism. In other words, in the oldest form of religion known in the Western world, polytheism, the gods are created in the image of human beings. A henotheism often represents an evolutionary stage between polytheism and monotheism. A henotheism, the Greek word *henos* meaning "one," elevates one god above all others but does not reject the reality of other deities. Historically, a henotheism usually ceases to exist or develops into a monotheism. The prefix *monos* does not mean "one" but "alone"; hence, monotheism involves the claim of exclusivity, that is, "One God Alone" or better "One and Only One God." While the difference between polytheism and monotheism is well known and clear, such is not the case between henotheism and monotheism. For clarification, consider the first commandment.

The two redactions of the Ten Commandments (the *Decalogue*, Greek for "Ten Words") are found in Exodus 20 and Deuteronomy 5.[5] In both, the first

---

[5]

One of the many problems that eventually led scholars to affirm the Documentary Hypothesis and reject the Mosaic authorship of the Pentateuch are differences in the two accounts of the Decalogue. While requiring careful reading, there are differences between the following commandments in Exodus and Deuteronomy: the fourth concerning keeping the Sabbath, the fifth concerning

commandment is the same and usually translated as "You shall have no other gods except [before or above] me." More correctly, the commandment is translated as "There shall be no other gods for you before my face." For the monotheist this commandment means something radically different than it does for the henotheist. Intrinsic to monotheism is the claim that there are no other gods; thus, the commandment means that believers are not to worship anything other than God, that is, believers are not to commit the sin of idolatry. For henotheists, however, because they do not reject the possibility that there are other gods, the commandment means that believers are to do one of two things: (1) place *Yahweh* above all other gods or (2) let no other gods intervene in the relationship between *Yahweh* and his people.[6]

Whoever were the ancestors of the Hebrews, they must have been polytheists because prior to the middle of the second millennium polytheism was the only religious orientation that existed in the Middle East, at least according to present archeological knowledge. As the Hebrews migrated into Canaan in the 13th century, they encountered polytheism in the Canaanites. While traditional scholarship on the pre-exhilic period usually affirmed the monotheism of the Jews, the better and more recent scholarship of individuals such as Mark Smith and Bernhard Lang argues most persuasively for monotheism as a 6th century (or later) development. This scholarship generally identifies four stages in the movement from polytheism to monotheism:

(1)   *Yahweh* polytheism--the pre-monarchial period (13th to 11th centuries, Moses

---

honoring father and mother, the ninth concerning false witness, and the tenth concerning coveting. Singular authorship cannot account for such differences.

6

For students of the **Hebrew Bible** who find the constant falling back into polytheism of the Hebrews as described in the collections of Samuel, Kings and Chronicles and are puzzled that even Solomon allowed altars and shrines of dozens of gods to built around the Temple, understanding the henotheism of the pre-exhilic period provides clarification. Once a people recognize monotheism there is little danger of returning to polytheism; rather the danger is idolatry. But during the stage of henotheism, there is a constant temptation to return to polytheism.

to David) in which the Hebrews worshipped *Yahweh* from among a number of other Canaanite deities such as *Baal, El, Asherah* (who may have been the female consort of *Yahweh* during this period), and *Chemosh*;

(2)   *Yahweh*-only party (that is, *Yahweh* henotheism)--the early monarch (10th and 9th centuries, David to the beginnings of Assyrian power just before the appearance of the great prophets of the 8th century) in which *Yahweh* was raised above all other gods as the national god of the Israelite nation and peoples;

(3)   Mono-Yahwism--the period in which the Hebrew faith began slowly to recognize that their national deity, *Yahweh*, was a god whose power extended to other nations (during the late monarchy, a period including the Assyrian destructions, the rise of the 8th century prophets and the destruction of Jerusalem and the Temple in the 6th century);

(4)   *Eloh-im* monotheism (The *Eloh-im* of Genesis 1)--the period from the exile to the writing of the last books included in the third part of the Masoretic Text, the *Ketub-im* (approximately 3rd century B.C.E.), the period in which the Jews affirmed that there was one and only God.

Regarding their final commitment to an unequivocal monotheism, there is a slowly growing Biblical literature on the part of scholars such as Hermann Vorlander, Morton Smith and Norman Cohn that argues for substantial influences of Zoroastrian monotheism on the Jewish religion during and after the exile.[7]

---

[7]

Norman Cohn's **Cosmos, Chaos, and the World to Come**, published by Yale University Press, 1993, is one of the best recent works. While considerable debate continues and will continue for decades, there is mounting evidence that several of the most cherished beliefs in these Western monotheisms may have originated among the Zoroastrians: moral monotheism, cosmic eschatology, a savior to come, the conflict between the Sons of Light and the Sons of Darkness (*Shaitan* is a Zoroastrian Son of Darkness), and realms of reward and punishment after bodily death. If these views are correct, then post-exhilic Judaism (especially the theology of the Pharisees) helped transmit considerable Zoroastrian influences into Christianity and Islam.

For purposes of this study, the four stages in the evolution of understanding the nature of God from pre-exhilic *Yahweh* polytheism to post-exhilic *Eloh-im* monotheism are reduced to the three historical periods previously described: pre-monarchial (*Yahweh* polytheism developing into *Yahweh* henotheism), monarchial (*Yahweh* henotheism developing into Mono-Yahwism) and post-exhilic (*Eloh-im*, monotheism). The general combining of the two intermediate stages (*Yahweh* henotheism and Mono-Yahwism) during the pre-monarchy and the monarchy does not compromise the theologies of war and peace that develop during these periods since the central ideas of chosenness, promised land and holy war are emphasized from the period of the Judges (Deborah) to the late monarchies. Further, this combining does no injustice to the major contrast at the center of this chapter, the differences between pre-exhilic (Hebrew) and post-exhilic (Jewish) theologies of war and peace and the apology for peace in the final chapter.. Thus, before exploring these theologies, a more adequate description of these differences is needed.

Examining the many terms (some are perhaps names) for the deity who came to be understood as Israel's god provides evidence for the movement from pre-monarchial Hebrew polytheism to post-exhilic Jewish monotheism. The earliest references involve the generic Semitic term *El* for the Hebrew deity in combination with several descriptive phrases. The root meaning of *El* is "power," and *El*-worship dominated the ancient Middle East. Among the various combinations of *El* in the **Hebrew Bible** are: *El Shaddai* (God of the Mountains), *El Elyon* (Most High God), *El Olam* (Everlasting God), *El Bethel* (God of Bethel), *El Roi* (God who Sees), *El Berith* (God of the Covenant), *El Eloke-Israel* (God of Israel), and *Eloh-im* (God or gods, the form is plural).[8] The many references in Genesis and Exodus to the "God (*El*) of your Fathers," that is, the "God (*El*) of Abraham, Isaac and Jacob are

---

[8]

While any Biblical Dictionary provides information on these various "names" of God, one of the better articles summarizing their uses is in **The Interpreter's Dictionary of the Bible**, edited by George Buttrick.

most likely references that occurred within a period of Hebrew polytheism. Thus, it is reasonable to conclude that these phrases dominated the oral tradition, that period when *Yahweh* polytheism was evolving into *Yahweh* henotheism, for during this time, the first identifications between the various *El*s and *YHWH* (*Yahweh*) most likely occurred. If the victory song of Deborah in Judges 3, which celebrated a victory over Sisera, is the earliest writing to survive in the Masoretic Text, then this identification between *El* and *Yahweh* occurred during the 12th century (the period of the *Shopet-im*, the Judges):

> 'Listen, you kings! Give ear, you princes! / From me, from me comes a song for *Yahweh*. / I will glorify *Yahweh*, God of Israel.
>
> . . . .
>
> Then Israel marched down to the gates / *Yahweh*'s people, like heroes, marched down to fight for him.
>
> . . . .
>
> "Curse Meroz," says *Yahweh*'s angel / "curse, curse the dweller's in it; / for they never came to the *Yahweh*'s aid, / to *Yahweh*'s aid among the warriors."
>
> . . . .
>
> 'So perish all your enemies, *Yahweh*! / And let those who love you be like the sun / when he arises in all his strength!' (verses 3, 13, 23, and 31)

While the term Israel may be an anachronism added by a later redactor--a national identity is almost 150 years in the future from the historical times of the Judges--it is clear that *Yahweh*, who became the covenant God of Israel, was identified with *El*. Once this identification was accomplished, the Hebrews took their first step from *Yahweh* polytheism to *Yahweh* henotheism. Once this occurred, the term *YHWH* dominated all others used in reference to the Hebrew deity. Once established as the term for the Covenant deity, it is used over 6800 times in the Masoretic Text. From the pre-monarchial period to the Exile, there was no prohibition against uttering this word. In fact, *Yahweh* became a war cry as the Hebrews confronted their enemies in battle, especially during the times before the monarchy. Also note, for future reference, that the elements of chosenness and holy war are celebrated in Deborah's song. The *Yahweh* God of Deborah was indeed a mighty warrior.

In the 9th century, the Elohist source introduced the use of the term *Eloh-im* for the Hebrew deity. Thus, from this century to the post-exhilic period, there were two major designations for the God of Israel: *Yahweh* and *Eloh-im*. The Priestly source, who wrote either near the end of the Exile or early during the return to Jerusalem, selected the term *Eloh-im* for the monotheistic God whose power created and extended throughout the whole universe, and the prohibition developed concerning utterances of the sacred *YHWH*. Many Biblical scholars find in the preachings of the great unknown prophet of the Exile, II Isaiah, the first clear utterances of Jewish monotheism. A key passage is Isaiah 45:14-25, which contains at least a half dozen monotheistic assertions identifying *Yahweh* of the Covenant with *Eloh-im* of the creation:

> I am *Yahweh*, unrivalled, / there is no other God besides me.
>
> . . . .
>
> I am *Yahweh*, unrivalled, / I form the light and create the dark. / I make good fortune and create calamity, / it is I, *Yahweh*, who do all this.
>
> . . . .
>
> I it was who made the earth, / and created man who is on it. / I it was who spread out the heavens with my hands / and now give orders to their whole array.
>
> . . . .
>
> 'With you alone is God, and he has no rival; / there is no other god'.
>
> . . . .
>
> Yes, thus says *Yahweh*, / creator of the heavens, / who is God, / who formed the earth and made it, / who set it firm, / created it

no chaos, / but a place to be lived in:

. . . .

Am I not *Yahweh*? / There is no other god besides me, / a God of integrity and a savior; / there is none apart from me. / Turn to me and be saved, / all the ends of the earth, / for I am God unrivalled. (verses 5, 7, 12, 14, 18, 21-22)

Even though the identity of this great prophet is unknown and there are significant differences in interpreting his teachings about the one who is to come and suffer (the "Suffering Servant" passages) between Jews and Christians, II Isaiah's proclamations represent the earliest, unambiguous references to Jewish monotheism. It is reasonable to conclude, then, that from the end of the Exile to the present day, the Jewish faith has remained a firmly committed monotheism with two major terms for its deity: *Eloh-im* and the unutterable *Yahweh*. From the advent of Islam in the 7th century C.E., it is only within Christianity that any questions have been raised concerning the monotheistic commitment to "only one God," and that is because of the doctrine of the Trinity mentioned earlier in discussing the Arian heresy. The journey from *Yahweh* polytheism to *Eloh-im* monotheism was a long, arduous one (approximately 700 to 800 years) for the Jews, but a journey that had and still has considerable impact on the other two monotheisms, Christianity and Islam.

Before turning to the analyses of war and peace, two further preparatory tasks remain: a general description of the differences between the beliefs of the Hebrews (pre-exhilic faith) and the Jews (post-exhilic faith)[9] and an analysis of the

---

[9]

Because the purpose of this discussion is providing background, it does not examine the literature and debates that continue to re-examine the nature of the pre-exhilic faith and its differences from the post-exhilic faith of the Jews. Many of the differences that are identified in this brief summary are still being debated, and, as is always the case, new archeological evidence will continue to change and modify present judgments. Of special significance will be new information concerning the Zoroastrians and their influence on the Middle East, especially post-exhilic Judaism.

relationships between henotheism, chosenness, promised land, and holy war. Based on the texts themselves in the **Hebrew Bible** and recent archeological evidence, the following represents a probable reconstruction of the beliefs of pre-exhilic Hebrew henotheism:

(1)   An emphasis primarily on the providential relationship between *Yahweh* and the Hebrew people as his chosen people;

(2)   A limited, anthropomorphic creation account (Genesis 2) which speaks of the creation of only a part of the universe, most particularly that part around a mythological Garden in the Middle East;

(3)   An absence of any cosmic eschatology because views about the end of the whole universe require a monotheistic God who has created the entirety of the universe--in other words, cosmic eschatologies do not develop within the religious structure of henotheism;

(4)   The first appearances of historical eschatology, that is, the belief that *Yahweh* will send a new David, a new Anointed One, as a response to the destructions of the 8th century Assyrians;

(5)   An inconsistent moral human dualism--a moral human dualism is the identification of the flesh as evil and the spirit as good--there are pre-exhilic passages celebrating the body as the temple of God as well as texts suggesting that the flesh, if not evil, is spiritually impure;

(6)   A vague human eschatology--a human eschatology is a collection of beliefs about what happens to the human spirit (soul, personality, consciousness) when the body dies--associated with a place of shadows, *sheol*, where there is neither reward or punishment after death;[10]

---

[10]

It is interesting to note that pre-exhilic Hebrews shared a similar belief with Greeks of the same historical period. In the **Iliad**, when he returns, Achilles describes the after-life as existence in a gray shadowy place where there is neither pleasure or pain, that is, neither reward or punishment for one's deeds. As stated earlier, there is growing evidence that it is among the Zoroastrians that the first

(7)   The absence of any cosmic dualism--a cosmic dualism is the view that there is a war occurring between the forces of evil, the Sons of Darkness, and the forces of goodness, the Sons of Light--which is usually attached to a cosmic eschatology leading to a final conflict and the victory of goodness over evil.[11]

For modern Jews, Christians and Muslims who take for granted their beliefs in the creation of the entire universe by one God, in a heaven and hell, in an evil power called Satan, in an end of time, and in a sinful perspective on the lusts of the flesh, the beliefs of the pre-exhilic Hebrews seem to come from another world. In other words, the Judaism known by contemporary Jews, Christians and Muslims is post-exhilic. Post-exhilic beliefs can be summarized as follows and are quite a contrast with those before the Exile:

(1)   A magnificent universal creation account (Genesis 1) that speaks of the creation of the entire cosmos (universe) through the power of God's Word overcoming chaos;

(2)   A well developed cosmic eschatology which integrates both historical

---

unambiguous beliefs in reward (a heaven) and punishment (a hell) developed in the Middle East. There is also a growing evidence that they were also the first to develop a firm cosmic eschatology.

[11]

The development of a cosmic dualism seems to be related to both monotheism and cosmic eschatology. Once the belief develops that there is only one God who created the whole universe, the stage is set for the end or the fulfillment of the whole created order. In other words, neither polytheism nor henotheism provides the theological structure for the development of either cosmic dualism or eschatology. In both polytheism and henotheism, the various gods are neither purely good or evil; rather they do good for their friends and evil to their enemies. However, once monotheism is established there must still be an explanation for evil; thus, the stage is set for introducing the existence of evil powers such as demons or evil angels, *Shaitan* for example. Recent studies of the Zoroastrian religion suggest that the Jewish, Christian, and Hebrew Satan may be a Persian transplant into post-exhilic Judaism. If so, then this raises several interesting questions about the theological role of this Prince of Darkness in these monotheisms; a role that has, in my judgment, created more problems than benefits, but that is another matter.

eschatology and human eschatology in beliefs about a *Mesiah* to come before the end of time and the resurrection of the dead;

(3)   A developed moral and theological dualism that views the flesh as at war with the goodness of the spirit;

(4)   A well developed human eschatology of reward (heaven) and punishment (hell) after the death of the body or at the resurrection of the dead at the end of time;

(5)   A powerful spirit of evil (*Satan*) leading the Sons of Darkness against the Sons of Light into a final conflict at the end of time when goodness shall prevail over evil.

While each of these outlines (pre-exhilic and post-exhilic) seems to describe radically different faiths, they represent the religious growth of a people over the course of nearly a millennium as they struggled to understand the nature of God and their relationships with the divine. As expected, most monotheists today are familiar with the end developments and ignorant of the historical processes that eventually led to Jewish monotheism. The first glimpses of Jewish monotheism were seen in the 8th century prophets, but the unequivocal affirmation of only one God was post-exhilic. Because of differences in pre-exhilic and post-exhilic views, a controversy began within two centuries after the Exile that continued well into the Common Era: the theological disputes between the Sadducees and the Pharisees. It was the Pharisees who most quickly incorporated these new elements of eschatology and dualism into their theology. The Sadducees considered many of these beliefs to represent Persian (Zoroastrian) pollution of their pre-exhilic faith.[12]

For purposes of this study the henotheistic theology in which the Hebrew belief in holy war developed is of paramount significance for both the remainder of

---

[12]
    This conflict has been the basis for one of the worst and most memorable puns used by teachers of religion when discussing these two religious groups of Jews. It can be stated as follows: "It is the Pharisees who believed in a resurrection to heaven, not the Sadducees, that is why they were "So-Sad-U-See."

this chapter and the argument presented in the last chapter concerning the relationships between holy war, promised land and chosenness TO HAVE. Thus, before turning to the Masoretic Text, it is important to understand the relationship between henotheism and holy war.[13]

The purpose of the following description is to summarize the relationships among henotheism, chosenness, promised land, and holy war. The chapter section on "Theologies of War" that immediately follows provides an in depth analysis of these relationships as well as the textual support for them. Beginning from the henotheistic foundation of believers affirming a special relationship with one god placed above all others leads to the central belief in henotheism: chosenness, that is, belief in being the Chosen People. This belief is of no small psychological consequence as the histories of the three monotheisms of the West indicate. Whether henotheist or monotheist, the belief that one belongs to the chosen ones of God is among the most powerful beliefs in the history of Western religion. While such a relationship is a natural development in henotheism --in fact, it almost seems to be a logical consequence that the god elevated above others must have a special relationship with those who do the elevating--the belief in chosenness is something significantly different in a monotheism.[14] Once the relationship of chosenness is established, it is usually understood in terms of a *Covenant* relationship involving responsibility as well as privilege. The latter part of the covenant understanding (privilege) leads to the controversial belief in *promised land*. If the Chosen

---

13

      The position taken in this study is that the belief in holy war is a natural development in a henotheism but represents a distortion in the theological context of a moral monotheism. In a similar manner, while beliefs in promised land and chosenness are intrinsic to henotheisms, they must be revised within the context of a moral monotheism. The henotheistic relation to holy war is examined in this chapter, the monotheistic one in the last chapter.

14

      See the last chapter for a discussion of the kind of chosenness that is morally consistent with monotheism.

122

(Covenant) People keep their part of the Covenant, then they receive many benefits such as victory in battle, protection from enemies, and promised land.[15] Once these theological connections are made between a people and their god, the next step is as logically natural: the Enemies of the Chosen People are also the Enemies of their god.[16] With this identification, then, the theological justification for the holy war is in place. To use an extended metaphor, if one views the beliefs in chosenness, promised land, the identification of enemies, and the holy war as the fingers of a glove, then it is the hand of henotheism the glove is made to fit. However, in order to force that same glove on the hand of monotheism, to use a questionable pun, it is first necessary "to cut off its **moral finger**." While the next section of this chapter fills in the details of the henotheistic glove more thoroughly, the concluding chapter

---

[15]

While humans kill one another for a multitude of reasons--for example, greed, lust, envy, anger, self-defense, etc.--one of the most fundamental reasons throughout the whole of human history is **LAND!** Land is so much more than wealth and power: land is identity. To use a contemporary African American metaphor, "Land is roots." A people without roots are like a tree without roots; they die, if not physically, then psychologically. Sociologists analyze this danger under the collective term *detribalization.* Clearly, one of the major complicating factors in the peace process in the Middle East are the claims that are made concerning sacred land (promised land).

[16]

Today, the reality that peoples have enemies is viewed in almost every news program reporting on world news; however, for many twentieth century Americans the idea that God (or a god) has enemies seems strange. However, during a time of religious henotheism, there is a most important sense in which other peoples (and their god or gods) represent a serious religious danger: the danger of seducing humans into the worship of their god(s). Thus, for *Yahweh,* not only did other peoples represent a political threat to the Hebrews, they represented a religious danger as well: the danger of placing another god above (in front of) *Yahweh.* In this sense, other peoples and their god(s) were the enemies of *Yahweh* as well as the Hebrews. This kind of religious thinking and situation produced the ban (*herem*) theology which occupies considerable space in the theology of war in the **Hebrew Bible.** Fundamentally, the purpose of the ban theology was to root out and eliminate any kind of religious uncleanliness, most especially that of placing another above *Yahweh* (see the section on "Pre-Monarchial Theologies of War" in this chapter).

reflects on the kind of glove that morally fits the hand of monotheism.

Theologies of War

Before proceeding to explore the theologies of war in this section, attention is called to "Appendix A: Index to Major Passages Concerning War (Battle) in the **Hebrew Bible**." Three preliminary observations emerge from this index: (1) political war and historical eschatological war dominate (over 190 references); (2) there is little concern about spiritual war (less than a dozen references); and (3) there is also little concern about cosmic eschatological war (less than two dozen references) and, with the exception of a couple of questionable texts, all are post-exhilic.

As an additional aid to the explorations of war in the **Hebrew Bible**, it is helpful to examine the various issues related to war and briefly provide a word study of three major terms: *milhama, saba'* and *herem*. Any adequate concordance indicates a multitude of usages and other issues related to war in the **Hebrew Bible**. Among these are: making war, repenting war, the Lord is a man of war, the noise of war, to go forth to war, the arms of war, men of war, rest from war, teaching war, hands of war, blood shed in war, war of God, army of war, mighty warriors, valor for war, declare war, war horse, time for war, death and war, day of war, etc.. These are only a few examples: some concordances list over forty different uses and combinations of war with other items. Clearly war permeates the **Hebrew Bible**. In addition to the many uses of war, there are also several different terms and their cognates which refer to war, battle, fighting, or killing enemies. Of these three stand out in significance.

The most commonly used term for war is *milhama*, and second to it in use is the term *saba'*. Each requires an etymological development. *Milhama*, which means "war," "battle" and "fight," derives from the verb *laham*, which means "to consume," "to fight," "to make war" and "to destroy."

While there are many passages in the **Hebrew Bible** in which "total destruction" is the nature of a particular war, there are also more limited kinds of war, and *milhama* is the generic term for these limited conflicts. In most of those where total destruction (genocide) is required, there is a special term used. Consequently, there is nothing significantly unusual in the use of the term *milhama* that requires further elucidation at this point. Second in use to *milahma* is the term *saba'*. This term has several meanings in the **Hebrew Bible**: "warfare," "war," "military service" and "time of military service" as well as "army" and "host" (usually in the plural form "hosts.") There is little substantive difference in the uses of *milhama* and *saba'* as terms for war or battle; however, in the sense of army or hosts, the term *saba'* is used over 200 times in the phrase "the Lord of Hosts (*Yahweh Sabaoth*)," literally, the "the Lord of Armies." Given the warrior nature of *Yahweh*, this identification is significant and is examined in this section of the chapter.[17]

17

There are, however, passages such as Isaiah 54:5, Psalms 46:7-9 and Psalms 24:7-10, in which the phrase *Yahweh Sabaoth* (*Yahweh* of Hosts) transcends its earlier nationalistic and militaristic uses in the pre-exhilic period. II Isaiah's exhilic use of *Yahweh Sabaoth* was most probably a redeemer God of the whole earth, rather than the militaristic *Yahweh* of the pre-monarchial period of conquest, when he wrote:

> For now your creator will be your husband, / his name, *Yahweh Sabaoth* [*Yahweh* of Hosts]; / your redeemer will be the Holy One of Israel / he is called the God of the whole earth.

In a similar non-militaristic theology, a psalmist wrote of a God whose purpose was to end wars in Psalm 46:

> *Yahweh Sabaoth* is on our side / . . . .
> Come, think of *Yahweh's* marvels, / the astounding things he has done in the world; / all over the world he puts an end to wars, / he breaks the bow, he snaps the spear.

While the writer of Psalm 24 may have been celebrating the *Yahweh* of Israel's wars, many commentators interpret his words as celebrating the *Yahweh* of the Heavenly Hosts who overcame the dark powers of chaos at creation when he wrote:

> Who is this king of glory? / *Yahweh* the strong, the valiant. / *Yahweh* valiant in battle! Gates, raise your arches, / raise, your ancient doors, / let the king of glory in!
> Who is the king of glory? / He is *Yahweh Sabaoth*, / King of glory, he!

Finally, attention must be given to a most interesting term that comes from the consonantal root *hrm*. As the verb *haram* it means "to dry up" or "to destroy" as well as "to dedicate" or "to consecrate." As the noun *herem* it means "curse" or "destruction" as well as "something devoted or consecrated."[18] The etymological connections between "being destroyed" and "drying up" need little explanation for a desert environment: what better way to describe the destructiveness of the desert than "drying up." However, the etymological connections between "to destroy" and "to consecrate" and between "curse" and "consecrated thing" is less clear. Footnote 18 provides a clue to this problem. For both Jews and Muslims, and Christians to a lesser extent, consecrated (sacred) areas and objects are subject to two possibilities: care and protection by the devoted and violation by the unclean, that is, by non-believers or the unchosen. Consequently, what is consecrated can become a curse or source of destruction if violated.[19] Combining these two apparently disparate but

---

While these gates can be interpreted as those of an earthy city or those of the heavens, scriptural evidence indicates that pre-exhilic references to *Yahweh Sabaoth* usually indicated hosts who were soldiers in the army of *Yahweh* engaged in conflict with his (and, thus, the Hebrews') earthly enemies while exhilic and post-exhilic uses of hosts became spiritualized as heavenly hosts (armies) engaged in a cosmic struggle between the forces of good and those of evil.

18

The same root is the basis for the Muslim term used to identify the Muslim Quarter of the Old Walled City of Jerusalem where the Mosque of Aqsa and the Dome of the Rock Mosque were built in the late 7th century C.E.. This area is called *Haram as-Sharif* or Noble (Consecrated, Sacred) Enclosure by Muslims. In other words, it is sacred as well as forbidden to the uncleanliness of unbelievers.

19

The belief expressed in these dual ideas of consecration and curse may originate in the primal concern of mana discussed in previous material. That which is sacred is often believed to be a source of great mana (power). Any violation of that power can result in the curse or even the destruction of the violator. As an example consider the taboo (curse, *herem*) of uttering the name of God that developed in the post-exhilic period. Vows to *Yahweh* were special matters of *herem*

126

closely connected ideas, the term *herem* is the word used to describe the **ban** in the **Hebrew Bible**, that is, the curse of genocide against those who occupy consecrated (promised) land. Unfortunately, the theology of the ban is an emphasized one, especially prior to the Exile.[20]

Utilizing the previous material concerning the movement from *Yahweh* henotheism to *Eloh-im* monotheism and the etymological studies of critical terms, now it is possible to examine in more detail the theologies of war that are presented in the **Hebrew Bible**. As stated earlier, the analysis of these theologies proceeds according to the three major historical periods encompassing the writing of the Hebrew scriptures: pre-monarchial, monarchial and post-exhilic.

Pre-Monarchial Theologies of War (Moses to David, 13th to 10th centuries)

The major difficulties in reconstructing pre-monarchial theologies of war are three-fold: (1) the paucity of pre-monarchial written records among the Hebrews; (2) controversies and debates among biblical scholars concerning the actual history

---

among the Hebrews. Or consider the case of Jephthah (one of the Judges) whose vow committed his only daughter as a sacrifice to *Yahweh* for a great military victory. Once the vow was made, the daughter was *herem*, that is consecrated-to-destruction (death). For Jephthah, to renounce the vow was to bring the curse of *Yahweh* (*herem*) upon himself and possibly his whole tribe.

20

Many biblical scholars such as Susan Niditch find in *herem* theology a religious view common to much of the Mediterranean world (Greeks and Hebrews for example) whose gods appreciated human sacrifice. Thus, the *herem* (ban) was the consecration-to-destruction of the most valuable spoils of war to the god or gods. Of all the spoils, the most valuable were the human beings captured; thus, the *herem* required their complete sacrifice to the divine; they were the deity's portion. Most probably, then, the *herem* (ban) originated among the Hebrews during their period of *Yahweh* polytheism and received additional emphasis and a prophetic theology during the period of *Yahweh* henotheism.

It should also be mentioned that there are many uses of the term *herem* which have no connection with war or the killing of enemies such as the execution of those who commit several kinds of crimes. Only the uses of *herem* that relate to war are examined in this study.

and religious beliefs of the Hebrews during this time; (3) and similar controversies concerning how accurately the monarchial writings reflect actual beliefs before the 10th century, especially the written source that is of major significance concerning war, the Deuteronomist. Scholars such as Smend, Weippert and Stoltz argue that the holy war (ban) is largely a Deuteronomic anachronism of the pre-monarchial age, while scholars such as Cross, Miller and Niditch argue that while the Deuteronomist "neatens up" (Niditch's wonderfully descriptive term) pre-monarchial theologies of war, his presentation is historically accurate. As stated earlier, this study takes a view similar to the latter scholars who accept that the written sources reflect with reasonable accuracy beliefs of earlier periods. There are two kinds of evidence for this position: the Song of the Sea (Miriam's Song) in Exodus 15 and the Song of Deborah in Judges 5, both of which probably date from the 12th century, and the similarity between Hebrew views of war (especially the ban) and those of their neighbors.

Since the Victory Songs of Miriam and Deborah are examined in depth as examples of pre-monarchial views of war, a brief description of similar views of war sets an appropriate background for the analyses which follow. According to Sa-Moon Kang, the idea of divine war (holy war)[21] originated in Mesopotamia as early

---

[21]

Kang dislikes the term holy war, as do some other scholars, because he thinks that there is a difference between *Yahweh* war and holy war. For him, the latter is a term more appropriate to the Deuteronomist's neatening up of a theology of war. While Kang has a good point, not only because of his views about differences between *Yahweh* war and holy war but also because of the over use of the term *holy war* today, this study does not make a distinction between *Yahweh* war and holy war. Justifications for this are two: first, the pre-exhilic Hebrew view of war is dominated by the ban which incorporates elements of both kinds of war and is examined in depth; and, second, for purposes of this study, the term *holy war* is defined as any war (conflict) in which at least one of the following is accepted by believers: (1) God (or a god) actually participates in the war; (2) God (or a god) commands a war; or, (3) a special relationship with God (or a god) is used to justify a war. Kang's distinction is not ignored in this definition because (1) and (2) are similar to his idea of *Yahweh* war and (3) to holy war.

128

as the third millennium as kingship became tied to both war and the gods:

> In the course of the transformation of the divine image war began to be recognized as a divine command. . . . In the cone inscription of Entemena (ca.2404--2375 B.C.E.), when Ush, the ruler of Umma invaded the boundary of Lagash, Ningirsu made war against Umma by the command of Enlil as follows:
>
> Ningirsu, the warrior of Enlil, made war against Umma by his righteous command.
>
> The above passage shows that the war was carried out by the command [of] Enlil, the father of the gods. (**Divine War in the Old Testament and in the Ancient Near East**, 11)

At a time even closer to the earliest Hebrew writings (The Songs of Miriam and Deborah), the Assyrian royal inscriptions often indicated divine help and support in war, as stated on the Adad-narari I (1307-1275) inscription:

> With the strong weapons of the god Ashur, my lord; with the support of the gods An, Enlil, and Ea, Sin, Shamash, Adad, Ishtar, and Nergal, most powerful among the gods, the awesome gods, my lords; I captured by conquest the city Taidu, his great royal city. . . .
>
> His son, Shalmaneser I showed a similar attitude; "with the support of Ashur and the great gods, my lords, that city I captured and destroyed. . . ." (Kang, 15)

While the pre-monarchial Hebrews did not link kingship to divine war as in the previous examples because the Hebrew tribes had no king, it is reasonable to conclude that even as a tribal groups they believed that their god(s) participated with them in war. Certainly, this was the case in the Songs of Miriam and Deborah. One of the best studies of war in the **Hebrew Bible**, Susan Niditch's **War in the Hebrew Bible**, takes many scholars to task for their refusal to comprehend how deeply imbedded in the Hebrew psyche was the acceptance of holy war:

> . . . the point needs to be made that deep in the mythological

framework of Israelite thought, war, death, sacrifice, the ban, and divine satiation are integrally associated. . . . To disassociate the Israelite ban from the realm of the sacred and from the concept of sacrifice is to ignore the obvious and yet this is precisely what many scholars have done. (40)

For students of the history of Western religions it is painfully obvious that a holy war theology linking death, sacrifice and divine satiation has emerged time and again and is still a religious factor in the Middle East today.

As evidenced in the previous pages, fundamental in pre-exhilic theologies of war was the ban (the *herem*). However, before examining this view, a brief statement of the historical situation of the pre-monarchial Hebrews is needed. The traditional view of this historical period was an uncritical acceptance of the books of Exodus, Joshua, and Judges. As presented in these writings, *Yahweh's* people were freed by his mighty arm from Pharaoh, wandered in the desert for forty years and with *Yahweh's* leadership and help in battle conquered Canaan during Joshua's tenure as *Yahweh's* chosen representative to the people. This view is accepted by few Biblical historians today. At present, there are two positions concerning the Hebrews and their eventual occupation of much of Canaan: the *revolt model* and the *pioneer-settlement model*. The former view argues that the Hebrews were already in Canaan and slowly revolted against other tribal groups eventually gaining control over sizeable areas of land. The latter view mirrors the American pioneer experience; slowly over decades, they moved into Canaan and conquered lands held originally by various groups of Canaanites. The major difference in these views is the Hebrew relationship with the Canaanites. The revolt model makes their relationship much closer than the pioneer-settlement model. Fortunately, whichever is the more historically accurate, the fundamental ban theology of warfare is little affected since the major thrust of war was the same: the conquest of land already occupied. Thus, the major situational influence on the formation of a religious view of war for the pre-monarchial Hebrews was the **conquest and occupation of land**. During the monarchial period, this situation changed with a consequent modifications in two new theologies of war: the **securing** of land rather than the **conquest** of land became the focus of war during the early monarchy and the use of war by *Yahweh* as a punishment for infidelity on the part of the Hebrews became the foci of the great prophets of the later monarchy.

While there are dozens of passages reflecting pre-monarchial theologies of war, six are pivotal: Exodus 15, the Song of the Sea (Miriam) celebrating the destruction of Pharaoh's chariots and the salvation of the Hebrews; Judges 5, the Song of Deborah celebrating a great victory over the Canaanites; Judges 7, the story of Gideon's miraculous victory over the Midianites; I Samuel 15, the account of Saul's revenge against the Amalekites; and Deuteronomy 20, which provides a comprehensive theology of warfare. Before examining the views of war presented in each, it is helpful to describe the most important features of holy war, since holy war is at the center of each passage. While Gerhard von Rad's **Holy War in Ancient Israel** has been thoroughly critiqued by much recent scholarship, his identification of the salient features of holy war is still generally accepted and provides a basis for an in depth analysis of these five fundamental passages. In the first chapter, von Rad describes the following features of holy war:

(1)   The troops were mustered by means of a *blast of the trumpet*.

(2)   Once gathered in camp the army was called *the people of Yahweh*.

(3)   The army itself, as the people of God preparing for war, was *consecrated to Yahweh*, that is, the troops were bound by severe sacred regulations.

(4)   Anticipating the coming battle the army *offered sacrifices awaiting a sign from Yahweh for the attack.* This sign was usually announced to the troops as follows: *Yahweh has given the _____ into our hands*.

(5)   As the army moved forward *Yahweh moved out ahead of them.*

(6)   The wars were *Yahweh's wars* and the enemies *Yahweh's enemies*.

(7)   When *Yahweh* engaged the enemy, they *lost courage*.

(8)   The battle opened with a *war cry* using the name(?) of *Yahweh.*

(9)   In the course of battle *divine terror overtook the enemy.*

(10)   The high point and conclusion of the holy war was the *herem, the consecrating of the spoils to Yahweh.*

(11)   The war ends with the dismissal, *To your tents, O Israel.*

While this list is not complete, nor are all the items listed above necessary for a holy war, it does provide a framework for examining the theology of warfare in the pre-monarchial period, a period when the primary purpose of war was conquest and occupation of land. This is the reason that the ban (*herem*) became the focal point concerning war.

As the theology of the ban (the total destruction of conquered peoples) evolved from *Yahweh* polytheism into the *Yahweh* henotheism of the monarchy and the eighth century prophets, its focus moved from the battle sacrifice which belonged to *Yahweh* for giving the Hebrews' battle victories to prophetic attempts to provide a religious justification for such brutal killings. At the same time, because the prophets also struggled with moral as well as religious issues, there developed a moral-psychological tension that led to a dual theology of the ban which likely appeared in the early monarchy if not earlier. Susan Niditch describes this tension and duality in these apt words:

> It is not easy for humans to kill others. To participate in mass killing is destructive of individual psyches and of the larger communities' mental health. The ban in either trajectory [as *Yahweh's* sacrificial spoils or *Yahweh's* justice] is a means of making killing in war acceptable. How do the ban as sacrifice and the ban-as-God's-justice differ in this regard? The ban as sacrifice is a part of war against those who are not of one's group, a means of securing God's aid in victory. The ban sometimes has to be imposed to win. God demands his portion and cannot be refused. The reasoning goes "If we offer them, we will be saved." Group solidarity is thus increased--better we should live than they--and guilt is reduced--God demands his

offerings--but the enemy is recognized as human, worthy of God's sacrifice. Inanimate booty can almost always be kept, because God has received the best portion. In contrast, the ban-as-God's-justice ideology actually motivates and encourages war, implying that wars of extermination are desirable in order to purify the body politic of one's own group, to eradicate evil in the world beyond one's group, and to actualize divine judgment. In the ban-as-God's-justice a sharp line is drawn between us and them, between clean and unclean, between those worthy of salvation and those deserving elimination. The enemy is thus not a mere human, an offering necessary to win the assistance of God, but a monster, unclean, and diseased. The ban-as-God's-justice thus allows people to accept the notion of killing other humans by dehumanizing them and the process of dehumanization can take place even within the group during times of distress, distrust, and anomie. (77)

In the ban as God's portion, that is, the sacrifice owed to *Yahweh*, no justification was required because in the earliest actions of *Yahweh* as warrior he won the battles without human aid. Consequently, to *Yahweh* alone belonged the spoils of war. This was the attitude of the earliest writings. However, as the Hebrews moved through the period of late conquest and the Judges (12th-10th centuries) and human soldiers became more important in contributing to *Yahweh*'s victories, the theology of the ban-as-*Yahweh*'s-justice began to emerge and would be given its most comprehensive formation by the Deuteronomist in the late monarchy.[22]

---

[22]

From Niditch's description it is obvious that the modern concept of holy war is related to the later development of the ban-as-God's-justice. It is this theology of holy war that has been previously described as grounded upon the equating of the People's enemies with God's enemies and seen as a natural, almost logical, development within a henotheism. Whether one uses the terms "ethnic cleansing," "genocide," or "holocaust" to descibe such a ban, the theology offered today to

Having set the historical and religious background, it is now time to examine five of the most important passages in the **Hebrew Bible** which reveal its developing theologies of war, especially holy war. The order employed is roughly chronological: Exodus 15 (13th century), Judges 5 (12th century), Judges 7 (12th century), I Samuel 15 (11th century) and Deuteronomy 20 (a 7th century synthesis of earlier views).

In order to understand the theology of war in the Song of the Sea (also called the Song of Miriam) in Exodus 15, there are several passages from the preceding chapter that are important as background to this well known story of the watery destruction of Pharaoh's chariots. In Chapter 14, attention is called to the following verses:

v.4   'Then I [*Yahweh*] shall make Pharaoh's heart stubborn and he will set out in pursuit of them. But I shall win glory for myself at the expense of Pharaoh and all his army, and the Egyptians shall learn that I am *Yahweh*.'

v.13-4 Moses answered the people, 'Have no fear! Stand firm, and you will see what *Yahweh* will do to save you today: the Egyptians you see today, you will never see again. *Yahweh* will do the fighting for you: you only have to keep still.'

v.18   'And when I have won glory for myself, at the expense of Pharaoh and his chariots and his army, the Egyptians will learn that I am *Yahweh*.'

v.19   Then the angel of *Yahweh*, who marched at the front of the army of Israel, changed station and moved to their rear. [This was to protect the Hebrews as they crossed the sea because the chariots of Pharaoh were approaching from the rear.]

v.25   *Yahweh* looked down on the army of the Egyptians from the pillar of fire and

---

"justify" such atrocities differs little from that of the pre-exhilic Hebrews. While it is the case that similar religious views were held by many of the Hebrews' neighbors, it is also true that it is through the influences of the **Hebrew Bible** and its view of God that theologies of holy war influenced the other monotheisms of the West. As stated earlier, it is the position of this study that the ban-as-God's-justice (the holy war) represents a distortion in a moral monotheism. The argument for this judgment occupies the last chapter.

cloud, and threw the army into confusion.

v.26   '. . . the Egyptians cried 'Yahweh is fighting for them [the Hebrews] against the Egyptians!'

v.28   The returning waters overwhelmed the chariots and the horsemen of Pharaoh's whole army, which had followed the Israelites into the sea; not a single one of them was left.

Following this miraculous saving of the Hebrews and total destruction of the army of Pharaoh, the Hebrews sang a song in honor of *Yahweh* called the Song of the Sea or Miriam's Song:

> 'Yahweh I sing: he has covered himself in glory, / horse and rider he has thrown into the sea. / 'Yah is my strength, my song, / he is my salvation / This is my God, I praise him; / the God of my father, I extol him. / 'Yahweh is a warrior; / Yahweh is his name. / . . . . / 'Your right hand, Yahweh, shows majestic in power, / your right hand, Yahweh, shatters the enemy. / So great your splendor, you crush your foes; / you unleash your fury, and it devours them like stubble. / . . . .
>
> 'Who among the gods is your like, Yahweh?' / . . . . / 'Canaan's inhabitants are all unmanned. / On them fall terror and dread; / through the power of your arm they are still as stone / as your people pass, Yahweh, / as the people pass whom you purchased.   (Exodus 15:1-28, sel.ver.)

Concerning the issues important in this study, there are several items to note in Exodus 14-15. First, there is clearly no curse associated with uttering the name(?) *Yahweh*. Indeed, it is sung to the heavens as a word of great power and glory. Second, the henotheistic structure of the pre-exhilic Hebrew faith is revealed in verse 11 of the Song: "Who among the gods is your like, *Yahweh*?" Third, of the eleven items previously identified as common to Hebrew holy wars, at least seven are present: the Hebrews are identified as the people of *Yahweh* (15:13, 16); *Yahweh* gives the Egyptians into the hands of the Hebrews (that is, in this account into the sea); *Yahweh* (that is, the angel of *Yahweh*) is first in front and then in the rear to protect the Hebrews (14:19); *Yahweh*'s enemies are the Hebrew's enemies (15:6, 7, 15-18); the enemy loses courage (14:25-6); the enemy experiences terror (14:26 and 15:14-15), and the enemy experiences total destruction (14:28 and 15:8-9). While the term *herem* is not used in this account, the theology of the ban-as-*Yahweh*'s-portion of the victory is implied by the total destruction of the army of Pharaoh. As described in this narrative, because *Yahweh* **ALONE** accomplishes the total destruction (ban), there is no need for the Hebrews to dedicate the conquered army to *Yahweh* and then destroy them; *Yahweh* has already accomplished the consecrated destruction. This destruction raises a fourth point of importance. In the earliest theologies of holy war, *Yahweh* requires no assistance from Hebrew soldiers; *Yahweh* alone, through his miraculous powers, brings the enemy to total destruction. The Song of the Sea is only one early example. Another well known war of conquest is the account of the destruction of Jericho. Because the holy war aspects of Jericho are similar to that of the Sea, especially the *Yahweh* alone motif, it is passed over in order to examine the powerful victory Song of Deborah in Judges 5.

As in the Exodus account, the previous chapter, Judges 4, sets the stage for the victory Song. Among the items in Judges 4 of importance are the following:

(1)   The story introduces a new theme--because the Hebrews have been unfaithful to *Yahweh*, he allows them to be "handed over" to Jabin the king of the Canaanites whose general is Sisera. The Hebrews cry to *Yahweh* for help after twenty years oppression.

(2)   *Yahweh* informs the prophetess Deborah that he will free the Hebrews by tricking Sisera at wadi Kishon.

(3)   Deborah summons Barak to raise a force of 10,000 warriors from the tribes of Naphtali and Zebulum. Note that this holy war involves only two of the twelve tribes; however, unlike the destructions at the Sea and Jericho, Hebrew soldiers are involved in actual battle with *Yahweh*'s enemies.

136

(4)   Because Barak hesitates in believing the promise of *Yahweh*, *Yahweh* punishes him by preventing him from killing his adversary Sisera; instead, he will be killed by a woman, Jael.

(5)   *Yahweh* marches at the head of Barak's army.

(6)   *Yahweh* strikes terror into Sisera and all his troops, and Sisera flees the field of battle.

(7)   Sisera's entire army is destroyed by the edge of the sword. Note that unlike the destruction in Exodus, the Hebrew soldiers must enforce the ban, the total destruction of the enemy even though the victory really belongs to *Yahweh*. Finally, *Yahweh* using the Hebrew army, completely destroys the kingdom of Jabin the Canaanite.

Following these great victories over Sisera and Jabin, Judges 5 contains the Song of victory:

'That warriors in Israel unbound their hair, / that the people came forward with a will, / for this bless *Yahweh*!

'Listen, you kings! Give ear, you princes! / From me, from me comes a song for *Yahweh*. / I will glorify *Yahweh*, God of Israel.

. . . .

'My heart beats fast for Israel's chieftains, / with those of the people who stood forth boldly. / For this, bless *Yahweh*!

. . . .

'There they extol *Yahweh*'s blessings, / The blessings of his reign in Israel. / (*Yahweh*'s people marched down to the gates.)

. . . .

'From high in heaven fought the stars, / fought from their orbits against Sisera.

'The torrent of Kishon swept them away, / the sacred torrent, the torrent of Kishon. / Trample, my soul, with might and main! / 'The horses' hoofs beat the ground; / galloping, galloping go his steeds.

"Curse Meroz," says *Yahweh*'s angel / "curse, curse the dwellers in it; / for they never came to *Yahweh*'s aid, / to *Yahweh*'s aid among the warriors."

. . . .

'So perish all your enemies, *Yahweh*! / And let those who love you be like the sun / when he arises in all his strength!' (2, 3, 9, 11, 20, 23, 29-31)

Regarding the aspects of holy war, the destructions of the Egyptians at the Sea and the Canaanites at the wadi Kishon are strikingly similar except for the significant use of Hebrew warriors at Kishon. In both there is no prohibition against speaking the name(?) *Yahweh*; rather, *Yahweh* verbally rings with power and glory, and both examples emphasize the supernatural powers of *Yahweh* in accomplishing the destructions of the enemy. Interestingly enough, water has a significant role in the destruction of both Egyptians and Canaanites. In Exodus the closing of the path through the Sea destroys the army of Pharaoh and in Judges 5 the flooding of the river Kishon neutralizes the chariots of Sisera and eventually throws the soldiers and horses into a panic that utterly destroys them. The victory song even mentions that *Yahweh* used the stars against Sisera. Finally, all the elements of the holy war in Exodus 14-15 are present in Judges 4-5 plus at least one more: 5:14 mentions that the warriors "unbound" their hair. This was a ritual preparation for battle still practiced among some Bedouin in the Middle East today. If the final statement in the narrative that the "land enjoyed rest for forty years" is equivalent to the Hebrew warriors being dismissed to their tents, then the only missing elements that are usually part of a holy war are: the blast of a trumpet and the war cry. The key aspects, however, are clearly emphasized: *Yahweh* is the warrior who wins the battle by confusing and striking terror in the enemy, and *Yahweh*'s enemies (also the Hebrews' enemies) are utterly destroyed, that is, *Yahweh*'s portion, the ban, has been fulfilled. What makes the account in Judges significantly different than those of the Sea and Jericho is that *Yahweh*'s enemies are destroyed with the help of *Yahweh*'s

138

Hebrew soldiers. The soldiers and their swords rather than the waters do the actual killing, and the Song of Deborah glorifies the fact that "*Yahweh's* people, like heroes, marched down to fight for him," (5:13). While the theology of the ban unequivocally declares that all victories belong to *Yahweh*, the increasing importance of the Hebrew army in these conflicts and the increasing prophetic interest in these wars are two factors which slowly bring about a movement from the ban-as-*Yahweh's*-portion to the ban as *Yahweh's* justice. With the addition of the human element, the division of the spoils also undergoes some change as well, but this is to get ahead. The next account which needs analysis is the story of Gideon and the Three Hundred in Judges 6-8.

Compared to the majority of other war narratives in the **Hebrew Bible**, the account of Gideon is unusually rich in terms of length and details, occupying three chapters. Because of its length, rather than cite extensive passages, it suffices to outline the details of the conflict and stress those that are either new or of special significance for the holy war.

(1)   As with all the narratives of the Judges,[23] the story of Gideon begins with the theological formula describing a people who have been unfaithful to *Yahweh*, and, consequently, *Yahweh* gives them into the hands of the Midianites for an oppressive seven years. The story even elaborates on the nature of their infidelity, which involves the worship of *Baal* and other gods of the Amonites (6:10). It further details

---

23

The English term *Judges* is the common translation of the Hebrew term *Shopet-im*. This translation is unfortunate because it is misleading. The figures identified as *shopet-im* in the book of Judges have little to do with the role of present day judges. They are all warriors (Deborah is an exception but she calls Barak to be *Yahweh's* holy warrior) who fulfill the commands of *Yahweh* with a sword rather than a gavel. In other words, the judges are in reality the warriors of *Yahweh*, that is, holy warriors. Their narratives present some of the most interesting stories in the **Hebrew Bible**, especially the accounts of Gideon, Jephthah and his vow, and the extended narrative of the powerful but irresponsible *shopet-im* Samson. The book of Judges, then, is more accurately described as the book of *Yahweh's* Holy Warriors.

how *Yahweh* through Gideon destroys the altar to *Bal* (6:25-29). Because of this destruction a coalition forms against Gideon that includes the Midianites and the Amalekites.

(2)   When the people cry to *Yahweh* for deliverance, a prophet comes to Gideon and reminds him of *Yahweh's* deliverance of the Hebrews from Egypt (6:7-9), and later an angel comes to Gideon and identifies him as *Yahweh's* chosen warrior (*shopet-im*): "*Yahweh* is with you, valiant warrior." (6:12)   When Gideon responds by asking how *Yahweh* can be with "us" when the people are oppressed by Midian, *Yahweh* responds: "Go in the strength now upholding you, and you will rescue Israel from the power of Midian. Do I not send you myself?" (6:14) Gideon's response is interesting, especially when compared to that of Barak. Both men have doubts and want a sign. Because of this Barak is denied the honor of killing his adversary Sisera, but no such punishment happens to Gideon.   Indeed, *Yahweh* shows considerably more patience with Gideon's questions and doubts than those of Barak.

(3)   In overcoming his doubts Gideon makes several offerings to *Yahweh*. (6:18-22, 25-26)

(4)   As the battle nears, the spirit of *Yahweh* comes into Gideon, and he blows the war trumpet. (6:34) Later, the war trumpet is sounded again and again; 7:22 mentions the blast of 300 war trumpets.

(5)   The next element in the narrative is one of the best known, the paring down of the forces from 32,000 troops first to 10,000 and then to 300 warriors.[24]

---

[24]

Ordinarily numbers should not be taken literally in most religious texts. However, in order to understand the theology of war that is presented in the Gideon narrative, it is important to accept the numbers in a "literal theological" sense. At the end of the battle accounts, the writer of this story credited the 300 soldiers of Gideon with the destruction of 120,000 enemies of *Yahweh*. The theology is clear, even though human warriors were involved, it was *Yahweh* who won the battles. In other words, the purpose of paring down the army from 32,000 to 300 was to stress the human impossibility of winning against such odds; only the divine intervention of *Yahweh* could account for the destruction of such a large force of Midianites and

140

(6)   As the Hebrew force of 300 prepare to engage in conflict with a force of 120,000 (8:10), Gideon announces: "On your feet, for *Yahweh* has put the camp of Midian into your power." (7:15) This is followed by the blasting of the trumpets (8:22) and a war cry: "For *Yahweh* and for Gideon." (7:18, 21)

(7)   The miracle of 300 routing 120,000 soldiers is explained as the action of *Yahweh*: "While the three hundred kept sounding their horns, *Yahweh* made every man in the camp [of the Midianites and Amalekites] turn his sword against his comrade." (7:22) In other words, *Yahweh* creates such confusion and terror in the enemy camp that they kill one another, and those who survive this *Yahweh* caused self-slaughter flee with Gideon and his troops in hot pursuit.

(8)   There is an interesting twist in the narrative as Gideon's army, in pursuit of the fleeing survivors of the inter-camp massacre, seeks nourishment from two cities who both refuse to help them. Because of this, when the last of the enemy army is destroyed, the numbers are put at 120,000 (8:10), the cities who refused help are also punished.

(9)   The final element in the story is new, the offer of kingship to Gideon, but he must refuse: "It is not I who shall rule over you, nor my son; *Yahweh* must be your lord." (8:23)

As this outline indicates, the narrative of Gideon is quite extensive for a war narrative. In one place or another, each of the aspects of a holy war identified by von Rad is found in the Gideon story. Further, the paring down of the forces makes it clear that it is *Yahweh*'s war and the destruction of 120,000 enemies surely fulfills the *herem* required by the Hebrews pre-exhilic god. The next account examining Saul and the Amalekites is quite different in several respects.

The first contrast that stands out in the two war narratives is the meager description of Saul's battle, which is described in only nine verses:

Samuel said to Saul, 'I am the man whom *Yahweh* sent to

Amalekites.

anoint you king over his people, over Israel, so now listen to the words of *Yahweh*. Thus speaks *Yahweh Sabaoth*, "I will repay what Amalek did to Israel when they opposed them on the road by which they came up out of Egypt. Now, go and strike down Amalek; put him under the ban with all that he possesses. Do not spare him, but kill man and woman, babe and suckling, ox and sheep, camel and donkey".'

Saul summoned the people and reviewed them at Telaim: two hundred thousand foot soldiers (and ten thousand men of Judah). Saul went to the city of Amalek and lay in ambush in the river bed. Saul said to the Kenites, 'Go, leave your homes among the Amalekites or I may destroy you with them, for you were friendly to all the sons of Israel when they came up from Egypt'. So the Kenites moved away from the Amalekites.

Saul then defeated the Amalekites, starting from Havilah in the direction of Shur, which is to the east of Egypt. He took Agag king of the Amalekites alive and, executing the ban, put all the people to the sword. But Saul and the army spared the best of the sheep and cattle, the fatlings and lambs and all that was good. They did not want to put those under the ban; they only put under the ban what was poor and worthless. (I Samuel 15:1-9)

In addition to the considerable absence of battle details, there are several other contrasts in this account from the three already examined. Before describing these, a question needs answering: Why is the story of Saul and the Amalekites examined in this section on the pre-monarchy rather than the one on the monarchy?

While Saul is identified as the king of Yahweh's people, it is a pre-mature title for several reasons: first, Saul's forces, as large as they are, probably do not represent all of the tribes; second, while the Hebrews are approaching an identifiable nation-state, they fall short of that reality during the time of Saul because they have no clear borders nor anything resembling a national capital; third, it is only under the charismatic leadership of David that the tribal federation actually becomes a nation-state with a powerful king, has borders to defend and has a political capital. For these reasons, the account of Saul and his war against the Amalekites is closer to the wars of the *shopet-im* than those of the kings.

Because the details are so few, it is impossible to know what aspects of the holy war are involved in the actual battle against the Amalekites; however, it is not unreasonable to assume that Saul's war conduct did not differ significantly from that of his *shopet-im* predecessors, except for one absolutely crucial religious error on Saul's part, the *herem*, and the size of his forces. The size of his army, 210,000 soldiers (15:4), is likely exaggerated, but even so, the account evidences two changing realities: first, an army even half this size indicates a considerable movement toward the unification of the tribes into a nation-state; and, second, and of considerable religious significance given the tradition of the Hebrews requiring the active intervention of *Yahweh* to win their wars, Saul now has the forces to win a battle with the Amalekites without the need for divine intervention. This precedent became a feature of the wars of the monarchial period and may account for prophetic efforts to keep the theology of the *herem* alive during the monarchy when wars were often more political than religious. For Saul, however, the religious issue of the *herem* was absolutely critical.

While the period of transition from tribal times into the monarchy brought about many political and religious changes among the Hebrews, it was most likely the time that the ban-as-*Yahweh*'s-portion, that is, the consecration to death of the most valuable of the spoils of victory, began to evolve into the ban-as-*Yahweh*'s-justice, the theology of the holy war that plagues the histories of Christianity and Islam. The narrative of Saul and the Amalekites, at least as remembered and transmitted by later generations, provides evidence that the ban-as-*Yahweh*'s-portion was still fundamental before David and the monarchy. First, the command from *Yahweh* for total genocide, *herem*, against every living thing associated with the

Amalekites clearly indicates that they are *Yahweh*'s enemies, perhaps his oldest and most constant[25] enemies who must be totally consecrated-to-destruction. Second, the religious problem that arises over the spoils also indicates the dangers of violating the ban as that which is owed to *Yahweh*. The key verse is nine: "But Saul and the army spared Agag with the best of the sheep and cattle, the fatlings and lambs and all that was good. They did not want to put those under the ban; they only put under the ban what was poor and worthless." When Saul marches back to Shechem with his booty, the prophet Samuel is horrified. His horror is not only because Saul has disobeyed *Yahweh*'s command for the ban, but even worse, he has saved the best of the animals for the Hebrews and even dared to appease the ban by sacrificing the worst of the animals. In today's terms, this would be considered a double insult. For this, according to the account in I Samuel, Saul paid dearly: Samuel withdraws his support from Saul, refuses to see him, Saul is punished with an evil spirit, and he is eventually killed along with his son Jonathan in conflicts with

---

25

     As the Hebrews are on their journey to Sinai to receive the Law, Exodus 17:8-16 reports the origins of the enmity between *Yahweh* and the Amalekites together with a chilling declaration of war by *Yahweh* against Amalek:

     The Amalekites came and attacked Israel at Rephidim. Moses said to Joshua, 'Pick out men for yourself, and tomorrow morning march out to engage Amalek. I meanwhile, will stand on the hilltop, the staff of God in my hand.' Joshua did as Moses told him and marched out to engage Amalek. . . . As long as Moses kept his arms raised, Israel had the advantage; when he let his arms fall, the advantage went to Amalek. . . . With the edge of the sword Joshua cut down Amalek and his people. Then *Yahweh* said to Moses, 'Write this action down in a book to keep the memory of it, and say in Joshua's hearing that I shall wipe out the memory of Amalek from under heaven.' Moses then built an altar and named it *Yahweh-nissi* because he said, 'Lay hold of the banner of *Yahweh*! *Yahweh* is at war with Amalek from age to age!'

In the theology of war as presented in this account, even though human soldiers did the direct killing, it is important to note that the victory is as miraculous as the destruction of the Egyptians at the Sea. It is the "staff of God" that provides the victory, that is, without it, the Hebrews could not defeat the Amalekites.

144

the Philistines. In the pre-monarchial theology of holy war, *herem*, doubts can sometimes be overlooked, but never the brazen sin of denying the ban as *Yahweh's* portion.

Having examined the theology of the *herem* in the *Yahweh* wars of the Sea, the two *shopet-im* Deborah and Gideon, and the disgraced warrior Saul, the background is provided for considering the most comprehensive theological statement of war in the **Hebrew Bible**: Deuteronomy 20. Before doing so, however, one question needs a response: why include Deuteronomy in this section on the pre-monarchy since it was written during the latter part of the monarchial period? The answer has already been given: in following the work of Susan Niditch and others, this study accepts that the Deuteronomist, while incorporating material and views from the monarchial period into his document, nonetheless remains reasonable true to traditions that preceded the monarchy. For this reason, Deuteronomic passages that concern the *herem* are relevant to both the pre-monarchy and the monarchy. So important is the Deuteronomist's "neatening up" of Hebrew war theology in Chapter 20, the entire chapter is cited:

> 'When you go to war against your enemies and see horses and chariots and an army greater than your own, you must not be afraid of them; *Yahweh* your God is with you, who brought you out of the land of Egypt. When you are about to join the battle the priest is to come forward and address the people. He is to say to them, "Listen, Israel; now that you are about to join battle against your enemies, do not be faint-hearted. Let there be no fear or trembling or alarm as you face them. *Yahweh* your God goes with you to fight for you against your enemies and to save you."

> Then the scribes are to address the people in words like these:

> "Is there any man here who has built a new house and not yet dedicated it? Let him go home lest he die in battle and another perform the dedication.

"Is there any man here who has planted a vineyard and not yet enjoyed its fruit? Let him go home lest he die in battle and another enjoy its fruit.

"Is there any man here who has betrothed a wife and not yet taken her? Let him go home lest he die in battle and another take her."

The scribes shall also address the people like this:

"Is there a man here who is fearful and faint of heart? Let him go home lest he make his fellows lose heart too."

'And when the scribes have finished speaking to the people, commanders will be appointed to lead them.

'When you advance to the attack on any town, first offer it terms of peace. If it accepts these and opens its gates to you, all the people found in it shall do forced labor for you and be subject to you. But if it refuses peace and offers resistance, you must lay siege to it. *Yahweh* your God shall deliver it into your power and you are to put all of its menfolk to the sword. But the women, the children, the livestock and all that the town contains, all its spoil, you may take for yourselves as booty. You will devour the spoil of your enemies which *Yahweh* your God has delivered to you.

'That is how you are to treat the far-distant towns not belonging to the nations near you. But as regards the towns of those peoples which *Yahweh* your God gives you as your own inheritance, you must not spare the life of any living thing. Instead, you must lay them under ban [*herem*], the Hittites, Amorites, Canaanites, Perizzites, Hivites and Jebusites, as *Yahweh* your God commanded, so that they may not teach you to practice all the detestable practices they have in honor of their gods and so cause you to sin against *Yahweh* your God.

> 'If, when attacking a town, you have to besiege it for a long time before you capture it, you must not destroy its trees by taking an axe to them: eat their fruit but do not cut them down. Is the tree in the fields human that you should besiege it too? Any trees, however, which you know are not fruit trees, you may mutilate and cut down and use to build siege works against the hostile town until it falls.

In this chapter the Deuteronomist synthesizes the theologies of war that developed over many centuries. Several of the provisions in this chapter, such as the deferments from battle, the saving of the fruit trees and the peace treaties offered some cities, indicate the more settled times of the monarchy. On the other hand, verses (15-18) which lay under the ban those cities occupying promised land[26] reflect theologies of war during the period of conquest, the pre-monarchial period. Consequently, only those parts of Deuteronomy 20 that reflect the pre-monarchial period are discussed at this point. Other passages in this chapter that reflect theologies of war during the monarchy are examined later.

As indicated earlier, for pre-monarchial theologies of war, the key verses are 15-18 and especially verse 18 provides an additional religious reason other than *Yahweh*'s portion for the brutal act of genocide (the ban) against those peoples inhabiting towns in the promised land; a reason reflecting the religious danger of worshipping other gods during the period of *Yahweh* henotheism, that is, placing another god above ("in front of") *Yahweh*: ". . . so that they may not teach you to practice all the detestable practices they have in honor of their gods and so cause you

---

[26]

The theology of war expressed by Rabin's assassin, Amir, is based, in part, on the view that those who occupy promised land, or those who are willing to give promised land to others, are under the ban. In other words, based on passages such as Deuteronomy 20:15-18, Amir believed that killing Rabin was sanctioned by *Yahweh*. Unfortunately, his beliefs are not uncommon, either throughout the history of the three monotheisms of the West or today in many parts of the Western world. Indeed, there has been a considerable re-birth of such theologies of holy war among many of the extremist groups in Israel.

to sin against *Yahweh* your God." As the second commandment makes abundantly clear: "For I *Yahweh* your God, am a jealous God and I punish the fathers' faults in the sons. . . ." (Exodus 20:5 and Deuteronomy 5:9). Thus, a second reason for the ban developed during the later pre-monarchy: to prevent the placing of other gods above *Yahweh*.

From the preceding analyses, several conclusions follow concerning pre-monarchial theologies of war. First, the primary purpose of war was the conquest of land, and such conquests were often brutal exterminations of the conquered. Second, the primary understanding of the *herem* was that which was owed *Yahweh* for his power to achieve victory, that is, conquered people were *Yahweh's* booty, who were "consecrated-to-destruction." However, another theological justification was provided for the ban as necessary to prevent the worshipping of other gods. Third, in the earliest war traditions *Yahweh* required no human aid and accomplished the total destruction of the enemy by his miraculous powers over nature. Fourth, as the Hebrews moved closer to the monarchy, human soldiers became more important in the war tradition. Human activities in *Yahweh's* victories raised new questions about the dividing of the war booty. As a result and also because of the emerging importance of the prophets, the ban began an evolution into the *herem* as *Yahweh's* justice: the view dominating holy war theologies from the monarchy to the present day. Finally, as the monarchy approached, the pre-monarchial view that all wars are holy wars required modification because wars became more political than religious, but the fundamental war theology of the pre-monarchy was the *herem*, that is, a holy war theology. Before moving to the period of the monarchy, however, several observations are needed concerning the two other dimensions of war, spiritual and eschatological, during the pre-monarchy.

Pre-monarchial references in the **Hebrew Bible** to spiritual war, defined for this study as internal conflict, temptation and distress, are either unknown or non-existent. A quick glance at Appendix A identifies only four references to spiritual war, and all of these belong to the periods of the later monarchy (Lamentations) or after the destruction of Jerusalem and the Temple (Job, Psalms, and II Isaiah). The pre-monarchial period centered on the acquisition of land at any cost. Prophets during these times centered their messages on the ban and the costs of infidelity to *Yahweh*. The moral concerns that are so important in the **Hebrew Bible** are largely the product of the prophets who arose during the monarchy, especially those of the terrible eighth century. The message of justice received its fullest expression in the preachings of the great eighth century prophets and was related to both righteousness and the future.[27] Thus during the pre-monarchy, little attention was given to the inner spiritual needs of human beings.

Compared to pre-monarchial concern about holy wars, references to eschatological war are more numerous than those about spiritual war; however, these references are inconsequential. First, there are no unquestionable references during this period to cosmic eschatological war. The other references to historical eschatological (future) wars are limited to two kinds: general references to *Yahweh*'s victories against his enemies (for example, Number 32:20-23), who are also the enemies of the Hebrews, and references to victories against those to whom the ban applies (for example, Exodus 23:22-27, Numbers 14:41, Deuteronomy 20:15-18 and Joshua 3:9-11): the Hittites, Amorites, Canaanites, Perizzites, Hivites and Jebusites. In other words, since these passages were written during the monarchy, they represent in most instances the writers looking backward to past victories rather than future ones. However, pre-monarchial Hebrews warriors, within the structure of a henotheism, most likely believed their God *Yahweh* would be with them in their present and future wars of conquest as he was with them in their past victories of

---

[27]

Correspondingly, the pre-monarchial period had little to offer concerning spiritual peace. Again, this is not surprising, for it was a violent, brutal period. Concerns about spiritual war and spiritual peace compliment one another; thus, it was also among the eighth century prophets that the first significant concerns about spiritual peace, which are the products of both righteousness and justice, received their initial expressions.

conquest. If this is correct, then it is also probable that all pre-monarchial political wars were also holy wars, that is, wars dominated by the brutal atrocity of the ban.

Monarchial Theologies of War (David to the Destruction of the Temple, 10th to 6th centuries)

Knowledge concerning the theologies of war which developed during the monarchies is more certain than those of the pre-monarchy for two important reasons: (1) With the possible exceptions of the Songs of Miriam and Deborah, the writings eventually collected as the **Hebrew Bible** (Masoretic Text) were written throughout this period as well as after the destruction of the Temple. (2) With the kings of Israel, historical and archeological knowledge is more certain and complete than that of the pre-monarchial period. While theologies of war developing during the monarchial period began with and reflected those of the pre-monarchy and its oral traditions, there were several significant developments concerning war in the period between David and the destruction of the Temple. Before examining these, a brief statement of the historical and religious situation of this period is needed.

With the advent of the monarchy, several important religious changes began to occur. First, the office of political leader and religious leader split and widened. While the king ruled as *Yahweh's* king, his religious significance was replaced first by the prophet and later by the priest. The division of the united nation-state of Israel into a northern kingdom, Israel, and a southern one, Judah, further widened this difference, especially in the north. Second, the prophets of the eighth century brought a new moral concern into the religious main stream; one which would lead at times to their criticism of even kings for failing to keep the laws of God.[28] Third,

---

28

It is interesting to note the rather gentle treatment of Solomon as contrasted with a king such as Ahab by the prophet-priest writers of the **Hebrew Bible**. Sins against *Yahweh* that received the strongest censure by the prophets were those of worshipping other gods, a constant temptation in times of henotheism. Solomon, however, who allowed the building of hundreds of altars and shrines to other gods

the building of the Temple by Solomon and its destruction by Nebuchadnezzar over three centuries later were events of overwhelming significance for religious views of this period. Finally, the first glimmers of monotheism made their appearance in the teaching of the eighth century prophets. It would require the experiences of the Exile, and perhaps the influences of the Persian monotheism Zoroastrianism, to complete the move from *Yahweh* henotheism to *Eloh-im* monotheism after the Exile, but the eighth century prophets began the preparation for this change in understanding the nature of God.[29]

Major historical events during this period have been partly described in the religious situation. Historically, the most significant were: the emergence of the nation-state under David, the selection of Jerusalem as his political capital and his moving the Ark of the Covenant from Shechem to Jerusalem, which made Jerusalem the religious center of the Hebrew faith; the great building program of Solomon, a program that was economically disastrous and set the stage for a civil war at his death; the civil war which split the once united nation-state of Israel; the Assyrian invasions and massacres of the northern tribes in the 8th century; and the Babylonian conquest of Judah and Jerusalem in the late 7th century followed by the destruction of Jerusalem and the Temple in 586 B.C.E. as punishment for a rebellion against Babylon.

Concerning theologies of war, the religious situation and the historical events of the monarchy gave birth to two major new developments: (1) political non-holy wars whose purpose was not the conquest of new lands, but the securing of those already occupied resulting in a new emphasis on peace treaties; and (2) efforts on the

---

near the Temple, was never directly punished by *Yahweh* for this sin (see pages 151-52) while other kings were bitterly condemned and violently punished for lesser crimes against *Yahweh* (see the account of Ahab and Ben-Hadad on pages 154-56). But this is not surprising, the religious writers of these works would tend to overlook a multitude of sins on the part of the king who built the Temple.

29

See the previous section, "From the Warrior *Yahweh* to the Creator *Eloh-im.*

part of the prophets continuing the theology of the *herem*, but one modified into the *herem* as *Yahweh's* justice so his justice could explain theologically the increasing number of war disasters visited upon the Hebrews by the Assyrians and the Babylonians.

During the early monarchy,[30] the position of *Yahweh* as the national god of the nation-state Israel was firmly bonded together with the king as his chosen leader of the people. During this period, even though a prophet would occasionally chastise a king, there was never any doubt that both David and Solomon were men of God's choosing. After the division at Solomon's death during the later monarchy, the situation between king and *Yahweh* changed, especially in the north where the conflicts between kings and prophets intensified. Even in the south, there were times of conflict between the two, but since a direct descendent of David sat on the throne at Jerusalem, these conflicts were less religiously significant. During both monarchial periods given the henotheistic nature of *Yahweh's* identification as the national god of the Hebrews, *Yahweh's* involvement in war remained important for warriors on the battlefield who still needed the help of their god for victory. Further, any act of infidelity to *Yahweh* brought terrible consequences, as the Hebrews after Solomon's death discovered:

> When Solomon grew old his wives swayed his heart to other gods;
> his heart was not wholly with *Yahweh* his God as his father David's
> had been. Solomon became a follower of *Astarte*, the goddess of the
> Sidonians, and of Milcom, the Ammonite abomination. He did what
> was displeasing to *Yahweh*. . . . Then it was that Solomon built a
> high place for Chemosh the god of Moab on the mountain east of

---

30

For this section of the study, the phrase *early monarchy* is used to refer to the monarchy during the united kingdom, that is, to the reigns of David and Solomon (1000-922 B.C.E.), and the phrase *later monarchy* to refer to the period after the civil war, that is, the divided kingdoms of Israel and Judah (922-586 B.C.E.).

Jerusalem, and to Milcom the god of the Ammonites. He did the same for all his foreign wives, who offered incense and sacrifice to their gods.

Yahweh was angry with Solomon because his heart had turned away from *Yahweh* the God of Israel who had twice appeared to him and who had forbidden him to follow other gods. . . . *Yahweh* therefore said to Solomon, 'Since you behave like this and do not keep my covenant or the laws I laid down for you, I will most surely tear the kingdom away from you and give it to one of your servants. For your father David's sake, however, I will not do this during your lifetime, but will tear it out of your son's hands. Even so I will not tear the whole kingdom from him. For the sake of my servant David, and for the sake of Jerusalem, which I have chosen, I will leave your son one tribe. (I Kings 11:7-13)

Over two centuries passed before the righteous king Josiah destroyed the altars Solomon built to *Astarte*, *Chemosh* and *Milcom* (II Kings 23:13-14).

From Solomon to the destruction of the Temple, even though views of war became increasingly more secular, fundamental to victory over enemies was fidelity to *Yahweh* who, when human resources failed, that is, when Hebrew soldiers could not defeat the enemies of *Yahweh*, *Yahweh* saved his people in a manner similar to the earliest supernatural actions of the pre-monarchy. One instance that fits the paradigm of divine salvation was the war of the Assyrian king Sennacherib against the faithful descendent of David, King Hezekiah. Sennacherib's crime against *Yahweh* involved more than his attack against the people of *Yahweh* but also the king's insults against *Yahweh*:

Sennacherib sent messengers to Hezekiah again, saying, 'Tell this to Hezekiah king of Judah, 'Do not let your God on whom you are relying deceive you, when he says: Jerusalem shall not fall into the power of the king of Assyria. You have learnt by now what the kings of Assyria have done to every country, putting them all under the ban. Are you likely to be spared? What power to help did the gods have of those nations my fathers destroyed, Gozan, Haran, Rezeph and the Edomites who were in Tel Basar? Where are the king of Hamath, the king of Arpad, the kings of Sepharaim, of Hena, of Ivvah?' (II Kings 19:10-13)

Since the Assyrians believed that their god *Ashur* together with the gods *An, Enil, Ea, Sin, Shamash, Adad, Ishtar* and *Nergal* aided them in the destruction of numerous cities, symbolically Sennacherib has thrown down the gauntlet at the feet of *Yahweh*. In the Hebrew theology of war, such a brazen insult cannot go unpunished, thus II Kings records:

> That same night the angel of *Yahweh* went out and struck down a hundred and eighty-five thousand men in the Assyrian camp
>
> . . . .
>
> Sennacherib struck camp and left; he returned home and stayed in Nineveh. One day when he was worshipping in the temple of his god Nisroch, his sons Adrammelech and Sharezer struck him down with the sword. . . . (19:35-37)

Two aspects of this account are important for an 8th century theology of war: (1) *Yahweh* alone slaughters the Assyrians, an action unusual during the monarchy when wars usually involved large numbers of Hebrew warriors and the kings' attitudes helped secularize war. (2) The assassination of Sennacherib while worshipping in front of the altar of Nisroch indicates an extension of the power of *Yahweh* over other peoples, gods and geographical areas--an extension that evidences a slow development from henotheism to monotheism.

Because a division occurred between the kings views of war and the prophets' theologies of war from the early monarchy to the late monarchy, it is helpful to divide the analysis which follows in terms of this conflict. The major theological change, then, from the pre-monarchy to the later monarchy was the separating of secular wars from holy wars. This separation is seen in the fact that there were several political wars which the prophets refused to bless and sometimes even condemned. An excellent example occurs in the conflict between the much maligned king Ahab and an unknown prophet concerning the Israelite victory over Ben-Hadad of Syria in I Kings 20. At conflict were a prophetic view of the *herem* and a more pragmatic, political view concerned about national security and peace. The story is as follows.

Ben-Hadad makes unreasonable demands of Ahab, even though at the time Ahab is subservient to him: he demands all of Ahab's gold and silver as well as his wives and children, that is, the gold and silver, wives and children of the Israelites. Ahab calls the elders together and they agree to send the gold and silver but not the wives and children. As Ben-Hadad takes up his positions against the city of Ahab, an unknown prophet comes to Ahab and promises him that *Yahweh* will deliver the army of Ben-Hadad into his hands. With seven thousand soldiers, Ahab sends the forces of Ben-Hadad in a panicked flight just as *Yahweh* promised. However, the prophet warns Ahab that Ben-Hadad will return within months. This time the size of Ben-Hadad's army is identified as over 127,000 soldiers while Ahab's warriors are described as like two small herds of goats, but they win a stunning victory because of the power of *Yahweh*. At this point, the war resembles those of the pre-monarchy *herem*, and herein lies the problem for Ahab. For him the war is more political than religious; thus, Ahab concludes a truce with Ben-Hadad allowing him to live and offering generous terms of peace. Unfortunately for Ahab, he has ignored *Yahweh*'s *herem*, that is, Ben-Hadad belongs to *Yahweh*, he is "consecrated-to-death." There follows a strange prophetic play whose purpose is to inform Ahab that because he has denied God his ban, Ahab must be sacrificed in Ben-Hadad's place: "*Yahweh* says this, 'Since you have let the man escape who was under my ban, your life will pay for his life, your people for his people'." (I Kings 20:42) Later as the prophet Elijah prophesies, the "dogs will lick up the blood [of Ahab] and the prostitutes wash in it. . . ." (I Kings 22:54) Ahab's attitude reflects a developing understanding of war as a political rather than religious event; in other terms, the story of Ahab and Ben-Hadad indicates a secularizing of war.

Other indications of the secularizing of war during the monarchy are the new emphasis on peace treaties (as in the peace treaty between Ahab and Ben-Hadad), the deferments that are provided, the treatment of women as war booty, and ecological-economic concerns about such things as fruit trees. Before turning to the prophet's efforts to keep alive the *herem* theology, brief descriptions of these more secular concerns of the monarchy are needed. Since the peace treaties are more appropriate for the final section of this chapter, "Theologies of Peace," the study moves to the deferments from war.

As a document which synthesizes several centuries of Hebrew thinking about war, Deuteronomy becomes a gold mine of information concerning the theologies of war in both the pre-monarchial and monarchial periods, and Chapter 20 is the mother lode in the mine. As already noted, verses 15-18 summarize the theologies of the ban beginning in the pre-monarchial *herem* as *Yahweh's* portion and developing into the ban as *Yahweh's* justice during the monarchy. After beginning with a reminder of *Yahweh's* mighty acts in the exodus and a pep talk to keep faith in *Yahweh's* leadership in war and thus overcome fear, a most interesting series of deferments (excuses) from participating in battle are offered: anyone who has built a new house, or planted a vineyard, or wed a new wife, or is fainthearted is excused from battle. Not only do these deferments indicate the more settled life of the monarchy, they represent a striking contrast to the attitude about failing to participate in battle during the period before the monarchy: for example, the Song of Deborah curses those who fail to fight, and Gideon massacres those who refuse to provide food for his weary holy warriors. From the religious perspective, these deferments represent a secularizing of war while the cursing and killing of those who refuse to participate in pre-monarchial war results from being holy wars. In other words, there are deferments from serving the king but never any excuses for failing to serve *Yahweh*.

Deuteronomy 21:10-14 represents a considerable change from the *herem* of the pre-monarchy in its description of women captives:

> 'When you go to war against your enemies and *Yahweh* your
> God delivers them into your power and you take prisoners, if you see
> a beautiful woman among the prisoners and find her desirable, you
> may make her your wife and bring her to your home. She is to shave
> her head and cut her nails and take off her prisoner's garb; she is to
> stay inside your house and mourn her father and mother for a full
> month. Then you may go to her and be a husband to her, and she
> shall be your wife.

The secularization in this view of the spoils of victory are a stark contrast to the ban pronounced in Deuteronomy 20 where total destruction of the captives was necessary because they might teach the Hebrews "to practice all the detestable practices they have in honor of their gods and so cause you [the Hebrews] to sin against *Yahweh* your God." (20:18) In many places in the **Hebrew Bible** when the prophets rail against the temptations to worship other gods, they often center their concerns on the seductions encouraged by foreign wives: for example the previous explanation of Solomon's seduction into worshiping other gods. Politically and economically captive wives are a source of wealth, but religiously they always are presented as a serious threat of fidelity to *Yahweh*.

Finally, before exploring the prophets' struggles to keep the religious traditions of holy war alive, one additional secularization of war in the monarchy deserves attention: provisions for preserving the economic value of land in war. The last two verses in Deuteronomy 20 make a distinction between two kinds of resources, using trees as the major example. Fruit bearing trees are not to be cut down in sieging a town, only those which cannot provide a source of food for the army and future generations. The intent is clear: in any siege (thus, any war), it is important to minimize the destruction of natural resources for they are a source of power and wealth for the victors.

All of these provisions--peace treaties whenever possible, deferments from battle, the division of women captives and the protection of the land as future income--represent secular movements in war more palatable to kings than prophets. However, the religious aspect of war never disappeared during the monarchy, for even when the king had a sizeable force, it was *Yahweh* who gave victory. The prophets emphasized this in several ways which must now be examined.

One of the ways that prophets stressed a holy war theology during the monarchy was through the ritual aspects of war and the presence of *Yahweh* in battle, either through the strong arms of his Hebrew warriors or by his actions alone. The destruction of 185,000 Assyrians in Sennacherib's army (II Kings 19) at the gates of Jerusalem illustrates divine action alone saving the Hebrews. However, when large numbers of human warriors were involved, so were the prophets and the priests as is evident in Deuteronomy 20:

> 'When you go to war against your enemies and see . . . an army greater than your own, you must not be afraid of them; *Yahweh* your God is with you. . . . When you are about to join battle, the priest is to come forward and address the people. He is to say to them, "Listen, Israel; now that you are about to join battle against your enemies, do not be faint-hearted. Let there be no fear or trembling or alarm as you face them. *Yahweh* your God goes with you to fight for you against your enemies and save you." (20:1-4)[31]

In addition to the priestly (prophetic) blessing of the war, the religious dimensions are also indicated by the presence of the Ark of the Covenant (the visual sign of the presence of *Yahweh*) and the rituals of religious purifications for battle. An example of both of these religious elements of war during the monarchy is observed in a most

---

[31]   As noted in the preceding, after the priests' declaration of the presence of *Yahweh* who fights for his people against his and their enemies, that is the declaration of a holy war, another group of speakers informs the assembled troops of the deferments. It is important to note, it is not the priests who do this--they represent *Yahweh*--the deferments are offered by the scribes, who represent the monarchy.

interesting narrative: the considerable efforts on the part of King David to trick Uriah the Hittite into sleeping with his wife Bathsheba so her pregnancy by David can be hidden.

Twice David tries to deceive Uriah into bedding Bathsheba; the second time even inducing him into drunkenness. However, even drunk, Uriah does not forget his religious vows of purification for holy war. When David learns that his ruses have failed, the following conversation takes place:

> This was reported to David; 'Uriah' they said 'did not go down to his house'. So David asked Uriah, 'Have you not just arrived from a journey? Why do you not go to your home?' But Uriah answered, 'Are not the Ark and the men of my lord, are they not in the open fields? Am I to go to my house, then, and eat and drink and sleep with my wife? As *Yahweh* lives, and as you yourself live, I will do no such thing!' (II Samuel 11:10--11)

Uriah's reluctance is much more than empathy for the sufferings of his fellow soldiers. He has taken a religious vow of ritual purity as a preparation for battle; any sexual activity would violate that vow. Although it is never stated, it is also reasonable to assume that he has "unbound his hair" (Judges 5) as part of the ritual preparation for battle. This account is one of many indicating that the priests (and prophets) continued to emphasize the religious aspects of holy war during the monarchy. The presence of the Ark of the Covenant was a powerful religious icon in war, and sometimes a costly one, as indicated in the account of its capture by the Philistines during one of many conflicts with the Hebrews. However, due to the calamities which befell them during the seven months they had the Ark[32], it was

---

[32]

I Samuel 5 describes the disasters that come upon the Philistines while they keep the Ark. Among them are the destruction of the sacred statue of *Dagon*, the henotheistic god of the Philistines, an affliction of tumors on the Philistines and other terrors. As a result, I Samuel 6 reports the return of the Ark of the Covenant.

returned to the Hebrews. After building the Temple, the Ark was removed from its appearances in battle and placed in the Holy of Holies.

The other major way prophets continued the holy war theologies of the pre-monarchy served a much more significant purpose than keeping past views alive, for they consummate in the modification of the *herem* from *Yahweh*'s portion to *Yahweh*'s justice.[33] Their modification in the theology of holy war became necessary because of the terrible Assyrian destructions of the 8th century. These disasters were more than political and economic events for the Hebrews, for such events created a major theological crisis: how can these catastrophes be happening to *Yahweh*'s chosen people? In this desperate question, the prophets faced no small challenge. The prophets' responses were in terms of the ban as *Yahweh*'s justice. In other words, because the Hebrew people had been unfaithful to *Yahweh* and his commandments to practice both righteousness and justice, sins for which they had been forgiven numerous times only to repeat them, the Hebrews must be purged of their uncleanliness (their infidelity).[34] An excellent example of this new theology of the

---

[33]

As Susan Niditch points out, the ban-as-*Yahweh*'s-justice has the fundamental purpose of purification which can be actualized externally against the Other (the enemy, the evil outside one's group) or internally during times of "distress, distrust, and anomie." Externally, such actions are known today as "ethnic cleansing" or "genocide." Internally they are usually defended in terms of purgation (cleansing) or purification. At different historical times, usually times of distress and distrust, each of the three monotheisms of this study have engaged in holy wars against the external enemy as well as internal purgations of the unclean. The Christian Inquisition is a clear example of the distorted theology and human destruction of such an internal holy war against the religiously unclean.

[34]

Because the ban-as-*Yahweh*'s-justice is internal, that is, actualized upon the chosen people, it does not require their total destruction. While the purging must involve human destruction, a remnant will survive and eventually receive the blessings of *Yahweh*, at least in the views of the prophets. Since this is a terrible message for any people to hear and accept, the prophets also provided a message of hope as well, for without hope a religion dies.

ban is the account of *Yahweh*'s justice against King Manasseh and the unfaithful in Judah:

> Manasseh was twelve years old when he came to the throne, and he reigned for fifty-two years in Jerusalem. . . . He did what was displeasing to *Yahweh*, copying the shameful practices of the nations whom *Yahweh* had dispossessed for the sons of Israel. He rebuilt the high places that his father Hezekiah had destroyed, he set up altars to *Baal* . . . he worshipped the whole array of heaven and served it. He built altars in the Temple of *Yahweh* of which *Yahweh* had said, 'Jerusalem is where I will give my name a home'.
>
> . . . .
>
> Then *Yahweh* spoke through his servants the prophets, 'Since Manasseh king of Judah has done these shameful deeds, acting more wickedly than all the Amorites did before him, and has led Judah itself into sin with his idols, *Yahweh* the God of Israel, says this, "Look, I will bring such disaster as to make the ears of all who hear of it tingle. . . . I will scour Jerusalem as a man scours a dish and, having scoured it, turns it upside down. I will cast away the remnant of my inheritance, delivering them into the power of their enemies, and making them serve as prey and booty to all their enemies, because they have done what is displeasing to me and have provoked my anger. . . . (II Kings 21:1-18, sel.ver.)

The message is clear, the holy war (*herem*) is now to be turned against the very people of *Yahweh*, but not to total destruction, for notice the metaphor used: scouring a dish. In the process of scouring a dish is not destroyed.

Because their response to the crisis of the eight century must not only explain present disasters but also future ones and provide a religious dimension of hope, the pre-exhilic prophets mixed a message of political war (past and present wars) and historical eschatological war (future wars). The latter provided a foundation for the post-exhilic development of cosmic eschatological war which was itself a prophetic response to the overwhelming catastrophe of the destruction of Jerusalem and the Temple.[35] Before exploring the dimension of hope in their historical eschatologies, it is illustrative to examine three other passages which explicate the new holy war theology of purgation: Isaiah 8:5-8 (First Isaiah), Amos 2:4-5 and the book of Hosea.

First, Isaiah's prophecy of *Yahweh*'s cleansing in Chapter 8 is precipitated by King Ahaz's turning away from *Yahweh* and his prophet Isaiah and seeking help from the enemy Assyrians against an assumed attack from another enemy not clearly identified in the text. In seeking aid from Assyria, Ahaz rejects *Yahweh*, makes himself a servant of the Assyrians, pays them booty and even erects an altar to the Assyrian god. Consequently, in Isaiah's metaphorical words, both Ahab and Judah must be purged:

> *Yahweh* spoke to me again and said:
>
> > Because this people has refused the waters of Shiloah[[36]] /
> > which flow in tranquility, / and trembles before Razon /
> > and the son of Remaliah, / the Lord will bring up against
> > you / the mighty and deep waters of the River / (the king
> > of Assyria and all his glory), / and it will overflow out of its
> > bed / bursting all its banks; / it will inundate Judah, flow

---

35

In their theologies of purging, the prophets speak of *Yahweh*'s power extending over the Assyrians and the Babylonians as his instruments for purifying the Hebrews as preparation for future great events. Not only does this set the stage for cosmic eschatologies but also indicates movement from henotheism to monotheism, that is, from the tribal-national warrior deity *Yahweh* to the creator *Eloh-im*, the God of all creation.

36

Shiloah is Jerusalem's only spring; thus, it came to symbolize the hidden protection of *Yahweh*. In refusing to metaphorically drink from the spring, the Judaeans are refusing to put their trust in *Yahweh* during a time of impending war.

162

> over, pour out, / flooding it up to the neck, / and its wings
> will be spread / over the whole breadth of your country, O
> Immanuel. (8:5-8)

Prophecy or acute political analysis, Isaiah's metaphor was most apt: for almost a century the Assyrians burst their banks and inundated much of the Middle East. In Isaiah's theology of the ban in this passage, there are three items of special note: (1) the disastrous consequences of losing trust in *Yahweh*'s promises; (2) the identification of Assyria as an instrument of cleansing; and (3) the promise that Judah would not be completely destroyed, in Isaiah's words, Judah would be inundated "up to the neck."

The book of Amos opens with a series of *Yahweh*'s judgments against a multitude of cities and peoples in the Middle East: Damascus, Gaza and Philistia, Tyre and Phoenicia, Edom, Ammon, Moab and even against Judah and Israel. Such judgments and the coming punishments indicate that for the prophets the power of *Yahweh* is beginning to grow beyond the limitations imposed by henotheism. *Yahweh*'s judgment and punishment of Judah are stated in these words:

> *Yahweh* says this:

> > For the three crimes, the four crimes of Judah / I have made
> > my decree and will not relent: / because they have rejected
> > the law of *Yahweh* / and failed to keep his precepts, /
> > because the false gods which their ancestors followed / have
> > led them astray, / I am going to hurl fire on Judah / to burn
> > up the palaces of Jerusalem. (2:4-5)

In the immediately following judgment against Israel, *Yahweh* through the prophet is much more specific about the violated precepts, that is, about the unrighteousness and injustice brought by the judgment and purging of *Yahweh* upon his people: (1) "they have sold the virtuous man for silver"; (2) they have sold the "poor man for a pair of sandals"; (3) they "trample on the heads of ordinary people"; (4) they "push the poor out of their path"; (5) father and son lie with the same woman; (6) they "profane. . . [*Yahweh's*] holy name"; (7) they "have forced the Nazirites to drink wine," that is, they have forced them to violate their holy vows; (8) they abuse and try to silence the prophets. In other words, because of the sins of unrighteousness (crimes against *Yahweh*) and injustice (crimes against other human beings) *Yahweh* must purge his people of their uncleanliness.

The book of Hosea begins with a passionate metaphor symbolizing the relationship between *Yahweh* and his people: marriage.[37] Hosea is told to marry a prostitute because *Yahweh's* people have prostituted themselves to other gods. Further, Hosea is told by *Yahweh* to father three children through her, children whose names symbolically represent the fracture between *Yahweh* and his people because of their unrighteousness and injustice. In order, the children are named:

(1)   Jezreel because "it will not be long before I make the House of Jehu pay for the blood at Jezreel[38] and I put an end to the sovereignty of the House of Israel." (1:4-5)

(2)   Unloved because "No more love shall the House of Israel have from me in the future, no further forgiveness. (But my love shall go to the house of Judah and . . . I mean to save them." (1:6-7)

(3)   No-People-of-Mine because "You are not my people and I am not your God." (1:8-9)

As the symbolic account of Hosea's marriage to Gomer continues, she proves unfaithful to him, but he forgives her even as *Yahweh* announces his desire to forgive

---

37

Biblical scholars are still debating whether the story of Hosea and Gomer is only metaphorical or has a historical basis in the prophet's life. Fortunately, concerning the prophetic theology of the ban-as-*Yahweh's*-justice, it makes no difference. Historical marriage or not, the theology of *Yahweh's* just purification of his people is the initial focus of the book.

38

Jezreel was one of many residences of the kings of Israel as well as the location where King Jehu massacred the descendants of Omri.

his unfaithful wife Israel and bring her home, as he intends to do in the future:

> I will betroth you to myself with faithfulness, / and you will come to know *Yahweh*.
>
> When that day comes--it is *Yahweh* who speaks-- / the heavens have their answer from me, / and the earth its answer from them, / the grain, the wine, the oil, their answer from the earth, / and Jezreel his answer from them. / I will sow him in the country, / I will love Unloved; / I will say to No-People-of-Mine, 'You are my people'. / And he will answer, 'You are my God'. (2:22-24)

While the saga between Hosea and Gomer (that is, between *Yahweh* and his people) continues through other acts of infidelity, they are followed eventually by acts of forgiveness and reconciliation. Even though the book of Hosea speaks at great length about infidelity and the destructive punishments to come from Yahweh's purging justice, it is foremost a work of hope for forgiveness and reconciliation.

In the midst of the historical calamities and the religious crises of the 8th and 6th centuries, the prophetic interpretations of the ban as the enactment of *Yahweh's* justice, filled two desperate needs: theologically explaining the historical destructions of *Yahweh's* people and providing the hope necessary for faith to survive. Previous discussions illustrate the former and give a glimpse of the latter. It is now appropriate to examine a major focus of that hope, the future *Mesiah* of *Yahweh* who will lead *Yahweh's* chastened and cleansed people[39]. In this new hope, the pre-monarchial prophets wed old views of the holy warrior with historical eschatological ones which in turn provide a basis for the post-exhilic prophets to

---

[39]

It is informative to compare this pre-exhilic *Mesiah* of the Hebrews with the return of the Twelfth Shi'ite Imam of the Muslims: the *Mahdi*. See Chapter Four.

develop their cosmic eschatologies.[40]

In times of great change, especially dangerous times of both external and internal conflict, humans respond in different ways in order to satisfy the same psychological needs: the most important being security and stability, courage to face today, and hope for tomorrow. One such response can be described as the stoic response, that is, a turning inward to create stability and courage through extensive rational self-discipline. Another response is the mystical one, that is, another turning inward but this time, one that leaves the turmoil in the world behind through absorption into other dimensions of reality. Also, the Hebrews wishing for a return to the good old days when life was simple, secure, and safe, at least safer than the present illustrates another common response.[41] For the pre-exhilic Hebrews, the "good old days" were the reign of David during the united nation-state. It is not surprising then, that eschatological prophecies of the future originating in the 8th century linked the past with the future. For the Hebrew faith remembering what *Yahweh* had done for his people in the past was not only fundamental for keeping fidelity with *Yahweh*, such remembering was the basis for any future hopes. Thus, in the midst of prophecies of doom and destruction Isaiah of the 8th century spoke of a new son to come from the stump of Jesse:

> A shoot springs from the stock of Jesse, / a scion thrusts
> from his roots: / on him the spirit of *Yahweh* rests, / a spirit

---

40

In their hopes for a new David, a new *Mesiah*, the prophets not only provided a survival hope for their people but the prophecies that became central to the claims made by Christians for the son born to Joseph and Mary centuries later.

41

I have never forgotten the first time I heard one of my daughters refer to the "good old days." She was only four. I was stunned: if at the age of four the, good old days are behind you, what lies ahead? I asked her, "Jaimie, what were the good old days?" Her response referred to our life in Oklahoma before we had moved to Tennessee when the "Adams Family" (her favorite program) was on afternoon television.

of wisdom and insight, / a spirit of counsel and power, / a spirit of the knowledge and of the fear of *Yahweh*. / (The fear of *Yahweh* is his breath.) / He does not judge by appearances, / he gives no verdict on hearsay, / he judges the wretched with integrity, / and with equity gives a verdict for the poor of the land. / His word is a rod that strikes the ruthless, / his sentences bring death to the wicked.

. . . .

That day, the root of Jesse / shall stand as a signal to the peoples. / It will be sought out by the nations / and its home will be glorious. / That day, the Lord will raise his hand once more / to ransom the remnant of his people, / left over from the exile of Assyria, of Egypt, / of Pathros, of Cush, of Elam, / of Shinar, of Hamath, of the islands of the sea. / He will hoist a signal for all nations / and assemble the outcasts of Israel; / he will bring back the scattered people of Judah / from the four corners of the earth. / Then Ephraim's jealousy will come to an end / and Judah's enemies be put down; / . . . . / They will sweep down westward on the Philistine slopes, / together they will pillage the sons of the East, / extend their sway over Edom and Moab, / and make the Ammonites their subjects. / And *Yahweh* will dry up the gulf of the sea of Egypt / . . . . / to make a pathway for the remnant of his people / left over from the exile of Assyria, / as there was for Israel / when it came up out of Egypt. (Chapter 11)

The message of Isaiah is clear and most distinctly Hebrew: to remember the past is the foundation of any hope for the future. Once *Yahweh*'s ban has purged evil from the Hebrews, he will send a new David to lead them to victory over *Yahweh*'s enemies and establish a new Israel founded on *Yahweh*'s commandments for righteousness and justice. Not surprisingly, remembering Samuel's anointing of David as *Yahweh*'s chosen king over Israel, the one to come became known as the *Mesiah*,[42] which means "Anointed One." While a few other pre-exhilic prophets added to the hope for the *Mesiah* to come, the exhilic and post-exhilic prophets embellished the hope and integrated it into cosmic eschatology. For the pre-exhilic prophets, the *Mesiah* was most likely a new *shopet-im* (holy warrior) whose eschatological occurrence would be historical rather than cosmic.

Since the previous discussion has described the theologies of both political and historical eschatological war that developed in the monarchial period, most of the tasks of this section are completed. There are no unquestionable pre-exhilic references to cosmic eschatology, so the only dimension of war left to examine is spiritual war, that is, internal conflict. Unfortunately, there is little to describe. Unquestionably there were many figures in pre-exhilic times who knew internal conflict, that is, who were at war with themselves or with *Yahweh*. For example, Job[43] complains:

> For me, there is no calm, no peace; / my torment banishes
> rest. (3:26)

---

[42]

    As a result of the Hebrews fleeing from the Assyrians in the 8th century and the Babylonians in the 6th century and other factors which dispersed the Jews from Palestine, one of the most important of the Jewish communities in the 3rd century was at Alexandria, Egypt. From there, in the 3rd century many of the sacred Hebrew writings were translated into the Greek **Septuagint**. **Septuagint** scholars chose to translate the Hebrew term *Mesiah* into the Greek word *Christos*. For most writers of the Christian **New Testament**, the Greek **Septuagint** was their Old Testament.

[43]

    The authorship of the book of Job is a complicated matter. It is generally accepted by the best biblical scholarship that the first two chapters (the Prologue) and the final part of the last chapter (the Epilogue) were written in post-exhilic times, but that the body of the story (the forty plus chapters that are often called the Dialogue) came from an older source, perhaps as early as the 9th century B.C.E..

168

In a similar vein, Jeremiah laments:

> My soul is shut out from peace; / I have forgotten happiness.
>
> (Lamentations 3:16-17)

Surely these complaints are not unusual, for the role of prophet was one of continual unrest. Amos, Hosea, Jonah and many other figures must have experienced the trials of spiritual war throughout much of their lives. Regrettably, they do not tell us about their internal struggles in an detail. Again, this is not surprising when looking at the times. The figures and prophets of the pre-exile were not given to introspection; they had considerable external tasks to accomplish in violent and destructive times. Further, the prophets lived a faith that was characterized more by the keeping of external rituals and laws than by acts of internal devotion. Consequently, there is little material concerning either spiritual war or peace (as defined for this study) in the pre-exhilic period.

Post-Exhilic Theologies of War (586 B.C.E. to approximately 100 B.C.E.)

There were several historical events that had significant impact on the developing theologies of war in the late exile and post-exhilic period.[44] Among the most important were: the Babylonian destruction of the Temple in 586 B.C.E.; the Babylonian Exile, 586 to 539 B.C.E.; the return to Jerusalem and the rebuilding of the Temple under the leadership of Ezra and Nehemiah (late 6th and early 5th centuries); the Alexandrian conquest of the Middle East from 333-323 B.C.E.; the division of the Macedonian empire of Alexander between the Ptolemies, who ruled

---

[44]

In this final section on theologies of war, the term *post-exhilic* also includes the Exile. In other words, this part of the study examines those views of war that developed in the period between the Babylonian destruction of the Temple and the writing of the last works to be canonized in the Masoretic Text of the **Hebrew Bible**. It also includes the Apocryphal books of the Maccabees because of their significance for the re-emergence of holy war on the political level.

Egypt, and the Selecuids, who ruled Syria[45]; the desecration of the Temple by Antiochus IV Epiphanus in 167 B.C.E.; the Maccabean revolt in 167 B.C.E.; and the Maccabean independence from 142 to 63 B.C.E. that ended when Pompey established Roman rule over Jerusalem. These events covered a period of approximately five centuries.

During these five centuries, except for the period of independence under the Maccabees, there existed no independent Jewish nation-state and no standing Jewish army. As a result, excluding the eight decades of Maccabean semi-statehood, the prophets and priests who kept alive a holy war theology were left with only two options since the old *herem* theology required a "real" army: either a modification of the holy war into a theology of rebellion against religious and moral oppression (for example, the books of Daniel and the Maccabees) or the movement of the holy war from the historical eschatological realm into the cosmic eschatological realm (for example, the book of Joel). Both ban theologies underwent modifications during this time. The latter view, which came to be known as the *apocalypse*, depended upon the universalizing of both the nature of holy war and the power of *Yahweh*; thus, a brief comment is needed on the movement from *Yahweh* henotheism before the Exile to *Eloh-im* monotheism after the Exile.[46]

The movement from henotheism to monotheism began by the 8th century prophets, and possibly received a considerable input from the Zoroastrians during the 6th century, came to fruition after the Exile. While some biblical scholars such as von Rad see in Jeremiah a universalizing of holy war, most find the first references

---

45

During the last few centuries B.C.E., the term *Syria* was used to include not only all of modern day Syria, but much of Palestine, Jordan, and Iraq. In other words, during this historical period present day Israel was considered part of Syria.

46

See the previous section of this chapter, "From the Warrior *Yahweh* to the Creator *Eloh-im,*" which describes pre-exhilic henotheism and contrasts it with post-exhilic monotheism.

that evidence the evolution of the warrior god *Yahweh* into the creator god *Eloh-im* in the prophecies of II Isaiah of the Exile. Many scholars find in passages such as Isaiah 44:6; 45:5, 7, 12; 51:15; 54:5 and post-exhilic Psalms such as 46:7-9 and 24:7-10, especially in usages of the term *Yahweh Sabaoth*, references to the Lord of Hosts who is the One God who overcame the powers of chaos, created the world, and rules supreme in it.[47] The Priestly writers of Genesis Chapter One built upon this monotheism to convey through powerful metaphors such as the sea of chaos (the *tehom*, usually translated as the "deep" or the "abyss"), darkness and light, goodness and the image (the *selem*) of God the most influential theology of creation to develop in the Middle East. In other words, with the universalization of the warrior *Yahweh* into the *Eloh-im* of creation, the pieces were in place for post-exhilic prophets to preach a message of cosmic eschatology. Because there was no nation-state of Israel, except for the few decades of the Maccabeans, cosmic eschatology became the focus of the post-exhilic period.

To summarize, post-exhilic theologies of war did not abandon the *herem* (the holy war), but they took one of two tracks: political holy war became rebellion against oppressors, especially when those oppressors forced uncleanliness upon the Jews or their holy places, and universalizing of historical eschatological war into cosmic eschatological war. Perhaps because of the terrible human destruction of the Babylonian Exile and the evolution of *Yahweh* into *Eloh-im*, a new element of morality entered the area of political war in the writings of the Priestly document.

As was the case before the Exile, the post-exhilic prophets spent little time looking inward at spiritual war and peace. Where dimensions of either entered their theologies, they were usually related to the promise in cosmic eschatology that after

---

47

      Isaiah 54:5 is a typical example:
                For now your creator will be your husband, / his name, *Yahweh Sabaoth*; / your redeemer will be the holy one of Israel, / he is called the God of the whole earth.

the final holy war between the forces of good and evil, *Eloh-im* would transform creation into a world of righteousness and justice. Thus, the post-exhilic prophets continued a view of spiritual peace that was hinted at by the pre-exhilic prophets: peace of spirit comes from righteousness and justice. However, the post-exhilic prophets related such peace to the eschatological Day of *Yahweh*. Because spiritual war, as defined for this study, is a negligible concern in the post-exhilic period and almost always related to spiritual peace, further comments on it are developed in the next section which examines Theologies of Peace. Consequently, the analysis that follows develops according to the two tracks of political war and eschatological war.

Because the absence of a nation-state and a standing army seriously compromised any theology of political holy war, there was historically only one important example during the period under examination: the Maccabean revolt against the ". . . disastrous abomination. . . .." (Daniel 11:31 and 12:11) The situation was as follows. In 167 B.C.E., Antiochus IV Epiphanus, who ruled from 175-163 as the Selecuid king of Syria, attempted to unite his kingdom under one language, one religion and one culture. For the Jews living in Jerusalem this uniting was a religious disaster, for it meant that Antiochus tried to replace their religion and cultural traditions with Greek ideas, values and beliefs. On December 6, 167, he desecrated their most holy place by erecting an altar to the Greek god Zeus in the rebuilt Temple. In Daniel, this desecration is the "disastrous abomination" or "the abomination to desolation." While the book of Daniel responded to this religious defilement by offering an eschatological prophecy that at the end of time those who had desecrated the places and people of God would be punished, the Maccabeans provided a political response to the desecration, and inso doing, revitalized the political holy war. Their holy war theology, which harkened back to the pre-monarchial days, is aptly described by von Rad:

> In the era of the Maccabees the Jews unexpectedly intervened
> once again in the political events with weapons, and, as we may
> believe in the reporting of the first book of Maccabees, again waged

holy wars. Indeed, the external circumstances even approximated in a curious way the oldest forms of the holy war. No king commanded the army, nor was it organized by a state bureaucracy; it was not soldiers, but the mass of the Jewish rural population who fought for their faith and for the worship of the God of their fathers. (**Holy War in Ancient Israel**, 133)

With the Maccabees, holy war returned to the earthly sphere with one modification: unlike the pre-exhilic holy war, the divine intervention necessary for most past victories was missing. According to Emil Schurer, it is

. . . remarkable that the successes with which the Maccabean enterprises were crowned are almost nowhere [in the texts] attributed to any immediate supernatural intervention on the part of God, but are represented throughout as the result of the military skill and political wisdom of the Maccabean princes. (**A History of the Jewish People in the Time of Jesus Christ**, 7)

In this sense, the holy war of the Maccabees incorporated elements of both the pre-monarchy (a rural army led by a charismatic leader rather than the king or the general of the king) and the monarchy (victories resulting from the skill of God's warriors for the purpose of enacting God's justice against those who had defiled the sacred, that is, the *herem* as a purging action). With the invasion of the Romans in 63 B.C.E., holy war theology once again left the historical realm, except for periodic guerilla actions on the part of zealous Jews, and returned mostly to the cosmic eschatological realm.[48]

---

[48]

From 63 B.C.E. until the United Nations partition of British Palestine into a Palestinian State and a Jewish State (Israel) on December 29, 1947, there had been no Jewish nation-state and no standing Jewish military force since 586 B.C.E.. The immediate response, as it was in the partition of India by the U.N. in 1948, was considerable bloodshed between Israelis and Arabs. This violence continued for the next two decades and reached new levels of engagement during the six day war of

Before turning to cosmic eschatological war, one further development in the area of political war deserves mention: a development indicating a growing awareness of the moral aspects of killing human beings in the context of monotheism. Numbers 31 presents the Priestly account of a *herem* against the Midianites during the time of Moses. As presented in this chapter, *Yahweh* commands Moses to exact "full vengeance for the sons of Israel on the Midianites." (31:1) 12,000 troops are assembled, 1000 from each of the twelve tribes. Eleazar the priest accompanies the holy warriors "carrying the sacred vessels and the trumpets for sounding the alarm." (31:6) *Yahweh*'s warriors are victorious and proceed to kill all the kings of Midian and all the male warriors, but take the women and all young children as well as the flocks and other spoils as booty. The Hebrew warriors return to Moses. Moses then requires, as part of *Yahweh*'s *herem*, the killing of all male children and any woman who has slept with a man; only the virgins are spared from the ban: "Spare the lives only of those young girls who have not slept with a man, and take them for yourselves." (31:18) At this point, the account differs from the pre-exhilic view of the *herem* as *Yahweh*'s portion only in **not** taking the lives of the virgins. However as the story continues, a divergence from this older theology of holy war is evident: the late monarchial and post exhilic theology of the *herem* as

---

1967 and the war of 1973. As a result of such violent conflicts on both sides and in order to survive, Israel developed one of the most effective military machines in the modern world, and today has the fifth largest army in the world. Needless to say, with the re-emergence of a Jewish state and a standing army there has also been a revival of *herem* theology among a growing number of religious extremists in Israel and among the better publicized Islamic extremist groups as Hamas and Islamic Jihad. In other words, with the partition, holy war theologies have again descended from the cosmic (heavenly) realm into the political one for both Israelis and Arabs in the Middle East as well as elsewhere. *Herem* theologies of internal cleansing are developing in Indonesia as well as Africa. There is also a growing *herem* theology among some American Jews who have provided both immigrants and monetary support for the extremist movements among the settlers in the West Bank (see the **Time** article, November 4, 1996, "Over Their Dead Bodies," which concerns the extremist views of many Hebron settlers).

Yahweh's justice against the unclean emerges with considerable force and specific description. Fundamental to the theology of the post-exhilic Judaism was the distinction between the clean and the unclean, that is, the religiously pure and impure. Not only is this theological passion for purity evidenced in the sparing of the virgins, spared because they had not been polluted by sexual contact with the unclean, it is also accentuated by the need to purify the other booty. (31:21-24) Such purification was not a part of the theologies of the pre-exhilic ban. Of even more significance, however, is another necessary kind of religious purification, one that hints at a growing moral concern about killing human beings. The key verse is 19: "As for you [the warriors], you must camp for seven days outside the camp, all of you who have killed a man or touched a corpse." This represents something new in the theology of holy war. Purification rituals for **engaging** in battle antedate the monarchy, but the requirement of purification for **killing** in battle is a post-exhilic view. Niditch provides a concise analysis of this new moral element in the theology of the *herem*:

> The warriors themselves who have killed or touched a corpse
> must . . . be purified. . . . Generally in Leviticus, contact with
> corpses is not defiling, nor is blood from a wound [except for priests]
> . . . . In Numbers . . . the uncleanness-rendering capacity of a human
> corpse extends to all Israelites . . . reflecting the status of the people
> as holy warriors. . . . Thus for the [post-exhilic] tradition of
> Numbers, war necessarily is a defiling activity. To consider war
> defiling, albeit in the context of a world-view that divides the world
> into clean and unclean, nevertheless is an ethical perception of sorts.
> The enemy is after all human [the Priestly account of creation affirms
> that all human beings are created in the image of God][49]; the

---

49

    The fundamental monotheistic belief that all human beings have something of God in them, that is, are created in the image of God, is basic to the argument

shedding of human blood tears the whole fabric of the cosmos and must be duly marked off. . . .

. . . .

. . . . In Numbers 31, as in Deuteronomy 20, war on some level is ritual, and yet war in Numbers 31 is not cleansing or whole-making in the spirit of the extirpation of wayward Israelite cities in Deuteronomy 13 or the ban texts demanding erasure of idolaters from the land. Doubts have crept in about the whole enterprise, for in killing one becomes part of the abomination, the enemy one seeks to eliminate. Such are the complexities of the priestly ethics of violence in war found in Numbers 31.

. . . . Numbers 31 expresses genuine ambivalence concerning the ethics of war. The cause is holy, the war is ritualized, but the killing defiles. Thus as one enters war ritually one must exit with separation, cleansing, and sacrifices of atonement. (86-89)

To summarize, post-exhilic theologies of political war centered on the *herem* as God's justice in cleansing the impure and rebelling against foreign oppression (the unclean other), but they also evidenced a growing moral concern about killing other humans, a concern that is intrinsic to a moral monotheism but morally inconsequential in a henotheism.

It is now appropriate to examine the war theology which dominated the post-exhilic period: cosmic eschatological war, that is, in other terms, holy apocalyptic war. To begin with a pun, the scholarly pitfalls in any analysis of Jewish eschatology are **Legion**. Four of the most controversial areas concern the meaning of the terms *apocalypse* and *apocalyptic* (as applied to eschatology), the relationships between apocalyptic literature and Jewish wisdom literature, the relationship between

---

presented in the final chapter that the holy war, the *herem* either as 'Yahweh's portion or *Yahweh*'s justice, is a distortion in moral monotheism.

prophetic eschatology (the term *historical eschatology* is used in this study for this kind of literature) and apocalyptic eschatology (the term *cosmic eschatology* is used to refer to this kind of literature), and the significance of external influences on Jewish eschatology. Books and dozens of articles published every year argue these problems. While the non-technical student expects that scholars should at least be able to agree about the meanings of the terms *apocalypse* and *apocalyptic*, even this still eludes the scholarly field. Because this study cannot begin to do justice to these issues,[50] and because its major purpose is limited to an analysis of only two issues which appear in Jewish eschatology--war and peace, for pragmatic reasons, it divides eschatology into two categories: historical (what is often called prophetic) eschatology and cosmic (what is usually termed apocalyptic) eschatology. Further, it basically agrees with the general position on these two kinds of eschatology as taken by the writers and editors of the Anchor Bible series as well as their position on the external influence of Persian (Zoroastrian) religion on Jewish eschatology:

> Prophetic eschatology and apocalyptic eschatology are best viewed as two sides of the same continuum. . . . Prophetic eschatology . . . is the view that God's new order would unfold within the realities of this world. Periods of extreme suffering . . . tended to cast doubts on the effectiveness of human reform and thus to abet apocalyptic eschatology with its more rigidly dualistic view of divine deliverance, entailing destruction of this world and resurrection of the faithful to a blessed heavenly existence. (**The Anchor Bible Dictionary**, 281)
>
> . . . the Persians had a well-developed apocalyptic tradition,

---

50

    There is an excellent essay by Michael A. Knibb titled "Prophecy and the emergence of the Jewish apocalypses" in **Israel's Prophetic Tradition**, edited by Coggins, Phillips, and Knibb, Cambridge University Press, 1984, which describes and critiques many of the most important and controversial issues in the study of eschatological literature.

which has often been assumed to be the source of Jewish apocalyptism. . . . In recent years scholars have become reticent about positing Persian influence because of the notorious problems of dating. Most of the relevant Persian material is extant in Pahlavi works, which are as late as the 9th century [C.E.]. . . .

Despite the problems, the possible influence of Persian apocalyptism on Judaism cannot be discounted. A brief account of Persian religion attributed to Theopompus (about 300 B.C.E.) attests a belief in an on-going dualistic struggle between light and darkness, the activities of angelic and demonic beings, and the division of history into periods. Belief in a resurrection is indisputably old in Persian religion as is the motif of a heavenly journey. . . . Persian influence on the dualism of the Dead Sea Scrolls is widely admitted. The full relationship between Persian and Jewish apocalyptism . . . remains one of the major unresolved problems in the study of apocalyptism. (**The Anchor Bible Dictionary**, 285)

Based on this division of eschatological literature and the judgment that historical (prophetic) eschatology is mostly confined to the pre-exhilic period and cosmic (apocalyptic) eschatology to the post-exhilic period, the final task in examining theologies of war is to explore the general features of post-exhilic cosmic eschatology. However, any reasonable analysis of cosmic eschatology cannot ignore historical eschatology for two reasons: first, historical eschatology, together with other factors, some internal and some external, provided the roots from which cosmic eschatology grew; and, second, beliefs in the re-creation of a historical Israel and Temple together with a historical Messianic figure have major roles in cosmic eschatology, although the *Mesiah* assumes several non-historical features in cosmic eschatology, that is, attributes that are more than human..

Given the richness, diversity, and extensive metaphorical nature[51] of cosmic eschatological literature, an in depth analysis of its corpus in the **Hebrew Bible** is beyond the limitations and purposes of this study. Instead, the goal of the following examination identifies the major features of Jewish cosmic eschatology and relates these first to the theme of war and later to that of peace.

Given the considerable scholarly controversies over even defining the different kinds of eschatology, it not surprising to find that there is considerable disagreement regarding the basic features of cosmic eschatology. According to an article in **Israeli Prophetic Tradition** by Michael Knibb, the scholar K. Koch proposed the following eight essential features in 1970: (1) "an urgent expectation of the impending overthrow of all earthly conditions in the immediate future"; (2) "the end as a vast cosmic catastrophe"; (3) "a close connection between the end-time and previous human and cosmic history and the division of world history into segments, the contents which have been predetermined from creation"[52]; (4)"the intervention of an army of angels and demons in the affairs of this world"; (5) "a new salvation beyond the catastrophe for the righteous in Israel, but not restricted to Israel"; (6) "the transition from disaster to salvation as the result of an act issuing from the throne of God and bringing about the establishment of the kingdom of God on earth; the distinction between this age and the age to come"; (7) "the frequent

---

51

Historical eschatology in part, but cosmic eschatology as a whole, must revert to symbolic (metaphorical) language, often cast in the forms of dreams or visions, in order to talk about the future. While historical eschatology occasionally resorts to such figurative language, cosmic eschatology fundamentally depends on it, for it is impossible to describe dimensions of reality that transcend time and space in the empirical terms used to describe history, which is in time and space.

52

Note the monotheistic assumption in this feature. Neither polytheism nor henotheism provides a basis for cosmic eschatologies because the power and knowledge of the gods are much too limited to achieve such a predetermined fulfillment of the whole of creation.

presence of a mediator with royal functions"; and (8) "use of the catchword 'glory' in descriptions of the new age." (Knibb, 158) As expected, Koch's views soon were critiqued by others who offered different lists of essential features. In 1976, J.J. Collins argued for four essential features: (1) "a narrative framework in which the manner of revelation [visions, auditions, otherworldly journeys, writings] is described."; (2) "an otherworldly mediator and a human recipient--it is never simply a direct oracular utterance by either a heavenly being or human."; (3) "an eschatological salvation which is temporally future and presents otherworldly realities."; and (4) "The eschatological salvation is always definitive in character and is marked by some form of personal afterlife."[53] (Knibb, 52) As expected,

---

[53]
    This final feature of a personal afterlife becomes one of the most centrally precious beliefs in all three of the monotheisms in this study. Indeed, one of the points of greatest contention among them is what might be called the absence of "affirmative action policies" in each for those outside their circle of faith for entrance into Heaven (that is, eternal salvation). Occasionally there have been philosophers in each religion who, following Aristotle, argued for some kind of impersonal immortality, but this has always been rejected by the overwhelming majority in each faith. On the other hand, there have always been a few theologians who have opened the gates of Paradise for every being created in the image of God, that is for all humans. One of the first Christian thinkers to argue this position was Origen of Alexandria (2nd century C.E.). It is usually identified by the phrase *universal salvation* (that is, at the end of time all are saved by the infinite forgiving love of God), and usually declared heretical. Finally, it is worth noting that, although the belief in personal immortality is fundamental to most Jewish theologies of salvation today, it arrived rather late for the writings incorporated in the Masoretic Text of the **Hebrew Bible**. The first unmistakable reference to some kind of personal salvation related to one's actions on earth in Judaism occurs in Daniel 12:1-3, one of the latest writings to be included in the **Hebrew Bible**:

> 'At that time Michael will stand up, the great prince who mounts guard over your people. There is going to be a time of great distress, unparalleled since nations first came into existence. When that time comes, your own people will be spared, all those whose names are found written in the Book. Of those who lie sleeping in the dust of the earth many will awake, some to everlasting life, some to shame and everlasting disgrace'.

The more ancient Hebrew views centered on a gray shadowy place referred to as

another scholar, P. D. Hanson, offered a different list of basic features: (1) "the present world is evil"; (2) "a great judgment separating the good from the evil and marking the crossroads between the present world and the world to come is imminent"; (3) "a newly created world of peace and blessing ordained for the faithful lies beyond that judgment"; and (4) "a modified dualism." (Knibb, 171) Finally, one other example is illustrative. H. Gese argued for at least five essential features: (1) "most of the characteristics . . . [of cosmic eschatology] are to be found in night visions [e.g., those of Zechariah]"; (2) a "last great battle that would inaugurate the new era . . . taking place at the instigation of God and marking the beginning of the end-time"; (3) "the messianic hope [the mediator of the other positions presented]"; and (4) martyrdom at the end time" including that of a "suffering messiah." (Knibb, 173) All of these elements Gese finds in Isaiah 65.

While the preceding discussion indicates the scholarly complexities of examining cosmic eschatology, it also shows that they share certain features, and fortunately this part of the study of war needs to examine only those features which involve violence, conflict, or war. The ones that have such relevance are: (1) God's (*Eloh-im*'s) judgment (*herem*) on evil (or impurity) in the world; (2) a violent end to the present world order; (3) the dualism of good and evil which provides a basis for a final conflict (war); and (4) the Messianic mediator when he is understood as a warrior rather than a "suffering servant."[54] Each must now be illustrated by textual

---

sheol which was neither a place of torment or blessedness. In other words, beliefs in reward or punishment after death arrived so late in post-exhilic Judaism that they are barely mentioned in the **Hebrew Bible**, but they are given considerable space in the writings that occurred thereafter.

[54]

While a *Mesiah* who comes to enact God's will through suffering becomes the focus of Christian theologies of salvation, the Jewish community of the first century C.E. was still split over a warrior *Mesiah* or a "Suffering Servant" *Mesiah* who would initiate the new order of creation. The latter is examined in later sections of the study; it is only the former, the warrior *Mesiah*, that is of concern for the present analysis.

examples before concluding the chapter with an exploration of theologies of peace.

The sections of the **Hebrew Bible** which unquestionably portray a cosmic eschatology are few in number and small in size: a few chapters in Isaiah, 55-59; several sections of Daniel such as 7:13-14 and 23, 9:25-27, and 12:1-3 (most eschatological sections of Daniel can be interpreted as historical rather than cosmic eschatology); Zephaniah 1:14-18; and the book of Joel, which is for the **Hebrew Bible** the equivalent of the book of Revelation in the **New Testament** concerning cosmic eschatology. Compared to the whole of the **Hebrew Bible**, in terms of space, little attention is given to cosmic eschatology. This situation, however, changed radically during the last two centuries B.C.E. and the first few centuries C.E. in the Jewish faith, for in this period the passion for cosmic eschatology expanded geometrically. It occupies a considerable place in many of those works included in the **Pseudepigrapha**, especially the books of I and II Enoch as well as several other books found at Qumran among the Dead Sea Scrolls. However, since this study is limited to the canonized books of the Masoretic Text, an examination of several passages from Daniel, Zechariah, Zephaniah, and Joel suffices to uncover the role of war and the warrior in the Jewish cosmic eschatology included in the **Hebrew Bible.**[55]

Eschatological passages in the **Hebrew Bible** which speak of God's *herem* as His justice, that is, His cleansing of both external evil (the enemies of Israel) and

---

[55]

Such is not the case in either the Christian **New Testament** or the Muslim **Qur'an**. In the **New Testament**, the preachings of Jesus, the letters of Paul, most of the other letters (excluding that of James which is more stoic ethical philosophy than religious theology), and the book of Revelation, beliefs and concerns about the Day of Judgment abound. In the **Qur'an** there are very few *suras* which do not contain a reference to the Day of Judgment that lies at the end of time. Thus, cosmic eschatology, which occupies only a small place in the **Hebrew Bible** but a much larger place in writings outside the canonized Hebrew text, becomes in Christianity and Islam a major focus and for some groups, especially extremist ones, a dominating passion.

internal impurity (the unrighteous, unclean in Israel) are found in almost all of those just mentioned. As typical examples, consider the following passages from Ezekiel, Zephaniah, and Zechariah:

'That is how I shall display my glory to the nations, and all nations will feel my sentence when I judge, and feel my hand when I strike them. The house of Israel will know that I am *Yahweh* their God from that day forward for ever. And the nations will learn that the House of Israel was exiled for their sin in behaving so treacherously to me that I had to avert my face from them because they rebelled against me, and to hand them over to their enemies; and they all perished by the sword. I treated them as their filthy sins deserved and hid my face from them. And so, thus says the Lord *Yahweh*: Now I am going to bring back the captives of Jacob, now I am going to take pity on the whole house of Israel and show myself jealous for my holy name'. (Ezekiel 39:21-25)

On the day of the anger of *Yahweh*, / in the fire of his jealousy, / all the earth will be consumed. / For he means to destroy, yes, to make an end / of all the inhabitants of the earth [except the humble / who seek him in righteousness]. (Zephaniah 1:18)

See, a day is coming for *Yahweh* when the spoils taken from you will be divided among you. *Yahweh* will gather all the nations to Jerusalem for battle. The city will be taken, the houses plundered, the women ravished. Half the city will go into captivity, but the remnant of the people will not be cut off from the city. Then *Yahweh* will take the field; he will fight against these nations as he fights in the day of battle.

.... The ban will be lifted; Jerusalem will be safe to live in. And this is the plague with which *Yahweh* will strike all the nations who have fought against Jerusalem; their flesh will molder while they are still standing on their feet; their eyes will rot in their sockets; their tongues will rot in their mouths. And such will be the plague on the horses and mules, camels and donkeys, and all the animals to be found in that camp. When that day comes, a great terror will fall on them from *Yahweh*, each man will grab his neighbor's hand and they will hit out at each other. (Zechariah 14: 1-4 and 11-14)

Several *herem* elements stand out in these cosmic eschatological passages: First God's justice reaches out to destroy both internal impurity and external evil. Second, the destruction of external evil (Israel's enemies) approaches the total **consecration-to-destruction** of the pre-monarchial ban, while the punishment of internal impurity is to be abated before total destruction. Further for the pure who are saved, the remnant, they shall return to Jerusalem. Finally, while God uses war as one means of purgation, these passages concerning cosmic eschatology return to the pre-monarchial view of *Yahweh*'s supernatural power as the instrument through which he brings about destruction of the enemy: plagues and earthquakes. This latter sets the stage for the best known and most metaphorically colorful aspect of cosmic eschatology: the violent catastrophes that precede the end of time.

In Isaiah Chapter 54, the prophet speaks of the mountains departing (disappearing), but the best known metaphors of the violence of the apocalypse are to be found in the books of Daniel and Joel:

"The fourth beast / is to be a fourth kingdom on the earth, / different from all other kingdoms. / It will devour the whole earth, / trample it underfoot and crush it. (Daniel 7:23)

The sun will be turned into darkness, / and the moon into blood, / before the day of *Yahweh* dawns, / that great and terrible day. (Joel 3:4)

Sun and moon grow dark, / the stars lose their brilliance. / *Yahweh* roars from Zion, / makes his voice heard from

184

Jerusalem; / Heaven and earth tremble. (Joel 4:15-16)
These violent events, the signs known as the horsemen of the apocalypse, include the power of *Eloh-im* over nature as in the pre-monarchial *herem*, but also the involvement of human armies as well as supernatural hosts (armies) of God in the final conflict. Thus, as incongruous as it seems, these passages speak of the necessity for the violence of war, both political (human) and cosmic (supernatural), in preparing the way for universal peace at the predetermined end of time.

Significant passages which describe these wars (battles) are found in Zechariah and Joel:

> Then *Yahweh* will take the field; he will fight against these nations as he fights in the day of battle. On that day his feet will rest on the Mount of Olives,[56] which faces Jerusalem from the east. The Mount of Olives will be split in half from east to west, forming a huge gorge, half the Mount will recede northwards, the other half southwards. And the Vale of Hinnom will be filled up from Goah to Jasol; it will be blocked as it was by the earthquake in the days of Uzziah king of Judah. *Yahweh* your God will come, and all the holy ones with him.
>
> . . . .
>
> All who survive of all the nations that have marched against Jerusalem will go up year by year to worship the King, *Yahweh*

56

The Mount of Olives is located in the West Bank that is so often in the news. According to the U.N. partition and the Oslo Accords, this land belongs to the Palestinians. However, note its importance for the final battle that issues in the new age of God. This is one of many reasons that religious extremists in Israel are so violently opposed to returning any of the land in the West Bank to non-Jews. See footnote #118 in the fourth chapter which describes Muslim views concerning the importance of the Dome of the Rock Mosque and the Mount of Olives on the Day of Judgment. Arab neighborhoods in the Mount of Olives have become a recent focus for conflict as Jewish settlers slowly acquire property and houses there with the approval of the Israeli government.

Sabaoth [Lord of Hosts]. . . .   (Zechariah 14:3-6, 16)

Sound the trumpet in Zion / give the alarm on my holy mountain! / Let all the inhabitants of the country tremble, / For the day of *Yahweh* is coming, / yes, it is near.

. . . . / a vast and might host, / such as has never been seen before, / such as will never be again / to the remotest ages. In their van the fire devours, / in their rear a flame consumes. / The country is like a garden of Eden ahead of them / and a desert waste behind them. / Nothing escapes them. / . . . . / a mighty army in battle array.

. . . .

Like fighting men they press forward, / each marching straight ahead, / not turning from his path; / they never jostle each other, / each marches straight ahead: / arrows fly, they still press forward, / without breaking ranks. /

. . . .

As they come on, the earth quakes, / the skies tremble, / sun and moon grow dark, / the stars lose their brilliance. / *Yahweh* makes his voice heard / at the head of the army, / and indeed his regiments are innumerable, / all powerful is the one that carries out his orders, / for great is the day of *Yahweh*, / and very terrible--who can face it?   (Joel 2:1-11)

'Proclaim this among the nations. / "Prepare for war! / Muster the champions! / warriors advance, / quick march! / Hammer your ploughshares into swords, / your sickles into spears, / let the weakling say, 'I am a fighting man'. / Come quickly, / all you surrounding nations, / assemble there!" / (*Yahweh*, send down your champions!)

. . . .

> Host on host / in the valley of Decision / For the day of
>
> *Yahweh* is near / in the Valley of Decision.   (Joel 4:9-14)

The human (natural) and the cosmic (supernatural) are intermixed in these passages about the final conflict that issues in the new age of God: an age in which all those who survive the final battle come to worship God at Jerusalem.[57] As noted before, the eradication of evil (both internal and external) is an action that lies beyond human efforts;   thus, God must intervene with His hosts in order to bring the conflict between good and evil to a final consummation, that is, a final victory of good over evil. In this conflict as presented in Zechariah and Joel, human soldiers and heavenly warriors are involved. Both prophets speak of arrows flying, plowshares becoming swords and sickles becoming spears: the weapons needed by human soldiers in the battle on the Day of *Yahweh*. But both also emphasize the supernatural actions of God in dimming stars, sun and moon as well as make mention of God sending down his "champions" ("holy ones") who will be led by an "all powerful one" who will carry out the orders of God. These champions, holy ones, are the angelic hosts (army) of God. The "all powerful one" who leads them is the hoped for *Mesiah*, but clearly a *Mesiah* who is more than human. This leads, then, to the final issue which requires elaboration: the warrior *Mesiah* of cosmic eschatology.

57

  The reference to Jerusalem in these passages may or may not refer to the historical city. They are interpreted in two ways: Jerusalem as God's re-created earthly city of righteousness and justice or Jerusalem as a metaphor for the heavenly city of eternal salvation. Likewise, Jewish theological and philosophical thought split over the interpretation of these eschatological prophecies about rebuilding the Temple. For some, they mean rebuilding the earthly Temple; for others, the Temple of cosmic eschatology is a heavenly Temple. As an example of the latter, see the work of Philo Judaeus (25 B.C.E. to 40 C.E) who claimed that the true Temple is not a physical (that is, earthly) one. Whether his thoughts influenced Augustine is uncertain, but Augustine's view of the true Community of Saints (the true Church) were similar to Philo's views of the true Temple. Luther later used Augustine's theology to argue that the true Church is the invisible Church.

Other than the reference in Joel 2:11 to the "all powerful one" who directs the hosts of God, the best references to the cosmic *Messiah* are in two passages in the book of Daniel:

> 'I gazed into the vision of the night. / And I saw, coming on the clouds of heaven, / one like a son of man[58] / He came to the one of great age / and was led into his presence. / On him was conferred sovereignty, / glory and kingship, / and all the peoples, nations and languages became his servants. / His sovereignty is an eternal sovereignty / which shall never pass away, / nor will his empire ever be destroyed.' (Daniel 7:13-14)
>
> 'Know this, then, and understand: / from the time this message went out: / "Return and rebuild Jerusalem" / to the coming of an anointed Prince [Prince *Mesiah*], seven weeks / and sixty-two weeks, / with squares and ramparts restored and rebuilt, / but in a time of trouble. / And after the sixty-two weeks / an anointed one will be cut off[59]--and . . . will not be for him-- / the city and the sanctuary will be

---

58

The term *Son of Man* became a major term in Jewish apocalyptic literature of the last century B.C.E. and the first few centuries C.E. to describe the *Mesiah* who would re-establish Israel and rebuild the Temple. Some understood him as a warrior who must accomplish his tasks through war, and others envisioned a Messianic figure who fulfilled the purposes of God without such violence. Christians claimed that Jesus was this *Mesiah* from God: in the gospel of Mark there are several passages where Jesus identifies himself as the "Son of Man who has come upon the clouds."

59

Many of the early Church Fathers interpreted this verse as referring to the crucifixion of the Christ. But others interpreted the passage as a reference to cosmic eschatology, that is, to the end of time. It is still being argued by both Jewish and Christian biblical scholars.

> destroyed / by a prince who will come. / His end will come
> in catastrophe / and, until the end, there will be war / and
> all the devastation decreed.   (Daniel 9:25-27)

These two verses in Daniel Chapter 9 are among the most obscure and interpretively controversial in the whole of a most difficult book: do they refer to a historical, human *Mesiah* or to a cosmic, more-than-human *Mesiah*? Both have been argued. However, if correlated with those references in Chapter 7 to a Son of Man whose sovereignty is eternal, the Prince Messiah is most likely a cosmic one who comes to do battle with evil, that is, lead the forces of goodness in their final war with evil and God's ultimate victory over evil will create a new world of justice and righteousness. Whether this new kingdom of God is earthly or heavenly is, again, a matter of considerable dispute, and one that cannot be settled here. What does seem certain, however, is that post-exhilic Jewish cosmic eschatology continued the *herem* (holy war) theology as God's justice, and that the power of evil was such that God's justice required the violence of war, either natural or cosmic or both. Further, a Future One would be sent by God to lead the hosts (armies) of this conflict, God's *Mesiah*, and that His victory would establish a new order of eternal peace.

It is now time to explore the theologies of peace that are found in the **Hebrew Bible**.

Theologies of Peace

A brief comparison of Appendices A and B suggests that war, conflict, battle, and holy war receives twice the attention given to peace in the **Hebrew Bible**. Further, the preceding section of this chapter on "Theologies of War," which occupies almost 75% of the chapter material to this point, seem to indicate that war is a dominant, if not the dominant, theme in the **Hebrew Bible**. By comparison, peace seems almost inconsequential during the oral tradition and writing period of this sacred revelation. Unquestionably war, especially the *herem*, was a dominating concern because these centuries were violent and destructive times for the Jews whose political and religious focus was on the conquest of promised land, the securing and defense of that holy land often against superior armies, and ultimately the loss of sovereignty over the promised land. These were not times promoting thoughts about peace. Viewed only from the perspective of war, the **Hebrew Bible** would unquestionably be an influential sacred book: a kind of ancient Machiavellian handbook of holy war. In this sense, however, while important and influential, it would not be a great spiritual revelation. Fortunately, however, this is a stunted view, for almost from its first writings by the Yahwist to the post-exhilic prophets there is a spiritual theme whose importance far transcends that of death and war: peace. Even during the most destructive and terror filled times these pages describe, times when even glimpses of peace seemed to be buried beneath the despairs of human hearts and the corpses of thousands, the need for peace and the hope for peace were still there awaiting only the right voice (prophet) to bring them to awareness. While war stands at the fore-front in much of the **Hebrew Bible**, its spiritual foundation is peace because the reality which lies at its core is one that transcends the worst limitations of human frailty: a God who created humans for peace. Thus, the spiritual greatness and genius of **the Hebrew Bible** is found its awareness of the relationships among peace, righteousness, justice, salvation and God.[60] As an introduction to the explorations of these relationships consider the well known

---

[60]

The other two children of Abraham, as described in the next two chapters, inherited this spiritual greatness and genius as well as the plague of holy wars that also abounds in the pages of the **Hebrew Bible**. This apparent contradiction between war and peace should not be surprising: spiritual greatness when not distorted is the source for the growth of those most important aspects of the human spirit such as compassion, charity, forgiveness and justice. Unfortunately, the more sacred something is, the greater the human destruction when it is distorted into such atrocities as holy war. It is the contention of the concluding chapter of this study, that the **Hebrew Bible** has, as it were, a historical excuse for its pre-exhilic predisposition toward racial-religious bigotry and theologies of the *herem*--its henotheism; however, neither post-exhilic Judaism, Christianity or Islam can use such a defense, for they are monotheisms.

blessing in Numbers 6, the traditional Jewish prayer of peace, the *Sam Shalom,* and the *Alenu* prayer which is an act of hope and adoration at the close of most synagogue services:

> *Yahweh* spoke to Moses and said, 'Say this to Aaron and his sons:
>
> "This is how you are to bless the sons of Israel.[61] You shall say to them:
>
> May *Yahweh* bless you and keep you.
>
> May *Yahweh* let his face shine on you and be gracious to you.
>
> May *Yahweh* uncover his face to you and bring you peace."
>
> This is how they are to call down my name on the sons of Israel, and I will bless them.' (6:22-27)
>
> Grant us peace, thy most precious gift, O eternal source of peace, and enable Israel to be its messenger to the peoples of the earth. Bless our country that it may ever be a stronghold of peace and its advocate in the council of nations. May contentment reign within its borders, health and happiness within its homes.[62] Strengthen the

---

61

While in the context of Numbers this blessing is given only to the sons of Israel, as the understanding of the nature of the divine moves from the nationalistic *Yahweh* of the pre-exhilic period to the universalized post-exhilic *Eloh-im,* the God of all creation, the great prophets like II Isaiah realize that the blessings of peace are for all mankind, as is prayed in the *Sam Shalom.*

62

It is enlightening to compare this prayer for peace (and health and happiness within the borders of Israel) and the hope for peace based on holiness that Karen Armstrong advocates in her new book, **Jerusalem: One City, Three Faiths,** with the recent positions taken by Prime Minister Netanyahu and the Likud's political coalition with several extremist religious-political parties. Can there ever be peace without the holiness of justice? Or, to paraphrase the prayer: Can there be peace without the holy justice of both Israelis and Palestinians hallowing each others **"homes,"** not just their own homes but those which to belong to the other. The final chapter presents an argument for the kind of moral chosenness, chosenness **TO BE**

bonds of friendship and fellowship among the inhabitants of all lands. Plant virtue in every soul, and may the love of thy name hallow every home and every heart. Praised be thou, O Lord, Giver of peace. (Ferguson, **War and Peace in the World's Religions**, 97)

> May the time not be distant, O God, when thy name shall be worshipped in all the earth, when unbelief and error be no more. Fervently we pray that the day may come when all men shall invoke thy name, when corruption and evil shall give way to purity and goodness, when superstition shall no longer enslave the mind, nor idolatry blind the eye, when all who dwell on earth shall know that to thee alone every knee must bend and every tongue give homage. O may all, created in thine image, recognize that they are brethren, so that, one in spirit and one in fellowship, they may be forever united before thee. Then shall thy kingdom be established on earth and the word of thine ancient . . . [prophets] be fulfilled. The Lord will reign for ever and ever. (Ferguson, 97-9)

Often hidden by the spectacle of war, there is a foundation of spiritual greatness in the **Hebrew Bible** that can, and occasionally has, changed the world: a God of Peace. It is now appropriate to explore the theologies of peace in its pages.

Hebrew Terms for Peace

As with the exploration of the theologies of war, the first step is to examine the etymology of the term *shalom*, its cognates, other terms for peace and the various usages of these words which inadequately describe not only human conditions but also relationships. Before beginning, however, a warning is needed concerning the inadequacy of translations and the relationship between *shalom* and chaos. Paul

---

rather than chosenness **TO HAVE**, which is fundamental to "hallowing" the homes of others.

Hanson, in an article in the journal **Interpretation**, describes the relationships among chaos, peace and war:

> The notion of shalom is in turn the key to any effort to identify a biblical perspective on the issues of war and peace. It is important to note that the Hebrew word "shalom" cannot be simply identified with the English word "peace," for it is a much more comprehensive concept. Perhaps the best way to begin to understand shalom is to recognize that it describes the realm where chaos is not allowed to enter, and where life can be fostered free from the fear of all that diminishes and destroys. Similarly if we are to grasp what the Bible has to say about war, it is necessary to avoid a simple identification of *milhama* in the Bible with our definition of war. War in the Bible can be understood only in relation to shalom and chaos, and can best be described as that which transforms the realm of shalom into the condition of chaos. ("War and Peace in the Hebrew Bible," vol. XXXVIII, no.4, 347)

Hanson's warning concerning a simple identification between "peace" and *shalom* is important and substantiated by the etymological study which follows. His recognition about the relationships among chaos, peace and war is also significant as well as his general characterizations that peace is a state in which chaos, either internal or external, has been overcome or at least kept in control while war represents the return of chaos, either internal or external.[63] Because chaos is an ever

---

63

The fear of chaos is a primal fear as old as human consciousness and as new as a child's painful and frightening expulsion from the womb into the world. It never leaves individuals or societies. Most ancient religions attempted to allay this fear in two ways: the practice of magic and the accounts of creation. Since magic has already been described, it needs only be mentioned that one of the purposes of magic in ancient religions was to keep the forces of chaos at bay. Creation, however, was another matter.

Given the empirical and rational aspects of human nature, it is easy to

present power and threat for human beings, individually and collectively, that is, because political and spiritual peace is always a fragile threatened condition incapable of being maintained by human beings alone, the **Hebrew Bible** recognizes that peace must always come as a gift from God. Before examining the nature of God's gift of peace, it is necessary to examine the etymology and uses of the various terms for peace.

Etymologically, the term *shalom* comes from the ancient Semitic root *SLM*,[64]

---

understand the reasons chaos was identified in ancient religions with darkness, hiddenness, and formlessness (that is disorder). It is mostly through sight that humans attempt to order the universe in which they live. It is not accidental that the English word for idea etymologically comes from the Greek verb *eidos*, which means "to see." Most of the great creation mythologies understood creation as the actions of the supernatural (gods) overcoming chaos, usually in a violent conflict (battle, war), and creating pockets of order where human beings could live. As expected, Chaos was identified with darkness, hiddenness, and formlessness. As an example, consider the Shabaka Stone and Genesis 1.

In the Shabaka Stone, one of the Pyramid Texts written during the middle of the third millennium B.C.E., the god Ptah creates the city of Memphis by overcoming four forces: darkness, hiddenness, formlessness, and watery chaos. In Genesis 1, written during the middle of the first millennium, the magnificent *Eloh-im* overcomes the *tehom* (verse 3) which is hidden in darkness, voidness, and formlessness (verse 2). While the Hebrew *tehom* is usually translated as "the deep," "the waters," or "the abyss," it is most adequately translated as the "sea of chaos." In other words, in the most influential creation account to emerge from the Middle East, the created (that is, ordered) world comes into being when the power of *Eloh-im* overcomes chaos (the *tehom*). Understood in this sense, the creation of light on the first day acquires a most important significance. Clearly light cannot refer to what we mean by the term today, nuclear fusion from a star, because the luminaries are yet to be created. In fact, even the terms day and night cannot be taken to mean a 24 hour period without an earth or sun. When verse four claims, "Let there be light," it is claiming "Let there be ORDER in the midst of chaos." The overcoming of chaos requires the power of the divine, a point that is never lost sight of in the **Hebrew Bible**, for either internally or externally, peace (the absence of chaos) cannot be achieved by human beings alone; it is always the gift of God.

[64]

Since the original Hebrew alphabet was a consonantal alphabet, the roots of Hebrew words were two or three consonants, as was the case with early Arabic. Thus, the root of *shalom* (Hebrew for "peace") and *salaam* (Arabic for "peace") are

and it is found in several cognates in the **Hebrew Bible**. *SLM* when used as the root of a verb has several meanings: "to be entire," "to be sound, safe," "to preserve, keep uninjured," "to be complete, finished," "to recompense," and when used with the noun *'el* (god) "to submit oneself in peace."[65] *SLM* as an adjective means "whole," "perfect," "complete," "uninjured," and "sincere." As a noun it has a multitude of uses: "sound, well in health," "safe, secure," "prosperity," "peace," "friendship," "kindness," "salvation" and "salutation upon greeting or departing."

In addition to the root *SLM* and its various cognates, there are several other roots which are used to indicate various kinds of peace: *BRKH* (*berakah*) means "blessing," "peace" and "concord"; *MYSR* (*meyshar*) means "straightness," "uprightness," "equity" and "peace"; *RG`* (*rage`a*) means "still," "quiet" and "peaceful"; and *SLH* (*shalah*) means "to be at rest," "to be secure" and "to be at peace."

In its different roots and cognates, the various dimensions of peace are used over 350 times in the **Hebrew Bible**. The word *shalom* accounts for nearly half of these. As a salutation upon meeting (a greeting) or departing it is usually combined with half a dozen phrases: "depart in peace," "God give you peace," "Peace be unto you,"[66] "Peace, peace be to you," "Peace be within you," "Peace be multiplied to

---

the same root, *SLM*, which essentially means "peace." This is most important in understanding the meanings of the sacred revealed terms *Islam* and *Muslim*. Ironically, the name *Jeru-salem,* in Hebrew, means "City of Peace."

65

See footnote 64 in Chapter Four for the Arabic and Muslim significance of this combination.

66

Today in Arabic speaking cultures, the most common greeting is: *Assalamu 'alaykum* (Peace be upon you). The expected reply is: *Wa'alaykum assalam* (And upon you peace). The most common salutation upon departing is: *Ma'a salama* (Go with peace, safety). The response is: *Allah yisallimak* (May God make you safe). This seems to me to be a far superior salutation than the trite "Have a good day" that is said dozens of times daily in the United States, often to strangers at the end of a financial transaction.

you" and "Peace return to you." Usages other than as a salutation include the following: send away in peace, come in peace, peace in the land, covenant of peace, words of peace, seek peace, peace between _____, time for peace, peace from the Lord, come out in peace, gathered to your grave in peace, speak peace, righteousness and peace, peace of Jerusalem, Prince of Peace, ordain peace, peace and security, publish peace, joy and peace, way of peace, look for peace, take away peace, die in peace, visions of peace, sowing of peace, truth and peace, and peace and uprighteousness. While some of these usages of *shalom* (peace) have meaning for the individual person--for example, those referring to a long life, a healthy life, a prosperous life and a tranquil death, the overwhelming majority of the uses of peace are relational ones: either in terms of social relations with other human beings, where *shalom* is almost a synonym for justice, or in terms of political-national relations with other peoples (nations), where *shalom* basically means the absence of conflict, or in terms of the covenant relationship between the Jewish community (or the nation-state of Israel when one existed) and God, where *shalom* is essentially a synonym for righteousness (fidelity). With the fall of Jerusalem in 586 B.C.E. and the explosive rise of Jewish eschatology, *shalom* acquired a new sense: the eternal peace of salvation through righteousness. Finally, although a sense of individual spiritual peace is not lacking in the **Hebrew Bible**, especially the awareness that even individual spiritual peace must come from God, an explicit theology of individual-spiritual-inner peace awaits the rabbinic writings of the last few centuries B.C.E., writings which were most likely influenced by the Greek concentration on the inner person during the period of Hellenism (the period following Alexander's death in the 3rd century B.C.E.).

Because the understanding of *shalom* in the **Hebrew Bible** maintains a relational center with God from pre-monarchial to post-exhilic times, it is not necessary to divide the study of *shalom* into the historical periods that required such extensive development in the section on war. Instead, the best strategy for examining the nature of *shalom* is a four-fold division: *shalom* as a salutation, *shalom* as a political-communal relation, *shalom* as a spiritual relationship, and *shalom* as an eschatological belief and hope. The first division requires little attention.

The various phrases which use *shalom* as a salutation have already been described. What is important in these salutations is the religious and emotional depth when a person is greeted with *shalom* or departs with the blessing *shalom,* for it is indeed a blessing because its true source is God. In the apparently simple, "Peace be with you," there is expressed a personal wish for others' mental and physical health, financial security, and friendship as well as a prayer to God for their well-being and safety. Thus, *shalom* is a blessing, a thanksgiving and a prayer!

Shalom as a Political-Social Relation

Perhaps the oldest concept of peace in the **Hebrew Bible** is its use to celebrate a military victory. In Judges when Gideon leaves the city of Peneul which has refused to give his soldiers bread, he declares: "When I come again in peace [victory], I will destroy this tower [he destroys the tower of Peneul along with its townspeople]." (8:12) When the prophet Miaaiah's prophecy declares that Ahab will die in the battle at Ramoth-gilead, Ahab has him put into prison and given the following message: "'. . . feed him on nothing but bread and water until I come in peace [back safe and sound, that is victorious].' Miaaiah said, 'If you come back in peace [safe and sound], *Yahweh* has not spoken through me'." (I Kings 22:27-28) The prophet Jeremiah speaks of the Babylonian destruction of Egypt by Nebuchadnezzar in these terms: "He will set fire to the temples of the gods of Egypt; he will burn these gods or carry them off; as a shepherd picks his cloak clean of vermin, so he will pick Egypt clean and leave in peace [without interference, that is, in victory]." (43:12)

A more common early use of the term *shalom* in the sense of political peace is similar to its use today: an agreement of non-hostility or mutual aid between nations, a treaty. Early in Deuteronomy, Moses offers a treaty of peace to the king of Heshbon: "So from the wilderness of Kedemoth I sent envoys to Sihon king of

Heshbon with this message of peace. I mean to pass through your land. I shall go my way, straying neither to the left or right. What food I eat, sell me in return for money; and I will pay for the water I drink." (2:26) In the theology of war against those not occupying promised land, the Deuteronomist advocates efforts at peace first: "When you advance to the attack on any town, first offer it terms of peace. If it accepts these and opens its gates to you, all the people to be found in it shall do forced labor for you and be subject to you." (20:10) While we may find the peace terms unenlightened by modern standards, they represented a considerable moral improvement over the *herem*. As indicated in the previous section on monarchial theologies of war, the pragmatic monarchs of Israel were more often disposed toward a peace treaty than war. The priests and prophets, especially the pre-exhilic ones, were suspicious of peace because they feared such alliances as introducing foreign elements into Hebrew society and thus contributing to the worship of other gods.

Concerning only the nation of Israel, *shalom* often describes three most desirable conditions which result from fidelity to *Yahweh*: the absence of war, national security-safety and national prosperity. The story of Hezekiah is an example. Because previous kings have been unfaithful to *Yahweh*, Israel must be punished, but because Hezekiah has been a faithful king, the prophet Isaiah is sent to Hezekiah to tell him that after his death his sons "will be chosen to be eunuchs in the palace of Babylon," but during his lifetime there will be "peace and security [the absence of war]." (II Kings 20:19) The lesson is clear: fidelity brings peace and prosperity while infidelity results in disaster and destruction. When the prophet Jeremiah ridicules the false prophets of his time, he does so by condemning their lies that war will not come: ". . . the prophets are telling them [the people of Judah], 'You will not see the sword, famine will not touch you; I [*Yahweh*] promise you unbroken peace in this place'." (Jeremiah 14:13) Just before arriving at Sinai, Moses is commanded by God to select judges to be leaders over the Hebrews, and he tells his people that if they are faithful to God's judges (leaders) they will be kept safe and secure : "If you do this--and may God so command you--you will be able to stand the strain, and all . . . will go home in peace [safety and security]." (Exodus 18:23) Finally, *shalom* often indicates prosperity. In the description of the lands of the southern tribes, the Chronicler describes the finding of "good, fat pastures" as land that is "untroubled, peaceful." (I Chronicles 4:40) Psalm 37 promises the faithful of *Yahweh* a land that is good where they will "live in peace [prosperity]" and that the "humble shall have the land for their own to enjoy untroubled peace [abundant prosperity]." (37:11) Isaiah in speaking of the new Jerusalem declares: "Your sons will be taught by *Yahweh*. The prosperity [peace] of your sons will be great." (Isaiah 54:13) In his vision of Messianic salvation, the prophet Zechariah combines peace and prosperity: "It is I *Yahweh* who speaks. For I mean to spread peace everywhere; the vine will give its fruit, the earth its increase, and the heaven its dew." (8:13)[67]

In the previous discussion of peace as communal safety, security and prosperity, the most important dimension of political-communal peace, while glimpsed, still needs clarification. Israel's experience of and promise of peace is founded upon one truth and one alone: the **COVENANT** community of God. Human beings are incapable of creating peace; thus, Israel's peace depends upon fidelity to the covenant, and as an example, remember the reason Hezekiah knew peace in his days was his fidelity to God. The prosperity of the land, protection from its enemies, and internal security depend on fidelity to the covenant Leviticus 26 declares:

> "If you live according to my laws, if you keep my
> commandments and put then into practice, I will give you the rain
> you need at the right time; the earth shall give its produce and the

---

[67]

In an interesting and tragic way, Israel experienced the prosperity of peace before the recent election. According to most economic reports, the economy of Israel was booming because the peace-process was working under the leadership of Peres and Arafat. But this is not that surprising: peace is good for business. With the deterioration of the peace-process and the increase in violence, businessmen began to withdraw from investing in Israel.

trees of the countryside their fruits; you shall thresh until vintage time and gather grapes until sowing time. You shall eat your fill of bread and live secure in your land.

I will give peace to the land, and you shall sleep with none to frighten you. (26:3-6)

In several passages the terms *covenant* and *shalom (peace)* are used interchangeably: "Let there be a sworn treaty [peace] between ourselves and you, and let us make a covenant with you." (Genesis 26:28) Psalm 55 makes this point antithetically by interchanging the breaking of a covenant and war: "he has gone back on his word [violated his covenant] . . . he has war in his heart." (55:20) When Ezekiel envisions a reunited Israel and Judah, he does so in terms of a covenant of peace: "I shall make a covenant of peace with them, an eternal covenant with them." (37:26) In his vision of the new Jerusalem, II Isaiah speaks of an everlasting love that will establish a covenant of peace: ". . . but my love for you will never leave you and my covenant of peace with you will never be shaken. . . . " (54:10) In all the preceding passages and a multitude of others, the message is clear: both internally and externally the peace of Israel comes as a gift from God and requires fidelity to their covenant relationship. The rewards of fidelity are manifold, but the costs of infidelity are horrible and destructive. While fidelity demands many things, fundamental are righteousness and justice. These two expected human responses to the covenant of peace based on God's commandments (laws) are best explored in examining spiritual peace.

Shalom as a Spiritual State

Although little is explicitly said in the **Hebrew Bible** regarding the dimension of individual, spiritual peace, from at least the time of the Yahwist, there was an awareness of this dimension which was also an awareness of both the grandeur and the destructiveness of human nature. In this awareness the **Hebrew Bible** reaches its deepest level of spiritual insight: it is the state of internal war (absence of peace of mind and spirit) that is the cause of external war. To understand this, it is necessary to examine in detail the story of that well known ancient dysfunctional family from the garden.[68]

Before beginning an extensive exegesis of the account of Cain and Abel, it is helpful to understand the relationship between *shalom* (peace, wholeness) and creation[69] as understood by the oldest of the creation theologies in the **Hebrew Bible**, the account of the Yahwist. Peter Craggie in his study titled, **The Problem of War in the Old Testament**, has a chapter on peace which he introduces with a superb

---

[68]

In the analysis which follows it is important to note that the Yahwist's narratives of Adam, Eve and the Garden and Cain and Abel are not to be taken in a simplistic literal manner, that is, they are not an ancient "Days of Our Lives" story of a dysfunctional family. The King James translation in 1611 did considerable harm to the text when it translated *'adam* as Adam. To do so is to change the noun *'adam* into the proper noun (name) Adam. In Hebrew *'adam* is the noun for "man" in the generic sense. Further, everywhere the noun *'adam* occurs in the Hebrew text of Genesis 2, it is attached to the definite article *ha* (the). While there are many differences between a Semitic language like Hebrew and an Indo-European one like English, one feature they both share is that the definite article *the* is never used with a personal name. Thus, the correct translation of *ha'adam* is "the man" or "man." In other words, everywhere the noun *ha'adam* occurs ("the man" or "man"), it has the same meaning as the statement: "the whale is a mammal." Genesis 2-4, then, are not chapters about an individual family but a powerful narrative about human nature, the relationship between God and human beings, and the costs of sin, that is, alienation from God. Understood in this way, not only do the inconsistencies that have plagued literal interpretations of Genesis disappear, but the narrative becomes even more important, as the analysis of Cain's *'awon* (sin) should reveal. Speaking as a philosopher who has studied the major ethical theories of the West, I must honestly say that reflecting on the human drama of Genesis 2-4 has shed as much light on the moral nature and responsibilities of our humanness as most of the philosophical corpus. In simple dramatic form, the Yahwist identifies the fundamental moral question and the basic costs of human immorality as well as the causes of such immorality. Whoever he was, the Yahwist was one of the great writers of the Western world.

[69]

It is important to remember that the fundamental idea in creation is the overcoming of chaos and the establishing of order. See footnote 63 in this chapter.

description of the theological connections among peace, creation, human nature and the relationship between humans and God:

> *Relationship* is rooted in creation itself; man is created by God and placed in this world in order to enjoy relationship with God. In the language of Genesis, man in the garden enjoyed that relationship with God before the fall. Man's primary nature, as a creature of God, was that of wholeness or completeness [*shalom*]-- which is of the essence of peace, with both God and man. But the rebellion of man, represented [metaphorically] by the fall, introduced *alienation* between God and man; the primary condition of wholeness was exchanged for the fragmentation of life. . . . Complete relationship, with God and fellow man, is the original (or God-given) human condition. To express it differently, peace is the primary condition, and the memory of it and desire for it lingers within us all. But alienation has become the primary characteristic of the human condition, and alienation is a fragmentation of human life, rather than a wholeness. And among the many expressions of the fragmentation . . . war is but one. Alienation between man and God leads to alienation between man and man, and war is one manifestation of alienation between man and man.
>
> . . . .
>
> But, in those very years when the alienation of the Hebrew people from their God gained ascendancy over relationship, the seeds of *hope* were being sown. The prophets . . . perceived the true spiritual state of their people, of which the wars, defeats, and disasters of their times were but outward manifestations. Not only did man need a deep word of God within his heart if he was to be restored to a full and vital relationship with God, but also true peace would be found in God alone, and not in man. (86-87)

Craggie is basically correct when he notes that it was the prophets who were able to see beyond the violence of their times to the human condition of alienation which was the cause of such destructiveness, but it should also be noted that not all of the prophets possessed the vision to universalize this insight to include all human beings as the alienated children of God. However, even though this moral insight did not ripen into awareness until the post-exhilic period, the theological seeds for its universalization were present at least as early as the writings of the Yahwist in the 10th century B.C.E..

The story of Cain and Abel has been for centuries a paradigm of the tragic consequences of envy and anger externalized as murder. The etymologies of several key Hebrew terms in the account provide an even deeper spiritual knowledge of the consequences of alienation from God. The part of the narrative most illustrative is the following: (Words in bold print are for emphasis and later analysis)

> Time passed and Cain brought some of the produce of the soil as an offering for *Yahweh*, while Abel for his part brought the first-born of his flock and some of their fat as well. *Yahweh* looked with favor on Abel and his offering. But he did not look with favor on Cain and his offering, and Cain was very **angry** and downcast. *Yahweh* asked Cain, 'Why are you **angry** and downcast? If you are ill disposed, is not sin at the door like a crouching beast hungering for you, which you must master?' Cain said to his brother Abel, 'Let us go out'; and while they were in the open country, Cain set on his brother Abel and **killed** [murdered] him.
>
> *Yahweh* asked Cain, 'Where is your brother Abel?' 'I do not know', he replied. **'Am I my brother's guardian** [keeper]?'[70]

---

[70]

Cain's defensive rebuttal, "Am I my brother's keeper?," is the fundamental moral (ethical) question. The issue that lies at the heart of any ethical system or moral problem is Cain's question. The reason for this is straightforward: morality

Yahweh asked. 'Listen to the sound of your brother's **blood**, crying out to me from the **ground**. Now be accursed and driven from the **ground** that has opened its mouth to receive your brother's **blood** at your hands. When you till the **ground** it shall no longer yield you any of its produce. You shall be a **fugitive** and **wanderer** over the earth. Then Cain said to *Yahweh*, 'My **punishment** is more than I can bear. See! Today you drive me from this **ground'**. (Genesis 4:3-14)

In verse 13, Cain responds to *Yahweh* in these words: "My punishment (sin) is more than I can bear." In Hebrew, Cain says: "My *'awon* is more than I can bear." The Hebrew term *'awon* is especially rich in meaning, and more Oriental than Occidental in emphasis. It means: "iniquity," "sin," "guilt," "crime" and "punishment." These various meanings are important in understanding the richness of the term, the Oriental emphasis, and its difference from the more familiar Anglo-Saxon *synne* (etymological origin for the English *sin*). The Hebrew concept of *'awon* includes all of the following: (1) the wrongful act; (2) the guilt (or shame) of the actor, that is the Eastern emphasis upon wrong as basically an internal state or condition; and (3) the consequences of the act, that is, the punishment. The internal aspects of sin and the inevitable consequences of sin have tended to become externalized in Western religious thought, and, as a result, the term *sin* has come to refer mostly to the act. The Hebrew *'awon* does not separate the internal from the external, and this is most

---

concerns human relationships. Whatever principles an ethical theory argues, it must argue them in terms of their impact on human relationships. In other words, moral concerns are always transcendent, that is, they involve human relationships. In terms that may be too simplistic for some modern ethicists, morality centers on the ways in which we treat each other as human beings. From this perspective, Robinson Crusoe has no significant moral concerns until Friday arrives. This does not mean that he may not have several value concerns about his self-relationship and possibly relationships with his non-human environment, but these are not essentially moral in nature. Even if one admits moral concerns into the realms of animals and the environment, and there are persuasive reasons for doing so, the human-human dimension still remains the foundation for morality.

204

significant for understanding the deeper moral lesson in the narrative.

When Cain says, "My *'awon* is more than I can bear," he is referring to the wrongness of the act, the guilt he carries in relation to his brother and God, the shame he bears in relation to himself and the consequences (punishment) for his act. While the first three, the wrongness, guilt and shame, are of considerable religious and moral significance, it is the punishment that requires attention at this point. To understand the self-inflicted nature of Cain's *'awon*, there are three other Hebrew terms in the passage that require elucidation. They are: *dam*, which translates as "blood," *'adam*, which translates as "man," and *'adamah*, which translates as "ground" or "soil." An examination of each of these terms reveals that the root of the words for man (*'adam*) and ground or soil (*'adamah*) is the word blood (*dam*). In other words, the word for man (*'adam*) is constructed by adding the prefix *'a* to the term for blood (*dam*) and the word for soil is made by adding the suffix *ah* to the noun for man (*'adam*). This construction is not mere coincidence. Early Mesopotamian mythologies often identified the vital force (mana) which gives life to physical bodies with blood; thus, the identification between *dam* and *'adam*. Also, many of the earliest societies were aware that, at death, the body when placed in the ground decayed, that is, seemed to return to the soil; thus, the identification between *'adam* and *'adamah*.[71]

Given the power of imitation and similarity in primal thinking identified as the homoeopathic principle Sir James G. Frazer noted in the earliest forms of magic,[72] the body's returning to the soil must mean that it came from the soil. This

---

[71]

    This latter identification, perhaps correlation is a better term, is most likely the original meaning of the traditional "ashes to ashes, dust to dust" of the traditional Jewish and Christian burial services.

[72]

    While Frazer's evolutionary thesis about religion evolving from magic has been dismissed by most recent scholars, his identification of the patterns of Sympathetic Magic in his monumental work, **The Golden Bough**, are still accepted

idea is certainly the view of the Yahwist. Based on this homoeopathic principle and the rich internal-external meaning of the concept *'awon*, the significance of Cain's lament that his *'awon* is more than he can endure far exceeds any simple translation of *'awon* as either "punishment" or "sin." He means that his wrongful act, his guilt-shame, and his punishment are all more than he can endure.

But what is his punishment? This critical question reveals the depth of the Yahwist's understanding of human nature and the costs of alienation. According to the text of Genesis, his punishment is: "Now be accursed and driven from the **ground** . . . When you till the **ground** it shall no longer yield you any of its produce." Cain's punishment can be paraphrased as follows: Cain, the man (*'adam*), is cursed from the ground (*'adamah*). The ground (*'adamah*) will no longer yield to him its produce or strength. In other words, Cain's sin (*'awon*) has alienated him from not only the ground but also from himself, for the *'adam* and the *'adamah* are a whole, that is, alienated from one another, and they are fragmented. This fragmentation is one of the great moral lessons of all time. When any human (*'adam*) loses his inner wholeness (his inner peace, his *shalom*) and becomes fragmented by internal states such as envy and anger, states which are the causes of the violence externally actuated in murder and war, they become alienated not only from God but from their natural wholeness. Or, to restate this truth in terms of chaos, internal chaos causes external chaos. In this sense, Cain does not need an external punisher, his war with himself (his internal chaos) has murdered (fragmented) his wholeness (inner peace, his *shalom*), and thus, alienated him from both God and himself.[73] Thus, internal war (chaos) breeds external war (chaos). Since the power of this

---

as definitive patterns by most anthropologists, archaeologists, and scholars of the ancient world from other disciplines.

73

    For a more complete development of the internal states which are the causes of external destruction, see: Randall, Albert B. "The Seven Deadly Bad Faiths (Sins): An Existential Interpretation," **Journal of Interdisciplinary Studies,** vol.II, no. 1/2, 1990, pp.39-55.

internal chaos (sin) is so dominating, humans cannot achieve their wholeness (their *shalom*) without the help of God. It is for this reason that the great prophets identified *shalom* with righteousness, fidelity, justice, truth and love. Before considering the eschatological dimensions of *shalom,* it is important to examine these correlations.

Isaiah correlates both justice and righteousness with peace in a manner which identifies the source of both as a gift from God and as the foundations for *shalom:*

> Once more there will be poured on us / the spirit from above; / . . . .
>
> In the wilderness justice will come to live / and integrity [righteousness] in the fertile land; / integrity [righteousness] will bring peace, / justice gives lasting security [*shalom*]. (Isaiah 32:15-16)

The Psalmist claims that: "In his days [the promised *Mesiah*] virtue [righteousness] will flourish, a universal peace till the moon is no more." (72:7) In Malachi, the covenant of *Yahweh* with Levi is described in terms of peace, righteousness, justice and truth: "My covenant was with him; it stood for life and peace, and these were what I gave him; it stood for fear and trembling, and he respected me and stood in awe of my name [he stood in righteousness]. The teaching of truth was in his mouth. . . . He walked with me in integrity and virtue [righteousness and justice]." (2:5-6) In Zechariah, the prophet speaks a message from *Yahweh* which commands truth, peace and love: "These are the things that you must do. Speak the truth to one another; let the judgments at your gates be such as conduce to peace. . . . Love truth and peace." (8:16-19)

These examples indicate the Yahwist's implicit theology of peace is later deepened and enriched by the prophets: Since sin alienates human beings from themselves, other humans, and God, and the power of sin (internal war, chaos) is so dominating, only with the help of God can anyone overcome the predisposition of human nature for chaos (brokenness) and recover that *shalom* (wholeness) for which humans were created. This restored *shalom*, then, becomes the foundation for living in righteousness, justice, truth, and love. The message of *shalom* gives spiritual depth to the **Hebrew Bible** and offers a hope which is also central for the other two children of Abraham. Before exploring the theologies of war and peace developed by the second child, Christianity, it is necessary to examine the final dimension of peace in the **Hebrew Bible**, the eschatological one that had, and continues to have, a seminal influence on both Christians and Muslims.

Shalom as an Eschatological belief and Hope

In works of the 20th century French philosopher Gabriel Marcel are found some of the richest insights concerning hope that have been written. One of those insights is especially relevant to the development of Jewish eschatology. Marcel writes that it is only when there is the temptation to despair that hope is possible: the greater the temptation to despair the greater the hope.[74] For both individual Jews and the Jewish faith, the eighth and sixth centuries B.C.E. were times of such horrible destruction that the temptations to despair were immediate and intense.[75] Without a message of hope, a faith dies, and prophets arose in both of these times of destruction and despair to offer an astounding hope: a hope for more than just survival but for a new world of righteousness and justice, that is, a hope for a salvation transcending the finite limitations of human existence and restoring the

---

[74]

Gabriel Marcel's most important thoughts concerning hope were formed during the first world war when he became the leader of a small group within the Red Cross who attempted to determine the fate of French MIAs and when he accepted the responsibility for sharing his information with their despairing-hoping family members. His insights on despair and hope continued to develop as he experienced the Nazi occupation of France during the second world war.

[75]

In many ways, for both individual Jews and the Jewish community of faith, the Holocaust in our century confronted them with many of the same dangerous temptations to despair.

shalom of the human spirit. While some prophets were not able to see beyond a chauvinistic vision of this salvation for Israel alone which required a *herem* to eradicate evil, a few by the grace of God were able to envision a new world order that belonged to all mankind. Since the former have already been examined in the post-exhilic theologies of cosmic holy war, this final section of Chapter Two concentrates on the latter: those whose cosmic eschatologies transcended national and ethnic identifications. However, before doing so, one additional comment of fairness is required: even for those whose eschatological visions were predisposed to chauvinism, many of them evidenced a tension that received its first adequate resolution in the eschatological visions of the great unknown prophet of the Babylonian Exile, II Isaiah. A tension clarified by asking the following question: does the eschatological peace of salvation belong only to Israel or to all mankind?

Two tasks now remain: to relate the eschatological hope for peace to salvation and to examine the role of the *Mesiah* who initiates this new age, this new kingdom of God's *shalom*. Passages concerning the *shalom* of eschatological salvation abound, but among the most important are those in Ezekiel (which are predisposed to the national chauvinism mentioned earlier) and II Isaiah (whose greatness is found in his transcending the limitations of henotheism and ethnic-religious chauvinism). Ezekiel, in a vision that is less universal than that of II Isaiah, speaks of the reunion of Israel and Judah, their re-settling of the land and re-building of the Temple in the Messianic Age with a new David as their king in words that promise eternal salvation in God's covenant of peace:

> They will live in it [the promised land], they, their children, their children's children, for ever. David my prince is to be their king forever. I will make a covenant of peace with them, an eternal covenant with them. . . . I shall settle my sanctuary among them forever. I shall make my home above them; I will be their God, they shall be my people. And the nations will learn that I am *Yahweh* the

sanctifier of Israel, when my sanctuary is with them forever. (Ezekiel 37:26-28)

In this passage, Ezekiel presents a concise statement of the more chauvinistic tradition of eschatology which emerged near the end of the Exile and even more strongly in the period following the return to Jerusalem. In an earlier passage, he even uses the image of David as the shepherd of *Yahweh* and the people as the flock of *Yahweh*. Even though these pastoral images are quite peaceful, most likely, Ezekiel's *Mesiah* was to be a warrior first and a man of peace second.

Ezekiel's vision of the salvation of Israel stands in contrast to that of II Isaiah whose cosmic salvation extends beyond the borders of Israel and is accomplished by a servant who initiates the Messianic Age through suffering the brokenness of others in order to restore their *shalom* (wholeness). Isaiah 56 indicates the salvation of the Messianic Age is for all the righteous, not only Israel:

Thus says *Yahweh*; Have a care for justice, act with integrity [righteousness], for soon my salvation will come and my integrity be manifest.

Blessed is the man who does this and the son of man who clings to it: observing the sabbath, not profaning it, and keeping his hand from every evil deed.

Let no foreigner who has attached himself to *Yahweh* say, '*Yahweh* will surely exclude me from his people'. Let no eunuch say, 'And I, I am a dried-up tree'.

For *Yahweh* says this: To the eunuchs who observe my sabbaths, and resolve to do what pleases me and cling to my covenant, I will give in my house and within my walls, a monument and a name better than sons and daughters; I will give them an everlasting name that shall never be effaced.

Foreigners who have attached themselves to *Yahweh* to serve him and to love his name and be his servants--all who observe the sabbath, not profaning it, and cling to the covenant--these I bring to my holy mountain. I will make them joyful in my house of prayer. . . . for my house of prayer will be called a house of prayer for all the peoples.[76]

It is the Lord *Yahweh* who speaks, who gathers the outcasts of Israel: there are others I will gather besides those already gathered. (56:1-8)

In II Isaiah's vision of the new Age, all those who live in justice and righteousness are the people of God, and to them belongs the Messianic Age of peace, that is, the restoration of wholeness that is salvation. The importance of II Isaiah's universalizing the people of God can hardly be underestimated, but his identification of the Messianic figure who initiates this Age through suffering[77] rather than holy war raises his spiritual insights above all national and ethnic chauvinisms and elevates his message as belonging to the greatest spiritual visions of mankind. The key chapter is 53:

And yet ours were the sufferings he bore, / our sorrows he carried. / But we thought of him as someone punished, /

76

Phil Judaeus, 25 B.C.E. to 40 C.E., one of the most important Jewish philosopher-theologians of the Hellenic period interprets these comments concerning God's house of prayer as referring to the invisible Temple whose foundations are the heavens rather than the visible Temple at Jerusalem. This point is further examined in the final chapter.

77

Interpretations as to the identity of this "Suffering Servant" have been the cause of considerable controversy, especially between Jewish and Christian scholars. Jewish theology has tended to identify the Servant with Israel while Christian theology unquestionably identifies the Servant with the crucified Christ. It is the contention of this study, as developed in the final chapter, that the identification, which cannot be determined apart from the presuppositions of faith, is less significant than the awareness that God's peace and salvation come from love and suffering rather than holy war and belong to all human beings.

struck by God, and brought low. / Yet he was pierced
through for our faults, / crushed for our sins. / On him lies
a punishment that brings us peace [*shalom*], / and through
his wounds we are healed [made whole].

. . . .

Yahweh has been pleased to crush him with suffering. / If he
offers his life in atonement, / he shall see his heirs, he shall
have a long life / and through him what *Yahweh* wishes will
be done.

His soul's anguish over / He shall see the light and be
content. / By his sufferings shall my servant justify man, /
taking their faults on himself.   Hence I will grant whole
hoards for his tribute, / he shall divide the spoil with the
mighty, / for surrendering himself to death / and letting
himself be taken for a sinner, / while he was bearing the
faults of many / and praying all the time for sinners. (53:4-
5, 10-12)

In these two selections from II Isaiah, Jewish prophecy reached a pinnacle of spiritual
insight unencumbered by the limitations of henotheism and racial-national bigotry.
New spiritual dimensions of love, suffering, forgiveness, hope, salvation and *shalom*
were suddenly offered to all human beings. Unfortunately, the universal message of
salvation and peace in II Isaiah was lost in the conflicts and theological disputes
among the Jews after the Exile.[78] As a result, chauvinistic eschatologies of holy war
often overpowered those of universal eschatological peace.

In concluding his article on war and peace in **Interpretation**, Paul Hanson

---

[78]

It should also be noted that both Christians and Muslims have also during
times of distress and conflict lost sight of their messages of universal salvation, peace
and hope and as a consequence have reverted to theologies of holy war.

provides a concise statement of the "engulfing" of *shalom* by war in the post-exhilic period as well as a most challenging charge for the children of Abraham who live today:

> How can we explain this new vision of the future [that is, the one that quickly develops after the Exile], in which the fascination with *Yahweh*'s ruthless punishment of all those, within and without the people of Israel, who were regarded as enemies overwhelmed the earlier vision [that of II Isaiah] of immanent universal peace?. . . In the period after the return from the exile, the community was not united . . . but divided into factions. . . . Zadokites strove against Levites, pragmatists against visionaries, followers of one prophet against followers of another. With the loss of their primary grounding in allegiance to one authority, righteousness and compassion parted company. Striving parties defined righteousness in terms excluding all rivals, and compassion was reserved for fellow party members. Leaders more zealous for their own power than for Yahweh's reign of peace imposed their definitions of justice by force. And inevitably they redefined Yahweh to fit their own image.[79] As regards Israel's relation to other nations, it is not surprising that the influx of chaos into the heart of the community extinguished the light of Yahweh's salvation which Servant Israel had been called to bring to the nations. As regards the vision of Yahweh's return, shalom was engulfed by images of war. (360)

Following this historical description, Hanson concludes with a challenging

---

[79]

    It is disturbing how accurately Hanson's description of the post-exhilic time of return to Jerusalem fits dozens of periods in the history of Christianity and Islam. Additionally, it is also a fairly accurate description of the dangerous fragmentation that internally plagues the present nation of Israel and seriously endangers the peace-process as well as the spiritual health of the nation of Israel.

charge that is also a warning:

> Certainly a civilization possessing the technology both to end world
> hunger and to end human life on this planet should take seriously its
> own location midway between Second Isaiah's invitation to become
> servants bringing God's salvation to the ends of the earth and the
> apocalyptist's warning of the chaos hastened by the society which
> turns its back on God's righteousness and compassion. (361)

The appropriateness of this charge and warning gives moral substance and influence to the eschatological message of prophets as long as the message is a universalized hope for righteousness, justice and peace. In keeping with this moral hope, the eschatological vision of I Enoch[80] provides a suitable ending for this chapter on war and peace in the **Hebrew Bible** and a suitable transition to the next chapter on Christian views of war and peace:

> And that angel came to me and greeted me with his voice and said to
> me: 'You are the Son of man who was born to righteousness, and
> righteousness remains over you, and the righteousness of the Head of
> Days will not leave you.' And he said to me, 'He proclaims peace to
> you in the name of the world which is to come; for from there peace
> has come from the creation of the world; and so you shall have it for
> ever and ever and ever. . . . And so there will be length of days with
> the Son of Man and the righteous will have peace and an upright way
> in the name of the Lord of Spirits for ever and ever. (I Enoch 71:14-
> 17)

---

[80]

    I and II Enoch are eschatological books that were not included in the **Hebrew Bible**. They were later included in the **Pseudepigrapha**. Although not in the canon of the Masoretic text, these two writings had considerable influence on the development of Jewish and Christian eschatologies.

CHAPTER THREE
CHRISTIANITY AND THE ESCHATOLOGICAL
PRINCE OF PEACE

Paul Hanson's descriptive warning of the "engulfing" of peace by war and the consequent separating of righteousness from compassion when historical circumstances allow extremist theologies to achieve political power applies not only to post-exhilic Judaism but tragically to Christianity and Islam as well. When this happens, the *herem* (holy war) as God's justice (destruction of external evil and purgation of internal uncleanliness) re-emerges into new, but also old, forms of genocide, ethnic cleansing, pogroms and holocausts. The anthropomorphism of re-creating God in their own ethnic-religious image by extremist religious groups who believe themselves to be the Chosen Ones, and the distorted identification of their enemies as God's enemies is destructive in at least two significant ways: first, there is the mental and physical violence directed at the OTHER (the enemies of God) and the religious violence of Cain's *awon*. In other words, the Chosen Ones injure their own spirituality, that is, they destroy their spiritual potential to grow in the true image of God. In a tragically destructive way, the victimizers become their own victims, that is the Chosen become victims of their self-righteous chosenness. One of the most horribly destructive examples of this kind of distorted theology in the history of Christianity occurred in Germany during the first half of the twentieth century: the Aryan *herem* of the *Reichskirce* (the official state Church of Germany during the period of National Socialism) against the Jews of Europe.[1]

One of the clearest examples of the human destructiveness and religious distortion of this kind of religious theology was the notorious "Godesberg Declaration" of April 1939, which was incorporated in the program of the Research Institute into Jewish Influence on German Church Life. The Institute opened on May 6, 1939 with the aim of "dejudaising" the *Reichskirche*:

> The foundation of this Institute is based on the conviction that Jewish influence on all areas of German life, including therefore that of religion and of the church, must be brought to light and eliminated.
>
> Christianity has nothing in common with Judaism. From the Gospel of Christ on it has developed in opposition to Judaism and has always been attacked by the latter. Its eternal truth has been of decisive importance in our people's history of wedding Germany into one. The eternal power of this truth means that particularly in the Germany of our own day Christianity has the task of promoting a true renewal of genuine religious life in our nation. Since alien Jewish influences have gained a foothold within Christianity itself over the course of its historical development, the Dejudaization of the Church and Christianity has become the inescapable and decisive task for contemporary church life; it is the presupposition for the future of Christianity.
>
> With this aim in mind the task of the Institute is to make an exact and detailed investigation into the manner and the degree of Jewish influence on church life by thorough scholarly research.

---

[1]

One of the ironies of the Nazi Final Solution is it espoused a theology that was as old as the Christian **Old Testament**. Nazi theology was little more than a modification of the *herem* of pre-exhilic Judaism, that is, it fit well with the views of holy war in Judges, Samuel, and Deuteronomy.

Leading scholars and churchmen will work together side by side in their determination to carry our this task.

On the basis of the results of scholarly research it then will be possible to rid the church life of the German people of those elements which derive from Jewish influence and to clear the way for a faith springing from the unadulterated Gospel of Christ to place itself at the disposal of the German people for the creation of its religious community. (Peter Matheson, **The Third Reich and the Christian Churches**, 81-2)[2]

Just as many Christians today look back at Germany and question how such distorted theologies could have developed within Christianity, many black and Indian Americans look back at Christianity and question how it could ever have been used

---

2

If it were not for the much too common occurrence of such theologies of chosenness and holy war in the history of all three monotheisms, the historical ignorance and theological stupidity of such thinking would be laughable; but millions of victims of such *herem* cleansings throughout Western history cannot be so easily ignored, not without overwhelming costs to the human spirit. The Nazi revival of an ancient holy war theologies in their anthropomorphizing of God (re-creating God in the image of the Chosen), their identification of the Chosen Ones as the Germans (Aryans), their manifest destiny to rule the unchosen (the world was their promised land), and their program of ethnic cleansing of the unclean (the Jews, the killers of Christ) were not new events in the history of Western monotheism. Theologically, to completely "dejudaize" Christianity would be to destroy it. Whether Christians are comfortable with the relationship between Judaism and Christianity or not, there is no central belief in Christianity that does not have its origins in Judaism. To use a metaphor, to "dejudaize" the Tree of Christianity would be to cut out its roots, then the whole Tree would die. This, however did not stop the "scholars and theologians" of the *Reichskirche* from identifying the Aryans as the Chosen People and establishing the pure Aryan ancestry of Jesus. Their anthropomorphism is evident: they re-created God and the Christ in their own image. Thus, like Cain, they became victims of their own *awon* as did millions of other human beings. As noted before, when lived with humility and toleration, the sacred is a source for those beliefs and values that contribute to the growth of the human spirit, but when distorted, the human spirit looses its way, and the spiritual and historical destruction which so often results is often overwhelming.

to support the atrocities of slavery and the slaughters of manifest destiny. Part of the answer to these questions lies in understanding the historical circumstances that gave rise to such times of religious travesty; part of the answer is to be found in an awareness of what is sometimes called the darker side of human nature[3]; and, the final part of the answer must be discovered in the fundamental **canon** of Christianity, the **New Testament** and its theologies of war and peace. Since the roots from which these theologies grow is post-exhilic Judaism, especially the Hellenic and Roman periods, it is necessary to describe the historical and religious situation into which Christianity was born and nurtured.

Many of the more important historical events and religious aspects of the Jewish world as it entered the Common Era have already been mentioned: at his death, Alexander's conquests were divided between the Ptolemies and the Secculids; the Maccabees established for several centuries a quasi-Jewish state only to be conquered by the Romans who remained in control of Palestine long past the writing

---

[3]

Since human bigotry in its most common forms--ethnic, racial, religious, national and sexual--is evidenced throughout the entirety of human history, it is possible to argue that there may be a biological basis for the psychological division fundamental to such a universal phenomena: the division between "Us" and "Them," that is, between the "The People" and "The Other." Possibly that basis is: **xenophobia**, which is "fear of that which is different." Such xenophobia may itself be a biological survival technique, for such fear constantly keeps an animal alert to danger, the danger of that which is different. During times of internal turmoil or external threat, human groups (communities, nations, religions, etc.) experience a growth of xenophobia. This contributes to the dehumanizing of those who represent a threat to the security or purity of one's own group, and, thus, the destruction of the Other becomes more easily justified. It is important to understand, however, that finding a possible biological basis for human bigotry does not religiously or morally justify it; rather it alerts one to the constant danger of such thinking. This last thought can be put into the religious language of revelation: Since humans are created in the **image** of God, even though they share such traits as xenophobia with the beasts of the fields, they are expected to live in ways that far transcend bestial behavior. Or to use a more philosophical approach, even though human beings are animals, they are **thinking** animals; thus, they cannot blame or justify their destructiveness on their animal nature.

period of the **New Testament**; and, the Jewish Diaspora (the dispersion of the Jews around the Mediterranean) had three major centers--Alexandria (Egypt), Babylon (Mesopotamia), and Jerusalem (Palestine). Further, throughout the Mediterranean world the influences of the Greeks as transmitted by the Romans were invading many cultures.[4] The Alexandrian and Babylonian Jewish communities were partly insulated from the powerful and increasing eschatology of the Palestinian community for several reasons: their distances from the sacred, holy lands of the prophets, their wealth, their intellectual communities, and their more cosmopolitan environments. In Palestine, however, where Roman occupation was never religiously accepted, the end of the last century B.C.E. and the beginning of the Common Era evidenced a passion for eschatology approaching a religious fever among some religious groups as they anticipated and prayed for the long awaited *Mesiah*.

Religiously, the Jewish community of Palestine was fractured into many religious and political sectarian groups. Among the more important were: the Zealots, whose agenda was the political overthrow of the Romans[5]; the Sadducees, who represented the "old time" religion before the Exile; the Pharisees, who incorporated most of the new elements of post-exhilic theology into their religious

---

[4]

Historians refer to this influence as **Hellenizing**, that is, the spreading of Greek values, beliefs, philosophy, religion, and language throughout the Mediterranean. One immediate effect of Hellenizing on Christianity was the writing of the books of the **New Testament** in *koine* (common) Greek.

[5]

The Zealots had a momentary success in their political rebellion during the reign of Nero (54-68 C.E.) when they initiated the Jewish-Roman War of 66-70, and a smaller group gained control of Herod the Great's invincible fortress at Masada. The Masada Zealots survived the Roman retribution for several months past the destruction of Jerusalem and the Temple because of the almost insurmountable cliffs of Masada. However, after spending months building a dirt road to the top of the cliffs, the Romans invaded the fortress only to find the ritual suicide (sacrifice?) of over nine hundred men, women, and children. Today, Masada is a shrine for Israelis and a monument of Jewish resistance to oppression. Needless to say, that for the more extremist religious groups, Masada is also a holy war memorial.

rituals and thinking; and the Essenes, one of many separatist groups who judged both the Pharisees and the Sadducees to be polluted religious groups seduced by the wealth and power of the world, and, consequently, the Essenes withdrew from the world into ascetic, desert communities whose beliefs centered on an inward repentance and an immanent cosmic eschatology.[6]   Whenever the son of Mary and

---

[6]

    Regarding the Essenes there has been, and still is, considerable interest in their possible connections with Qumran, the ascetic desert prophet known as John the baptizer and Jesus.

    Each deserves a brief comment. Of the eleven caves in which the collection of ancient manuscripts called the Dead Sea Scrolls were found, six of them are within a hundred yards of the ancient community at Qumran. Scholars are still debating who built and resided at Qumran. There are three major positions today: (1) it was a desert retreat of the ascetic, eschatological Essenes who wrote and copied the Dead Sea Scrolls and hid them when the Romans destroyed Jerusalem and much of the surrounding territory in 70 C.E.; (2) it was a prosperous "Camel Pit-Stop" for the important caravan trade coming from the Gulf of Aqaba toward Damascus; or (3) it was the winter home of a group of wealthy Sadducees because Jerusalem is rather cold during part of the winter due to its altitude. The evidence today seems to better fit (1) than the others, but the question is still open.

    Although there is little information about the message of the desert preacher John the baptizer other than what is in the gospel stories, many scholars think John may have been an Essene or may have spent considerable time with them before he began his preaching of repentance, the immanent coming of the kingdom of God and the criticisms of Herod that may have led to his death. The **Qur'an** includes no passage which specifies the nature of John's death; consequently, most Muslim tradition believes that because he was a prophet of God, God would not allow one of His prophets to suffer the horrible death of be-heading described in the **New Testament**. Thus, according to common interpretations of the **Qur'an**, John died a natural death in old age, and Muslim tradition claims that his body was enshrined in the great Umayyad Mosque at Damascus. However, see footnote #131 in the fourth chapter for a variant interpretation by Yusuf Ali.

    Because of the similarity in the preachings of Jesus and John--the repentance that leads to rebirth, the spiritual cleansing of baptism, and the immanent coming of the kingdom of God--many Christian scholars think Jesus may have spent some time with the Essenes during that period of his life the gospel stories leave silent: from about 12 years of age until his early thirties.

Joseph came into the world,[7] he came into a Jewish environment in Palestine seething with political unrest, religious fever, and eschatological expectations and questions. Two of those questions were of utmost significance for the beginnings of Christianity. Was the Son of Man (that is, the *Mesiah*, the *Christos*) to be a Warrior *Shopet* from the historical lineage of David **OR** a Suffering Servant (a Prince of Peace)? Was the Son of Man to be a historical figure who would lead the Jews to a rebellion that would free them from the control of Rome and establish a new state of Israel **OR** a cosmic eschatological figure who would bring an end to the old order of creation and issue into existence the new kingdom of God? Palestinian Judaism was alive with such questions. Christianity, in the doctrine of the incarnation, essentially merged both Messianic views: the Son of Man was both a historical person (*Yeshua ben Yusuf*, Joshua the son of Joseph) and a Suffering Servant, cosmic eschatological savior (the *Christos*).[8] Thus, in the midst of expectations of apocalyptic events of

---

[7]

Because of a slight error in the gospel of Matthew in dating the reign of Herod the Great, the birth of Jesus must be placed between 6 and 4 B.C.E..

[8]

It is this claim, more than any other doctrine, that separates Christians from Jews and Muslims: the incarnation. Many Jews and all Muslims accept Jesus as a great prophet, but not the incarnate son of God. Among the claims Christians make for Jesus as the *Mesiah* that are rejected by both Jews and Muslims are: (1) that the death of Jesus on the cross in any way effects atonement for the collective sins of humanity or the sins of the individual; (2) that God became, or would become, incarnate in any human form; and (3) that, as Paul contends, the life and death of Jesus rendered the elaborate system of Jewish (and by extension, Muslim law) functionally useless for salvation. Further, for Jews, among the things expected of the *Mesiah* which Jesus did not accomplish are: (1) the end of Roman oppression of the Jews; (2) the restoration of the state of Israel with a Davidic king as its leader; (3) the miraculous return of the scattered exiles to Israel, that is, an end of the Jewish Diaspora; and (4) an endless era of world peace, justice and harmony. Muslim views about the *Madhi* are similar, although they interpret his actions in terms of Islam rather than Judaism: he will bring an end to the persecution of Muslims and create an eternal era of world peace, justice, and righteousness. Unfortunately, in both Jewish Messianism and Muslim Madhi'ism, many extremist groups believe that only through holy war can such an era of world peace become a reality.

both natural and historical violence and cosmic hopes of eternal peace, for Christians a child came into the world whose birth was announced in words affirming the victory of peace over war:

> In the countryside close by there were shepherds who lived in the fields and took turns to watch their flocks during the night. The angel of the Lord appeared to them and the glory of the Lord shown round them. They were terrified, but the angel said, 'Do not be afraid, I bring you news of great joy, a joy to be shared by the whole people. Today in the town of David a saviour has been born to you; he is Christ the Lord. And here is a sign for you: you shall find a baby wrapped in swaddling clothes and lying in a manger.' And suddenly with the angel there was a great throng of heavenly host, praising God and singing:
>
> 'Glory to God in the highest heaven,
>
> And peace to men who enjoy his favour'. (Luke 2:8-14)

Before exploring the theologies of war and peace in the **New Testament**, that is, before struggling with the question of "A Warrior *Mesiah*" or a "Suffering Prince of Peace," a brief comparison of Appendices A and C **and** B and D is illustrative. Significant references to war and peace in the **Hebrew Bible** and the **New Testament** are best compared and contrasted in a table format: (figures are approximate, "-" means less than; "+" means more than)

References to War

	Hebrew Bible	**New Testament**
Political War	190+	10-

Without ignoring the significance of this difference between Christians and Jews and Muslims, it is the contention of this study that there is still a solid enough foundation of shared beliefs and values to encourage dialogue and mutual respect rather than conflict and violence among these children of Abraham. The final chapter develops this argument in more detail.

Spiritual War	6+	8+
Eschatological War	100-	20+
	References to Peace	
Political Peace	80+	30-
Spiritual Peace	50-	50+
Eschatological Peace	40+	30+

In examining these figures remember the **New Testament** is slightly less than one-third the size of the **Hebrew Bible**. Thus, for example, 50+ references to spiritual peace in the **New Testament** compared to 50- references to spiritual peace in the **Hebrew Bible** equates to approximately three times as many references to spiritual peace in the former than in the latter when considering the size of each. However, of more significance than these simple contrasts is the ratio of war passages to peace passages in each Holy Book. In the **Hebrew Bible** there are twice as many references to war as peace, and in the **New Testament** there are five times as many references to peace as to war. Of equal comparative importance is the contrast between the two revelations on political war (which includes the category of historical *herem*, historical holy wars): more than 190 references in the **Hebrew Bible** compared to less than 6 in the **New Testament**.[9] Given the **New Testament**

---

[9]

Several reasons for this contrast have already been described. The majority of the books included in the **Hebrew Bible** were written during periods of conquest, occupation, destruction and *Yahweh* henotheism. These were violent periods when the Jews had tribal affiliations or a nation-state, historical and political enemies, and armies. During these times, war was more common than peace. Consequently, many of their values and beliefs were formed in times of political power, religious turmoil and expectations for a warrior *Mesiah*. On the other hand, the books of the **New Testament** were written during times that Christians had no national identity, no army, a suffering *Mesiah* and a universalized God of the whole creation. It is not surprising, then, that spiritual and eschatological peace are a more substantial concerns in the **New Testament** than in the **Hebrew Bible**. From the moral point of view, Christianity's non-political beginnings were an advantage, for the conflicts of the political world did not significantly intrude on the formation of its basic values. Even the political-religious persecutions in early Christianity did not result

concern for peace rather than war, it is surprising that there are more than 80 references to political peace in the **Hebrew Bible** and less than 30 in the **New Testament**. The reason is the political and religious environment in which Christianity was born, an environment aptly described by Victor P. Furnish in the conclusion to his article, "War and Peace in the New Testament":

> [As the church understood its mission through at least the first century, it was] . . . to proclaim, by word and by witness its own life as a believing community, the gospel of a Christ whose kingdom was not of this world and who in life and in death had demonstrated that true greatness consists not in one's ability to rule over others but in one's commitment to serve them (Mark 10:35-45). That the church made no attempt, this early, to ask in what ways its gospel was relevant to the issue of war and peace was due partly to political conditions in general [the Pax Romana], partly to the church's status as minority movement largely without access to political power, and partly to the kind of eschatological hope to which it clung. **(Interpretation**, vol.XXXVIII, no.4, 379)

Theologies of War

While the examination of theologies of war in the **New Testament** follows the same pattern as in the preceding chapter, that is, beginning with an etymological word study of the primary terms for war, an analysis of the various usages of war and explorations of theologies concerning political, spiritual and eschatological war, there are three significant differences in the approach taken for the **New Testament**. First,

---

in a political holy war theology but rather in an increased passion for eschatological peace. In the formation of its basic beliefs and values Islam shared a situation more similar to that of Judaism than Christianity, for from the first revelation to Muhammad in February 610 C.E., the political world constantly interacted with the religious revelations of the Prophet. The next chapter examines this in more detail.

since the oral tradition and writing period is little more than a century there is no need to separate the analysis into different periods. Second, except for the early church's introduction of the doctrine of the trinity, there was no question about the universalized monotheism of Christianity from the initial teachings of Jesus to the closing of the **New Testament**; and, thus, there was no significant theological evolution in thought concerning the nature of God in Christianity that complicates the study of the **Hebrew Bible**. Third, while the analysis does not require division into various periods, it is useful to separate each of the three theologies of war-- political, spiritual and eschatological--into two categories: the teachings of Jesus[10] and the views of the early Christian writers, especially Paul, as they were incorporated in the non-gospel books of the **New Testament**.[11]

There are three terms, plus their cognates, used in the Greek **New Testament** to indicate conflicts such as war or battle. Over 75% of these involve the noun, *polemos*, or the verb, *polemeo*. The other two terms are: *antistrateuomai*, which means "to oppose" or "to set against," hence, "to be at war with" and *strateuma*,

---

[10]

As noted in the first chapter, it is impossible to recover the actual words of Jesus. What is included in the gospels are the earliest traditions concerning the teachings of Jesus. However, even given this problem, there is general agreement among Christian scholars concerning the central core of Jesus' preachings: (1) his eschatological proclamation of the imminence of the Kingdom of God; (2) his equating of this Kingdom with non-worldly salvation; (3) his understanding that the power of God is expressed in forgiveness, mercy, and love; (4) his call to repentance and rebirth through placing one's trust in God rather than the world; (5) his radical call to love not only one's neighbor but also one's enemies; (6) his opening of the Kingdom of God to those who were the despised and religiously unclean of his society; and (7) his affirmation of the Kingdom arriving through love and suffering rather than violence and war, that is, his crucifixion as the *Mesiah*.

[11]

While the majority of the letters in the **New Testament** were written by Paul, or attributed to Paul, it is the non-Pauline letters which provide a gold mine of information about the beliefs and the values of the early church. Unfortunately, these letters are least studied part of the **New Testament** by contemporary Christians.

which means "army" or "troops." While the term *antistrateuomai* is ordinarily used to indicate human conflicts, Paul uses it in the **New Testament** in regard to a spiritual conflict within the human being. The noun, *strateuma* is used in several books to refer to human soldiers and in Revelation to heavenly ones. While the preceding terms are scantly used, the cognates of *polemeo* and *polemos* are the predominant terms for war and conflict. *Polemos* occurs 16 times (9 of them in Revelation) and *polemeo* occurs 7 times (6 in Revelation). The verb means "to make war" and the noun means "armed conflict," "war," "battle," "fight," "strife," and "conflict."

As in the **Hebrew Bible**, the terms for war are used in many phrases. Among the more important are the following: "wars and rumors of wars," "encounter in war," "hear of wars and tumults," "mighty in war," "at war," "war against (make war)," "war arose in heaven," "judges and makes war," and "war in your members." As expected in most of these usages, *polemos* predominates.

Before turning to an examination of the theologies of war in the **New Testament**, three additional issues help provide background: (1) a description of the general significance of the **Old Testament**[12] on Christian theologies of war; (2) a general statement of the major problems for any Christian theology of war; and (3) a brief clarification about what this chapter does not include concerning Christian views of war.

Unquestionably, **the Old Testament** exerted considerable influence on Christian thinking. One of the first major crises facing the early church, mostly

---

[12]

As stated in the second chapter, the term **Old Testament** is rejected for most of this study because of the problems of religious chauvinism and the intolerance such attitudes breed. However for this chapter on Christianity, and it alone, the term **Old Testament** is appropriate because the subject is the Christian **New Testament** for whom the **Hebrew Bible** is the **Old Testament**. In other words, in this chapter alone it is appropriate to place a Christian interpretation on the revelation communicated through the Jews.

because of Paul's missionary success in the gentile world, was the problem: must a gentile convert be circumcised before he can be baptized? As strange as this question seems to modern Christians, there was a major theological issue and crisis behind it, for the question really was: what is the relationship between Christianity and the Jewish faith? Acts Chapter 15 records the early church's response, which was to affirm the revelation to the Jews as sacred and authentic but not limiting. In other words, Christians were to understand the Jewish revelation (**Covenant**) as having come from God, but that in Jesus God had accomplished a **New** revelation (**Covenant**) which could not be confined to the **Old** one. Although the church had no **New Testament** at the time this determination was made, the decision made in Acts 15 committed Christianity eventually to having an **Old Testament** (**Covenant**) and a **New Testament** (**Covenant**). Consequently, since the Jerusalem Council, Christian thinking has needed to take the **Old Testament** into account, especially concerning war.[13]

13

    Because there was no canonized Christian Bible until long after the first century C.E. and no canonized **Hebrew Bible** until 90 C.E., the major influence of the **Old Testament** on Christian views of war has been on Christian thinkers from the fourth century to the present age. It has been these thinkers who were forced to struggle with worldly issues of war that inevitably resulted from the political power that Christianity began to acquire from the time of Constantine to the modern period. Augustine used Exodus 32:26-28 to justify a limited *herem* (holy persecution) of heretics as did the Inquisition. John Calvin used the same passage to justify the participation of the elect (God's Chosen) to engage in war against evil, and John Knox took Calvin's views and acted on them in Scotland to produce Presbyterianism. However, of all the destructive influences of the **Old Testament** *herem* in the history of Christianity, the Crusades are at the top of the list of those atrocities Christians have used the **Old Testament** to justify. Consider the first Crusade. According to Christian historians, the defeat of the Muslim defenders of Jerusalem on July 15, 1099 led to the slaughter of tens of thousands. Over 10,000 Muslim warriors were beheaded near the Mosques of Aqsa and the Dome of the Rock. Further, these same historians recorded the beheadings were the cause for shouts of great joy and applauding that justice had finally been done to the infidel by God's new holy warriors. For these warriors, the Crusades were a *herem* (that is, God's justice against the evil infidel), and the church found theological justifications for such

228

As already noted, there is little difficulty in theologizing war in the **Hebrew Bible** because of the perspectives of henotheism, chosenness, promised land, nation-states, armies and the enemies of God. The **New Testament**, however, provides none of these same perspectives, and, thus, presents Christian theologians with several considerable problems for any efforts to legitimize war on the political level-- the spiritual and eschatological dimensions of war are another matter. John Lanagan, in an essay in Kelsey and Johnson's excellent anthology, **Just War and Jihad: Theoretical and Historical Perspectives on War and Peace in Western and Islamic Tradition**, provides an impressive list of the problems confronting any Christian effort to justify war: ("The Western Moral Tradition on War: Christian Theology and Warfare," 76-77)

(1)   *"The moral character of God."* The God preached by Jesus is a God characterized by forgiveness, justice, infinite love and mercy. Surely such a God would not condone holy wars or any kind of intentional destruction of human beings.

(2)   *"The power of God. "* If God is omniscient and infinite love, then the evil of war potentially indicates that God cannot be omnipotent.

(3)   *"The unity of God."* Since God is one, how can Christians explain their obedience to God in light of their divisions and hostilities toward one another?

(4)   *"The justice of God."* Since God is infinite love, it follows that God must be perfectly just. Justice requires that goodness be rewarded and evil punished. However, in the destructiveness of war and the exigencies of peace, it often happens that terrible suffering is visited on the innocent, and the victors who caused such suffering often go unpunished and reap the spoils of war.

(5)   *"The kingdom of God. "* Unquestionably, Jesus preached the coming kingdom of God as a kingdom of peace and justice. If, as the Church has often interpreted, the kingdom came in the person of Jesus, then divisiveness among his

---

bloodshed mostly in the Christian **Old Testament**. Fortunately, the early church was so apolitical that such uses of the **Old Testament** *herem* would have seemed inconceivable to them.

disciples and war in the world should be non-existent. Yet, the Christian world continues to be plagued with divisiveness and war. Can this be reconciled with the Church's claim that Jesus is the *Mesiah*?

(6) *"The commandment of love."* Over and again, Jesus tells his disciples that they are "to turn the other cheek" and "to love their enemies" as well as their friends. Since any war, just or other wise, represents deliberate harm and destructiveness against other human beings, can any kind of war be reconciled with the numerous commandments of love in the **New Testament**?

(7) *"The example of Christ."* At the heart of Christian salvation is the cross, that is, the Christ's willing sacrifice of his life. According to the **New Testament**, Christians are to pick up their crosses and follow Jesus. Surely, making war represents a violation of such cross bearing.

(8) *"The teaching of Christ."* Representing a major advance from previous Western moralities, in many places but especially Matthew 5-7, "The Sermon on the Mount," Jesus emphasizes that his disciples are to forgive those who harm them by never returning evil with evil but with goodness. How can any war fulfill this command of goodness?

These are difficult hurdles, but nonetheless, throughout the history of Christian theology there have been many theologies of a just war, and in most of them the Christian **Old Testament** exerts considerable influence.

Finally, given the problems noted in the preceding paragraph, it is helpful to remember that this study is limited to the three canons, that is, the three Holy Books. Consequently, the analyses of the theologies of war which follow do not attempt to examine those efforts to justify war that have plagued Christian thinkers after the writing of the **New Testament.** For those who are interested in these efforts, there are several good works available, but two of the best are the anthologies of John Kelsay and James T. Johnson: **Cross, Crescent, and Sword: The Justification and Limitation of War in Western and Islamic Tradition**, Greenwood Press, Westport, Conn., 1990; and, **Just War and Jihad: Historical and Theoretical**

Perspectives on War and Peace in Western and Islamic Tradition, Greenwood Press, Westport, Conn., 1991. With this background, a more in depth study is now possible.

Theology of Political War

Teachings of Jesus in the gospels interpreted as references to political war are found in these passages: Matthew 10:34-35, Luke 12:51-52 (which is the synoptic parallel of the teaching in Matthew 10) and the puzzling Luke 22:36-38. Since the Matthew 10 and Luke 12 passages are basically the same, only one of them is examined together with the statement in Luke 22:[14]

> 'Do not suppose that I have come to bring peace to the earth; it is not peace I have come to bring, but a sword. For I have come to set a *man against his father, a daughter against her mother, a daughter-in-law against her mother-in-law. A man's enemies will be those of his own household.*' (Matthew 10:34-36)
>
> He said to them, 'When I sent you out without purse or

---

[14]
> There is a statement attributed to John the baptizer in Luke 3:14 which has implications for war, at least as regards military service:
> > When all of the people asked him, 'What must we do, then?' He [John] answered, 'If anyone has two tunics he must share with the man who has none, and the one who has something to eat must do the same'. There were tax collectors too who came for baptism, and these said to him, 'Master, what must we do?' He said to them, 'Exact no more than your rate'. Some soldiers asked him in their turn, 'What about us? What must we do?' He said to them, 'No intimidation [no robbing by violence]! No extortion [no robbing by false witness]! Be content with your pay!' (Luke 3:10-14)
> Two points can be made concerning John's statement to the soldiers: first, they are expected to treat others with justice; and, second, the enigmatic "Be content with your pay" taken together with Jesus statement about "rendering to Caesar" (Luke 20:22) has often been used to justify Christian participation in the military, hence in war. However, given other teachings such as "loving one's enemies," these two do not decisively settle the issue of Christian military service or just war.

haversack or sandals, were you short of anything?' 'No' they said. He said to them, 'But now if you have a purse, take it; if you have a haversack, do the same; if you have no sword, sell your cloak and buy one, because I tell you these words of scripture have to be fulfilled in me: *He let himself be taken for a criminal.* Yes, what scriptures says about me is even now reaching its fulfillment.' 'Lord,' they said 'there are two swords here now.' He said to them, 'That is enough!' (Luke 22:35-38)

For those seeking a scriptural justification for Christian participation in the military and a just war, these two passages have become central. But do they unequivocally argue for Christian participation in political war?

While some great theologians, such as Augustine, used these passages as scriptural support for a Christian theology of just (holy) war, many others have argued that the term *sword* should not be understood in a literal sense but has a symbolic meaning placing the saying outside the dimension of political war and therefore is consistent with both Jesus's actions immediately after his arrest in Gethsemane and his emphasis on love and forgiveness in the Sermon on the Mount.[15] An excellent argument made by Victor Furnish in **Interpretation** for a figurative (symbolic) meaning of the term *sword* in both passages clearly rejects any connection

---

[15] Although many literalists still understand Matthew 5-7 as a single sermon which Jesus delivered to a multitude gathered at a "Mount," the best Biblical scholarship recognizes that the content of these three chapters does not come from a single presentation by Jesus. Rather, the writer of Matthew chose to introduce the reader to what he (and most likely the early church) understood to be the core of Jesus teachings as a preparation for telling the story of Jesus. In this sense, then, the so-called "Sermon on the Mount" is most likely a compilation of Jesus' most important teachings, perhaps some of them from the Q-document that is no longer extant. Whatever the writer's purpose, these three chapters have touched the hearts and minds of not only Christians but many non-Christians throughout the world. Gandhi once said that the two most important spiritual writings in the history of humanity are the **Bhagavid Gita** and the "Sermon on the Mount."

between Jesus' teachings and the political *herem* theologies of the first century Zealots:

> Jesus proclamation of the Kingdom of God as a gift stood in direct contradiction to the Zealots' conviction that the Kingdom could be established by means of a militant revolution; his teachings about loving one's enemies stood in direct contradiction to the Zealots' advocacy of the use of violence to overthrow one's enemies. . . .
>
> Nor do the so-called "sword sayings" of Matthew 10:34 and Luke 22:36 require any qualification of what has already been noted about the ideological distance between Jesus and the Zealots. The former, "Do not think that I have come to bring peace on earth; I have not come to bring peace, but a sword," is certainly to be understood figuratively, perhaps as a general reference to the conflict and hostility which those who follow Jesus may expect to encounter. This is suggested by the interpretation . . . in the Lucan parallel [12:58] . . . where "division" stands in place of "a sword". . . . More particularly, the sword could be a metaphor for martyrdom. . . .
>
> The charge of Jesus to his disciples to arm themselves with swords (Luke 22:36) is more difficult. Here, too, the sword could be a metaphor for conflict and affliction, and the point that Jesus disciples must prepare to endure that.   If so, the disciples misunderstand, because they show him they already have two swords. In this case Jesus' response, "It is enough," would best be interpreted as a rebuke, cutting off the conversation. The argument has also been made for a literal meaning. . . . But a literal meaning, whether it has to do with being prepared to defend oneself or with taking up arms to resist one's enemies is so difficult to reconcile with what is known otherwise about Jesus' teaching. . . . (**Interpretation**, vol.XXXVIII, no.4, 369-70)

J. Carter Swain, in rejecting a literal interpretation that the sword refers to political war, offers an even more symbolic interpretation of the problematic term *sword*:

> In Israel's early history, no distinction can be made between tools and weapons. An ax, used for felling trees and shaping lumber, could be used to ward off wild beasts. . . . Daggers could not be distinguished from hunting knives. . . .
>
> A weapon-tool similar to a dagger is used in many cultures [including that of the Jews]. . . . This throws light on a strange saying attributed to Jesus. On his last night with his friends, he said, ". . . 'let him who has no sword sell his mantle and buy one.' . . . ." This saying has long troubled the church. Can we really believe that words like these were spoken by the Prince of Peace?
>
> One of the ancient versions of this account contains a different reading. In place of "Let him who has no sword sell his mantle and buy one," it has "Love your enemies"--and that would seem to be more in character for the Savior of the world on the eve of cross-bearing. The men of his time, too, carried a short knife--dirk, dagger, panga--useful in warding off wild animals and for as many domestic purposes as a Boy Scout knife. About to confront the might of the Roman empire, symbolized by Pilate and his minions, Jesus wants to drive home the point his friends seem to have missed, namely, that his sword is his truth, his shield is his love, he needs no armies. In a moment of melancholy playfulness, he assures them that two small knives--one for Israel, one for Rome--will be all they need to conquer the kingdoms of the world. (**War, Peace, and the Bible**, 52-53)

Whether Jesus' words reflected a "moment of melancholy playfulness" is questionable, but given the consistency of his teaching on forgiveness and love even of one's enemies[16] and his rebuking of Peter for drawing his sword (knife) in Gethsemane (Matthew 26:53), it is reasonable to conclude that Jesus' sword sayings have nothing to do with a theology of political warfare.[17] Even when Jesus praises the faith of the Centurion in Matthew 8:5-13 and (its synoptic parallel) Luke 7:1-10, "I tell you solemnly, nowhere in Israel have I found a faith like this," he does not praise or condemn the Centurion for his profession; rather Jesus praises him for his faith in the healing power of God. The moral focus, the eschatological emphasis, the spiritual concern and the apolitical nature of Jesus' teachings provide no substantive theology concerning political war. The early church also took a similar perspective.

As with the teachings of Jesus, there are only a few passages from the other books written by the early church that might have implications for political war: Acts 10:1-9, Hebrews 11:30-40, James 4:1-5 and those passages of Paul that make

---

[16]

Jesus' teaching that love extends even to one's enemies is his most radical ethical teaching. Such an ethic represents a considerable break with past ethical views in the Western world. A brief set of contrasts helps in understanding the radical nature of this teaching about love. From the Hammurabi Code (second millennium B.C.E.) of "An eye for an eye, and a tooth for a tooth," the normative moral rule was: "Do good to friends and evil to enemies." In the Greek city-state of Athens, a troublesome stone mason turned philosopher, Socrates (died 399 B.C.E.), on the eve of his execution, proposed to a young friend of his, Crito, a moral rule that was radical for its time: "It is never just (moral) to pay back one wrong with another wrong." In other words, Socrates rejected the old "eye (evil) for an eye (evil)" morality of the past. This moral principle, however, did not require one to return "a good for an evil," just not to return "an evil for an evil." However, Socrates's view falls considerably short of Jesus' radical teaching stating one is expected to return "a good for an evil." While this principle makes its appearance in Eastern thought in the sixth century B.C.E. in the thoughts of Siddartha Gautama (the Buddha) and Mahavira (the founder of Jainism), Jesus is the first to make it a focus of moral behavior in the West.

[17]

In addition to his teachings about love and forgiveness, there are many scholars who interpret Jesus' sayings in Luke 9:24 and 17:33, "For anyone who wants to save his life will lose it; but anyone who loses his life for my sake, that man will save it," as denying the use of violence even for self-defense.

reference to war, battle and the weapons of such conflict: Philemon 2:25; I Corinthians 4:8, 9:7; II Corinthians 10:3-5; and I Thessalonians 5:8. While literal interpretations have sometimes been given to Paul's passages, there should be no question that Paul's uses of war in these passages is symbolic, and he is referring to either spiritual war (in most instances) or eschatological war; thus, these passages are examined in the next two sections on theologies of spiritual and eschatological war.

The passage in Acts 10 is similar to those already examined in the sayings about the Centurion. Cornelius is a Roman soldier who has become a Christian, is given a vision from God to send for Peter and is praised for his faith, not his profession. While this passage implies that military service may not be inconsistent with the Christian faith, it requires a rather giant leap to use it to justify a Christian theology of political war.

The passage in Hebrews 11:32-40 is a little more promising for glimpsing a view of political war:

> Is there any need to say more? There is not time for me to give an account of Gideon, Barak, Samson, Jephthah, or of David, Samuel and the prophets. They were men who through faith conquered kingdoms, did what was right and earned the promises. They could keep a lion's mouth shut, put out blazing fires and emerge unscathed from battle. They were weak people who were given strength, to be brave in battle and drive back foreign invaders. . . .
> (Hebrews 11:32-35)

Here, at last, is a passage which speaks of "real" (political) war and brave warriors. This passage, then, seems to provide a **New Testament** basis for a theology of political war, but the account ends with a judgment that their actions did not make them righteous before God: "These are all heroes of faith, but they did not receive what was promised, since God had made provision for us to have something better,

236

and they were not to reach perfection [salvation[18]] except with us." (Hebrews 11:39-40) The passage clearly indicates that war, even though it be fought by the faithful, does not lead to salvation. It can certainly be interpreted to allow Christians to participate in war, but rejects one of the often accepted premises of the *herem* (holy war): that the shedding of blood can accomplish salvation.

Finally, the passage in James 4:1-3 is a passage that does indeed refer to political wars does so but for a spiritual reason:

> Where do these wars and battles between yourselves [political wars] first start? Isn't it precisely in the desires fighting inside your own selves? You want something and you haven't got it; so you are prepared to kill. You have an ambition that you cannot satisfy; so you fight to get your way by force. Why you don't have what you want is because you don't pray for it; when you do pray and don't get it, it is because you have not prayed properly, you have prayed for something to indulge your own desires.[19]

18

This verse about not reaching "perfection," that is salvation (for Christians, Heaven and for Muslims, Paradise) based on their activities as warriors is an interesting contrast to the promise that Popes' offered Christian holy warriors during the Crusades, and *Imams*' offered their *mujihads* (holy warriors) during the same wars: the promise that any warrior killed in a holy cause would have their sins forgiven and immediately enter the salvation (Heaven or Paradise) prepared by God. This promise remains a powerful motivation for those extremist religious groups in the Middle East who continue to carry forward the distorted tradition of the holy war.

19

The statement made by the writer of James in this passage about "prayed properly," that is, about the proper nature of prayer is captured wonderfully by the philosopher Gabriel Marcel when he states that one may pray to **BE** more (loving, forgiving, generous, etc) but not to **HAVE** more. The spiritual principle that accounts for this distinction also applies to the belief in **Chosenness**: one is **not Chosen to HAVE** (things like promised land that others do not have) but **Chosen to BE responsible** for sharing the power and love of God in their life. The final chapter returns to this most important principle.

In other words, this passage continues the spiritual insight first glimpsed in the writings of the Yahwist: the fundamental cause of political (external) war is spiritual (internal) war.

As indicated in the preceding explorations, neither in the gospels nor the other books of the **New Testament** is there an unquestionable foundation for a theology of political war, although many efforts have been made to interpret certain texts to support such a theology. Thus, to use a pun, for Christian theologians who wish to found a theology of political holy war on the writings of the **New Testament**, "when they turn their ploughshares into swords, they are going to have a tough row to plough."

Theology of Spiritual War

Unlike Paul for whom military metaphors abound, Jesus seldom makes use of either the term *polemos* (war) or military metaphors. An exception is found in a parable:

> 'Or again, what king marching to war against another king would not first sit down and consider whether with ten thousand men he could stand up to the other who advanced against him with twenty thousand? If not, then while the other king was still a long way off, he would send envoys to sue for peace. So in the same way, none of you can be my disciple unless he gives up all his possessions.' (Luke 14:30-33)

While Luke's attempt to impose the theme of "renouncing possessions" as a condition for true discipleship on the parable of the king preparing for war[20] is questionable,

---

[20]

Had this parable occurred in the **Hebrew Bible**, it would most likely have been cast in the traditional form of the *herem*, and, thus, the two to one odds would have been inconsequential in considering victory, that is, the odds would have been no cause for seeking peace. Jesus' use of this parable, however, concerns spiritual war rather than political.

238

the parable clearly calls disciples to consider the costs of discipleship. In this sense, Jesus shows an awareness of the internal battle (conflict) preceding the decision to become a disciple: the battle to overcome selfishness and possessiveness. This conflict is a common theme for him.

Although the term *polemos* is seldom used by Jesus to describe spiritual war, internal conflicts (battles) of conscience occupy a considerable place in his spiritual teachings. One of the best places to evidence this kind of spiritual war is in the "You have heard it said" statements in the Sermon on the Mount. One of them should clarify the emphasis Jesus places on the internal spirit of the human being[21]: "You have learnt how it was said to our ancestors: *You must not kill*; and if anyone does kill he must answer for it before the court. But I say this to you: anyone who is angry with his brother will answer for it before the court. . . ." (Matthew 5:21-22) The spiritual insight Jesus reveals in this teaching is similar to that in the Yahwist's account of the sin of Cain: internal conflict (war) leads to external conflict. However, Jesus goes one step beyond the Yahwist: for both the externalized act of murder is a sin, but for Jesus the internal condition of anger is itself the sin, the sin that if not conquered leads to external acts of violence, such as murder.

As in many other teachings, the emphasis of Jesus on the internal struggles of the spirit is his focus rather than their destructive external consequences. For this reason, when Jesus speaks of this kind of struggle (spiritual war) he uses the term

---

21

Two characteristics shared by most of the great religious reformers and mystics of both the East and the West are: (1) a critical rejection of reducing religious belief to matters of law and external ritual--a reduction that had been commonplace during their times; and (2) a call to return to the inner spirit of the human being, that is, a recognition that true spirituality must first confront (do battle with) such internal states as anger, lust, greed, hubris, etc.. Western religions have understood this as the battle against sin and Eastern ones as the struggle against an inner chaos that leads to destructive actions. Jesus, the Buddha and Mahavira are only three of the great religious reformers who rejected the reductions of religious belief to external ritualism and called human beings to seek their inner spirit.

peirasmos (or a cognate), a noun meaning "test," "trial," "temptation" and "enticement." For Jesus, then, the primary way that he explores spiritual war is through the term *peirasmos*.[22] Not only did Jesus attempt to teach his followers about the destructiveness of spiritual war (internal conflict), he experienced such in his own life. The following two examples, one just before his period of public teaching and the second just before his crucifixion, are powerful examples of his struggles with *peirasmos*: the temptations in the desert and the agony in Gethsemane.

There are two accounts of Jesus' temptations by the devil (see footnote 22) in the wilderness before he begins his period of public teaching, Matthew 4 and Luke 4:

> Filled with the Holy Spirit, Jesus left the Jordan and was led
> by the Spirit through the wilderness, being tempted there by the devil
> for forty days. During that time he ate nothing and at the end he was
> hungry . . . . [There follows the temptation to turns stones into bread,
> for which Jesus responds] *Man shall not live by bread alone.*

22

From the perspective of this study, it is unfortunate that in many instances where Jesus examines the temptations of the human spirit, and Paul the temptations of the flesh, that these internal struggles (wars) are given an external source: Satan. In agreement with much of the new scholarship emerging which indicates that the Jewish belief in an external evil power, the *satan* (the adversary in the prologue to Job), was absent before the Exile and most likely was introduced into post-exhilic Judaism through Zoroastrian sources, and then passed from Judaism into both Christianity and Islam, this study treats references to Satan as reifications. In other words, it is the position of this study that references to Satan are not to be understood in a literal way; rather Satan is a metaphor for that part of human nature which is absorbed by selfishness, arrogance, greed, lust, moral chaos, etc. It is the position of this study that: (1) the belief in an external power of evil, Satan, contributes nothing to the healthy spirituality of monotheism; unfortunately it seems to provide some with a supernatural cop-out, "The devil made me do it"; and (2) these three Holy Books speak of such a being because those were the terms in which human beings understood the universe at the time they were revealed and written and not because a being of supernatural evil actually exists.

.... [Next follows the temptation for earthly power, for which Jesus responds] *You must worship the Lord your God, and serve him alone.*

.... [Finally there is the temptation to tempt God into providing a miracle, for which Jesus responds] *You must not put the Lord your God to the test.* Having exhausted all these ways of tempting him, the devil left him, to return at the appointed time. (Luke 4:1-13)

Whether one accepts the references to *diabolos* (the devil) in this passage as external (literal) or internal (metaphorical), the war Jesus must fight is not external; Jesus must conquer his internal fears and doubts in order both to begin and later to fulfill his purpose in life. This battle becomes agonizingly evident in his struggles (temptations) with fear and loneliness in the Gethsemane prayer: "'My Father,' he said 'if it is possible, let this cup pass by me. Nevertheless, let it be as you, not I, would have it'." (Matthew 26:39) Matthew records that as Jesus leaves the disciples and struggles with his fears, he describes his spiritual war: "'My soul is sorrowful to the point of death'." (Matthew 26:38) Luke describes the spiritual anguish in words the Yahwist would have appreciated: "In his anguish he prayed even more earnestly, and his sweat fell to the ground like great drops of blood." (Luke 22:44) The spiritual war he fights is reasonably clear: the fear of death, the loneliness of dying, the temptation to have God let the "cup pass" and the search for the courage and hope to accept death. The prayer is concise, but reveals the true nature of prayer: To **Be** (that is to find the courage to fulfill his life's purpose) rather than to **Have** (the cup pass from him). In his teachings as well as his life, Jesus knew the struggles of spiritual war, but in almost as dramatic a way, so did the fanatic Pharisee who became a Christian missionary, Paul.

Paul and the writer of Revelations show the greatest fondness for military terminology in their communications: Paul's usage concerns mostly spiritual war and Revelation's usage is almost extensively in regard to eschatological war. The following are representative passages in which Paul uses military terminology as metaphors for spiritual war:

(1)   "We live in the flesh, of course, but the muscles that we fight with are not flesh. Our war is not fought with weapons of the flesh, yet they are strong enough, in God's cause, to demolish fortresses." (II Corinthians 10:3-5)

(2)   "Put God's armor on so as to be able to resist the devil's tactics. For it is not against human enemies that we have to struggle, but against the Sovereignties and the Powers who originate the darkness in this world, the spiritual army in the heavens."[23] (Ephesians 6:12)

(3)   ". . . let us put on faith and love for a *breastplate*, and the hope of *salvation* for a *helmet*."[24] (I Thessalonians 5:8)

(4)   "Timothy, my son, these are the instructions that I am giving you: I ask you to remember the words once spoken by the prophets, and taking them to heart to fight like a good soldier with faith and good conscience for your weapons," (see footnote 24). (I Timothy 1:18-19)

(5)   "Fight the good fight of the faith and win for yourself the eternal life to which you were called when you made your profession and spoke for the truth in front of many witnesses."[25] (I Timothy 6:12)

---

[23]

While the focus of this verse is eschatological, it also implies the internal struggle (spiritual war) with temptation; thus, in these words is an example of two dimensions of war. This is the case with other passages in the **New Testament** which related both spiritual war (temptation and trial) with eschatological war (the conflict of "Sovereignties and Powers").

[24]

While war or battle are not specifically used in this passage, the implication is clear: faith and love (the breastplate) and hope of salvation (the helmet) are the weapons for believers' struggles with both internal temptations and external Powers, in Paul's words: "fight the good fight of the faith."

[25]

While the good fight (battle) of faith means confronting external Powers, for Paul, as he makes abundantly clear in Romans 7:14-25, the major battle of faith is a

242

Although some of these passage have eschatological implications, it is clear that they refer to that internal battle characterized as spiritual war in this study.

There are several other writers in the **New Testament** who share Paul's insights concerning spiritual war; for example, consider the letters of James and I Peter:

(1)   "I urge you, my dear people, while you are *visitors and pilgrims[26]*, to keep yourselves free from the selfish passions that attack (wage war against) the soul." (I Peter 2:11)

(2)   "Where do these wars and battles between yourselves first start? Isn't it precisely in the desires fighting inside your own selves?" (James 4:1-2)

This last passage from James is similar to one of the greatest analyses of human nature and human struggles with spiritual war in the **New Testament**: Romans 7:14-25.

So important are the insights about human nature in these words of Paul to the Romans that they require an extensive citation:

> The Law, of course, as we all know is spiritual; but I am unspiritual; I have been sold as a slave to sin. I cannot understand my own behavior. I fail to carry out the things I want to do, and I find myself doing the very things I hate. When I act against my own will, that means that I have a self that acknowledges that the Law is good, and so the thing behaving in that way is not myself but sin

---

spiritual war.

26

The terms *visitors and pilgrims* reflect the view of the early church that Christians were **in** the world but not **of** it, that is, life in the flesh was but a stage in the journey (pilgrimage) toward God. This is one of the reasons that Christian writings of the first century C.E. did not address the issue of political war. However, this same perspective placed a considerable emphasis on spiritual war--overcoming those temptations and internal conflicts that separated one from God--and eschatological war--living in a way that prepared one for the end of time and the final salvation of God.

living in me. The fact is, I know of nothing good living in me--living that is, in my unspiritual self--for though the will to do what is good is in me, the performance is not, with the result that instead of doing the things I want to do, I carry out the sinful things I do not want to do. When I act against my will, then, it is not my true self doing it, but sin which lives in me.

In fact, this seems to be the rule, that every single time I want to do good it is something evil that comes to hand. In my inmost self I dearly love God's law, but I can see my body follows a different law that battles against the law which my reason dictates. This is what makes me a prisoner of that law of sin which lives inside my body.

What a wretched man I am! Who will rescue me from this body doomed to death? Thanks be to God through Jesus Christ our Lord!

In short, it is I who with my reason serve the Law of God, and no less I who serve in my unspiritual self the law of sin. (Romans 7:14-25)

Few passages in Paul's writings have received as much comment as these astounding verses. Whether one agrees with Paul about the human condition of sin and the implied dualism of flesh and spirit and the human inability to overcome sin, his insights about the battles of the human conscience (spiritual war) are well known by anyone who has struggled to "do the right thing!" In passages such as this and Jesus's teachings in the Sermon on the Mount, which focus on those conflicts and temptations of the spirit, the **New Testament** achieves a spiritual and moral greatness which transcends Christian claims about the divine nature of Jesus. This is the reason many non-Christians find teachings of spiritual depth and moral guidance for their lives in this Holy Book.

244

Theology of Eschatological War

As noted in the previous section, Jesus' statements about bringing a "sword" rather than "peace" most likely refer to conflicts in personal relationships (that is, his message will bring conflict between father and son, etc.) and spiritual war (that is, the decision to become a disciple involves the internal battle against the darker side of human nature described so thoroughly by Paul in Romans). However, they also might refer to the conflicts, both internal and external at the end of time. For this reason, Matthew 10:34-5 and its synoptic parallel Luke 12:51-2 may have eschatological significance. While there are eschatological teachings of Jesus scattered throughout the gospels, his most important cosmic eschatological statements are found in Mark Chapter 13 and its synoptic parallel Luke Chapter 21: the Little Apocalypses. Before turning to these, it is useful to examine the "Wedding Feast" metaphor for the Kingdom of God at the end of time in Matthew 22:1-14.[27]

The Wedding Feast parable is an extensive one which raises a nagging question concerning violence, as do the Little Apocalypses in Mark and Luke. This question is examined after the cosmic eschatologies of Mark and Luke are explored. The parable is as follows:

> Jesus began to speak to them in parables once again. 'The kingdom of heaven may be compared to a king who gave a feast for his son's wedding. He sent his servants to call those who had been invited, but they would not come. Next he sent some more servants. "Tell those who have been invited" he said "that I have my banquet all prepared, my oxen and fatted cattle have been slaughtered, everything is ready. Come to the wedding." But they were not interested; one went off to his farm, another to his business, and the

---

[27]

The use of a "Banquet" or "Feast" as a metaphor for the end of time was not original with Jesus. In fact, it was a common metaphor in much of the cosmic eschatology derived in the Middle East.

rest seized his servants, maltreated them and killed them. The king was furious. He despatched his troops, destroyed those murderers and burnt their town. Then he said to his servants, "The wedding is ready; but those who were invited proved to be unworthy, go to the crossroads in the town and invite everyone you can find to the wedding." So these servants went out on to the roads and collected together everyone they could find, good and bad alike; and the wedding hall was filled with guests. When the king came in to look at the guests he noticed one man who was not wearing a wedding garment, and he said to him, "How did you get in here, my friend, without a wedding garment?" And the man was silent. Then the king said to his attendants, "Bind him hand and foot and throw him out into the dark, there will be weeping and grinding of teeth". For many are called, but few are chosen.'

In this parable of the Wedding Feast, murder and violence seem to be more common than celebration and food, and it ends with a dire warning: "few are chosen." It is easy to see why the parable has been a source of comfort throughout the ages for those who believe they are the chosen, but a source of dread and fear for those who are unsure. Whatever its meaning, and as is the case with parables, there are many interpretative meanings that are possible, it is a good example of a common metaphor in cosmic eschatology. Using it as background, the Little Apocalypses of Mark and Luke require analysis.

Since Luke 21 is a parallel of Mark 13, the one in Mark suffices for understanding the teachings of Jesus about war, violence and cosmic eschatology. Luke 21, along with two other passages--Matthew 24:4-8 and Luke 19:14--are included in the following examination when they add new elements to what is in Mark. Since Mark 13 is cosmic eschatology from beginning to end, rather than cite the entire chapter, it is adequate to summarize the major views in it:

(1)   The chapter begins as Jesus and the disciples are leaving the Temple, and a

disciple comments on the size of the stones used in its construction. Jesus responds that not "a single stone will be left on another; everything will be destroyed." (13:2) (2) This statement later prompts a question from the disciples: "when is this going to happen, and what sign[28] will there be that all this is about to be fulfilled?" (13:4)

(3) Jesus then warns the disciples about several of the signs that will come: false prophets (deceivers), "wars and rumors of wars," earthquakes, famines and persecutions of the faithful. (13: 5-10) After this dire pronouncement, Jesus offers comfort to the disciples promising them when these terrible times come, they will not be alone, the Holy Spirit will be with them to tell them what to say and that those who are "hated on account of my name . . . will be saved." (13:11-13) Matthew 24:13 makes the same promise of salvation.

(4) Jesus next predicts an additional desecration of the Temple in Jerusalem and describes the horrible suffering that will occur: "For in those days there will be *such distress, until now, has not been* equalled since the beginning when God created the world, nor ever will be again." (13:14-19) In Luke 19:41-44, Jesus weeps tears over the destruction coming to Jerusalem and offers an old prophetic explanation (theodicy?) for its occurrence: "As he drew near and came in sight of the city he

---

28

   One of the more common elements of Western cosmic eschatologies is the belief in signs. This belief is one of the reasons that these end of the world views are called *apocalypses*: the term *apocalypse* derives from the Greek verb *apokalyptein*, which means "to uncover." For the believer, it is the "signs" that uncover (reveal) that the end of time has commenced. First century Christian cosmic eschatology was inherited from post-exhilic Jewish eschatology which emphasized signs of violence --wars, plagues, famines, earthquakes, etc.--as indicators of the coming terrible Day of *Yahweh*. Consequently, the Four Horsemen of the Apocalypse (War, Famine, Disease and Death) have ridden at the center of most Christian cosmic eschatologies. One undesirable consequence of the belief in apocalyptic signs is that every major natural disaster has usually been declared as a sign of the coming end. Even the end of a millennium has been interpreted as a sign of the coming *eschton* (that is, end of time).

shed tears over it and said, 'If you . . . had only understood . . . the message of peace! But alas, it is hidden from your eyes! Yes, a time is coming when your enemies . . . will dash you and the children inside your walls to the ground; they will not leave one stone standing on another within you. . . .' "

(5) Following another warning concerning false prophets, Jesus describes additional signs that would have been very familiar to any first century Jewish audience: "But in those days . . . of distress, the sun will be darkened, the moon will lose its brightness, the stars will come falling from the heavens. . . . And then they will see the Son of Man coming in the clouds with great power and glory . . . he will send the angels to gather his chosen . . . from the ends of the world to the ends of heaven." (13:24-27)

(6) Jesus continues with a parable involving a fig tree and a warning about the time of the end: "As for that day or hour, nobody knows it, neither the angels of heaven, nor the Son; no one but the Father." (13:28-32) The Little Apocalypse in Luke includes an interesting variant on the time: "I tell you solemnly, before this generation has passed away all will have taken place. Heaven and earth will pass away, but my words will never pass away." (21:32-33)[29]

(7) Finally, Jesus concludes his eschatological teachings with another warning to be alert, for no one other than God knows the day of its arrival. (13:33-37)

While the early church gave a central place to these eschatological teachings and placed considerable hope in them, as the generations passed and the world continued, slowly the church moved them from the center to the periphery (fringe)

29

The early church apparently took the tradition included in Luke more seriously than that in Mark, for there is considerable evidence in the letters of Paul, especially those to Thessalonica, and the other letters that many believed that the return of the Son of Man and his initiation of the events of the cosmic eschatology would occur in their lifetimes. Paul provides some good practical, moral advice for those who would claim to know too much about the appointed time. His advice is examined after completing the analysis of Jesus' eschatological teachings.

of Christian theology and life. However, during times of massive destruction--wars, plagues, famines, earthquakes, etc.--these teaching often leaped from the fringes of Christianity back to the center.

Whether a central focus or a fringe issue in Christianity, one of the most troubling aspects of these teachings is their violence: in other words, they seem inconsistent with the message of forgiveness and love, even of enemies, from the Prince of Peace. One response to this concern has been to adopt the old prophetic explanation for the violence and suffering as suggested in the parable of the Wedding Feast: only the wicked will suffer such horrible ends, the faithful (the chosen) will be saved. Another response has been to interpret most of the signs of violence as metaphors rather than literal descriptions. As an excellent example of such a symbolic interpretation, consider the following passage by J. Carter Swain:

> [When] Jesus says to his little community: "When you hear of wars and rumors of war, do not be alarmed--don't panic!" He is not predicting the inevitability of war at the end of time. If he were, he would be denying the kingdom that he had come to establish and in the proclamation of which he gave his life.
>
> At times of crisis people, eager to find some way out, are easily misled, and charlatans quick to take advantage of the anxiety and uncertainty. . . .[30] [Consequently] Jesus warns about . . . false Christs. . . . Do not be led by any of these, whether they call themselves Jim Jones or Sung Myung Moon. . . . [Passions] about "last things" can lead us astray from first things, which must always

---

30

A tragic example of the vulnerability of people during such times occurred in Kuwait when Hussein and the Iraqi army invaded it. The 400,000 Palestinian refugees in Kuwait were easy prey for the seductions of Hussein; consequently they attached themselves to his "star." When the Iraquis were forced to retreat, the refugees were also forced to return to Iraq with his beaten army. The poor and the displaced are always tragically vulnerable to wild and irrational hopes.

be our concern: doing justice and loving mercy and walking humbly with God.

Although the word was never upon Jesus' lips, talk of Armageddon [the apocalyptic final battleground for the war between good and evil] is another way by which people can be distracted from things that always matter, and so be led astray. It is curious that Armageddon should be so much talked about, because in the whole of scripture it occurs only once . . . (Rev.16:16). . . .

. . . .

In any case, the derivation of Armageddon [which is very uncertain] is not of primary importance. It was and is the symbol of cosmic conflict between good and evil, not the name of a land-based battle we are about to witness. It is symbolic of the clash not between armies but between powers and principalities--and the New Testament does not doubt that victory has already been decided [in the victory over death through the crucifixion and the resurrection].

(War, Peace and the Bible, 54-55)

Since the nature of the wars and the violence, whether literal or metaphorical, of Christian eschatology is mainly in the interpretative eye of the believer, further discussion of this problematic issue is not needed for two reasons: first, Jesus' teachings concerning eschatological peace are of much more importance than his teachings concerning eschatological war, and they are developed later in this chapter; and, second, Paul provides additional perspectives on the nature and problems of eschatology.

Before moving to Paul's writings, a summary of Jesus's views concerning the three dimensions of war is helpful. First, concerning any theology of political war, the recorded teachings of Jesus provide, at the very best, a highly questionable foundation for a theology of just war. Second, concerning any kind of *herem*, internal or external, the teachings of Jesus clearly repudiate such violence. Third, the teachings of Jesus provide a significant and insightful foundation for a theology of spiritual war. Finally, concerning eschatological war, while the literal interpretation of violence has been common, it is the conclusion of this study that interpreting Jesus' teachings concerning cosmic eschatology as symbolic in a manner similar to that suggested by Swain is more consistent with the whole of his message of eternal forgiveness and infinite love than any literal approach.

Unlike Jesus, Paul had to struggle with interpreting eschatology for a generation whose expectation of its immanence was unfulfilled. His letters to various Christians reveal that, although Paul believed in cosmic eschatology, he was more concerned with the future of the Christian church than the end of time as Christians struggled with the tension between being **in** the world rather than **of** it. Consequently, rather than examine Paul's specific beliefs about the signs and events of the end of time, which were not significantly different from those already noticed in the teachings of Jesus and the Jewish prophets, it is more important to examine the practical, moral advice Paul offers concerning the end of time. Whether he understood the "wars and rumors of war" as actual future events or as symbols of the ongoing conflict between good and evil, again, lies in the interpretative eye of the beholder. Whichever is the case, Paul warns about making eschatology too central in one's spiritual life. Three brief passages should suffice to describe Paul's views: Ephesians 6:10-17, I Thessalonians 5:1-2, 14 and II Thessalonians 3:11-12. The passage in Ephesians, in part, has already been cited in the section on spiritual war. In this passage Paul uses numerous metaphors to describe the weapons that Christians have to "fight the good fight of the faith." Among them are: "*truth bucketed around your waist,*" "*integrity* [righteousness] *for a breastplate,*" "*the shield of faith,*" and "*salvation from God to be your helmet.*" These weapons, while largely references to the Christian's struggle (spiritual war) with internal temptation (that is, sin), can also be interpreted as weapons to be used in the eschatological war (cosmic) against "Sovereignties and Powers."

The two passages to the Christians in Thessalonica which follow are more concerned about the problems and dangers eschatological beliefs were causing the early church than in the occurrence of the events themselves:

> You will not be expecting us to write anything to you, brothers about 'times and seasons', since you know very well that the Day of the Lord is going to come like a thief in the night. . . .
>
> . . . .
>
> Be at peace among yourselves. And this is what we ask you to do, brothers: warn the idlers; give courage to those who are apprehensive, care for the weak and be patient with everyone. . . . (I Thessalonians 5:1-2, 14)
>
> We gave you a rule when we were with you: not to let anyone have food if he refused to do any work. Now we hear that there are some of you who are living in idleness, doing no work themselves but interfering with everyone else's. In the Lord Jesus Christ, we order and call upon people of this kind to go quietly on working. . . . (II Thessalonians 3:11-12)

Paul's message for those who stopped working and sat in idleness awaiting the coming of the Son of Man on the clouds is clear: " Get back to work; God's purpose will be fulfilled in God's time." Unfortunately, this warning has often been forgotten by those groups who give too central a focus to cosmic eschatology.

Before examining **THE** book of cosmic eschatology in the **New Testament**, a brief recapitulation of Paul's views on war is needed. First, like Jesus, Paul says little concerning political war or any kind of *herem*. Second, his views about cosmic eschatology are mostly concerns about the effects of such beliefs in the lives of Christians. He never questions the traditions that are a part of his Jewish heritage and Christian environment, but as a missionary he is passionately involved in planning future journeys to spread the faith rather than awaiting the end of time. Finally, Paul's greatest spiritual insights concern his understanding of spiritual war. The passage in Romans 7 ranks among the greatest passages on this issue in the religious literature of mankind.

An appropriate conclusion to the theologies of war in the **New Testament** is an examination of the book of Revelation, for it is, whether interpreted literally or symbolically, the most war oriented book in the **New Testament**. The book of Revelation, its Greek title is the "Apocalypse of John," is one of the most intimidating books in the whole of the Christian Bible. Since an *apocalypse* is an "uncovering," that is, a *revelation*, the Apocalypse of John became known as the Revelation. Like Joel, the major apocalyptic book of the **Hebrew Bible**, Revelation is filled from beginning to end with a rich symbolism communicated through dreams and visions. Further, because the book is written at a time of persecution during the first century C.E., (possible dates are during the persecutions of Domitian, about 95 C.E., or perhaps earlier during the persecutions under Nero, before 70 C.E.), it was written in cryptic (hidden) language. In addition, the text itself presents many difficulties of interpretation: extensive repetitions, interruptions in the dreams and visions, passages divorced from their contexts, and inadequate transitions. These problems have led many Biblical scholars to argue the book of Revelation in the **New Testament** is a compilation from two different apocalypses, possibly written by the same author at different times and later fused into one by another author. Fortunately, this study need not struggle with all these issues since its concern is the use of the term *polemos* and its view of eschatological war. As in the previous discussion of eschatological war in Jesus and Paul, the study need not get "bogged down" in the arguments over a literal or symbolic interpretation of such issues as the final battle at Armageddon. Thus, the method employed is outlining the major passages that concern violence and war and leaving their interpretations to the reader. However, it should be stated that this study accepts a symbolic interpretation of this end of time violence (see page 249-50 and the concluding comments on cosmic eschatology in the teachings of Jesus).

While there are numerous passages in Revelation that either speak directly of war or conflict, there are seven which are of considerable significance:

(1)   "And now war broke out in heaven, when Michael with his angels attacked the dragon. The dragon fought back with his angels, but they were defeated and driven out of heaven. The great dragon, the primeval serpent[31], know as the devil or Satan, who had deceived all the world was hurled down to the earth and his angels hurled down with him." (12:7-9) (See footnote 22 describing the perspective on Satan accepted by this study.)

(2)   "Then the dragon was enraged with the woman[32] and went away to make war on the rest of her children, that is, all who obey God's commandments and bear witness for Jesus." (12:7)

(3)   "It [the beast who has been given authority to act for the dragon, that is, for Satan] was allowed *to make war against the saints and conquer them, and given power* over every race, people, language and nation; and all people of the world will worship it, that is, everybody whose name has not been written down since the foundation of the world in the book of life of the sacrificial Lamb [the elect, the saved]. If anyone has ears to hear, let him listen: *Captivity for those who are*

31

   The identification of the devil or Satan as the dragon (primeval serpent) occurred in late Jewish eschatological literature and rabbinic interpretations of Genesis. Christianity inherited this identification and, consequently, Christians for centuries have usually interpreted the serpent in the garden of Eden who tempted Eve as Satan in disguise. Competent Biblical scholarship offers two serious problems with such an identification: (1) it requires a literal interpretation of the great narrative of the Yahwist in Genesis 2-4 (see footnote 68 in Chapter Two); and (2) the identification is an anachronism, that is, the forcing of a present meaning or interpretation upon the past. When the Yahwist wrote, the Hebrew faith included no belief in an independent evil power who constantly confronted a henotheistic god. The term *satan* does not make its appearance into Jewish religious writings until the Exile and post-exhilic periods. Consequently, the serpent in the garden could not have been Satan when the Yahwist wrote.

32

   The writer of Revelation continues with his anachronistic interpretation of the garden story and the punishing of all involved in the sin of the forbidden fruit: "Then *Yahweh* God said to the serpent . . . I will make you enemies of each other, you and the woman. . . . " (Genesis 3:14-15)

destined for captivity; the sword for those who are to die by the sword."[33] (13:7-10)

(4)   "Then from the jaws of dragon and beast and false prophet I saw three foul spirits come; they looked like frogs and in fact were demon spirits, able to work miracles, going out to all the kings of the world to call them together for the war of the Great day of God the Almighty. This is how it will be: I shall come like a thief . . . . They shall call the kings together at a place called, in Hebrew, Armageddon." (16:13-16)

(5)   "They [the ten kings] are all of one mind in putting their strength and their powers at the beast's disposal, and they will go to war against the Lamb; but the Lamb is *the Lord of lords and the King of kings*, and he will defeat them and they will be defeated by his followers, the called, the chosen, the faithful." (17:13-14)

(6)   The First Battle of the End:

> And I saw heaven open, and a white horse appear; its rider was called Faithful and True; he is a *judge with integrity* [righteousness], a warrior for justice. His eyes were flames of fire, and his head crowned with many coronets; the name written on him was known only to himself; *his cloak was soaked with blood.* He is known by the name, The Word of God. Behind him, dressed in linen of dazzling white, rose the armies of heaven on white horses.. From his mouth came a sharp sword to strike the pagans with; he is the one *who will rule them with an iron scepter*, and tread out the wine of Almighty God's fierce anger. . . .
>
> I saw an angel standing in the sun, and he shouted aloud to all the birds . . . 'Come here, *gather together at the great feast* that God is giving. *There will be the flesh* of kings for you. . . .

---

[33]

    There is a variant translation of this last statement which provides a significantly different perspective: *"he who kills by the sword must die by the sword."*

Then I saw the beast, with all the kings of the earth and their armies, gathered together to fight the rider and his army. But the beast was taken prisoner, together with the false prophet who had worked miracles on the beast's behalf. . . . These two were thrown alive into the fiery lake of burning sulphur. All the rest were killed by the sword of the rider, which came out of his mouth, and *all the birds were gorged with their flesh.* (19:11-21)

(7)   The Second Battle of the End:

When the thousand years[34] are over, Satan will be released from his prison and will come out to deceive all the nations in the four corners of the earth, *Gog and Magog*[35], and mobilize them for war. His armies will be as many as the sands of the sea; and they will come swarming over the entire country and besiege the camp of the saints, which is the city that God loves[36]. *But fire will come down on them from heaven* and consume them. Then the devil, who misled them, will be thrown into the lake of fire and sulphur, where the beast and the false prophet are, and their torture will not stop, day or night, for ever and ever. (20:7-10)

34

It is this verse in Revelation identifying a thousand years (a millennium) as the period of time between the first cosmic eschatological battle and the second one that has been the basis for the predictions of the end of time at the end of each millennium.

35

These names are usually interpreted as symbolic names referring to all the infidel (that is, non-believing) kings whose armies will be led by Satan in the final battle between the Sons of Light (Powers of Good) and the Sons of Darkness (Powers of Evil).

36

Throughout most of the Christian Bible, the beloved city of God is identified as Jerusalem, but in this passage it refers to the New Jerusalem, that is, in Christian eschatological literature, the New Jerusalem is usually a symbol for the Church.

Finally, this second battle and victory of the armies of God concludes in the appearance of a *"new heaven and a new earth,"* (21:1), that is, the Heavenly, Messianic Jerusalem.

What distinguishes the cosmic eschatological visions of Revelation from the teachings of Jesus and Paul are the powerful images of war and violence. While Jesus and Paul do not ignore these metaphors, in Revelation they dominate so powerfully that the Suffering Servant, Prince of Peace *Mesiah* seems swallowed up by the Warrior *Mesiah* of God's *herem* against evil. Although Revelation ends with a vision of eschatological peace, the metaphorical (or for some literal) violence and destruction preceding the New Jerusalem is as spine chilling as the **Hebrew Bible**'s *herem*.

As stated earlier, and even literalists agree that much of the book must be understood metaphorically, these visions, dreams and prophecies are best interpreted as symbolic when placed within the total context of the central message of the **New Testament**: unconditional, infinite love and compassion. It is, however, easy to understand why this book has provided hope for Christians during times of persecution: first, they are experiencing the horrors of destruction and death which are described in many of the visions; and, second, the book promises that such violence is but a prelude to eternal peace (salvation). In remaining consistent with the view it is this peace rather than war which lies at the heart of the Christian revelation, it is now appropriate to consider the theologies of peace in the **New Testament**.

Theologies of Peace

Both within the **New Testament** and the life of the church, there have been many titles and descriptions given to Jesus: the Christ (that is, the *Christos*, the *Mesiah*, the Anointed One), the Son of Man, the Lord, the Word of God, the

Incarnate Word, the Savior,[37] and the Prince of Peace are but a few of the more important ones. While they are all appropriate, there is a special significance to the title Prince of Peace because of the depth of the meaning of peace in the **New Testament**. As noted earlier, it is not unimportant that there are five times as many references to peace as to war in the Christian revelation.

There are over 100 individual uses of the term *peace* in the **New Testament** and 95% of them use either *eirene* or a cognate of this term. The other terms for peace are: *ataraxia*, which means "undisturbedness," that is, "unstirred-upness"; *esuchia*, which means "quietness," "rest," and "silence"; and *siopao*, which means "to keep silent," and "to make no sound." While the sense of these latter three terms is a state of calmness or rest, in the **New Testament**, the word *eirene* acquires a spiritual depth[38] far beyond these three and its usual meaning in Greek thought. Originally, *eirene* was used by the Greeks as the opposite of *polemos* (political war), that is, the absence of strife between peoples. However with Socrates and the later Stoics and Epicureans, *eirene* acquired an internal dimension understood by the Stoics as *apatheia* (the calm peacefulness that comes from controlling the passions, that is, *a + pathos*, which means "not + suffering") and the Epicureans as *ataraxia*

---

[37]

For the church, the descriptive title **Savior** has been one of the most cherished of all titles, so much so that it became a fundamental part of the sacrament of Baptism: "Do you accept Jesus Christ as your Lord and Savior?" It is surprising how little use of this title is made in the **New Testament**. The Greek term *soter*, which means "savior" is used in referring to Jesus less than a dozen times: Luke 2, Acts 5 and 13, Ephesians 5, Philippians 3, II Timothy 1, Titus 1 and 2, II Peter 1 and I John 4. Although little used by the **New Testament**, the title Savior is not only a superbly descriptive term for Christian beliefs about Jesus but also etymologically descriptive of his name *Jesus*. Mary and Joseph named their son *Yeshua*, that is, Joshua, which means in Hebrew "God saves." In Greek, the Hebrew name *Yeshua* is translated as *Iesous*, which becomes Jesus in English. Thus, the name *Jesus* etymologically means "God saves."

[38]

The religious significance of *eirene* is attested by the fact that it is used in every book in the **New Testament** except the book of I John.

(that is, *a* + *tarache*, which means "not + stirred up"). For both Stoics and Epicureans these two states of mental peace were achieved through self-discipline, the acceptance of certain rational principles and dedication to specific life styles. For the Christian, however, the peace of *eirene* was something quite different.

One way to understand the spiritual depth of Christian *eirene* (peace), in contrast to its traditional Greek connotations as political calm or reflective peace of mind, is to examine the various phrases which involve peace: "let your peace return to you," "bring peace," "go in peace," "be at peace," "peace among men," "peace be upon you," "son of peace," "Prince of Peace," " peace in heaven," "good news of peace," "come in peace," "enjoy peace," "grace and peace," "honor and peace," "life and peace," "righteousness and peace," "God of peace," "called to peace," "love and peace," "love, joy, peace, patience, kindness, goodness," "peace and mercy," "preaching peace," "bond of peace," "gospel of peace," "peace of Christ," "king of peace," "peacemakers," and "grace, mercy and peace." In this list are to be found the essential characteristics of the Christian life as well as a richness that goes considerably beyond the traditional Greek concept of peace.

The use of the term *eirene* in the **New Testament** was greatly influenced by the fact that the translators of the **Septaugint**[39]selected the Greek word *eirene* as the translation of the Hebrew term *shalom*. Consequently, the rich spirituality and diversity of the Hebrew term became attached to the Greek noun *eirene* (see pages 191-207): wholeness, health, friendship, security, completeness, safety, etc. As a term of salutation, it became the **New Testament** equivalent of the various Hebrew salutations using *shalom*, especially the *shalom* of God. Almost everyone of the letters opens with a salutation such as "To you . . . who are God's beloved . . . called

---

[39]

    The **Septuagint** was the 3rd century B.C.E. translation of Hebrew scriptures into middle Greek. It is the most important translation of these scriptures ever made. Because the **New Testament** was written in koine Greek, the **Septuagint** became the **Old Testament** for the church.

to be saints, may God our Father and the Lord Jesus Christ send grace and peace [*eirene*]" (Romans 1:7) and often ends with a salutation such as "Be united; live in peace, and the God of love and peace be with all of you" (II Corinthians 13:11).

Because *eirene* is associated with every major characteristic of the Christian life in the **New Testament**, it is always understood as a gift from God. This gift is one of the features of **New Testament** peace which separates it from the traditional Greek usage. For the Stoics and the Epicureans internal peace (*apatheia* and *ataraxia*) were not gifts from a transcendent source but individual human accomplishments. For the **New Testament** *eirene* in all three dimensions--political peace, spiritual peace and eschatological peace--is beyond human achievement: peace can be realized only through the grace (gift) of God. In an essay in **Peace, War and God's Justice**, Paul Hammer provides an excellent description of the **New Testament** understanding of peace as the gift of God:

> "Peace" relates to the whole biblical witness to God's creating, liberating, renewing action in human history. New Testament writings portray Jesus as bringer of God's peace, who reconstitutes God's covenantal relationship with Israel as the "good news of peace" (Acts 10:36) for all the world. . . .
>
> Paul presents peace as God's gift, though its reception leads inseparably to human response. God's gift intends a healthy change in human relationships in the present, though the promise of complete fulfillment lies in the future.
>
> As Paul presents peace as God's gift, it is not surprising that he links it with such other concepts as grace, justification, and the Holy Spirit. To examine them is to reveal characteristics of peace more clearly.
>
> From earliest times, "peace" has been a greeting in the Near East, and Paul uses it in all his letters. However, he precedes it with "grace," thereby reflecting his Greek heritage. His use is more than

convention, for he relates the two terms distinctly to God and Jesus. For him Jesus as Lord is the historical focus and climax of God's grace and peace (II Cor.4:5; Phil.2:11). . . .

In a sense, this greeting embraces Paul's entire theology: grace points to the unmerited gift of God's love that accepts us sinners as we all are (Rom.5:8); and peace points to the new and whole relationships between God and us, and between us and our fellow human beings, which results from appropriating that gift. The grace of God's love, received in faith . . . brings the peace of healed relationship with God; and this "faith working through love" (Gal 5:6) is to effect peace (health, well-being, wholeness, harmony) in all human relationships.

. . . .

Paul links justification and peace closely in Romans: "Therefore, since we are justified by faith, we have peace with God through our Lord Jesus Christ" (Rom.5:1). . . .

. . . .

Peace does not mean passivity. After speaking of peace in Romans 5 Paul proceeds immediately to speak of hope, suffering, endurance, character (Rom.5:2-5). God's gift of peace does not deliver us from the struggles of life. . . .

. . . .

Paul closely connects the Holy Spirit and peace in Romans 8: "To set the mind on the flesh is death, but to set the mind on the Spirit is life and peace" (Rom 8:6). . . . The Spirit bridges the historical distance between Jesus Christ in the past and all subsequent futures, between God's peace then and God's peace now.

. . . .

The gifts of the Spirit (see I Cor.12) have as their purpose the mutual attainment of the common good, this is, of life in the full relationship Paul calls love (I Cor.13). . . .

. . . .

Elsewhere Paul writes: "Be at peace among yourselves" (I Thess.5:13). This does not mean passivity; for Paul follows immediately with "admonish the idle, encourage the faint-hearted, help the weak, be patient with them all. See that none of you repays evil with evil, but always seek to do good to one another and to all. Rejoice always, pray constantly, giving thanks in all circumstances; for this is the will of God in Christ Jesus for you" (I Thess.3:14-18). Peace is the active concern for one another even to the point of returning good for evil, both within and beyond the Christian community.

. . . .

What about individual, inner peace? Paul writes: "And the peace of God, which passes all understanding, will keep your hearts and minds in Jesus Christ" (Phil.4:7). . . .

Paul seems to suggest that worship and prayer are sources of God's peace. God's peace overcomes anxiety in the human heart and mind. . . .

. . . .

Another text suggests that peace is a process toward wholeness: "May the God of peace sanctify you wholly; and may your spirit and soul and body be kept sound and blameless at the coming of our Lord Jesus Christ" (I Thess.5:23).   ("The Gift of Peace in the New Testament," 18-22)

As clearly evidenced in this extensive citation from Hammer, the peace of God is a promise and a reality that lies at the center of the **New Testament** and the Christian life. Beginning from this fundamental understanding, it is now possible to explore in more detail the various dimensions of peace in the **New Testament**. Since the use of *eirene* as a salutation has already been noted and is essentially the same as the Hebrew *shalom*, this study moves next to the dimension of political peace. As in the explorations of the theologies of war, each dimension begins with an examination of the teachings of Jesus, then those of Paul and finally the other books in the **New Testament**.

Theology of Political Peace

For the same reasons he said little concerning political war, Jesus says very little directly about political peace: Jesus' emphasis is on spiritual peace. The clearest direct reference to political peace on the part of Jesus occurs in the Sermon on the Mount where the term *eirevopoios* (peacemaker) has its only occurrence[40] in the **New Testament**: "Happy are the peacemakers: they shall be called the sons of God." (Matthew 5:9) Certainly this statement of a fundamental value refers to those who encourage peace among humans: the birth of Jesus was even announced in terms that expressed this value and constant human need: "Glory to God in the highest heavens, and peace to [among] men. . . . " (Luke 2:14) While it is possible that the "peacemaker" beatitude may have eschatological connotations, it definitely affirms that those who work for both political and spiritual peace among human beings are doing the work of God.

While the word *eirene* does not occur in either of the preceding, there are two other significant passages which indirectly affirm the importance of political peace and the disciples' responsibilities for helping create such peace among humans: "You

---

[40]

James 3:18 uses the terms *poiousin eirenen*, which are often translated as "peacemakers," but they are more accurately translated as "those who make peace." Thus, Matthew 5 is the only passage which contains the term *erienopoios*, which means "peacemaker." However, regardless of the translations made of the Greek words, the value and belief are the same in Matthew and James: those who work for peace among humans are doing God's work.

have learnt how it was said: *You must love your neighbor* and hate your enemy. But I say this to you: love your enemies and pray for those who persecute you; in this way you will be sons of your Father in heaven. . . . " (Matthew 5:43-44) "'Well then,' he said to them 'give back to Caesar what belongs to Caesar--and to God what belongs to God'." (Luke 20:25) Although neither one of these passages explicitly mentions political peace, they both affirm values and actions that contribute to the creation of peace in the community: the first by asserting the value of love over revenge, and the second by advocating the importance of authority as a condition for social stability. It should be noted that the statement about rendering to Caesar does not grant Caesar control over one's spiritual life, "render to God what belongs to God," but it does affirm Christian responsibility to do whatever is possible to maintain civil (political) peace. Even when the political authorities abuse their power, these two teachings of Jesus most likely affirm only passive resistance, but this issue has been and continues to be debated among Christians.

As noted in the studies of war, Paul's theology of political peace is more developed than that of Jesus for several reasons. First, because of the non-occurrence of the cosmic end of time, Christians had to struggle with their being **in** the world rather than **of** it. As humans **in** the world they were members of social and political communities as well as a religious community. Second, Paul's missionary successes considerably broadened Christians' involvement in the gentile world. For these reasons, Paul develops a theology of political peace functioning on two levels: the community of Christians and the more expansive social-political community of the gentile world. More than any other writer in the **New Testament**, Paul emphasizes that God is a God of peace: "May the God of peace be with you all!" (Romans 15:33) "Prophets can always control their prophetic spirits, since God is not a God of disorder but of peace." (I Corinthians 14:33) ". . . and that peace of God . . . will guard your hearts and your thoughts, in Jesus Christ. . . . Then the God of peace be with you." (Philippians 4:7-9) "May the Lord of peace himself give you peace all the time and in every way. . . ." (II Thessalonians 3:16) For Paul, the

God of peace is the source of peace for the community as well as the individual person.

In several passages Paul appeals to Christians to keep peace among themselves as the community of God:

> In short, you must not compromise your privilege [freedom], because the Kingdom of God does not mean eating or drinking this or that,[41] it means righteousness and peace and joy brought by the Holy Spirit. If you serve Christ in this way you will please God and be respected by men. So let us adopt any custom that leads to peace and our mutual improvement; do not wreck God's work over a question of food. Of course all food is clean, but it becomes evil if by eating it you make somebody else fall away. (Romans 14:16-20)

Paul's intent is clear: Christian actions within the community of faith are those contributing to peace, encouraging those who are weak in faith, and promoting the growth and development of the spirit. In his communications to the church at Corinth, Paul emphasizes the importance of the church living in peace: "In the meantime, brothers, we wish you happiness; try to grow perfect; help one another. Be united; live in peace, and the God of both love and peace will be with you." (II Corinthians 13:11) In one of his letters to the church at Thessalonica, a church experiencing internal strife (divisions), Paul writes: "Be at peace among yourselves . . . give courage to those who are apprehensive, care for the weak and be patient with everyone. Make sure that people do not try to take revenge; you must think of what is best for each other. . . . Be happy . . . pray constantly; and for all things give thanks to God. . . . " (I Thessalonians 5:14) For Paul, peace within the church was a mark of righteousness, and, given the power of sin (both as internal and external conflict)

41

This reference to "eating and drinking" is another indication of the struggles of early Christianity to understand its relationship to the Jewish revelation (especially its religious laws) and its own unique teachings about righteousness.

in human nature, such peace could only come from God as Christians opened their hearts and minds to the presence of God.

Christians, however, are also members of social-political communities, and, consequently, Paul often writes of the need for peace among all humans. In keeping with Jesus' teachings to love enemies and pray for those who persecute Christians in his letter to Rome, Paul encourages Christians "to live at peace with everyone":

> Bless those who persecute you: never curse them, bless them. Rejoice with those who rejoice and be sad with those in sorrow. Treat everyone with equal kindness; never be condescending but make real friends with the poor. Do not allow yourselves to become self-satisfied. Never repay evil with evil but let everyone see that you are interested only in the highest ideals. Do all you can to live at peace with everyone. . . . Resist evil and conquer it with good.[42]
> (Romans 12:14-21)

Paul affirms the same commitment to political peace in many of his other letters.

In Ephesians, Paul confirms that one of God's purposes through the Christ is to bring the message of peace between Jew and gentile: "In his own person [the Christ] he killed hostility . . . he came to bring the good news of peace, *peace to those who were far away and peace to those who were near at hand.*"[43] (Ephesians

---

42

Unfortunately in the 12th chapter of Romans, while Paul rejects vengeance as a Christian action, he does not do so for God: "leave that [vengeance], my friends, to God's anger. As scripture says: *vengeance is mine --I will pay them back,* the Lord promises." (Romans 12:19) Not only is such a statement troublesome because of its anthropomorphism, "God's anger," it seems to present a vindictive picture of God that is inconsistent with Jesus' commandment to love even one's enemies.

43

In his theology of the "single New Man" in this passage, Paul also has an eschatological message of peace as well as a political one. The passage affirms that God through the Christ has begun the process of overcoming the hostilities that separate humans and providentially moving the world to a fulfillment of unity and peace at the end of time.

2:16-17) Recognizing that political stability is a necessary condition for political peace, Paul's letters to both Timothy and Titus emphasize Christians' responsibilities toward political authorities[44]: "My advice is that, first of all, there should be prayers for everyone--petitions, intercessions and thanksgiving--and especially for kings and others in authority, so that we may be able to live righteous and reverent lives in peace and quiet. To do this is right, and will please God. . . ." (I Timothy 2:1-3) "Remind them that it is their duty to be obedient to the officials and representative of the government; to be ready to do good at every opportunity; not to go slandering other people or picking quarrels, but to be courteous and always polite to all kinds of people." (Titus 3:1-2) For Paul, Christians' responsibilities to promote political peace (peace among humans) do not stop at the door of the church!

The book of the Acts of the Apostles has three references to political peace: 9:31; 12:20; and 24:2. Each is descriptive of a period of peace. 9:31 refers to a period when the "churches throughout Judaea, Galilee and Samaria were now left in peace, building themselves up. . . . " 12:20 speaks of a treaty of peace between King Herod and the Tyrians and Sidonians. Finally, 24:2 includes a complimentary reference by one of Paul's accusers, Tertullus, to the governor Felix for providing a period of "unbroken peace." These references, then, contribute nothing of substance to a theology of political peace.

Three other letters speak of political peace: Hebrews 12:14-16, James 3:17-

---

[44]

For Paul, living at a time when the political authority of Rome was moderately tolerant of religious practices throughout the Mediterranean, civil authorities presented only occasional obstacles for the practice of one's religious faith. The persecutions that followed Paul, the division of the Mediterranean world into several nation-states during the modern period, the conflict between Catholic and Protestant forces in the 15th-16th centuries C.E. and the abusive totalitarian regimes that rise and fall after the Medieval Ages presented Christian thinkers of these periods with difficult moral and theological issues concerning Christians' responsibilities to civil authorities as well as, at times, religious authorities. The challenges are still there for current theologians and Christians who are struggling to understand how Christians are **in** the world but not **of** it.

18 and I Peter 3:10-11. *"Always be wanting peace* with all people, and the holiness without which no one can ever see the Lord. Be careful that no one is deprived of the grace of God and that no *root of bitterness should begin to grow and make trouble*; this can poison a whole community." (Hebrews 12:14-16) "Whenever you find jealously and ambition, you find disharmony, and wicked things of every kind being done; whereas the wisdom [from God] . . . is full of compassion and shows itself by doing good. . . . Peacemakers [*poiousin eirenen*, those who make peace], when they work for peace, sow the seeds which will bear fruit in holiness." (James 3:17-18) Finally, I Peter also affirms the Christian duty to promote political peace in a manner that recognizes peace with other humans beings first requires spiritual peace, (peace, wholeness with oneself), whose source is God:

> Finally: you should all agree among yourselves and be sympathetic; love the brothers, have compassion and be self-effacing. Never pay back one wrong with another, or an angry word with another one; instead, pay back with a blessing. That is what you are called to do, so that you inherit a blessing yourself. Remember: *Anyone who wants to have a happy life and to enjoy prosperity[45] must banish malice from his tongue, deceitful conversation from his lips; he must never yield to evil but must practice good; he must seek peace and pursue it. Because the face*

45

Passages such as this one, which promise "prosperity" for those who believe and practice the faith, have been badly interpreted throughout much Christian history. Too many Christians have understood the term *prosperity* as referring to material (physical, economic) prosperity. To do this is to fall prey to the "Big Bribe Theory" for which Christianity has so often been condemned by those who have not understood its spiritual message: that is, Christianity is just a Big Bribe that says if you are good God will reward you in this world and give you salvation in the next. It should be reasonably clear that when such passages speak of the prosperity that comes from belief in God, the prosperity is a spiritual one, which is best characterized by the term *shalom* or *eirene* in all the rich depth of their meanings, especially spiritual **WHOLENESS!**

> *of the Lord frowns on evil men, but the eyes of the Lord are turned*
> *towards the virtuous.* (I Peter 3:8-12)

I Peter's awareness that political peace requires spiritual peace, then, provides a suitable transition for turning to the dimension of peace most important in the **New Testament**: spiritual peace.

Theology of Spiritual Peace

Before exploring the spiritual dimension of peace (*eirene*), it is wise to recall Paul Hanson's reminder that the opposite of *shalom* is not so much war as it is chaos, that is, war is but one form that chaos assumes. The same is true of the **New Testament** use of *eirene*: its opposite is chaos, which may take the forms of violent external destructions such as wars, earthquakes and famines or internal forms such as lust, anger, greed, uncontrolled passions, fear, confusion and despair. Paul indicates his awareness of the opposition between peace and chaos when he writes the Corinthians: ". . . God is not a God of disorder [chaos] but of peace." (I Corinthians 14:32) Jesus communicates a similar view in the Sermon on the Mount when he speaks of the spiritual turmoil when one attempts to serve two masters, that is, when they are spiritually and mentally fragmented: "No one can be the slave of two masters: he will either hate the first and love the second, or treat the first with respect and the second with scorn. You cannot serve God and money [that is, non-spiritual things]." (Matthew 6:24)

Because internal chaos has the power to destroy individuals, human relationships and even whole communities, part of the greatness of both Jesus and Paul is they recognize two truths about this spiritual disorder: the first they share with many of the great Greek philosophies of life; the second they inherit from the spirituality of the Jewish faith. First, together with the Stoics and Epicureans, they both realize the greatest battle one must fight is with themselves, that is, the struggle against the forces of internal chaos.[46] This battle is the focus of Paul's great analysis of the fundamental battle of the human spirit in Romans 7: "I cannot understand my own behavior. I fail to carry out the things I want to do, and I find myself doing the very things I hate. . . . [Every] single time I want to do good it is something evil that comes to hand . . . ." (Romans 7:14-25) Second, both Jesus and Paul unequivocally assert that God is the source of peace, that is, God is the source of the power to overcome chaos. One of the most important elements of the Priestly creation account is the creative power of God in overcoming the *tehom*, the sea of chaos. In other words, Genesis 1 affirms that the natural state of the creation is one of order and peace. Since humans have fallen from the peace and order of creation through sin (internal chaos), there is only one road back to spiritual wholeness (peace): God. For this reason, spiritual peace begins with righteousness, that is, with one's right relationship with God. For Christians, unlike the Jewish prophets, righteousness involves a mediated relationship through a suffering-dying Prince of Peace.

Before examining those passages in which Jesus uses the term *eirene* as spiritual peace, it is helpful to explore two passages from the Sermon on the Mount: one which evidences his emphasis on the internal dimensions of sin (internal chaos, war) and the second his unequivocal affirmation that only through trust in God can humans overcome the internal chaos that results in spiritual brokenness, infidelity in human relationships and conflict both within societies and among societies. In the Sermon on the Mount there are six "You have heard it said . . ." statements which reflect Jesus' awareness of the inner spiritual condition of humankind as well as criticize the external, legalistic reduction of spirituality so evident in the Judaism of his day. The first two, concerning murder and adultery, and the final one, concerning love, stand out:

---

[46]

The Muslim **Qur'an** asserts the same truth. There are four kinds of *jihads*, and the most precious one in the eyes of Al-Lah is the *jihad* fought by the heart, that is, the struggle against internal chaos.

(1)   "You have learnt how it was said to our ancestors: *You must not kill*; and if anyone does kill he must answer for it before the court. But I say this to you: anyone who is angry with his brother will answer for it before the court. . . ." (Matthew 5:21-22)

(2)   "You have learnt how it was said to our ancestors: *You must not commit adultery*. But I say this to you: if a man looks at a woman lustfully, he has already committed adultery with her in his heart." (Matthew 5:27-28)

Jesus' meaning in these statements is twofold. First, healthy spirituality (spiritual wholeness, *eirene*) cannot be realized through the mere keeping of laws, even valuable spiritual and social laws, because laws can only place conditions on external behavior. In other words, one can keep the law concerning murder even though he hates his neighbor if he finds the discipline not to act on his hate. While such discipline is laudatory and contributes to social stability, hate is a form of internal chaos (sin) that fragments the spiritual *eirene* (peace) of the hater. What was suggested by the Yahwist in the story of Cain and Abel becomes for Jesus a fundamental spiritual truth: the loss of internal *eirene* (the loss of wholeness, that is, spiritual war) leads to external violence and destruction.

The last of the six statements is, in many ways, a description of the spiritual foundation for all of them: love.

(3)   "You have learnt how it was said: *You must love your neighbor* and hate your enemy. But I say this to you: love your enemies. . . ." (Matthew 5:43-44)

The lesson is clear: the experience of love opens the spirit to both forgiveness and then peace. In other words, the experience of love opens the human spirit to the presence of God.

Given the power of internal chaos in human lives and the assertions by both Jesus and Paul that alone human beings are incapable of any final victory over their spiritual brokenness, how, then, does the battle for spiritual *eirene* begin? The well know "lilies of the fields" metaphor provides an initial answer:

'That is why I am telling you not to worry about your life and what you are to eat, nor about your body. . . . Surely life means more than food and the body more than clothes. Look at the birds of the sky. They do not sow or reap . . . yet your heavenly Father feeds them. Are you not worth much more than they are? Can any of you, for all his worrying, add a single cubit to his span of life. . . . Think of the flowers [lilies] growing in the fields; they never have to work or spin; yet I assure you that not even Solomon in all his regalia was robed like one of these. Now if that is how God clothes the grass in the field . . . will he not much more look after you. . . . Your heavenly father knows [what] you need. . . . Set your hearts on his kingdom first, and on his righteousness, and all these other things will be given you as well.' (Matthew 6:25-33)

For Jesus, as well as Paul, the battle for spiritual *eirene* begins with trust in God, that is, with the decision to open one's life to the presence of God.[47]

In those passages where Jesus refers to spiritual peace (*eirene*), he relates it to faith, love and the peace which he brings, a peace that is not only spiritual but eschatological. Mark 5:34-35 describes an encounter between Jesus and a woman who has been suffering "from a hemorrhage for twelve years."[48] The account states:

---

[47]

Muslims understand this act of trust as essentially one of surrender or submission to *Al-Lah*, a surrender which brings peace (*salaam*). This is examined in the opening pages of the next chapter in connection with the sacred meaning of the terms *Islam* and *Muslim*.

[48]

Modern readers of this healing account often miss one of the most important religious aspects of the story. In almost all ancient Middle Eastern societies, the loss of blood was not only a serious health problem but often a religious one, especially for women. Levitical law declared that during her menstrual flow a woman was religiously unclean, and, consequentially could not touch a male over eight days old nor any food or utensils that a male would eat or use. The woman in the account had been unclean for 12 years, and for her to even touch the robe of Jesus was for the Jews of his day a terrible sin.

> She had heard about Jesus, and she came up behind him through the crowd and touched his cloak. 'If I can touch even his clothes,' she had told herself 'I shall be well again.' And the source of bleeding dried up instantly. . . . Immediately aware that power had gone out from him, Jesus turned . . and said, 'Who touched my clothes?' . . . . Then the woman came forward, frightened and trembling, because she knew what had happened to her, and she fell at his feet and told him the whole truth. 'My daughter,' he said 'your faith has restored you to health; go in peace and be free from your complaint.'

" . . . your **faith** has restored you to **health [wholeness]**; go in **peace**. . . . " The usual departing salutation, "Go in peace," means something much more in this context than a mere parting courtesy. The woman leaves in a state of spiritual *eirene* because her faith has helped to heal her brokenness, that is, she is now spiritually whole. In another passage, Luke 7: 36-50, Jesus indicates that both faith and love are necessary for spiritual peace:

> One of the Pharisees invited him to a meal. When he arrived . . . a woman came in who had a bad name in the town.[49] She waited behind him at his feet, weeping, and her tears fell on his feet, and she wiped them away with her hair; then she covered his feet with kisses and anointed them with the ointment.
>
> When the Pharisee who had invited him saw this, he said to himself, 'If this man were prophet, he would know who this woman is that is touching him and what a bad name she has.' [Simon, the Pharisee host, believes that Jesus has allowed himself to be polluted by being touched by an unclean woman, see footnote 48. Jesus

---

49

Some Biblical commentators think the reference to the"woman with a bad name" is Mary of Magdala. The surmised cause of her bad name was her profession as a prostitute.

responds to Simon with a parable]. . . .

The he turned to the woman. 'Simon,' he said 'you see this woman. I came into your house, and you poured no water over my feet, but she has poured out her tears over my feet and wiped them away with her hair. You gave me no kiss, but she has been covering my feet with kisses ever since I came in. You did not anoint my head with oil, but she has anointed my feet with ointment. For this reason I tell you that her sins, her many sins, must be forgiven her, or she would not have shown such great love.' Then he said to her, 'Your sins are forgiven'. . . . 'Your faith has saved you; go in peace.'

". . . her many sins, must have been forgiven her, or else she would not have shown such **great love** . . . . Your **faith** has saved you; go in **peace**'." Again, as with the woman who suffered from 12 years of bleeding, the parting salutation is more than a social convention; it is a description of her spiritual *eirene* which comes from love and faith.

There are several passages where Jesus speaks of the *eirene* which he brings as a peace that is both spiritual and eschatological. In John 14:27-28 Jesus offers to the disciples a peace that transcends the world: "Peace I bequeath you, my own peace I give you, a peace the world cannot give, this is my gift to you. Do not let your hearts be troubled or afraid." Following this gift of peace Jesus describes his going to the Father and returning to bring the Father's love which will ultimately and eternally overcome the powers of evil (chaos) in this world. In John 16:33, Jesus reiterates his teaching in John 14: "I have told you all of this so that you may find peace in me. In the world you will have trouble, but be brave: I have conquered the world." In these passages as well as many others, Jesus offers peace to his followers, a peace which is both spiritual ("Do not let your hearts be troubled or afraid") and eschatological ("I have conquered the world [that is, the powers of chaos, evil].").

Like Jesus, Paul realizes that the fundamental religious task is the struggle for spiritual peace, that so powerful is sin (spiritual *polemos*, conflict) in human nature

274

spiritual *eirene* must come as a gift from God and that the battle for spiritual peace is fought with spiritual gifts such as love, hope and faith which create righteousness and justice. While Romans 7 is Paul's greatest passage concerning the struggle for spiritual peace, he addresses this battle in several other places. In Romans 8:5-6, Paul writes: "The unspiritual are interested only in what is unspiritual, but the spiritual are interested in spiritual things. It is death to limit oneself to what is unspiritual; life and peace can come only with concern for the spiritual."[50] Even though there are biblical scholars who interpret Paul's comments in this passage about death as referring to physical death, they also describe the death of spiritual *eirene* when one's life centers on the unspiritual things of the world. In Galatians Paul provides his most expansive description of those unspiritual things which must be overcome in order to find spiritual peace:

> Let me put it like this: if you are guided by the Spirit you will be in no danger of yielding to self-indulgence, since self-indulgence is the opposite of the Spirit. . . . When self-indulgence is at work the results are obvious: fornication, gross indecency and sexual irresponsibility; idolatry . . .; feuds and wrangling, jealousy, bad temper and quarrels; disagreements, factions, envy; drunkenness, orgies and similar things. I warn you now, as I warned you before; those who behave like this will not inherit the kingdom of God. What the Spirit brings is very different . . . peace. . . . (Galatians 5:16-21)

Paul's point is clear: the fundamental spiritual battle is against the internal chaos

---

[50]

Many commentators on the **New Testament** find in this statement by Paul an affirmation of his theology of the fall. In other words, there are passages where Paul, in interpreting the Yahwist garden of Eden story, argues that the consequence of sin is physical death, that is, death came into the world because of the sin of the first Adam. But God, in order to overcome the power of sin and its consequence, death, sent a second Adam (the Christ) to die for the sins of humankind. See Romans 5.

experienced through such states as self-indulgence, envy, anger, lust, etc.. Without achieving victory in this battle, spiritual peace is impossible. Further, no victory is possible in the spiritual war with chaos without the help of God.

For Paul, God achieves victory over the powers of chaos through the death of Christ on the cross and his resurrection to eternal life. In his death and resurrection, spiritual and eschatological peace become gifts offered to those who believe. Paul's begins his instructions to the church at Colossius by reminding them of God's victory over chaos and death:

> As he is the Beginning, / he was first to be born from the dead, / so that he should be first in every way; / because God wanted all perfection / to be found in him / and all things to be reconciled through him and for him, / everything in heaven and on earth, / when he made peace / by his death on the cross. (Colossians 1:18-20)

Certainly the peace Paul writes about in this passage has eschatological meaning, that is, the promise of eternal peace, but it also involves the promise of spiritual peace for those who have been freed from the power of death. For Paul, then, the peace God offers humans cannot be separated from righteousness and justice. In Romans 5:1-3, Paul relates peace and righteousness: "So far then we have seen that, through our Lord Jesus Christ, by faith we are judged righteous and at peace with God, since it is by faith and through Jesus that we have entered this state of grace in which we can . . . look forward to God's glory."[51] In Romans 2:10-11, Paul indicates that peace

---

51

In this passage and dozens of others, Paul's recognition that faith is not something human beings accomplish on their own, that is, Paul's knowledge that faith is a gift from God, should serve to correct two of the most common "fallacies of faith": the Rationalistic fallacy and the Voluntaristic fallacy. The first makes the mistake of reducing faith to a deductive argument; consequently, it wastes considerable time and effort in attempts to rationally prove the existence of God. While the arguments have some informative value, they miss Paul's point: faith cannot be achieved by an act of intellect alone. That melancholy Dane, Kierkegaard,

cannot be separated from justice: ". . . renown, honour and peace will come to everyone who does good [does justice]--Jews first, but Greeks as well. God has no favorites." Since the source of spiritual peace is God (the Spirit) for Paul, it follows that through this peace God creates unity among believers: "Bear with one another charitably, in complete selflessness, gentleness and patience. Do all you can to preserve the unity of the Spirit by the peace that binds you together. there is one Body, one Spirit, just as you were all called into one and the same hope. . . ." (Ephesians 4:2-5)

In the same passage where Paul describes the consequences that result from the loss of spiritual peace, he also describes the gifts of the Spirit that both provide spiritual peace and are actualizations of spiritual *eirene*: "What the Spirit brings is very different: love, joy, peace, patience, kindness, goodness, trustfulness, gentleness, and self-control." (Galatians 5:22-23) In his last advice to the Christians at Philippi in Philippians 4:4-9, Paul shares his understanding of the spiritual peace that comes as a gift from God and the creative force for good such peace has in human lives:

> I want you to be happy, always happy in the Lord; I repeat,
> what I want is your happiness. Let your tolerance be evident to
> everyone: the Lord is very near. There is no need to worry; but if
> there is anything you need, pray for it, asking God for it with prayer
> and thanksgiving, and that peace of God, which is so much more than
> we can understand, will guard your hearts and thoughts, in Jesus
> Christ. Finally, brothers, fill your minds with everything that is true,

---

criticized such efforts in one of his wonderfully delightful "Dipsalmata" in his book, **Either**, when he wrote that standing on one leg and attempting to prove God's existence is not the same thing as going down on one's knees and thanking Him. The second fallacy concerns the human will. It makes the mistake of thinking that faith can be accomplished through will power. In other words, one can will himself to believe something if only his will power is strong enough. Paul Tillich's **Patterns of Faith** provides an excellent critique of the Voluntaristic fallacy.

everything that is noble, everything that is good and pure, everything that we love and honour, and everything that can be thought virtuous or worthy of praise. . . . Then the God of peace will be with you.

From God, then, comes a peace that heals the internal brokenness of the person, that overcomes the conflicts that fracture human relationships and that provides hope for the future. This peace is the force of Paul's prayerful petition for the Christians at Rome: "May the God of hope bring you such joy and peace in your faith that the power of the Holy Spirit will remove all bounds to hope." (Romans 15:13)

References to spiritual peace are less common in the rest of the **New Testament** than they are in Paul, but there are a few which deserve comment before turning to eschatological peace. The Acts of the Apostles and the non-Pauline letters commonly characterize the good news of the gospel as the good news of peace. Peter's sermon at the house of Cornelius in Acts 10 is a representative example: "It is true, God sent his word to the people of Israel, and it was to them that *the good news of peace was brought* by Jesus Christ--but Jesus Christ is Lord of all men." (Acts 10:36) The letter to the Hebrews concludes with a prayer which further clarifies the good news of peace as the news of the resurrection: "I pray that the God of peace, *who brought* our Lord Jesus *back* from the dead *to become the great Shepherd of the sheep by the blood that sealed an eternal covenant*, make you ready to do his will in any kind of good action. . . ." (Hebrews 13:20-21) Additionally, the book of Hebrews presents an interesting relationship between suffering and peace and communicates it by using a metaphor of parental discipline:

Have you forgotten that encouraging text in which you are addressed as sons? *My son, when the Lord corrects you, do not treat it lightly; but do not get discouraged when he reprimands you. For the Lord trains the ones that he loves and he punishes all those that he acknowledges as his sons.* Suffering is part of your training. . . . Besides, we have all had our human fathers who punished us, and we respected them for it: we ought to be even more willing to submit

> ourselves to our spiritual father, to be given life. Our human fathers were thinking of this short life when they punished us, and could only do what they thought best; but he does it all for our own good, so that we may share his holiness. Of course, any punishment is most painful at the time, and far from pleasant; but later, in those on whom it has been used, it bears fruit in peace and goodness. (Hebrews 12:10-13)

That punishment helps build character and thus encourages goodness is not a new idea; but the writer of Hebrews does something much more interesting: he argues that punishment and suffering bear the fruit of peace, a most interesting thought. Certainly if suffering and punishment can lead to goodness, they also contribute to peace for goodness helps create both political and spiritual peace. However, the writer may also have in mind an ancient view that punishment of wrong doing is necessary to re-establish the moral balance of the universe: that is, evil (sin, wrong doing) leads to chaos, punishment corrects this state, and, thus, punishment returns a state of peace. It is certainly true that unpunished wrongs in a society often lead to social chaos.

While there are a few other references to spiritual peace in these books, they contribute neither additional insights nor depth to the understandings of Jesus and Paul concerning spiritual *eirene*. For this reason, it is now appropriate to consider the last dimension of peace: eschatological peace. As we approach the year 2000 C.E., the millennium, speculations and prophecies concerning eschatological peace as well as eschatological war will likely evidence a geometric growth among the more extreme groups in Judaism and Christianity. Since the Muslim calendar is different, the Islamic world should not see such a dramatic increase in millennial theologies.

Theology of Eschatological Peace

Because there are four fundamental features of cosmic eschatology emphasized in the **New Testament**, the strategy for examining eschatological peace differs from the preceding approaches for political and spiritual peace. Rather than beginning with the views of Jesus, then those of Paul and concluding with the understanding of peace in other parts of the **New Testament** as in previous sections, it is more advantageous to organize this final section of the chapter in terms of four major aspects of cosmic eschatology: (1) the return of the Messianic Savior (the *Christos*); (2) the crushing of evil (Satan); (3) the creation of the New Jerusalem and the New Man; and (4) descriptions of those who will receive the eternal peace of salvation. Selections from the gospels, the letters of Paul and the book of Revelation are used to illustrate these features of **New Testament** cosmic eschatology.

In keeping with the cosmic eschatology inherited from the Jewish apocalypses, the **New Testament** identifies many of the same signs whose purpose indicates the new age has commenced. Most of these have been examined in the section on cosmic eschatological war in the **Hebrew Bible**. From the perspective of the **New Testament**, the most important of these signs is the arrival of the *Mesiah* Savior, that is the return of the crucified and resurrected *Christos*. In John 14, after telling the disciples to " not let your hearts be troubled or afraid," Jesus informs them that he will leave them only to return:

> I am going away, and shall return.[52] / If you love me you
> would have been glad to know that I am going to the Father,
> / For the Father is greater than I. / I have told you this now
> before it happens, / so that when it does happen you may

52

  Jesus' comment about going away and returning has a double meaning in this passage: (1) his crucifixion (going away) and resurrection (returning) and (2) his returning at the end of time. His II Coming (returning) is clarified later in the passage when he talks about "going to the Father" and the "prince of this world" (Satan) who is on his way. Since Jesus states in the gospels that between his first going away (his death) and his returning (the resurrection) he has not yet ascended to the Father, his returning in this passage refers to the II Return (Coming) to overcome evil at the end of time.

> believe. / I shall not talk with you any longer, / because the
> prince of this world is on his way. / He has no power over
> me, / but the world must be brought to know that I love the
> Father / and that I am doing exactly what the Father told me.
> (John 14:28-31)

In Ephesians, Paul writes of the power of the risen *Christos* for this age and the "age
to come":

> This you can tell from the strength of his [God's] power at work in
> Christ, when he used it to raise him from the dead and to make him
> sit at his right hand, in heaven, far above every Sovereignty,
> Authority, Power, or Dominion . . . not only in this age but also in the
> age to come. He has put all things under his feet, and made him the
> ruler of everything . . . the fullness of him who fills the whole
> creation. (Ephesians 1:19-23)

In II Thessalonians, while warning the church to stay calm and not be alarmed
by false predictions and prophecies, Paul affirms the II Coming of the Messiah Christ
in terms also emphasizing the second aspect of Christian cosmic eschatology:

> To turn now, brothers, to the coming of our Lord Jesus Christ
> and how we shall all be gathered round him: please do not get
> excited too soon or alarmed by any prediction or rumour . . implying
> that the Day of the Lord has already arrived. Never let anyone
> deceive you in this way.
>
> It cannot happen until the Great revolt has taken place and the
> Rebel,[53] the Lost One has appeared. This is the Enemy, the one
> who claims to be so much greater than anything that is worshipped,

---

53

Later Christian tradition identifies this "Rebel," (also called the"Lost One,"
the "Enemy") as the Anti-Christ who becomes, metaphorically, the general of Satan's
army of evil.

that he enthrones himself in God's sanctuary and claims that he is
God. . . . The Lord will kill him with the breath of his mouth and will
annihilate him with his glorious appearance at his coming.

But when the Rebel comes, Satan will set to work: there will
be all kinds of miracles and a deceptive show of signs and portents,
and everything evil that can deceive those who are bound for
destruction because they would not grasp the love of truth that would
have saved them. The reason why God is sending a power to delude
them . . . is to condemn all who refused to believe in the truth and
choose wickedness instead. (II Thessalonians 2:1-12)

The appearance of the Anti-Christ is but a prelude to the Second Appearance
of the *Mesiah* Savior who returns to crush evil. In the gospel of John, Jesus comforts
the disciples in words which indicate his final victory over evil:

Listen; the time will come--in fact it has come already-- /
when you will be scattered, each going his own way / and
leaving me alone. / And yet I am not alone, / because the
father is with me. / I have told you all this / so that you may
find peace in me. / In the world you will have trouble, / but
be brave: / I have conquered the world. (John 16:32-33)

As before, Jesus' comments have a two-fold referent: the events surrounding Passion
week and the end of time. By "world" in this passage is meant the destructive
powers of evil in the world. Concerning the final destruction of evil, Paul concludes
his letter to Rome with a most concise statement: "The God of peace will soon crush
Satan beneath your feet. The grace of the Lord Jesus Christ be with you." (Romans
16:20) The implication in this passage is once evil (Satan) is crushed, the creation
will return to its original state: **PEACE!**

When God crushes Satan (Evil) through the *Mesiah* Savior, the New
Jerusalem will rise as the home of the New Man. In Ephesians, Paul declares that the
New Man is neither Jew or gentile:

> For he [the *Christos*] is the peace between us, and has made the two
> [Jew and gentile] into one and broken down the barrier which used to
> keep them apart, actually destroying in his person the hostility caused
> by the rules and decrees of the Law. This was to create one single
> New Man in himself out of the two of them and by restoring peace
> through the cross to unite them in a single Body and reconcile them
> with God. . . . Through him, both of us have in the one Spirit our way
> to come home to the Father. (Ephesians 2:14-18)

While the passage identifies the *Christos* as the New Man, it also implies in the New
Jerusalem there will be neither Jew nor gentile but a New Human who is the child of
God, that is, the New Man is not only a metaphor for the *Christos* but for citizens of
the New Jerusalem. The rising and the nature of the New Jerusalem[54] provides the
content of Revelation 21:

> Then I saw a new heaven and a new earth; the first heaven
> and the first earth had disappeared now, and there was no longer any
> sea. I saw the holy city, and the new Jerusalem, coming down from
> God out of heaven. . . . Then I heard a loud voice call from the
> throne, 'You see this city? Here God lives among men. He will make

---

[54]

    The nature of the New Jerusalem has been a subject of considerable
controversy throughout the history of Christianity. For some, it is a physical city re-
created on the same ground as ancient Jerusalem; for others, the New Jerusalem is
a metaphor for Heaven. This study agrees with the latter view, a point that is
important for the final chapter and has implications for the New Temple that is to be
rebuilt in the New Jerusalem. For some, the New Temple is a physical Temple
rebuilt on the site of Solomon's Temple (for Jews, Temple Mount; for Muslims the
present location of the Dome of the Rock Mosque and the Mosque of Aqsa, the
Haram as-Sharif, the Noble Enclosure); for others, such as Philo Judaeus (died in 40
C.E.), the True Temple is a spiritual one whose pillars are the sky. This issue and
controversy are important in considering the political and religious future of
Jerusalem. The final chapter, in its theological argument for chosenness **TO BE**
rather than chosenness **TO HAVE**, agrees with Philo concerning the nature of the
True Temple and the view of the New Jerusalem stated in the following footnote.

his home among them; they shall be his people, and he will be their God; his name is God-with-them. He will wipe away all tears from their eyes; there will be no more death, and no more mourning or sadness. The world of the past has gone.　　(Revelation 21:1-4)

Later the writer of Revelation declares that in the New Jerusalem all who are thirsty (for righteousness, justice and holiness) shall drink of the "water of life": "'Come'. Then let all who are thirsty come: all who want it may have the water of life,[55] and have it free." (Revelation 22:17) These passages metaphorically describe the New Jerusalem and the New Man. This leaves only one further issue that needs brief description: the citizens of the New Jerusalem who inherit the promise of eternal peace.

In John 14, Jesus prepares the disciples for his crucifixion with words of comfort and hope for the future:

> Do not let your hearts be troubled. / Trust in God still, and trust in me. / There are many rooms in my Father's house; / if there were not I should have told you. / I am going now to prepare a place for you, / and after I have gone and prepared you a place, / I shall return to take you with me; / so that where I am / you may be too. / You know the way to the place where I am going. (John 14:1-4)

While the "you" in this passage explicitly refers to the disciples, in the story of the repentant thief who is crucified along with Jesus, Jesus opens the doors of the New Jerusalem to all those who repent and ask God for forgiveness, that is, all who seek righteousness:

55

 References to there being "no more death" and freely drinking form "the water of life" strongly suggest that the New Jerusalem is a metaphor for eternal life in Heaven, and, thus, should not be taken literally as a physical city. See previous footnote.

> One of the criminals hanging there abused him. 'Are you not the Christ?' he said. 'Save yourself and us as well.' But the other spoke up and rebuked him. 'Have you no fear of God at all?' he said. 'You got the same sentence as he did, but in our case we deserved it: we are paying for what we did. But this man has done nothing wrong. Jesus' he said 'remember me when you come into your kingdom.' 'Indeed, I promise you,' he replied 'today you will be with me in paradise.' (Luke 23:39-43)

Paul affirms the same openness of paradise to those who do good and promises the peace that awaits them: ". . . renown, honour and peace will come to everyone who does good--Jew first, but Greeks as well. God has no favorites."[56] (Romans 2:9-11) The book of Revelation also describes the inhabitants of the New Jerusalem as those who do good:

> The One sitting on the throne spoke: 'Now I am making the whole of creation new' he said 'Write this: that what I am saying is true and will come true. . . . I am the Alpha and the Omega, the Beginning and the End. I will give water from the well of life to anybody who is thirsty [for righteousness and goodness]; it is the rightful inheritance of the one who proves victorious; and I will be his God and he a son to me.' (Revelation 21:5-7)

Finally in several passages, Paul speaks of the eschatological future of those who have already died. The following passage from the Corinthian correspondence is

---

[56] This passage should serve as a corrective for that salvation arrogance which characterizes too many Christian groups who claim only those like them are saved. Fortunately, the **New Testament** provides a better affirmative action policy of salvation than many church groups have preached. In fairness, it should also be stated that many Jewish and Muslim groups adhere to a similar chauvinistic view of salvation which also distorts and is inconsistent with the spiritual depths of their sacred revelations.

typical:

> Or else, brothers, put it this way: flesh and blood cannot inherit the kingdom of God: and the perishable cannot inherit what lasts forever. I will tell you something that has been secret: that we are not all going to die, but shall all be changed. This will be instantaneous, in the twinkling of an eye, when the last trumpet sounds. it will sound and the dead will be raised,[57] imperishable, and we shall be changed as well, because our present perishable nature must put on imperishability and this mortal nature must put on immortality. (I Corinthians 15:50-53)

The **New Testament**, then, as a whole affirms a cosmic end to the present dimension of existence which results in the ultimate and final defeat of evil and the consequent creation of a New Jerusalem populated by those who love God (those who are righteous) and their fellow human beings (those who do justice). Their existence in the New Jerusalem is one filled with joy, wonder, blissfulness and, above all, characterized as a life of eternal peace. Over and over again, when the **New Testament** speaks of the Day of the Lord, the term *eirene* is included, as in I Thessalonians when Paul closes his letter with what is both a hope and a prayer:

57

Christians have been divided over the timing of the celestial journey to Heaven since the first century because of passages like this in Paul and references in other passages (for example, I Corinthians 15:51; I Thessalonians 4:14-15; Ephesians 5:14) to the soul "sleeping with the body." Most Christians today believe that the soul's journey begins at the death of the body. Roman Catholics and most Protestant Christians accept this view although they differ concerning the purifying place of purgatory that created such conflict during the Protestant Reformation. A small minority of Christians accept the position that the soul sleeps with the body until the Last Day at which time the saved are raised in a spiritual body to Heaven and the damned to Hell. Muslim theology accepts the view that the soul sleeps with the body until *Al-Lah* gives it a new body on the Day of Judgment. There is, however, an interesting and troubling exception to this in Islam: the belief that a *mujihad*, a person killed in a holy war, immediately enters Paradise. The next chapter examines this belief.

"May the God of peace make you perfect and holy; and may you be kept safe and blameless, spirit, soul, and body, for the coming of our Lord Jesus Christ. God has called you and he will not fail you." (I Thessalonians 5:23)

Having explored the theologies of war and peace in the **New Testament**, it is now time to examine the theologies of war and peace that developed among a group of people whose historical situation was more similar to pre-exhilic Jews than the first century Christians: the Arabs of the Arabian peninsula. Among them a Prophet named Muhammad arose and created a social and religious revolution: Islam. The fact his situation was as political as it was religious had a major impact on the development of theologies of war and peace that emerged in this third child of Abraham.

CHAPTER FOUR

ISLAM AND THE PEACE OF SUBMITTING ONE'S
LIFE TO GOD

Unfortunately, for many Americans the very term *Muslim* conjures up images of holy warriors storming crusader castles,[1] suicidal terrorists who cowardly slaughter civilians with bombs,[2] patriarchal savages who brutalize women through atrocities such as clitoral circumcism,[3] despotic, wealthy sheiks and ignorant, poverty

---

[1]

As a whole, Americans know little about the crusades other than the distorted and chauvinistic views they have received from films or Christianity. In their views, the crusaders were holy men who saved the holy land from the bloodthirsty ravages of Islam. The historic facts are quite different. While atrocities were committed on both sides during this disastrous and disgraceful period in the history of the West, Christian crusaders were guilty of much more bloodshed than Muslim *mujihads* (warriors). Karen Armstrong's book, **Holy War: The Crusades and Their Impact on Today's World**, published by Anchor Books in 1988, is an excellent and unbiased study of the crusades.

[2]

The media is largely responsible for this stereotype because it seldom covers events in the Middle East except when some kind of violence has occurred. Groups like Hamas and Islamic Jihad represent only a minuscule portion of Islam. Most Muslims are like human beings throughout the world. They laugh and love, suffer and cry, and most of all, they want their children to live happy and healthy lives.

[3]

While such mutilation is still found in such places as Egypt and more commonly in Africa, it is not practiced because of Islam. The practice of clitoral

stricken populations,[4] and militant religious fanatics who preach intolerance.[5]   In a

---

circumcism, as well as the clothing practices associated with Islam, were cultural practices in the Middle East and Africa long before Islam arrived. The **Qur'an** neither requires the wearing of a veil nor condones the barbaric practice of female circumcism. As Islam spread from Arabia into the Middle East and Africa, it syncretized local customs into its traditions. This has always been the case with missionary religions, Christianity included. For its time, the 7th century C.E., the **Qur'an** provided women with rights of divorce and inheritance unequalled anywhere in the Christian world. Until the beginnings of the modern period in Europe, the status of women in Christianity was barbaric compared to Islam. Unfortunately during the 13th-14th centuries C.E., the world of Islam was driven back into a dark age from which it has yet to emerge while Europe began an enlightenment in these same centuries that continues today.

4

While much of the Muslim world is struggling to rise out of their dark ages, for approximately four centuries (650 to 1050 C.E.), the most intellectually alive culture in the West was Islam. During this time, the best science (especially medicine) and philosophy was produced by Muslim thinkers. One of the reasons for this was that much of the science, mathematics and philosophy of the Greeks which was lost to the Christian West was known in the world of Islam. During these 400 years, the international language of learning in the Mediterranean world was neither Latin nor Greek, but Arabic. As an example, consider Moses Maimonides (13th century). The greatest philosopher in the history of Judaism wrote his philosophical and medical works in Arabic. Indeed, while most historians date the Renaissance in Europe from the end of the 13th century, intellectually the philosophical Renaissance began in the 11th century when Latin translations of the Muslim Aristotelians challenged the church. During this period, the Europeans and Christians were the philosophical, intellectual and scientific barbarians.

5

All three of Abraham's children have been guilty of preaching and practicing intolerance. Compared to the other great religions of the world, it is the monotheisms which have been the most intolerant. Of the three, Islam has been historically the most tolerant. The theology of the *herem* (ban) indicates a strong tendency within Judaism of intolerance, while Christian acts of intolerance, especially against Jews, have helped create the kind of environment for pogroms and final solutions. Of the three children, Muslims have treated both Jews and Christians with considerably more religious toleration than they have reciprocated. This is not to claim that Islam has not also been guilty of religious bigotry and intolerance, but especially as contrasted with Christianity, Muslims has fewer historical sins for which they must atone than Christians.

similar manner, Americans think of the **Qur'an** as a brutal, judgmental, repetitive manual of Holy War against the enemies of Islam.[6] If there is any word that Americans do not associate with either Islam or the **Qur'an**, it is **PEACE**. However, notice the title of this chapter: "Islam and the Peace of Submitting One's Life to God."

There are many reasons for the distorted image of Islam dominating American perceptions of this great monotheism. Most have already been mentioned in previous sections: the distortions created by the mass media,[7] the confusing of religious fundamentalism with religious extremism, the chauvinism of Christianity (at least that of many Christian groups), the historical ignorance of many Americans (especially their ignorance of world history), American political and economic arrogance, and the intellectual laziness of thinking in terms of stereotypes. Since the subject of this study is a religious one, an additional problem of distortion needs to be mentioned: that of confusing what a religion **actually teaches** with the manifold ways that religious groups **use (distort)** religious beliefs and values for their own

---

[6]

The study of the theologies of war and peace in this chapter should suffice to establish that there is much more to the **Qur'an** than war, and that, even when the **Qur'an** discusses war, it presents a theology that is much more civilized than that of the pre-exhilic Hebrews. As indicated earlier, the **New Testament** in its views of war had several, considerable moral advantages over the Holy Books of both Jews and Muslims: the two most important being that the early church had no political power and no standing army to influence its theologies of war and peace.

[7]

Probably because of the media, a new term has been coined: *factoid*. This term may be illustrative of the problem of media created stereotypes because a factoid is a simple sentence supposedly stating a fact, but one presented without a context. Most media reports are a collection of factoids, that is, stories hastily written to meet a deadline which present the "facts" (factoids) without adequate context. For facts to be meaningful, they must be presented within an adequate context. The average 1-3 minute "sound bite" media report can hardly provide an adequate context for an intelligible and comprehensive understanding of what is reported.

benefit.[8] In other words, it is no more reasonable, accurate, or moral to reduce Islam to Hussein and Khomeini (or to Hamas and Hizbollah) than it is to reduce Christianity to Jimmy Swaggert and Jimmy Baker (or the white supremist "Christianity" of the militia groups who advocate overthrow of the U.S. government). **What a religion teaches** can be quite different than the way its beliefs and values are used by self-justifying groups.

As an introductory corrective to the usual distorted and stereotypical images of Islam, consider the following three examples that more clearly and adequately indicate the true spirit of Islam: the first from Muslim history and the next two from the **Qur'an**. In her anthology of materials on the Zoroastrian religion, Mary Boyce includes the following description of an incident recorded by an anonymous Persian historian during the reign of the Umayyad caliph Mu'awiya (about 1060 C.E.), which concerns the interaction between Islam and Zoroastrianism:

> [Ziyad ibn Abih, the governor of Basra has sent one of his officials, 'Obayd Allah, to Sistan where there is a Zoroastrian community and fire temple.]
>
> Before his departure, Ziyad gave the following order: 'When you go there, kill Shabur, the chief priests of the fire temples, and stamp out their fires.' So 'Obayd Allah went to Sistan to carry out his assignment. Consequently, the small landlords and the (other) Zoroastrians resolved that they would rebel because of this.

8

As examples of such distortions consider the uses of Christianity to justify anti-Semitism, the Hebrew belief in the ban, and the arguments used by Christians in the past (unfortunately, also by some groups in the present) to justify slavery. These are but a few of the many ways that noble and compassionate religious beliefs and values can be distorted for personal or group advantage. In Israel such arguments are presently being used by the religious extremists to drive Palestinians from Jerusalem and their homes in the West Bank. However, there are thousands of Israelis who speak out against the continued occupation of Palestinian land, against their government's expansionist policies and for the rights of Palestinians.

Whereupon the Moslems of Sistan said: 'If our Prophet (the blessings of God be upon him!) or the first four caliphs have done this to a group which had made peace with them, then we shall carry out the order; but if this has not been the case, then we must not act on this matter contrary to Islamic law and our peace (agreement).' So they wrote a letter to the court [in Damascus] in this regard, and the reply came, saying: 'You must not (harm them) because they have made a treaty of friendship with us and those places of worship are theirs.[9] The Persians say: "We worship God and we have our fire temples and our sun. But it is not the sun and the fire temple we worship; on the contrary, they are ours in the same way that the altars [of mosques, i.e., the mithrab] and the Ka'ba are yours." In as much as this is so, you should not exterminate (their temples), since they have fire temples in the same fashion that Jews have synagogues and the Christians their churches. Since they are all Peoples of the Book , what difference does the place of worship make, since we worship God? . . . . Furthermore they resent the destruction of any object or any building of ancient standing. If our Prophet (the blessings of God be upon him!) had so desired he would have permitted none of these to exist, but would have exterminated all the infidels and all religions other than Islam. However, he did not do so, but made peace with them on the basis of a capitation tax (jizya). . . .' 'Obayd Allah did not carry out the orders, and acted in the capacity of both administrator

---

9

The analyses of theologies of peace which are examined in the last section of this chapter clearly indicate that the **Qur'an** always recommends peace above war, toleration for religions who worship one God and have a "Book," and views the individual violation of an oath or the community violation of a treaty of peace (friendship) are sins severely punished by *Al-Lah* (God).

and judge. (**Textual Sources for the Study of Zoroastrianism**, 117)

Notice that the political governor, Zayad ibn Abih, tries to use religion to destroy the Zoroastrians, but the Muslim community as a whole is more concerned with remaining true to the beliefs and values of Islam: values clearly indicating the importance of keeping one's treaties and religious toleration for those who worship God. In this incident, we find the spirit of peace fundamental to the **Qur'an**. Further, the religious toleration evidenced in this incident is quite a contrast to the lack of toleration that has historically characterized the Christian world, where there has been as much intolerance within Christianity among competing groups as for those who are not Christian.[10]

There are many passages in the **Qur'an** that emphasize peace over war and forgiveness over hate. In the two selected as examples, the first is a Qur'anic variation of the Cain and Abel story and the second a wonderful moral lesson about righteousness. The account of Cain and Abel in the **Qur'an** adds an important religious value to the story absent from the **Hebrew Bible**--Abel's response to Cain just before his murder:

> Recite to them the truth / Of the story of the two sons / Of Adam. Behold! they each / Presented a sacrifice (to God): / It was accepted from one, / But not from the other. / Said the latter: / "Be sure I will slay thee." / "Surely," Said the former, / "God Doth accept of the sacrifice / Of those who are righteous.

10

It should be noted that the considerable intolerance in Christianity that developed after the church gained political power represented a distortion of the teachings of Jesus concerning love and that in every decade there were individual voices who protested the distortions and impurities which had entered Christianity. It is often in these voices, voices which seem to be crying in the wilderness, that each generation is provided with an opportunity for spiritual growth. The final chapter presents an apology for such an opportunity today in recognizing the **moral universality** of the message of monotheism in the chosenness **TO BE**.

"If thou dost stretch they hand / Against me, to slay me, / It is not for me to stretch / My hand against thee / To slay thee: for I do fear / God, the Cherisher of the Worlds.

"For me, I intend to let / Thee draw on thyself / My sin as well as thine, / For thou wilt be among the / Companions of the Fire, / And that is the reward / Of those who do wrong."

The (selfish) soul of the other / Led him to the murder / Of his brother: he murdered / Him, and became (himself) / One of the lost ones. (V: 30-33)

In his commentary on this amazing speech from Abel, A. Yusuf Ali writes:

> Abel's speech is full of meaning. He is innocent and God-fearing. To the threat of death held out by the other, he returns a calm reply, aimed at reforming the other. "Surely," he pleads, "if your sacrifice was not accepted, there was something wrong in you, for God is just and accepts the sacrifice of the righteous. If this does not deter you, I am not going to retaliate, though there is as much power in me against you as you have against me. I fear my Maker, for I know He cherishes all His creation. Let me warn you that you are doing wrong. I do not intend even to resist, But do you know what the consequences will be to you? You will be in spiritual torment."
>
> **(The Holy Qur'an**, 251)

Note the emphasis on the holiness of all creation and the righteousness (atonement) that comes from not striking back against a wrong. Abel's speech could almost have come from the cross of Jesus. There is a significant emphasis in the **Qur'an** on forgiveness and the religious merit of enduring injustice rather than violently striking back. Later in the same *sura*, this point is again emphasized:

> We ordained therein for them [the reference here is to the Law of Moses]: / "Life for life, eye for eye, / Nose for nose, ear for ear, / Tooth for tooth, and wounds / Equal for equal." But if / Anyone

> remits the retaliation / By way of charity, it is / An act of
> atonement of himself. . . . (V:48)

The lesson is clear: there is greater religious merit in forgiveness and charity (love) than in retaliation or vengeance.[11] As a beginning background, these three examples should suffice to establish there is much more to Islam than war and intolerance. Now the rich spiritual meaning of the terms *Islam* and Muslim can be explored.

The Peace-Surrender of Islam and the Muslim[12]

From the Medieval period into the 20th century there has been an ignorant

---

[11]

The lessons in this *ayat* are strikingly similar to the teachings of Jesus in the Sermon on the Mount concerning the old law, the righteousness of forgiveness and charity toward enemies.

[12]

Because of the importance of Hebrew (the language of the **Hebrew Bible**) and Greek (the language of the **New Testament** as well as a considerable corpus of works in philosophy, history, science and literature which had considerable influence on European civilization), transliterations of Hebrew and Greek words into English, French and German have been standardized for centuries. Unfortunately, the same situation is not the case concerning Arabic. After the 14th century, the knowledge of Arabic in Europe almost disappeared. Interest in Arabic materials has only recently revived. As a result, transliterations of Arabic words into English have not yet been standardized. Consequently, the Arabic term for the Holy Book is still transliterated as either *Koran* or *Qur'an.*. Another example is the term for the one who accepts the revelations of the **Qur'an**. The Arabic term is variously transliterated as *Moslem* or *Muslim*. Because the purpose of a transliteration is to pronounce the term, most Americans recognize that **Koran** and **Qur'an** are the same terms. Sometimes, however, the transliterations into English are different enough to be confusing: for example consider the two common transliterations for Muhammad's flight from Mecca to Medina in 622 C.E.: *Hegira* or *Hijrah*. This study uses those transliterations which are most likely to become the standardized ones. However, for reasons already stated, Islam and Muslim are not italicized as transliterations except where such is grammatically appropriate or for emphasis. For an excellent description of the problems of transliteration see Marshall G.S. Hodgson's **The Venture of Islam, vol 1: Conscience and History in a World Civilization**, published by The University of Chicago Press, pages 3-12.

use of the term *Muhammadean* to refer to a *Muslim,* and correspondingly the term *Muhammadism* to refer to *Islam,* by non-Muslim Europeans and Americans. For Muslims the use of these two words is more than inaccurate, it is religiously offensive for two reasons. First, Muslims believe the two nouns *Islam* and *Muslim* were given (commanded) by God in a revelation to Muhammad during the last few months of his life.[13] Second, because the term *Christian* means "one who worships the Christ as the Son of God," many Muslims believe the term *Muhammadean* implies that Muslims worship Muhammad. Nothing could be further from the truth. While Muslims revere Muhammad more than any other prophet sent from God, they would never commit the sin of *shirk*: the sin of attributing partners to God, that is, the sin of worshipping Muhammad as well as God.[14] Excluding the atypical period of the "Satanic Verses,"[15] the revelations of Muhammad represent the

---

13

     As described in Chapters One (see footnote #11) and Two, while nouns have always occupied a special place in human language and thought, proper nouns (names) possessed a religious significance in the ancient world that was far different than their significance today. Nouns (or names) which came from God were more important than all others: for example *Jacob* being given the name *Isra-el* by the angel of God was a naming with monumental religious meaning. So it is with the nouns *Islam* and *Muslim*, which for Muslims are **Arabic** words that came to Muhammad from God. See the next section for the significance of this: "The Arabic Voice of God in the **Qur'an**."

14

     From the Muslim perspective, the Christian doctrine of the Trinity is a distortion of the monotheistic revelation sent by God through Jesus. Consequently, they believe Christians are guilty of the worst of all sins, *shirk.*

15

     Approximately four years after the Night of Power and Glory (the night of the first revelation from God, late spring or early summer 610 C.E.), Muhammad made the house of al-Arqam the center of his preaching activities. Although his early preaching (reciting of the revelations from *Al-Lah*) centered on one God, prayer and charity, the absolute monotheism of his claims was not yet clear to Muhammad, the small Muslim community or the non-Muslim Meccans. This fact probably prevented much opposition to his teaching during these first years. Sometime during 614 C.E. an interesting event occurred in his life, the "revelation of the Satanic Verses." This

clearest and most adamant monotheism in the history of the West. Even the

---

"revelation" and the following revelation which abrogated (replaced and corrected) it were decisive for Muhammad in two ways: first, the ambiguous monotheism of his first four years preaching was definitively rejected in terms of an unequivocally clear monotheism; and, second, the opposition to Muhammad by the powerful in Mecca intensified geometrically.

Briefly, the incident of the Satanic Verses can be described as follows. Muhammad received a revelation which apparently encouraged the worship of divine beings other than *Al-Lah*:

> Did you consider al-Lat and al-Uzza / And al-Manat, the third, the other? / Those are the swans [divinities] exalted; / Their intercession is expected; / Their likes are not neglected. (W. Montgomery Watt, **Muhammad: Prophet and Statesman,** 60)

This revelation was more consistent with henotheism than monotheism: *Al-Lah* was still the God above all others, but *al-Lat*, *al-Uzza* and *al-Manat* (three of the major deities of the Arabic polytheistic pantheon who had major shrines in Mecca and Medina) were also to be remembered. While this revelation was clearly inconsistent with monotheism, it was one which would have allayed many of the fears of the Meccan polytheists and merchants who made a living from the pilgrim trade to the polytheistic shrines of Mecca.

Sometime later, Muhammad received a revelation abrogating the previous one:

> Did you consider al-Lat and al-Uzza / And al-Manat, the third, the other? / For you males and for Him females? / That would be unfair sharing. / They are but names you and your fathers named; / God revealed no authority for them; / they follow only opinion and their souls' fancies, / though from their / Lord there has come to them guidance. (Watt, 60)

The second revelation clearly affirmed that these three are only "names you and your fathers named," that is, the correcting revelation (LIII:19-23) rejected any other divinities: *Al-Lah* alone is God. From this point there was never any question about the absolute monotheism of Islam.

However, Muhammad and the Muslim community had a problem: why and from whom came the Satanic Verses. Their answer was one that was not inconsistent with either Jewish or Christian beliefs: the false revelation came from Satan whose purpose was to confuse and harm both the Prophet of God and the community of Muslims. Throughout the histories of post-exhilic Judaism and Christianity the powerful figure of Satan constantly attempted to harm holy men and confuse God's chosen communities.

announcement of his death by Abu Bakr to the Muslims of Mecca reinforced the absolute monotheism of Islam: "O ye people, if anyone worships Muhammad, Muhammad is dead, but if anyone worships God, He is alive and dies not." (W. Montgomery Watt, **Muhammad: Prophet and Statesman**, p.228)[16]

In order to understand the deep religious significance of the terms *Islam* and *Muslim*, two tasks are required: first, an etymological examination of the consonantal root *SLM¹⁻* of both terms and the most important Qur'anic *ayats* which reveal their meanings. It will, then, be possible to translate their meanings into English.

The Semitic root *SLM* should be familiar because it is the same root for the Hebrew word *shalom*. Its fundamental meaning is "peace." When the vowels *I* and *A* are added, the root becomes *ISLAM*, translated by many writers as "submission" or "surrender." Such translations are highly inadequate, for the term *Islam* means so much more. Some translators, therefore, attempt to capture both ideas and indicate that the word *Islam* means "peace-surrender." But even this is inadequate for understanding the rich religious meaning of both this word and the noun *Muslim*. Before attempting to translate this richness into English, a brief examination of several key *ayats* from the **Qur'an** is helpful.

16

There are several biographies of Muhammad available in English. One of the best is the two volume biography by W. Montgomery Watt, **Muhammad at Mecca** and **Muhammad at Medina**. In 1960 Oxford University Press published a condensed version of these two volumes with the title **Muhammad: Prophet and Statesman**. From a slightly different perspective, Karen Armstrong's biography, **Muhammad**, published by Harper Collins in 1992 gives more attention to the person and family of Muhammad than the historian Watt. Together, both provide a historically accurate and fair treatment of this great human being, social reformer and prophet.

17

A more thorough etymological study is provided for this consonantal root as it is the root of the Arabic term for peace, *salaam*, in the final section of this chapter: "Theologies of Peace."

Regarding the term *Islam*, there are three key passages:

> But your God is One God: / Submit then your wills to Him / (In
> Islam): and give thou / The good news to those / Who humble
> themselves,--
>
> To those whose hearts, / When God is mentioned, / Are filled with
> fear, / Who show perseverance / Over their afflictions, keep up /
> Regular prayer, and spend / (In charity) out of what / We have
> bestowed upon them. (XXII:34-35)
>
> For me, I have been / Commanded to serve the Lord / Of this City,
> Him Who has / Sanctified it and to / Whom (Belong) all things:
> / And I am commanded / To be of those who bow / In Islam to
> God's Will,-- (XXVII:91)
>
> (A voice will say:) / "This is what was / Promised for you,-- For
> everyone who turned / (To God) in sincere repentance, / Who kept
> (His Law),
>
> "Who feared (God) / Most Gracious unseen, / And brought a heart
> / Turned in devotion (to Him):
>
> Enter ye therein / In Peace and Security; / This is the Day Of
> Eternal Life!" (L:32-34)

In his footnote commentaries on these *ayats*, Ali clarifies the nature of the believer
in *Al-Lah* and the promise of Peace:

> The description of the righteous [that is, the Muslim] is given
> in four masterly clauses: (1) those who turned away from Evil in
> sincere repentance; (2) those whose new life was good and righteous;
> (3) those who in their innermost hearts and in their most secret doings
> were actuated by God-fearing love, the fear that is akin to love in
> remembering God under his title "Most Gracious" and (4) who gave

up their whole heart and being to Him. . . .[18]

The true meaning of Islam: peace, security, salutation, and accord with God's Plan in all Eternity. **(The Holy Qur'an**, 1416) To understand the Qur'anic basis for the sacred term *Muslim*, there are two key passages:

> "Our Lord! make of us / Muslims, bowing to Thy (Will), / And of our progeny a people / Muslim, bowing to Thy (Will); / And show us our places for / The celebration of (due) rites; / And turn unto us (in Mercy); / For Thou art the Oft-Returning, / Most Merciful. [This is part of Abraham's Prayer in this *sura*.] (II:128)
>
> And strive in His cause / As ye ought to strive, / (With sincerity and under discipline). / He has chosen you, and has / Imposed no difficulties on you / In religion; it is the cult / Of your father Abraham. / It is he who has named / You Muslims, both before / And in this (Revelation); / That the Apostle may be / A witness for you, and ye / Be witnesses for mankind! / So establish regular Prayer, / Give regular Charity, / And hold fast to God! / He is your Protector-- (XXII:78)

These two selections establish several crucial beliefs: (1) Abraham was the first to be given the designation *Muslim*; (2) the term *Muslim* is God's descriptive name for those who bow to him in prayer; and (3) Muhammad has been told to use the term *Muslim* for those worship the One True God.

These passages should suffice to establish the sacredness of both terms, *Islam* and *Muslim*, as well as indicate the error in referring to a Muslim as a Muhammadean. Further, they suggest the rich spirituality that both words have for Muslims. Guided by these insights, it is now possible to suggest better, although still

---

[18]

Such a description of the righteous could just as well have come from the **Hebrew Bible** or the **New Testament**.

inadequate, translations: *Islam*, which is the name of the religion, means "The **peace of spirit** that comes from **submitting one's life** to the **will of God**." Since *MU* is a prepositional prefix to *SLM*, the Muslim is the "**One who has found peace of spirit in submitting his life** to the **will of God**."[19] Understanding the sacredness of these two words provides a background for the next section of this chapter; a section that addresses an issue hinted at in the first chapter: the sacredness of Arabic as compared with Hebrew and Greek.

The Arabic Voice of God in the Qur'an

As indicated in the last section of Chapter One, "The Holy Books," applying the tools of textual criticism to the Arabic **Qur'an** raises a difficulty not encountered in using these tools for study of the **Hebrew Bible** and the Greek **New Testament**. Before exploring the theologies of war and peace in the **Qur'an**, this difficulty must be addressed. As a typical view of the origin of and nature of the **Qur'an**, consider the following statement from an article on John the baptizer in the July 1996 edition of the journal, **Review of Religions**, by Maha Dabbous[20]: (words in bold print are for emphasis and later reference)

---

[19]
Two additional observations are worth stating: (1) the series of posture that are ritually a part of the Muslim daily *salat* (prayer) are symbolic of the "submitting of one's life to God"; and (2) given the meaning of the term *Muslim*, faithful Jews and Christians are also those who submit their lives to God, that is, they are also *Muslims* in a significant spiritual sense.

[20]
Dabbous article and the journal in which it is published, **Review of Religions**, both represent a rather chauvinistic missionary attitude toward the other monotheisms. While such an attitude is inconsistent with the principles of this study, his statement is cited because it represents a traditional view that is common to much Muslim theology. Fortunately, there are more enlightened views in the Muslim world as well. Finally, to be fair, the same kind of chauvinism has characterized much of Judaism and Christianity historically as well as experienced a modern regrowth in all three monotheisms.

Yet it is not surprising to know that today, the wise and honest people among the Christians--and so also most probably among the Jews as well--know it for certain that the Bible, as it stands today, is not the [actual] word of God. Moreover, they also know that through the centuries, the Bible suffered countless interpolations and changes in its text before it reached us in its present form. . . . God has not protected its text from corruption because it was not meant to guide the future generations. It was meant to benefit only the generations who witnessed its original form. As for the people who came after that, there was another book. It is 'the book', which fulfilled their needs and is fulfilling the needs of the present day generations and will continue to be the only true divine guidance for all the people until the end of time. This is the Holy Qur'an, the perfect and final revealed book from our Creator.

The Holy Qur'an is the **pure word** of God without **not even one letter influenced by a human hand**. This is our eternal guidance to the perfect truth. God has called His book 'Al-Furqan' which is an Arabic word that means 'what differentiates between what is true and what is false'. God **said**: Blessed is he Who has sent down Al-Furqan to His servant, that he may be a Warner to all the worlds. He to Whom belongs the Kingdom of the heavens and the earth. (Chapter 25:2-3) (44-45)

Although the religious chauvinism of Dabbous' statement is unfortunate and his misunderstanding of the consequences of applying the scholarly methods of higher and lower criticism to the **Hebrew Bible** and the **New Testament** is highly questionable, his citation is informative for several reasons: (1) it represents a traditional Muslim view about the scriptures of the two other monotheisms, and (2) it implies the issue of **Arabic literalism** as applied to the **Qur'an**. Both of these issues require examination before turning to the theologies of war and peace.

Many introductory books and public lectures on Islam often use an analogy in describing the view the **Qur'an** takes regarding the **Hebrew Bible** and the **New Testament** as similar to the view the Christian **Testament** takes regarding the **Old Testament**: that is, the **Qur'an** accepts both the **Hebrew Bible** and the **New Testament** as revelations from God, but revelations that are incomplete and, therefore, fulfilled by the **Qur'an**. Although this analogy is not false,[21] it is weak because what the **Qur'an** means by the revelations (books) to the Jews and the Christians is something quite different than their written Holy Books. The **Qur'an** affirms in many passages that God has sent revelations to both religious groups, and many Muslim scholars have extended this belief to the Zoroastrians as well, but what the **Qur'an** means by these revelations is something different than Jews and Christians mean when they refer to their holy revelations.

References in the **Qur'an** to the revelations God gave the Jews identifies them by the Arabic term *Taurat*. Generally, the *Taurat* refers to the **pure, true** revelation given to the Jews in oral form, through many prophets but primarily Moses. Thus, the *Taurat* is neither the *Torah* (that is, the first five books identified in Greek as the *Pentateuch*) nor the written **Hebrew Bible**. In other words, the *Taurat* basically refers to the original revelation from God in oral form, much of which over the centuries became lost, and thus, what survived was re-interpreted in the written form of the canonized **Hebrew Bible**. From this religious perspective, then, although the **Hebrew Bible** contains written revelations from God, they have lost their original oral meaning over the centuries and consequently been distorted

---

21

It is important to realize that analogies are neither true or false; consequently they neither establish the truth or falsity of a statement or the validity of an argument. The basic form of an analogy is "X is like Y." For this reason, logicians analyze analogies as strong or weak. A strong analogy is one in which the similarities between X and Y are more significant than the differences. A weak analogy is the reverse. While analogies cannot prove or disprove an issue, they can serve the purpose of aiding the understanding of an unfamiliar issue("X") by comparing it ("is like") to a more familiar one ("Y"), as long as the analogy is not weak.

and misunderstood by the Jews in their written form. This view does not reject the **Hebrew Bible** as a source of true revelation, but critiques it as incomplete, at times misleading, and most often misunderstood. Further, the **Qur'an** claims to have re-claimed the original meaning of the oral revelation[22] given to the Jews through dozens of prophets.

In those many passages where the **Qur'an** makes references to the revelation from God through the Christ, the Arabic term *Injil* is used and translated as "Gospel." However, as with the term *Taurat*, the *Injil* does not refer to the written revelation that Christians accept as canonical (that is, as authoritative). In an appendix, A. Yusuf Ali, concisely states the Qur'anic position concerning the *Injil*:

> The *Injil* (Greek, Evangel=Gospel) spoken of by the Qur'an is not the New Testament. It is not the four Gospels now received as canonical. It is the single Gospel which, Islam teaches, was revealed to Jesus, and which he taught. Fragments of it survive in the received canonical Gospels and in some others, of which traces survive (*e.g.,* the Gospel of the Childhood or the Nativity, the Gospel of St. Barnabas, etc.). Muslims are therefore right in respecting the present Bible (New Testament and Old Testament, though they reject [many of] the peculiar doctrines taught by orthodox Christianity or Judaism. The claim to be in the true tradition of Abraham, and therefore all that is of value in the older revelations, it is claimed, is incorporated in the teaching of the Last of the Prophets. (**The Holy Qur'an**, 287)

22

In an interesting way, Jews are more familiar with this kind of religious thinking than Christians. For many Jews there are two *Torahs* that are both true revelations from God. There is the written, canonized Masoretic Text of the **Hebrew Bible**, and there is the unwritten **oral** *Torah* that has been passed from one generation of rabbis to the next since the time of Moses. In some ways, the Qur'anic understanding of the *Taurat* is similar to the Jewish understanding of this unwritten revelation. For Christians there is no unwritten Gospel.

Even though this view reveals a religious chauvinism concerning the content and nature of true revelation, it is a theological perspective not significantly different from that of either Jews or Christians. Further, even if somewhat reluctantly, it affirms that both the **Hebrew Bible** and the **New Testament** are sources of religious truth, belief and value, albeit sources that are confused and misunderstood by believers.[23] In all three religions, there are those who reject any possibility for meaningful, tolerant trialogue because of these differences concerning the three Holy Books, but, fortunately, there are many Jews, Christians and Muslims who, accepting these differences, nonetheless hold out a hand of toleration and respect. Yusuf Ali is one of these, for in the paragraph following the quotation above, he writes:

> In ... [V:85] we are told that nearest in love to the Believers
> [Muslims] among the Peoples of the Book are the Christians. I do not
> agree that this does not apply to modern Christians. . . . I think that
> Christian thought . . . has learned a great deal from the protest of
> Islam against priest domination, class domination, and sectarianism,
> and its insistence on making this life pure and beautiful while we are
> in it. We must stretch a friendly hand to all who are sincere and in

---

23

While the **Qur'an** states that Jews and Christians have incomplete and inaccurate revelations from God and, consequently, have abused and misunderstood them, there is a sense in which any Jew or Christian of reflecting, good conscience would agree for two reasons. First, thinking Jews and Christians know that God's activities can never be limited to the pages of a written book, no matter how great a book. Several years past the term *Bible-alotry* was coined to describe those who worship the Bible rather than the Reality that lies behind it, that is, those who worship the Book rather than God who can never be confined to a book. Second, given the weaknesses of human nature (what these three monotheism call sin), humans of good conscience realize that confusions and distortions of sacred truth occur everyday, intentionally and unintentionally. Persons of reflecting good conscience know this and constantly seek religious truth through thinking and praying for guidance. In fairness, then, it should be stated that Muslims, who are fallible human beings just like Jews and Christians, also misunderstand and distort their revelation as well.

sympathy with . . . [these] ideals. (**The Holy Qur'an**, 287)

Ali's point cannot be underestimated: although there are significant differences among the children of Abraham, they share a common enough core of beliefs concerning righteousness and values regarding the practice of justice that the hand of friendship can and should be extended to all those who struggle to make "this life pure and beautiful while we are in it."[24]

It is now time to examine the controversial and difficult issue of scriptural **literalism**. As stated in the "Prologue," this study rejects the intelligibility of the position of scriptural literalism. Such a rejection is less problematic for Jews and Christians than for Muslims. Although there are Jews and Christians who still believe in the literalism of their scriptures, for many the positions of literalism and inerrancy (see footnote #6 in the "Prologue") are red herrings. In other words, for many Jews and Christians rejecting literalism and inerrancy does not deny the **Hebrew Bible** or the **New Testament** as revelations from God and, therefore sources of religious truth and guidance for one's life. Few knowledgeable Jews believe that God spoke Hebrew; rather, God inspired the prophets and they interpreted this to their people. This idea is one of the reasons many find the prophets so inspirational, for their personalities, that is, their hopes, needs, fears and passions become a part of the prophetic message. Knowledgeable Christians are aware that because Jesus preached in Aramaic and his teachings were later recorded in Greek, his words cannot be taken literally since they are already in translation in the **New Testament**. Consequently, the controversial positions of literalism and inerrancy are maintained usually by those who know the least about the formations and transmissions of those works which come to comprise their Holy Books. For Islam, however, the issue is different.

The traditional Muslim view of the origin and transmission of the **Qur'an** has

---

24

The final chapter returns to this sentiment in its "Apology for Peace Among the Children of Abraham."

already been described in the first chapter. This description indicates that inerrancy and literalism are fundamentally traditional positions within Islam. Since each **Arabic** word in the **Qur'an** came from the Mouth of God (forgive the anthropomorphism), then the **Qur'an** must be inerrant. Since the position of inerrancy is logically prior to that of literalism, most Muslim's have argued for a literal reading of the text as have those Jews and Christians who accept the inerrancy of the Bible. Since the rational unintelligibility of these two positions in Judaism and Christianity has already been discussed, it is time to address both positions as regards Islam and the **Qur'an**. There are two important points needing clarification, for they indicate that many of the same problems with inerrancy and literalism apply to all three Holy Books.

First, the position of Qur'anic inerrancy must be questioned for at least two historical reasons. To begin with, there is an oral tradition associated with Muhammad's earliest preaching which may be over a decade. Because he was illiterate and could not write his revelations and because for the first few years hardly anyone payed much attention to his preaching, it is reasonable to assume many of Muhammad's early teachings must have been written later from memory by his earliest disciples. Consequently, there is a considerable possibility some of the earliest revelations written from memory may vary from their original utterances.[25] Further, why did the third caliph, Uthman (644-656 C.E.), during whose leadership the **Qur'an** was codified and canonized, order the burning of thousands of palm leaves containing the written revelations of Muhammad to prevent controversy about the authoritative **Qur'an**. If there had been no variances among these thousands of

---

[25]

On this issue Christianity has a much more difficult problem because Muhammad's recited revelations in Arabic were written in Arabic while Jesus' Aramaic preachings were written in Greek. There is also the further difficulty for Christianity that between Jesus' oral teachings and their written form was a period of several decades, while for Muhammad it was less than one decade for some of his oral preachings.

palm leaves, then why would they have needed to be destroyed.[26]

Second, even if one ignores the issue of inerrancy, the effort to maintain literalism encounters an interesting Qur'anic difficulty. Internally the **Qur'an** affirms that not all verses can be taken literally, that is, at face value. The third *sura* contains a most important *ayat*:

> He it is Who has sent down / To thee the Book: / In it are verses / Basic or fundamental [that is, clear verses] / (Of established meaning); / They are the foundation / Of the Book: others / Are allegorical [that is, unclear, open to different interpretations]. But those / In whose hearts is perversity follow / The part thereof that is allegorical, / Seeking discord, and searching / For its hidden meanings, / But no one knows / Its hidden meanings except God. / And those who are firmly grounded / In knowledge say: "We believe / In the Book; the whole of it / Is from our Lord:" and none / Will grasp the Message / Except men of understanding. (III:7)

In their excellent collection of **Textual Sources for the Study of Islam**, Andrew Rippin and Jan Knappert translate ten different interpretations from the history of Islamic commentary on the meaning of the **clear** (Ali, "basic or fundamental") verses and the **unclear** (Ali, "allegorical") verses. Therefore, *ayat* 7 affirms not only that there are parts of the **Qur'an** that cannot be taken literally but also "only those firmly grounded in knowledge" can understand its message. Further, if one wishes to

---

26

While the burning of these palm and the position of Qur'anic inerrancy inhibited the scholarly development of the same kind of Critical Apparatus for the **Qur'an** as exists for the **Hebrew Bible** and the **New Testament** (see footnote #5 in the "Prologue"), such an action strongly suggests textual variances. However, because of the hand copying of the **Qur'an** for centuries, it is reasonable to conclude that many of the same kinds of copying errors as summarized in the Critical Apparatus of these other two Holy Books also appeared in the thousands of pre-printing copies of the **Qur'an**.

maintain the position of Qur'anic literalism, then how does he explain the Shi'ite doctrine of *wayalat*²⁷ (the doctrine that there is both a superficial and an esoteric, hidden meaning in each *ayat* in the **Qur'an**), and the historical fact that both within Sunni and Shi'a Islam developed many diverse schools of theology based on different interpretations of the **Qur'an**. Clearly Muslim history as well as the **Qur'an** indicate there is no **one literal** meaning that can be given by all readers to the *ayats* of the **Qur'an**. Consequently, Muslims, like Jews and Christians, face many of the same scholarly issues concerning both the inerrancy and literalism of their great Holy Books.

In closing, it is worth reiterating that none of the preceding discussion is a criticism or rejection of the **Qur'an** as a holy revelation and a source of spiritual truth and guidance. Rather just as with the **Hebrew Bible** and the **New Testament**, if the words in these great revelations cannot be taken literally, then Muslims like Jews and Christians must use their minds to struggle with the revealed truths in their Holy Books.

Theologies of War (Jihad)

When most non-Muslim Westerners think of the *jihad*, they historically imagine a warrior Muhammad commanding the slaughter of tens of thousands in the name of *Al-Lah* as well as envision the mangled bodies of children lying in the streets after the explosion of a terrorist bomb.²⁸ Because these powerful images are

---

27

One of the scriptural sources for this Shi'ite doctrine is III:7.

28

Certainly there have been many instances of such bombings throughout the Middle East on the part of extremist groups such as Hizbollah and Hamas, but to be fair, the mangled bodies of innocent children left in the streets after the recent punitive bombings by Israeli jets in southern Lebanon are, for those who must bury their children, also acts of terrorism. It matters little to the parents of an Arab child or an Israeli child whether the bomb came from a jet or a planted suitcase on a bus: both are terrorist actions for the parents.

reinforced constantly by the media, it is important to accomplish three tasks before beginning a direct analysis of the Qur'anic message concerning war: (1) a description of the nature of war during the time of Muhammad; (2) a study of the Arabic terms for war (conflict, fighting) in the **Qur'an**; and (3) a brief statement of the kinds of *jihad* found in the **Qur'an**. For most Americans, the information in (1) and (3) should provide information significantly different than their usual media-promoted stereotypes of both Muhammad and Islam.

From Ghazw to Jihad During the Time of Muhammad

In pre-Muhammadean Arabia (before 570 C.E.) there were a series of decimating wars between the Byzantine empire (Asia Minor, Syria, Egypt, southeastern Europe to the Danube River and other small parts of Europe and north Africa) and the Persian (Sasanian) Empire (Iraq to Afghanistan to the Oxus River). Because these conflicts exhausted both empires, while influenced by both cultures, Arabia was not controlled by either. As a result, Mecca became a wealthy commercial center because it controlled the caravan routes from Yemen (the Arabian Sea) to Damascus. This provided the Meccans, Muhammad included, with ample opportunities for commerce with a wide variety of cultural and religious traditions (especially Judaism, Christianity and Zoroastrianism).

Given the importance of the major oases--Mecca, al-Taif, Medina--in the desert environment, they became centers for commerce and religion, but centers without any centrally controlling authority. Tribal affiliation was the dominant factor not only among the nomadic groups (Bedouin) but also for those dwelling in the cities. Consequently, tribal affiliation became the cornerstone of social order and stability. Within this order a power structure developed among the various tribal clans. Those with sources of power such as numerical superiority, military advantages (horses, camels and weapons), monetary resources and land wealth (especially grazing pastures or water) were usually able to impose their will in limited ways on the weaker clans.

In this social, economic and military situation, unless there were existing treaties among tribal clans, it was assumed that a kind of war existed. However, this kind of war was significantly different in several ways from modern states of war. First, since the harshness of the environment usually controlled population growth, actual conflicts among tribal clans usually involved a limited number of warriors. For example, in the three major battles Muhammad and his Muslim forces fought against the Meccans--Badr, Uhud and The Trench--the body count on each side from all three conflicts was less than one hundred.

Second, since the loss of life was minimal in these wars (battles) among tribal clans, they served to maintain a kind of retributive justice among the clans.[29] Since these conflicts provided for a system of justice and promoted social order, fidelity to treaties was essential.[30]

Third, in many ways, these conflicts among tribal groups were as much a kind of sport as a type of warfare. Remembering that the precursors of the Olympic Games were a kind of military training for war, tribal battles and raids were a type of Arabian Olympic Games. As such, they encouraged several virtues. Among the more prized virtues were military prowess, courage bordering on recklessness, generosity in victory and honor. Unnecessary violence such as harming non-combatants was a taboo.[31] It was considered more honorable and courageous to

---

29

Traditionally historians have described this kind of unwritten law as a "blood for blood" tribal retribution. In other words, if a member of one tribe harmed another, the pay-back would be in kind. In order for this kind of "law" to keep an uneasy peace among tribes, it was important that it not over-retribute, for then, this would require retribution in return. Functioning without any central authority to enforce social stability, this informal kind of legal structure operated moderately well in maintaining social order and stability.

30

As later analysis shows, the **Qur'an** considers the breaking of an oath or treaty of peace to be among the worst of all human sins.

31

The **Qur'an** not only continues this tradition but strengthens it as a

wound rather than kill an opponent in battle. The former took more daring and skill than the latter.

In this situation where tribal conflicts and raids were more a kind of military sporting event than war, the poet became as important as the warrior. Arabic poetry centered on two themes: military valor and romantic love. The warrior need the poet to immortalize his heroic exploits, and the poet need the warrior as content for his poetry.

Fourth, these hybrid tribal battle--sporting events functioned according to rules centered on fairness and generosity. As uncomfortable as it is for most Westerners to accept, the taking of hostages for ransom was an honorable rule of the game. Not only did this honorable rule contribute to the welfare of those conquered in battle, it made good economic sense. A killed clan member could be the basis for a retaliatory raid but a ransomed clan member satisfied both sides.[32] The rules of the game also stressed generosity by making the killing of non-combatants a taboo. While this prohibition included the elderly, the physically and mentally ill as well as other classifications, the most important prohibition made the harming of women and children a major dishonor.[33] Again, this made good moral as well as economic sense. In an environment whose harshness produced high infant mortality rates, children were a most valuable resource. Additionally, captured women were potential child bearers who also broadened the gene pool.

---

prohibition from *Al-Lah* that is severely punished when violated.

[32]

The taking of hostages for ransom, a practice so abhorred by most non-Muslim Westerners, was, and to some extent still is, an accepted social custom. As a custom, however, there were serious taboos against further harming a hostage. The **Qur'an** allows the taking of hostages but places serious restrictions against their abuse and places significant responsibilities concerning their humane treatment upon their captors.

[33]

There are several passages in the **Qur'an** (examined later) that describe *Al-Lah*'s commands for the honorable treatment of women and children in warfare.

Finally, the rules of the game placed serious limitations on the destruction of vegetation. In an environment constantly struggling against hunger, and in certain situations against starvation, any destruction of vegetation was serious. The most serious, however, was the destruction of food bearing plants. Consequently, the wanton destruction of food supplies was a dishonorable act.

Because of the wealth and power of Mecca, for several decades before Muhammad's birth until the Battles of Badr (March 15, 624 C.E.), Uhud (March 23, 625) and the Trench (which commenced on March 31, 627) there had been no major wars[34] in Arabia, that is, there had been no significant challenge to the powerful family clans at Mecca. During these decades the sport of the *ghazw* (the razzia) continued as a outlet for martial valor as well as a means of increasing tribal wealth and expanding the gene pool.

Persecutions of the small group of Muslims in Mecca and plots against the life of Muhammad led to his flight from Mecca to Medina in the summer of 622[35]. Arriving in Medina several days later, Muhammad and a small group of Muslims who joined him later began the struggle to build a religious community. They were few, poor and with little political clout. Given their grim situation, one of the traditional and honorable ways to increase their wealth and social standing was the *ghazw*. A natural target for such activities was Mecca and its many caravans to and

---

[34]

For an excellent historical description and analysis of these three major battles of Muhammad and the Muslims against the Meccans see W. Montgomery Watt's **Muhammad: Prophet and Statesman.**

[35]

Muslims refer to this flight as the *Hijrah*. For them it is the religious event used to chronologically organize world history: that is, 622 C.E. is 1 A.H. (year of the *Hijrah*). A note of warning, however, is needed. Because the Muslim calendar is a lunar calendar of 12 months alternating between 29 and 30 days, a lunar year is several days shorter than a solar one. Consequently, the Muslim year cannot be figured by subtracting 622 from the Gregorian one used by Europe and the United States. As an example, Gregorian 1984 was for Muslims the beginning of the 15th century, 1400 A.H.

from Damascus. Thus during 622-623, Muhammad and the Muslims at Medina made several such caravan raids. Then in late spring 624, a golden opportunity arose: a very wealthy Meccan caravan was enroute from Damascus to Mecca. This caravan offered an unprecedented economic and political opportunity for Muhammad and his Muslims to gain both wealth and prestige. As events unfolded, however, a planned *ghazw*, that is, a caravan raid, developed into something of much more religious and historical significance: the first political *jihad*, that is, a battle between believers against non-believers.

Without describing the details of the battle at Badr,[36] the eventual outcome was politically and religiously monumental. With a force of about 300 young men, Muhammad won a decisive victory over a force which had a considerable advantage in cavalry (camels and horses), number of warriors and weapons. Muslim losses numbered approximately 14; the Meccans lost between 45-70 men killed in conflict and an equal number taken hostage for ransom. For the small group of Muslims, this overwhelming victory over vastly superior odds was more than a political-economic victory, it was a "Gideon-like" *furquan*, a sign that Muhammad was indeed the chosen Prophet of God. Two *ayats* in *sura* III of the **Qur'an** emphatically declare Badr to be a *furquan*:

> "There has already been / For you a Sign / In the two armies / That met (in combat): / One was fighting in the Cause / Of God, the other / Resisting God; These saw / With their own eyes / Twice their number. / But God doth support / With His aid whom He pleaseth. / In this is a warning / For such as have eyes to see. (III:13)

> God had helped you / At Badr, when ye were / A contemptible

---

36

    See W. Montgomery Watt's biographies for an excellent description and analysis of all three Battles: Badr, Uhud and the Trench.

little force; / Then fear God; thus / May ye show your gratitude.
(III:123)

Badr confirmed the prophetic call of Muhammad and set the stage for one of the four kinds of *jihad* that are an integral part of the **Qur'an**.

The powerful few who limped home to Mecca now knew that Muhammad was a force which must be eliminated. Consequently in March 625, they left Mecca with an impressive army, by Arabian standards, with one objective in mind: to destroy the upstart prophet in Medina. Their numbers exceeded 3000 warriors, 700 of them in coats of mail, over 200 horses and a like number of camels. For the infrequent warfare in Arabia, this was an imposing army. Muhammad had approximately 700 warriors who possessed only a few dozen mounts and were severely under-armed.[37] Although Muhammad did no wish to engage such a vastly superior force, several incidents required his leaving Medina to engage the Meccans. The two forces met in combat at the hill of Uhud on March 23. Because of Muhammad's superior strategic abilities and several command problems in the Meccan forces, Muhammad's small army nearly won the day until at a crucial time they lost heart and retreated. The result was a victory on the battlefield for the Meccans: the Muslims lost in excess of 70 men and the Meccans less than 30. For them, this was a decisive victory, and, consequently, instead of following up and destroying Muhammad, they retired to Mecca singing the poetry of victory and believing the career of that troublesome prophet in Medina was over.

This judgement was premature, but the loss on the field of battle presented Muhammad with a major religious crisis, for his small but growing group of Muslims had come to expect a "Gideon-like" victory anytime *Al-Lah*'s Prophet led them into battle. Muhammad's survival was most likely the results of his tremendous abilities as a statesman and an explanatory revelation for the Muslim loss at Uhud that could

---

[37]

For details see W. Montgomery Watt' s biographies.

have come from the eighth century prophets of Judaism: *Al-Lah* had allowed the Meccans victory because the Muslims lost faith at a critical time in the battle and retreated. *Sura* III explains the punishment of the Muslims for this lapse of faith in *Al-Lah*:

> How many of the Prophets / Fought (in God's way), / And with them (fought) / Large bands of godly men? / But they never lost heart / If they met with disaster / In God's way, nor did / They weaken (in will) / Nor give in. / And God Loves those who are / Firm and steadfast. (III:147)

Two years later, aware that Uhud had not destroyed Muhammad, the Meccans raised one of the largest armed forces in the history of Arabia: approximately 10,000 men, with nearly 600 horses and several hundred camels. They set off for Medina with little advance planning and a divided leadership, but nonetheless confident because of their astounding numbers.[38] Their siege of Medina was a disaster of over-confidence, ill planning and indecisive, incompetent leadership. Reported casualties from the Battle of the Trench were: 6 Muslims and 3 Meccans.[39] The Meccan army returned in a state of incompetent disgrace. Less than three years later, in 630 C.E.,

---

[38]

Again, see Watt for an excellent description of the details.

[39]

It is interesting to note the casualty numbers in these three pivotal battles: Muslim losses = approximately 95 and Meccan losses = approximately 100. More than likely, the forces of Desert Storm took more Iraqi lives in the first 24 hours of bombing than the total lost on both sides in the Muslim-Meccan wars. Had the bombings not been limited to strategic military targets in Desert Storm, given the weapons available today, there could have been tens of thousands of lives lost. As described later, the **Qur'an** places significant restrictions on warfare which attempt, in part, to limit the number of casualties. The terribly destructive weapons of modern warfare disturb the consciences of many Muslims as well as Christians today. This appropriate moral concern about the power of modern weapons provides a common ground for fruitful conversation among those of good conscience in all three of the monotheisms.

Muhammad rode into Mecca as the Prophet of God without a single life lost. When he died in 632, the empire of Islam was limited to a small area of land along the caravan route between Mecca and Medina, a distance of just over 250 miles. [40]

While warfare under the leadership of Muhammad moved from the *ghazw* (limited tribal raiding against other tribes) to the political *jihad* (the battle against external evil, that is, non-believers), even the political *jihad* as understood by Muhammad was circumscribed by several moral concerns, especially the limiting of bloodshed.[41] Although the preceding has not examined all of the influences that contributed to Muhammad's understanding of warfare,[42] it has served to show that Muhammad's understanding was considerably different than modern perspectives. With this understanding as background, it is now appropriate to examine the terms for war in the **Qur'an**.

---

[40]

As small as the empire of Islam was at the death of Muhammad, its growth over the next century was astounding. One hundred years after Muhammad's death, the empire of Islam spread from Arabia through the Middle East westward through North Africa into Spain and southern France. If Charles Martel had not stopped the advance of Islamic forces into France at the Battle of Tours in 732 C.E., many of us who are European Americans might have grown up reading the **Qur'an** rather than the Christian **Bible**. Moving eastward, the forces of Islam conquered Persia and extended into the Indus Valley in India. This represents the most astonishing expansion of a religion and culture in the history of the West.

[41]

Given the value placed on human life in the **Qur'an** and the evidences of Muhammad's sensitivities for living beings as illustrated in his love for children and even animals, one cannot help but think that the Prophet would be horrified by the terrible destructiveness of today's weapons as well as brought to tears by the number of human lives (especially those of children) slaughtered in the conflicts between Christians and Muslims in the Crusades and the terrorist activities by extremist Israelis and Muslims in the Middle East.

[42]

See Fred Donner's article in Kelsay and Johnson's **Just War and Jihad** for an excellent description of the Byzantine, Sasanian and Zoroastrian influences on Muhammad's view of war.

Arabic Terms for War (Conflict)

There are six important Arabic words for various kinds of human conflict: *fitna*[43], which came to mean "internal strife" or "civil war"; *tha'a*, means "vendetta" or "revenge"; *qital*, generically means "fight"; *harb*, which is the general term for "war"; *ghazw*, which refers to a "tribal or caravan raid"; and, *jihad*,[44] which generally means any kind of struggle against something specific but because of its religious context in the **Qur'an** has come to mean a "struggle or striving against evil." Of these six, the two most important for the analyses which follow are *harb* and *jihad*. In the **Qur'an** these two terms represent quite different kinds of conflict: *harb* refers to conflicts (wars, raids, etc.) undertaken for personal, political or selfish reasons; *jihad* refers to a struggle or war against evil whose purpose is religious rather than economic, political or personal gain.

Since the term *jihad* is the most important one for this study, two other etymological comments are needed. First, the noun *jihad* is based on the verb *jahada*, meaning "to struggle" or "to strive." In the **Qur'an**, both the noun and the verb acquired a religious meaning significantly different than their previous more secular usage in pre-Islamic Arabia. Since a striving requires a striver, two terms

---

43

In pre-Islamic Arabia and the **Qur'an**, the term *fitna* meant "test," "trial" or "temptation." However, thirty years after the death of Muhammad the Muslim community erupted in a civil war which was won by the Umayyads, a victory which established the Umayyad dynasty. As a consequence of this internal conflict, the term *fitna* acquired a new meaning: civil war. There was a religious logic in this usage, for according to the Prophet Muhammad, every Muslim is a brother to every other Muslim; thus, for Muhammad war among Muslims could never be a *jihad*, a battle against evil. Instead, for him, Muslims killing other Muslims was an evil, and one which would "test" the community of Islam far beyond anything he could have imagined. One cannot help but wonder what Muhammad would think of the many declarations by the Ayatollah Khomeini (also transliterated as *Khumayni*) that the war against Iraq was a religious war (a *jihad*).

44

The Arabic term is also transliterated as *djihad*.

developed to describe the person involved in a *jihad*: an old term for a raider engaged in a *ghazw* was borrowed and used to refer to a warrior involved in a *jihad*, a *ghazzi*. The second term was directly related to the noun *jihad*, a *mujihad*. This noun was formed by adding the prepositional prefix *mu*, the same one added to form the term *Muslim*, to *jihad*, hence *mujihad*. Although the analysis of war in this study is limited to the **Qur'an**, it should be noted that each generation of Muslim *imams* (religious leaders) and political leaders have interpreted and re-interpreted the meaning of the *jihad* to fit their historical situations and needs. Muhammad's limited views of the *jihad* have often been revised to include war against other Peoples of the Book (the Crusades) as well as war against other Muslims (the 20th century Iran-Iraq War). As is always the case with significant religious values and beliefs, they never remain stagnant. Consequently, the task of analyzing the ever changing uses, meanings and interpretations of the term *jihad* throughout the history of Islam would require an entire volume if not more. This is a task beyond the purpose of this study whose goal is more limited: an examination of the Qur'anic uses and meanings of the *jihad*. As in Chapters Two and Three, the strategy used is basically the same: a three-fold analysis in terms of political war, spiritual war and eschatological war. However, because the term *jihad* is so deeply rich in Qur'anic meanings, one other distinction helps provide additional background: the four kinds of *jihad* found in the **Qur'an**. This distinction applies to each of the three dimensions of war.

In his important study of **War and Peace in the Law of Islam**, Majid Khadduri cites a well known **hadith**: "The jihad is the peak of religion." (51) He declares the Qur'anic purpose of the *jihad* is to transform the *dar al-harb*, the world of non-Muslims, into the *dar al-Islam*, the world of Muslims. In other words, the ultimate object of the *jihad* is the establishment of a world of peace and justice united in religious submission to the will of God: "Like Christianity, it [Islam] sought to achieve the salvation of mankind; but unlike Christianity, it began to achieve it first on earth." (Khadduri, 141-2) While the actual establishment of this vision of peace and justice has been unrealized historically in the relationships between the *dar al-*

harb and the *dar al-Islam* as well as within the *dar al-Islam* itself, and the *jihad* has been as badly abused within Islam as outside it, Muslim commentary and scholarship on the **Qur'an** has never wavered in its affirmation that the purpose of the Qur'anic *jihad* is peace and justice.[45] It is for this reason a **Hadith** declares: "The jihad is the peak of religion." Because of the religious significance of the *jihad*, Qur'anic commentators have analyzed the "struggle against evil" according to many different typologies. A most common one distinguishes between the physical *jihad* and the spiritual *jihad*. Some use the terms lesser *jihad* and greater *jihad* to describe the same distinction. Another useful typology integrated into the analyses that follow is a four-fold one mentioned on the previous page:

(1)　　the *jihad* fought by the heart, which is the struggle against internal evil, that is, the struggle against sin and temptation;

(2)　　the *jihad* fought by the mouth, which is the struggle against evil by speaking openly against injustice and spreading the universal message of peace through submitting to the Will of *Al-Lah*;

(3)　　the *jihad* fought by the hand, which is the non-violent struggle to correct an injustice or reconcile a wrong[46];

(4)　　the *jihad* fought by the sword.

The explorations of the three dimensions of war that follow make use of this four-

---

45

In slightly different ways, both the **Hebrew Bible** and the **New Testament** affirm a similar theology: the purpose of creation is peace, humans have fallen from peace (that is, into chaos) and God is moving His creation firmly from chaos toward eternal peace. Although they disagree about how His final purpose of creation will be fulfilled, they share a common vision of salvation as consisting of an eternal world of both peace and justice. Surely this provides a common ground for respect and conversation among the children of Abraham.

46

For those who think of the *jihad* as only an act of violence, it is illustrative to note that the world's best known *mujihad* (holy warrior) engaged in these first three *jihad*s is most likely Mother Teresa.

320

fold typology:

(1)   the dimension of political war most clearly includes the *jihad* fought by the sword but also aspects of *jihads* fought by the mouth and the hand;

(2)   the dimension of spiritual war is basically equivalent to the *jihad* fought by the heart;

(3)   the dimension of eschatological war includes aspects of *jihads* fought by the heart, the mouth and the hand and, unfortunately, by the sword.[47]

Before turning to political war, one additional comment is important: Qur'anic commentary has also consistently affirmed that the most important *jihad* is the one fought by the heart and the *jihad* fought by the sword is the last in religious merit.[48]

Political War

In a September 1990 article in **Atlantic Monthly**, a noted writer on Islam, Bernard Lewis, espoused the traditional and incorrect stereotype of the *jihad*:

> If the fighters in the war for Islam, the holy war "in the path of God," are fighting for God, it follows that their opponents are fighting against God. And since God is in principle the sovereign, the supreme head of the Islamic state--and the Prophet and, after the Prophet, the caliphs are his viceregents--then God as sovereign commands the army. The army is God's army and the enemy is God's enemy. The duty of God's soldiers is to dispatch God's enemies as

---

47

The importance of the *jihad* fought by the sword in the dimension of eschatological war is especially important in Shi'ite theologies of war. They are examined in the final section on war.

48

Unfortunately, many of the Muslim extremist groups in the Middle East have reversed this order of religious merit and given priority to the *jihad* by the sword over that by the heart. In doing this they have also used torturous interpretations of the **Qur'an** to defend bombings and hostage taking as defensive *jihads*.

quickly as possible to the place where God will chastize them--that

is to say, the afterlife. ("The Roots of Muslim Rage," 49)

Such comments are most unfortunate because they help perpetuate a distorted perspective of the Islamic theology of war, that is constantly reinforced by the superficiality of media coverage of conflict in the Middle East. Although there is an internal logic to Lewis' argument, one which is more readily applicable to the **Hebrew Bible** than the **Qur'an**, the statement is both theologically and historically wrong. The analysis of political war which follows should suffice to reveal the flaws in Lewis' view.[49]

Because Lewis' incorrect stereotype is so influential in American perceptions of Islam, it is helpful to examine several other sources which explode this fiction. In 1964, Abd al-Rahman Azzam, who served as Secretary General of the Arab League from 1945-52, published a monograph, **The Eternal Message of Muhammad**, in which he described the Muslim position concerning legitimate war:

In sanctioning war, Islam defined its aims and purposes: to

suppress tyranny, insure the right of a man to his home and freedom

within his nation, prevent persecution in religion, and guarantee

freedom of belief to all people.

This freedom for all people is manifest in the Koran's citation

of all places of worship for the various religions--monasteries and

churches for Christians, synagogues for the Jews, and mosques for

Muslims. Islam permitted war to safeguard all these . . . as well as its

own, against the attacks of aggressors.

---

[49]

In some ways, the considerable limitations placed on *jihad* in the **Qur'an** represent not only a moral contrast to the theology of the *herem in the* **Hebrew Bible,** these limitations are so enlightened for the 7th century C.E. that they can analogously be compared to the Geneva Conventions of the modern era: Conventions whose general purpose has been to limit the occurrences and destructiveness of war.

. . . .

Once Muslims were left with no alternative but war, and their right [moral right] to that became clear, war was sanctioned, and peace became its supreme objective; in the words of the Almighty, "But if they desist, then let there be no hostility except against wrongdoers." "And if they incline to peace, incline thou also to it, and trust Allah."

. . . .

It is therefore evident . . . [in the **Qur'an**] that Islam does not sanction any war of aggression, nor does it unleash war to acquire worldly gains, for with God there are many treasures. . . . The aims of Islam are humanitarian and universal: its blessing should extend to all people; and the outlook of Islam is a lofty one: it regards the whole of mankind as one family to be secured against injustice. Almighty God is not the God of Muslims alone, but of the entire universe. (129-32)

It would not be incorrect to state that in the **Qur'an**, war is a "hated necessity": hated because all humans are the children of God; necessary because of human sin, that is, because there are human beings who through their greed or lust for power create situations of injustice and violence.[50] There is an important *ayat* in the second *sura* identifying internal conflict as the source of external conflict in a manner echoing the great insight of Paul in Romans concerning the conflict between the "flesh and the spirit" that leads to human violence:

Fighting is prescribed / For you, and you dislike it. / But it is possible / That ye dislike a thing / Which is good for you, and that

---

[50]

This same seminal insight concerning human nature was noted earlier in the Yahwist account of Cain and Abel.

> ye love a thing / Which is bad for you. / But God knoweth, / And
> ye know not. (II:216)

Although this verse is subject to varied interpretations, Ali provides one shedding
light on the spiritual nature of the *jihad*:

> To fight in the cause of truth is one of the highest forms of
> charity. What can you offer that is more precious than your own life?
> But here again the limitations come in. If you are a mere brawler, or
> a selfish aggressive person, or a vainglorious bully, you deserve the
> highest censure. If you offer your life . . . [for righteousness] you are
> an unselfish hero. God know the value of things better than you do.
> **(The Holy Qur'an**, 84)

In *sura* XLVIII, the **Qur'an** condemns those who fight for plunder and the love of
destruction, that is, the selfishness of military glory in such activities as the sport of
the *ghazw*:

> Say to the desert Arabs / Who lagged behind: "Ye / Shall be
> summoned (to fight) / Against a people given to / Vehement war:
> then shall ye / Fight, or they shall submit. / Then if ye show
> obedience, / God will grant you / A goodly reward. . . .
> (XLVIII:16)

Ali's commentary is again most enlightening:

> The desert Arabs loved fighting and plunder, and understood
> such motives for war. The higher motives seemed beyond them.
> Like ignorant men they attributed petty motives or motives of
> jealousy if they were kept out of the vulgar circle of fighting for
> plunder. But they had to be schooled to higher ideals of discipline,
> self-sacrifice, and striving hard for a Cause.
>
> . . . .
>
> . . . you shall go forth to war if you learn discipline, not for
> booty, but for a great and noble Cause. For if your opponents submit

to the cause, there will be no fighting. . . . (**The Holy Qur'an**, 1395)
The preceding are only two from many passages that affirm a difference between
harb (war fought for secular reasons such as greed, lust for power, etc) and *jihad*
(war fought against evil).

Since the difference between *harb* and *jihad* is of major significance, and
because most Americans collapse the two categories into each other, further
examination of their difference is important. Wars fought by Muhammad and the
caliphs known as "Rightly Guided,"[51] because their purpose was to bring the world
under *Al-Lah*'s guidance and thus create a world of peace and justice, became known
as *jihads*. Originally these conflicts never intended to force conversions to Islam.[52]
In other words, these *jihads* were to fight injustice and establish the rule of God.
Other kinds of war used the term *harb*.[53] As indicated in footnote #52, while there

---

[51]

The designation "rightly guided" is used to indicate the first four caliphs after
the death of Muhammad: Abu Bakr (June 632 to August 634); Omar (August 634
to November 644); Uthman (November 644 to June 656), the caliph under whose
leadership the **Qur'an** was codified and authorized and who tragically ordered the
burning of all the palm leaves on which were recorded the revelations of God as
recited by Muhammad; and Ali (June 656 to January 661), the first cousin and son-
in-law of Muhammad through which the Shi'ites trace the history of their holy
imams.

[52]

The **Qur'an** denounces the forced conversion of any monotheist to Islam.
Instead it grants religious freedom to the Peoples of the Book, although they are to
pay a tax to support the needs of the Muslim state and would be harshly punished for
any act of treason. Further, the **Qur'an** recognizes that forced conversions are not
honest conversions, for God will not change a man until he is willing to change
himself.

[53]

Although there have always been religious and political leaders in the Muslim
world who have reduced the Noble cause of *jihad* into a political *harb*, a sinful
distortion well evidenced in the other two of Abraham's children, prior to the
Crusades, many of the leaders of the Muslim world remained faithful within their
historical limitations to the religious parameters of the Qur'anic *jihad*. In one sense,
this worked to Muslim disadvantage as the Crusaders roared out of Europe into the

have been Muslim leaders who reduced the spiritual *jihad* to the political *harb,* even at a times trying to use it as a justification for exterminating whole groups of people, there have always been religious leaders who remained true to the message of the **Qur'an** and condemned such actions.

Since the fundamental form of political war that occupies the **Qur'an** is the *jihad* rather than the *harb,* the following analyses concentrate on the former. Further, since the *jihad* by the sword is the one most misunderstood by almost all non-Muslims, and, unfortunately by some Muslims, the examination of political war concentrates on the *jihad* by the sword. However, in the numerous passages from the **Qur'an** cited in the following analyses, it is important to remember that they also have meanings for political *jihads* fought by the mouth and by the hand as well as the sword. Any Muslim, or non-Muslim for that matter, who finds the courage and conscience to speak out against the various forms of injustice that inevitably occur in any social-political situation are *mujihads.* When such speaking out about injustice imperils their lives, they are holy warriors in the truest sense of the **Qur'an**. When Muslims or non-Muslims work in non-violent ways to correct injustice, especially when doing so involves great sacrifice, they are truly *mujihads.* Finally, it is worth remembering that according to the most consistent interpretations of the **Qur'an**, those whose *jihads* are by the heart, mouth or hand are those most blessed by God.[54]

Middle East. At first, Muslims of this period could not comprehend the Crusader theology of slaughtering thousands for the glory of God, that is, their *herem* mentality. However, as often happens, they learned to fight fire with fire on both battlefields: the theological one and the geographical one.

[54]

Since the ultimate purpose of the *jihad* is the creation of justice and peace, those *mujihads* of the heart, mouth and hand are also those whom Jesus blessed in the Sermon on the Mount, "Blessed are the peacemakers, for they shall be called the children of God." *Mujihads* of the sword, however, are not as clearly included in this beatitude, but this is a problem that Christian theology has also struggled with ever since the church because integrated into the political world: "Can the soldier also be

The examination of political *jihad* that follows is divided into several aspects: (1) who may be a *mujihad*; (2) against whom can a *jihad* be fought; (3) what are the Qur'anic rewards and punishments related to a *jihad*; (4) what are the religious and moral limitations imposed by the **Qur'an** on a *jihad*; and (5) miscellaneous Qur'anic views about the *jihad* not included in the first four categories. In citing passages from the **Qur'an** illustrating these aspects, extensive use is made of the exigetical comments of A. Yusuf Ali in his excellent translation and commentary, **The Holy Qur'an**.

Who may fight in a *jihad* by the sword?[55] Based on either *suras* in the **Qur'an** or *matns* in important **hadiths**,[56] Majid Khadduri describes the necessary

---

a peacemaker?" Christian debate on this issue continues, especially since there are situations of terrible injustice in the world that seem to require military action in order to bring an end to the human suffering created by such human evil and bring peace to an environment of chaos and suffering. With the demise of the old Soviet Union, many American military actions have been conceived of and justified as "peace-keeping" deployments.

[55]

Since the criteria for eligibility concern the physical abilities to endure the rigors of actual combat, it is possible for there to be political *mujihads* whose battles are fought by the mouth and the hand who would be incapable of those fought by the sword. Certainly a child is capable of speaking out about an injustice long before being able to endure the physical trials of battle. Likewise, the elderly who may not be competent to engage in a political *jihad* by the sword are certainly capable of political *jihads* by the mouth or the hand.

[56]

Hadiths are reports of other teachings of Muhammad and revelations *of Al-Lah* through Muhammad not included in the codified **Qur'an**. For Muslims they comprise a secondary set of scriptures that are greatly valued and almost as fundamental for determining proper Muslim living as is the **Qur'an**. Each **hadith** contains an *isnad*, that is, a chain of transmission such as "Ali heard it from Abu Bakr who heard it from Muhammad who heard it from *Al-Lah*," and a *matn*, which is the lesson or teaching. One of the priceless aspects of many **hadiths** is that the personality of the Prophet Muhammad is revealed in ways that go far beyond the **Qur'an**. In the *shari'a*, Muslim law, the **hadiths** have almost as much authority as the **Qur'an**.

qualifications for a *mujihad* fighting in a political *jihad* by the sword: (1) the *mujihad* must be a believer, that is, a Muslim; (2) the *mujihad* must be mature and of sound mind, that is, children and the mentally ill are excluded[57]; (3) the *mujihad* must be physically capable of enduring the rigors of battle; (4) traditionally the *mujihad* must be male although women could contribute in indirect ways (there is a **hadith** that states, "The *jihad* of women is a pilgrimage"); (5) the *mujihad* must be economically independent--if he is a slave, then he must be freed and if he is in debt to another, then he must be released from his debt[58]; (6) the *mujihad* must have his parents permission except in the event of surprise attack when such permission is not possible[59]; and (7) the *mujihads* motives must be religious rather than personal, that

---

[57]

This second characteristic is a consequence of the first, for a believer is one who submits his life to *Al-Lah* as exemplified in the daily prayer. Two of the conditions for Muslim *salat*, that is, prayer or worship, is that persons be mentally sound and mature. Children are not encouraged to participate in prayer until they can understand the nature of their submission. With very few exceptions throughout the history of Islam, children have been protected from either participating as soldiers in a *jihad* or being killed by *mujihadists*. The recent and abominable use of children as soldiers in the Iran-Iraq War was condemned by a vast majority of Muslims outside both countries as well as some Muslims within both countries who found the courage to become *mujihads* by the mouth, that is, who found the courage to speak out against a horrible travesty of Muslim justice. Those who did speak out about this abuse of children often did so at peril to their lives.

[58]

The fundamental reason for this condition is to make sure that the Muslim who participates in a *jihad* does so as a matter of free choice, that is, that no one be forced to participate. Unquestionably, there have been many times throughout Muslim history when political leaders have ignored this condition.

[59]

There are most likely two reasons for this condition: first, it continues the protection of children mentioned in condition (2), and, second, it emphasizes the central value given to the family in Islam and especially to a familiar commandment: to honor one's mother and father.

is, his motives must be to serve God rather than personal gain or revenge.[60] (**War and Peace in the Law of Islam**, 84-86)

Using Khadduri's list of conditions for a *mujihad*, it is enlightening to turn to the *ayats* of the **Qur'an** for better understanding who may fight in a *jihad* by the sword. As indicated earlier, the most fundamental condition for being a *mujihad* is that one believes, trusts and submits his life to *Al-Lah*. The necessary faith of *mujihads* is extolled in many *suras* by emphasizing the proper motives for participating in a *jihad*.[61] As indicated in footnote #61, several of the most important passages concerning the motive have already been examined. Consider the following *ayat* in *sura* IV which rejects any **individual** motive for a *jihad* by the sword:

> O ye who believe! / Take your precautions, / And either go forth in
>
> parties / Or go forth all together. (IV:71)

While this *ayat* commands *mujihads* to enter battle with forethought and planning, that is, without foolish recklessness, according to Ali, its most important prohibition concerns motive: "No fight should be undertaken without due preparations and

---

[60]

Unquestionably, in those conflicts which continue for years--unfortunately, sometimes for several generations--it is a characteristic of human nature that personal revenge overwhelms all other motives for continued conflict. This aspect of human nature is as common in Christianity and Judaism as it is in Islam. It is also a continuing hazard for the peace process between Israelis and the Palestinians. Some of Rabin's spiritual greatness was revealed in his overcoming such motives which fuel continuing war; this must have been a difficult spiritual struggle for an old warrior. One of the most troubling questions which must be asked about the future of Israelis and Palestinians is: "Do the new generations assuming leadership among their peoples have the courage to engage in the same spiritual struggle and to face the same brutal honesty that led an old warrior like Rabin to acknowledge the 'cancer of occupation' and set aside decades of enmity in order to seek peace?" On the Palestinian side, "Are there new leaders emerging who have the spiritual greatness to cast aside terrorism and seek peace?"

[61]

Several of the most important *ayats* which concern the religious motives of a *mujihad* have been examined: II:216; III:121 and 146; and XLVIII:16.

precautions. . . . But we must go forth in a collective spirit, and not in a selfish spirit --either in small parties or all together as our leader determines." **(The Holy Qur'an,** 210) Again emphasizing the motive, *sura* II reminds the *mujihad* that no one can hide his true motives from God:

> Then fight in the cause / Of God, and know that God / Heareth and knoweth all things. (II:244)

In further supporting the necessity for purity of motive, several *ayats* emphasize that those who truly believe and participate in battle cannot lose in a righteous cause[62]:

> Apostle! rouse the Believers / To the fight. if there are / Twenty amongst you, patient / And persevering, they will / Vanquish two hundred: if a hundred / They will vanquish a thousand / Of the Unbelievers . . . . (VIII:65)

The preceding should be sufficient to answer the first question: Who may fight in a *jihad* by the sword? Before turning to the second question, however, it is important to recognize a group of people who have a special justification for participating in a *jihad*: those who have been wronged. *Suras* II and XXII provide concise descriptions of the kinds of wrongs and injustices which justify a *jihad*:

> Those who believed / And those who suffered exile[63] / And fought (and strove and struggled) / In the path of God,-- / They have the hope / Of the Mercy of God: / And God is Oft-forgiving, / Most Merciful. (II:218)

62

Several *ayats* that explain the loss at the battle of Uhud make the same point by declaring that the battle was lost because the fighters failed to trust *Al-Lah*.

63

These words have special meaning to Palestinians living in exile in refugee camps in Jordan, Syria and Lebanon as well as those in the occupied territories. However, many Jews also believe that they have been living in exile for centuries and have just recently returned to their true home. Unquestionably, the beliefs and passions associated with exile and homelessness are powerful forces in the conflict between Israelis and Palestinians. The final chapter returns to this subject.

To those against whom / War is made, permission / Is given (to
fight), because / They are wronged;--and verily, / God is Most
Powerful / For their aid;--

(They are) those who have / Been expelled from their homes[64] /
In defiance of right,-- / (For no cause) except / That they say, "Our
Lord / Is God". Did not God / Check one set of people / By
means of another, / There would surely have been / Pulled down
monasteries, churches, / Synagogues, and mosques, in which / The
name of God is commemorated / In abundant measure God will /
Certainly aid those who / Aid His (cause);--for verily / God is Full
of Strength, / Exalted in Might, / (Able to enforce His will).
(XXII:39-40)

These fundamental *ayats* are clarified by Ali as follows:

Several translators have failed to notice that *yugataluna* . . .
is in the passive voice, "against whom war is made",--not "who take
up arms against the unbelievers". . . . Verse 40 . . . [further clarifies
those wronged in *ayat* 39]. The wrong is indicated: 'driven by
persecution from their homes, for no other reason than that they
worshipped the One True God.' This was the first occasion on which
fighting--in self-defense--was permitted. (**The Holy Qur'an**, 861)

While both *suras* describe the religious right for *jihad* against oppression and
injustice, the two *ayats* in *sura* XXII are of special importance for indicating the
defensive nature of the *jihad* by the sword; a viewpoint already discussed in the

---

64

This *ayat* has special meaning for Palestinians who have been forced from
their homes in the West Bank because of the War of 67 and the continuing building
of Israeli homes in this area. The growing population of Israel and its need for West
Bank land is a most problematic aspect of the Peace process and a potential powder-
keg in Israel.

preceding.[65] The character of the *mujihad* and the descriptions of those who have special justifications for a *jihad* provide insights for responding to the second question.

Against Whom may a *jihad* be fought? As already stated, a *jihad* may be waged against those who prohibit worship, those who create injustice and those who force believers into exile. In general, the **Qur'an** identifies three major categories of those against whom a *jihad* may be fought: those who oppress or prohibit the worship of God; those who break treaties or oaths of peace; and, those who oppress through various kinds of injustice. Unquestionably, the most grievous offense that justifies a *jihad* is religious oppression.

Suras II and XXII contain strong *ayats* which not only justify but require *jihad* against those who prohibit and oppress the practice of religion. Both passages also share a common historical situation: the religious oppression of the Meccans, especially their denying Muslim access to the *Ka'ba*.[66] The second *sura* declares:

> And slay them / Whenever ye catch them, / And turn them out /
> From where they have / Turned you out; / For tumult and

---

[65]

That the *jihad* by the sword is justified only as defensive war is a theological interpretation almost unquestioned in Qur'anic exegesis. Unfortunately, however, what is meant by a defensive action is subject to considerable debate and varied interpretation. To use a football phrase: "The best defense is a good offense." Jews, Christians and Muslims have all used this interpretation to justify such military actions as "pre-emptive strikes," and "police actions," as defensive engagements. As is always the case with the Holy Books of all three of Abraham's children, interpretations are influenced by numerous non-textual issues and historical situations.

[66]

The *Ka'ba* is a cylindrical building in the center of the Grand Mosque at Mecca. It is, to use an analogy, the equivalent of the Jewish Holy of Holies for Muslims. For this reason, it is the most *haram*, that is sacred and forbidden, place in the whole of the Muslim world. Meccan refusal to allow Muslims in Medina during the time of Muhammad free access to the *Ka'ba* was a religious oppression beyond description.

oppression / Are worse than slaughter; / But fight then not / At the
sacred Mosque, / Unless they (first) / Fight you there. . . . (II:191)

Ali's note concerning the *ayat* is most enlightening:

> This passage is illustrated by the events that happened . . . in
> the sixth year of the Hijra. . . . The Muslims were by this time a
> strong and influential community. Many of them were exiles from
> Mecca, where the Pagans [the polytheists] had established an
> intolerant aristocracy, persecuting Muslims, preventing them from
> visiting their homes, and even keeping them out by force from
> performing the Pilgrimage during the universally recognized time of
> truce. This was intolerance, oppression, and autocracy to the last
> degree. . . .
>
> In general, it may be said that Islam is the religion of peace,
> goodwill, mutual understanding, and good faith. But it will not
> acquiesce in wrong-doing, and its men will hold their lives cheap in
> defense of honor, justice, and the religion which they hold sacred.
> Their ideal is that of heroic virtue combined with unselfish gentleness
> and tenderness, such as is exemplified in the life of the Apostle. They
> believe in courage, obedience, discipline, duty, and a constant striving
> by all means in their power, physical, moral, intellectual, and
> spiritual, for the establishment of truth and righteousness. (**The
> Holy Qur'an**, 76)

Muslim passion for *jihad* against those who oppress the worship of God is well
known.[67] What is less well known are the Qur'anic emphases on first doing

---

[67] This passion for fighting those who oppress religion, according to many
Qur'anic scholars, extends to fighting against even Christians and Jews who oppress
the worship of God. Since they are also Peoples of the Book who worship the true
God, although in their ignorance they often misunderstand God's Word and
commandments, nonetheless, their religious oppression is also cause for a just war.

everything possible to establish peace, but if war is unavoidable, then ending physical violence as quickly as possible. *Sura* VIII contains two significant *ayats* emphasizing these elements of peace:

> Say to the Unbelievers / If (now) they desist (from Unbelief), / Their past would be forgiven them; / But if they persist, the punishment / Of those before them is already / (A matter of warning for them).
>
> And fight them on / Until there is no more / Tumult or oppression, / And there prevail / Justice and faith in God / Altogether and everywhere; / But if they cease, verily God / Doth see all that they do. (VIII:39-40)

As in the previous *ayats*, while the term "Unbelievers" refers specifically to the polytheists at Mecca in their persecution of Muslims and their prohibiting of Muslims' access to the *Ka'ba*, but by extension the noun also refers to all who

---

Abd al-Rahmam Azzam emphasizes this in the following:
> In sanctioning war, Islam defined its aims and purposes: to suppress tyranny, insure the right of a man to his home and freedom within his nation, prevent persecution in religion, and guarantee freedom of belief to all people.
> This freedom for all people is manifest in the Koran's citation of all places of worship from the various religions--monasteries and churches for the Christians, synagogues for the Jews, and mosques for Muslims. Islam permitted war to safeguard all these religious freedoms, as well as its own, against the attacks of aggressors. . . . [Islam] limits the aims of war to repelling tyranny and dictates the cessation of war as soon as the aggressor ceases his indulgence in persecution of people because of their faith. Thus, war is not renewed or perpetuated except against a tyrant who insists on acts of tyranny, compelling people to abandon their religion. Persecution, forced conversion, and the deprivation of religious freedom are more distasteful to God than the taking of life. . . . (**The Eternal Message of Muhammad**, 129)

practice the same kind of intolerance toward freedom of religion.[68] It is important to note that the two *ayats* encourage efforts at peace (" their pasts would be forgiven them") and encourage a speedy end of hostilities ("until there is no more tumult or oppression") in order to minimize the bloodshed.

Because during his lifetime there was no persecution or oppression of Muslims by either Christians or Jews, it never occurred to Muhammad that the other two children of Abraham would ever prohibit Muslim worship. Before his death he became aware that his revelations were not going to convert Jews to Islam, nor did he experience any significant opportunities to discover how well the message of Islam would be received among Christians. Consequently, the very idea that some day Christians would oppress Muslims would have seemed incongruous to him. Nor did he conceive of Muslims prohibiting either Christians or Jews from worshipping the One God.[69] Consequently, a political *jihad* by the sword against either Christians or Jews for persecuting Muslims was a foreign idea to the Prophet. However, a *jihad* against any group who broke a treaty, monotheists or not, was another matter. In this case the justification for a *jihad* was not religious oppression but the failure to maintain a treaty of peace.[70]

In Islam, the greatest sin committed by humans is *shirk*, the attributing of partners to *Al-Lah*. Consequently, the polytheistic Meccans--variously referred to

---

[68]

Also by extension, as indicated by other *ayats* such as XXII:239-40, the freedom of Jews and Christians to worship God is affirmed.

[69]

While Muhammad's view about the Zoroastrians is unclear, after his death many of the *ulama* (the religious scholars and leaders) extended the phrase *People of the Book* to include the monotheistic Zoroastrians.

[70]

One of the most troubling events in the life of Muhammad, and one of the most criticized actions by European writers, was the incident concerning the violation of a treaty (alliance) by a Jewish tribe, the banu Quraiza, at Medina after the War of the Trench. See W. Montgomery Watt, **Muhammad: Prophet and Statesman** for an unbiased description of this event.

in the **Qur'an** as "Pagans" or "Unbelievers"--were guilty of this terrible affront to God. Yet not even the seriousness of their polytheistic sin against *Al-Lah* was justification for violating a treaty with them:

> (But the treaties are) not dissolved / With those Pagans with whom / Ye have entered into alliance / And who have not subsequently / Failed you in aught, / Nor aided any one against you. / So fulfill your engagements / With then to the end / Of their term: for God / Loveth the righteous. (IX:4)

However, if they violate their treaties (oaths, alliances), then a *jihad* is required:

> But if they violate their oaths / After their covenant, / And taunt you for your faith,-- / Fight ye the chiefs of Unfaith: / For their oaths are nothing to them: / That thus they may be restrained.
> Will ye not fight people / Who violated their oaths, / Plotted to expel the Apostle / And took the aggressive. . . .
> Fight them, and God will / Punish them by your hands, cover them with shame, / Help you (to victory) over them, / Heal the breasts of believers. (IX:13-15)

These *ayats* historically refer to treaty violations by the polytheists in Mecca, but by extension they refer to all parties who violate such alliances. The next citation specifically refers to a group of monotheists at Medina and a tragic incident during and after the Battle of the Trench: the Jewish tribe of the banu Quraiza.

> They are those with whom / Thou didst make a covenant, / But they did break their covenant / Every time, and they have not / The fear of God.
> If ye gain the mastery / Over them in war, disperse, with them, those / Who follow them, / That they may remember.
> If thou fearest treachery / From any group, throw back / (Their Covenant) to them, (so as / To be) on equal terms: / For God loveth not the treacherous. (VIII:56-58)

Ali's exigetical note clarifies the meaning of these *ayats* about those who violate their covenants:

> The immediate occasion was the repeated treachery of the Banu Quraiza after their treaties with the Muslims. But the general lesson remains. . . . Treachery . . . endangers many lives [especially during times of war]. Such treachery should be punished in a way that it gets no chance again. Not only the actual perpetrators but those who follow their standard should be rendered powerless. And the broken treaty should be denounced so that the innocent party can at least fight on equal terms [that is, the aggrieved party now has the right to renounce their oath]. From actual physical warfare we can carry the same lesson to spiritual warfare. A truce or understanding is possible with those who respect definite principles [especially the worship of One God and the practice of human justice], not with those who have no principles and are merely out for oppression and wickedness. (**The Holy Qur'an**, 429)

The **Qur'an**'s position on violating treaties is unequivocal: not only is a political *jihad* permitted, it is required and doubly so if the treaty is violated during times of war. Ali describes the historical danger of the acts of treachery by the banu Quraiza during the Battle of the Trench as follows:

> After a close investment of two to four weeks, during which the enemy was disheartened by their ill success, there was a piercing blast of the cold east wind. It was a severe winter . . . [Medina with an altitude of over 3000 feet can be bitter even into early spring]. The enemy's tents [Meccans] were torn up, their fires extinguished, the sand and rain beat in their faces, and they were terrified. . . . They had already . . . fallen out amongst themselves, and beating a hasty retreat, they melted away. The Medina fighting strength was no more than 3000, and the Jewish tribe of the banu Quraiza, who were in

their midst was a source of weakness as they were treacherously intriguing with the enemy. (**The Holy Qur'an**, 1105)

Medina, like Mecca, had no central authority; instead there were several tribes (*banu*, that is, clans) which existed by way of treaties (alliances) of peace. In order to survive in Medina, the emigrant Muslims established treaties with the major tribes. At a time of great danger, when the Meccans had besieged Medina with approximately 10,000 troops, the Jewish Quraiza violated their treaty with the Muslims. The reasons for their violation are mostly unknown, but given the difference in the number of troops, quite possibly the Quraiza anticipated a Meccan victory. What ever the reasons for their breaking the alliance, the results were disastrous for the Quraiza, as described by the historian W. Montgomery Watt:

> As soon as it was clear that the Meccan confederacy had finally departed, Muhammad issued a fresh summons to the Muslims . . . . They were to meet him before evening in front of the strongholds of the Jewish clan of Qurayzah [Watt's transliteration of *Quraiza*]. The Muslims responded and a siege was instituted which lasted twenty-five days. The reason . . . was that . . . they had been intriguing with Muhammad's enemies and at one point and been on the verge of attacking Muhammad in his rear. They had thus been guilty of treasonable activities against the Medinan community. . . .
>
> [The Quraiza surrendered after offering little opposition and even with an advance hint that their treason would be punished with extreme severity. Approximately 600 men were executed and the women and children sold as slaves][71]

71

This incident has been the cause of several major criticisms of Muhammad which claim he adopted a policy of executing or selling as slaves all of the Jews of Medina just because they were Jews. Watt provides a corrective to this erroneous view in his concluding paragraph to the situation of the Jewish Quriaza at Medina:

The continuing presence of at least a few Jews in Medina is

338

. . . .

After the elimination of Qurayzah no important clan of Jews was left in Medina, though there were probably several small groups.
(Muhammad: Prophet and Statesman, 171-74)

Before examining the third question concerning the rewards and punishments of *Al-Lah* for the righteous and the unrighteous engaged in a *jihad*, it is important to explore several *ayats* which reveal a moral dimensions of the *jihad* as the fight against injustice and in behalf of the oppressed. *Sura* IV provides a compelling statement regarding the *jihad* against injustice:[72]

> And why should ye not / Fight in the cause of God / And of those who, being weak, / Are ill-treated (and oppressed)?-- / Men, women, and children, / Whose cry is: "Our Lord! / Rescue us from this town, / Whose people are oppressors; / And raise for us from Thee / One who will protect; / And raise for us from Thee / One who will help!
>
> Those who believe / Fight in the cause of God, / And those who reject faith / Fight in the cause of Evil. . . .   (IV:75-6)

---

an argument against the view sometimes put forward by European scholars that in the second year after the Hijrah Muhammad adopted a policy of clearing all the Jews out of Medina just because they were Jews. . . . It was not Muhammad's way to have policies of this kind . . . . The occasions of his attacks . . . [on the Quriaza] were no more than occasions; but there were also deep underlying reasons. The Jews in general by their verbal criticisms [sometimes using ridicule and insult]. . . of the Qur'anic revelation were trying to undermine the foundation of the whole Islamic community; and they were also giving political support to Muhammad's enemies. . . . In so far as the Jews abandoned these forms of hostile activity Muhammad allowed them to live in Medina unmolested. (**Muhammad: Prophet and Statesman**, 175)

[72]

When *ayat* 75 states that the Muslim should "Fight in the cause of God," this *jihad* can just as well be undertaken by the mouth and the hand as well as the sword.

This *ayat* is an emotional and clear call from God for Muslims to fight against injustice. Ali's note makes the call even more passionate:

> Even from the human point of view the cause of God is the cause of justice, the cause of the oppressed. In the great persecution before Mecca was won again, what sorrows, threats, tortures, and oppressions were suffered by those whose faith was unshaken? Muhammad's life and that of his adherents was threatened; they were mocked, assaulted, insulted and beaten; those within the power of the enemy were put into chains and cast into prison; others were boycotted and shut out of trade, business and social intercourse; they could not even buy the food they wanted, or perform their religious duties. The persecution was redoubled for the believing slaves, women, and children after the Hijrah. The cry for a protector and helper from God was answered when Muhammad the Chosen One brought freedom and peace to Mecca again. (**The Holy Qur'an,** 202)

Sura II advocates the *jihad* against injustice in an interesting manner stressing the importance of charity:

> O ye who believe! / Fear God, and give up / What remains of your demand / For usury, if ye are / Indeed believers.
>
> If ye do it not [fear God], / Take notice of war / From God and His Apostle: / But if ye turn back, / Ye shall have / Your capital sums: deal not unjustly, / And ye shall not / Be dealt with unjustly.
>
> If the debtor is / In a difficulty, / Grant him time / Till it is easy / For him to repay. / But if ye remit it / By way of charity, / That is best for you / If ye only knew. (II:278-280)

These *ayats* deal with a common modern kind of oppression: economic oppression. The **Qur'an**, then, advocates a political *jihad* against those who would enslave through economic means. Notice also the tremendous emphasis put on charity. The following **hadith** states that in forgiving a debtor, one's sins (debt's with God) are forgiven:[73]

> On the authority of Abu Mas-ud al-Ansari (may Allah be pleased with him), who said that the Messenger of Allah (may the blessings and peace of Allah be upon him) said:
>
> A man standing from among those who were before you was called to account. Nothing in the way of good was found for him except that he used to have dealings with people and, being well-to-do, he would order his servants to let off a man in straitened circumstances [from repaying his debt]. He said that Allah said: We are worthier than you of that. Let him off.[[74]] (**Forty Sacred Hadiths**, 68)

The moral aspects of the *jihad* by the sword as a war against injustice are also emphasized in the limitations on war commanded in the **Qur'an**. Before exploring these limitations, it is appropriate to examine briefly the relationship between the *jihad* and the Hereafter.

What are the Qur'anic **rewards** and **punishments** related to a *jihad*? One of the better known, controversial and also misunderstood aspects of Islam is the nature of Paradise.[75] As with post-exhilic Judaism and Christianity, those human beings

---

73

In the **hadith** which follows, the first paragraph is the *isnad*, the chain of transmission, and the second paragraph is the *matn*, the moral and spiritual lesson.

74

The lesson in this **hadith** is similar to an important part of the Lord's Prayer in the "Sermon on the Mount": "Forgive us our debts as we forgive our debtors."

75

The **Qur'an** employs several descriptive terms for the Muslim equivalent of the Christian Heaven: described by such terms as *Paradise*, the *Garden*, the *Garden of Bliss* and the *Hereafter*. There are many passages in the **Qur'an** which describe the blessings of Paradise: cool streams, beautiful maidens, wine that does not intoxicate, luscious fruit, etc.. On the other hand, Hell is most commonly described as a place of eternal fire and excruciating immolations of unbelievers and unrepentant sinners. As is the case with Christianity, the theologically unsophisticated tend to understand these descriptions in a literal manner, while the more theologically sophisticated understand these descriptions as symbolic, metaphorical. In an important appendix, pages 1464-70, Yusuf Ali corrects the major Western misconceptions of the Muslim Heaven:

> . . . some ignorant critics of Islam imagine that Islam postulates a sensual heaven, and they press into service some garbled versions of what some of our more material-minded brethren have said on the subject.

> Our doctrine of the Hereafter is not strictly a doctrine of Rewards and Punishments. . . . Certainly whatever good we do benefits our own souls , but the motive with which we should do it should be only as "seeking the glory (literally, Face, Countenance) of God." [That is, the Muslim motive for goodness is not the bribe of Heaven or the fear of Hell, but the love of God. Many Christians and critics of Christianity have made this same mistake: accusing Christianity of either the Big Bribe--be good and get to Heaven or the Big Fear-be good or burn in Hell.]

> . . . . But as the light of Islam illuminates the soul more and more, it is seen that virtue is its own reward and evil its own punishment. . . . But "repentance" does not mean sackcloth and ashes, or putting on a gloomy pessimism. It means giving up disease for health. . . . It is akin to love, and is a purification of our will. . .

> . . . . Our Heaven is independent of Time, or Place, or fleeting Circumstance. No one can know precisely now the spiritual delights hidden in reserve for him (XXXII:17). But we must necessarily use terms that imply all these three conditions. Therefore they can only be expressed by allegory or imagery. . . .

> The simplest and yet the most far-reaching allegory that we can employ is that of the Garden--the Garden of Bliss. . . .

> . . . . All those whom we loved in this life--mothers, wives, sisters, relatives, children, friends--will add to our joy by their company in a transformed Love as superior to earthly love as in the Garden of Heaven to an earthly Garden. . . .

> . . . . [The Garden of Bliss is a place of] purity, grace, beauty, innocence, truth, and good-will. . . .

> . . . . [The happiness there] will not be solitary, but will be shared in association, on thrones of dignity and peace. . . .

> . . . . While the memory of love and all good in this life will endure, it will be purged of all old fears and anxieties in the supreme realization . . . that God is the One Reality--the Good, the Beneficent

whose lives are characterized by righteousness[76] and justice[77] are candidates for the salvation of eternal bliss. For Islam, since the fundamental nature of the *jihad* is the struggle with evil (**external**, that is, against oppression and injustice and **internal,** that is, against sin and temptation), it follows that the *mujihad* who struggles by the heart, mouth, hand or sword is the Muslim analogy of the Christian saint, the one whose destiny is eternal salvation with God. The **Qur'an** contains many passages which proclaim salvation for those who struggle against evil, and it places a special emphasis on those whose lives are lost in the struggle, that is, martyrs.[78]

---

and the Merciful. The souls in Heaven will realize in the highest spiritual sense the Presence of God. (**The Holy Qur'an**)

[76]

All three monotheisms recognize that the power of sin is such in human life that no human being is completely free of it; consequently, beyond human efforts to live righteously, eternal salvation requires the forgiveness of God. Of the three, however, it is Christianity which finds the power of sin so overwhelming that more is needed than just God's forgiveness, eternal forgiveness requires the sacrifice of the Christ. While Judaism and Islam emphasize the power of sin, the necessity of repentance and the forgiving love of God, they also have more faith in the human ability to overcome sin through the keeping of law. Consequently, the Christian view of human helplessness to conquer sin--thus, requiring the action of God in the Christ--presents less of a theological problem for Islam and Judaism concerning the Pelagian question that became a major theological conflict in Christianity: the question concerning how much a human being could contribute to his own salvation. Finally, it should be noted, that while all three religions emphasize the importance of righteousness, each develops slightly different understandings about what it means to "be-right-with-God," that is, righteousness.

[77]

While the understanding of righteousness differs among Abraham's children, there is very little difference in their understanding of justice.

[78]

It is important to remember that the promise of Paradise for a *mujihad* is not only for the Muslim whose life is lost in a *jihad* by the sword but also for those involved in the other three kinds of *jihads*. This promise has been historically one of the most misunderstood and criticized beliefs in the **Qur'an** by non-Muslims. Part of this misunderstanding is the result of an inaccurate limiting of the promise to the political *jihad* by the sword and part because of religious chauvinism. Remembering

Of the many passages which promise paradise, the following two are representative. *Sura* III speaks of the slain as not really dead and of the glory of the martyrs:

> Think not of those / Who are slain in God's way / As dead. Nay, they live, / Finding sustenance / In the Presence of their Lord; They rejoice in the Bounty / Provided by God: / And with regard to those / Left behind, who have not / Yet joined them (in their bliss), / The (Martyrs) glory in the fact / That on them is no fear, / Nor have they (cause to) grieve. (III:169-70)

Ali's note on these two *ayats* presents a view of the spiritual glory of losing one's life in the cause of justice and righteousness that could just as well have come from the pen of a Jewish or Christian theologian:[79]

---

that all *mujihads* who lose their lives, not just warriors in battle, are promised Paradise should suffice to correct the misconception of Paradise as a kind of Viking Valhalla. Remembering that Christian leaders, especially during the Crusades, made similar promises to their "holy warriors" should suffice to correct the second problem of religious bias.

Finally, a word is needed concerning the timing of this promise. As in Christianity, there has been a difference of interpretation in Muslim thought as to when the slain *mujihad* enters Paradise. In general, Islam holds that the human soul remains with the body until the end of time when the angel Israfil sounds the Trumpet of Doom which initiates the sequence of events which will culminate in the resurrection of all soul-bodies from their graves and their final judging for either Paradise or Hell. However, some Muslim *ulama*, especially among the Shi'a *ulama*, have maintained that the slain *mujihad* receives Paradise immediately rather than at the end of time. Christian eschatology has also struggled with the timing of the soul's journey to Heaven because of passages in the **New Testament** which speak of the soul "sleeping with the body."

79

In many ways, Ali's commentary cited above expresses a belief reminiscent of the final words of the Christian martyr Dietrich Bonhoeffer who was hanged at the Prison at Flossenberg three day before the allies liberated it on April 11, 1945. Payne Best, an English prisoner with Bonhoeffer described the events as follows:

> Bonhoeffer . . . was all humility and sweetness, he always seemed to me to diffuse an atmosphere of happiness, of joy in every smallest

A beautiful passage about the Martyrs in the cause of truth. They are not dead; they live--and in a higher and deeper sense than in the life they have left. Even those who have no faith in the Hereafter honour those that die in their cause, with the crown of immortality in the minds and memories of generations unborn. But in Faith we see a higher, truer, and less relative immortality. . . . In their case, through the gateway of death, they enter, the true real Life, as opposed to its shadow here. Our carnal life is sustained with carnal food, and its joys and pleasures at their best are those which are projected on the screen of this material world. Their real life is sustained from the ineffable Presence and Nearness of God. . . .

The Martyrs not only rejoice at the bliss they have themselves attained. The dear ones left behind are in their thoughts: it is part of their glory that they saved their dear ones from fear, sorrow, humiliation, and grief, in this life, even before they come to share in the glories of the Hereafter. (**The Holy Qur'an**, 167)

Sura IV reinforces the message in *sura* III:

---

event in life, and a deep gratitude for the mere fact that he was alive . . . . He was one of the very few men that I have ever met to whom his God was real and close to him. . . . The following day, Sunday, April 8th, 1945, pastor Bonhoeffer held a little service and spoke to us in a manner which reached the hearts of all, finding just the right words to express the spirit of our imprisonment and the thoughts and resolutions which it had brought. He had hardly finished his last prayer when the door opened and two evil-looking men in civilian clothes came in and said: "Prisoner Bonhoeffer, get ready to come with us." Those words "come with us"--for all prisoners they had come to mean only one thing--the scaffold.

We bade him goodby--he drew me aside--"This is the end," he said. "For me the beginning of life". . . . (**Letters and Papers From Prison**, 11)

Dietrich Bonhoeffer, in the richest sense of the term, was a *mujihad* of the heart and tongue.

Let those who fight / In the cause of God / Who sell the life of this
world / For the Hereafter. / To him who fighteth / In the cause of
God,-- / Whether he is slain / Or gets victory-- / Soon shall We
give him / A reward of great (value). (IV:74)

Ali's note on this *ayat* could have come from the pen of Paul who declared that not
even death was a victor over the power of God:

It is not everyone . . . who is fit to fight in the cause of God.
To do so is a privilege, and those who understand the privilege are
prepared to sacrifice all their interests in this life, and this life itself;
for they know that it is the sacrifice of something fleeting and of little
value, for the sake of something everlasting, and of immense value.
Whether they win or lose, in reality they win the prize for which they
were fighting . . . honour and glory in the sight of God. Note that the
alternatives here are death or Victory! The true fighter knows no
defeat. (**The Holy Qur'an**, 202)

Other significant *ayats* which emphasize the promise of Paradise for the *mujihad* are
III:142, III:156-58 and II:214.

On the other hand, Paradise is not the only Hereafter, for like the **New
Testament**, there are many passages that mention the fires (a metaphor) of eternal
damnation for several sins. To begin with, there are several *suras* such as IV:93
which declare that Hell is the destiny for anyone who intentionally kills a believer
whether the killing is part of a *jihad* or not. If the killing is unintentional, and the one
responsible repents and recompenses the family of the one killed, Hell is not a
punishment.[80] Just like Judaism and Christianity, then, Islam has several ways to

---

[80]

This provision of recompense for a family who has lost a member due to
unintentional death is a feature of pre-Islamic Arabia. In fact, even when the killing
was intentional such as in a *ghazw*, there were sometimes provisions for a
recompense that did not require a life for a life. Muhammad syncretized these kinds
of traditional "unwritten laws" from pre-Islamic Arabia into the Constitution of

deal with the taking of life outside a *jihad*. Since war, however, is the subject of this study, it is necessary to examine only those passages which concern the *jihad*.

There are several *ayats* which unconditionally declare that hell is the eternal destiny for those who wage war against *Al-Lah*, unless they repent. The two following are representative:

> This because they contended / Against God and His Apostle: / If any contend against God / And His Apostle, God / Is strict in punishment.
>
> Thus (will it be said): "Taste ye / Then of the (punishment): / For those who resist God, / Is the penalty of the Fire." (VIII:13-14)
>
> The punishment of those / Who wage war against God / And His Apostle, and strive / With might and main / For mischief through the land / Is: execution or crucifixion, / . . . . / That is their disgrace / In this world, and / A heavy punishment is theirs / In the Hereafter;
>
> Except for those who repent / Before they fall / Into your power: / In that case, know / That God is Oft-forgiving, / Most merciful. (V:36-37)

The punishment for those who defy God is clear: eternal damnation often described metaphorically as the Fire. The **Qur'an**, however, identifies three special classes of individuals whose destiny is eternal Fire: cowards in a *jihad*, those who cause internal discord among Muslims and Unbelievers, that is, non-monotheists. *Sura* VIII: 15-16 declares the penalty for cowards:

> O ye who believe! / When ye meet / The Unbelievers / In hostile array, Never turn your backs / To them.
>
> If any do turn his back / To them on such a day-- / Unless, it be a stratagem \ Of war, or to retreat / To a troop (of his own)-- / He

---

Medina.

draws on himself / The wrath of God, / And his abode is hell,-- / An evil refuge (indeed)!

Sura VIII:25 declares the punishment of God for those who cause internal dissent:

And fear tumult [*fitnat*, internal discord or civil war] or oppression, / Which affecteth not in particular / (Only) those of you who do wrong: / And know that God / Is strict in punishment [a phrase for Hell].

Finally, VIII:36-7 unequivocally declare the punishments of Hell for Unbelievers:

The Unbelievers spend their wealth / To hinder (men) from the path / Of God, and so will they / Continue to spend; but / In the end they will have / (Only) regrets and sighs; / At length they will be overcome: / And the Unbelievers will be / Gathered together in Hell.

In order that God may separate / The impure from the pure, / Put the impure, one on another, / Heap them together, and cast them / Into Hell. They will be / The ones to have lost.

The message is clear: Paradise for those who fight in the cause of God, that is, strive against evil with the heart, mouth, hand or sword; Hell for those who oppose God.[81]

What are the **religious** and **moral limitations** imposed by the **Qur'an** on a *jihad*? These limitations on war were one of the moral highlights of the Middle Ages: to use an analogy, they were the "Geneva Conventions" for Muslims of the Middle Ages. Unfortunately, just like twentieth century nations and groups involved in warfare, more peoples in the Middle Ages engaged in war chose to ignore rather

---

[81]

While the medium of the message is different, Arabic poetry, there is little in these views of Paradise and Hell and of the occupants of both places presented in the **Qur'an** that differs significantly from similar messages in the **Hebrew Bible** and the **New Testament**: the righteous and just receive eternal bliss; the unrighteous and unjust, unless they repent, are destined to eternal damnation. The major difference among Abraham's children is over the nature and content of righteousness.

than follow these moral limitations. Nonetheless, they represent a major advance in efforts to limit the bloodshed and destruction of warfare. If the Christian Popes and Rulers had followed them, there would probably have been no Crusades, or Crusades whose bloodshed would have been considerably less.

Given that the fundamental Qur'anic purposes of a *jihad* are creating of justice and peace, as previously noted in IX:4 and VIII:56-58, the **Qur'an** unequivocally forbids a *jihad* against those with whom Muslims have a treaty of peace:

> Except those who join / A group between whom / And you there
> is a treaty / (Of peace), or those who approach / You with hearts
> restraining / Then from fighting you / As well as their own /
> People. If God had pleased, / He could have given them / Power
> over you, and they / Would have fought you: / Therefore if they
> withdraw / From you but fight you not, / And (instead) send you
> / (Guarantees of) peace, then God / Hath opened no way / For you
> (to war against them).   (IV:90)

Not only does this *ayat* prohibit war against those with whom there is a treaty of peace, it also prohibits a *jihad* against those who wish to negotiate an honorable treaty of peace.

A second limitation on the *jihad* is the prohibition against killing other believers. This limitation has already been noted in the previous section on rewards and punishments related to a *jihad*. (See also IV:92-93.) Fundamental to Islam is the message that every Muslim is a brother to every other Muslim, that is, the message of unity. Muhammad's last message to the people of Mecca shortly before he died centered on this unity, a unity based on faith in *Al-Lah* (righteousness) and justice.[82]

---

[82]

As many observers of the Muslim world know, the **Qur'an**'s prohibition of a *jihad* against other believers has often been distorted by both political and religious leaders. Some of the clearest examples have been the Iraq-Iran War during the eighties, Desert Storm and the conflicts between North and South Yemen during the nineties. In fairness it should be noted that Christian Europe for centuries

A third limitation, perhaps the **Qur'an**'s most morally important one, is the prohibition against the killing of non-combatants. In his note to II:190 which warns the believer against transgressing the limits imposed by *Al-Lah* on war, Ali provides a concise list of protected persons and things:

> War is only permissible in self-defense, and under well-defined limits. When undertaken, it must be pushed with vigor, but not relentlessly, but only to restore peace and freedom for the worship of God. In any case strict limits must not be transgressed: women, children, old and infirm men should not be molested, nor trees and crops cut down, nor peace withheld when the enemy comes to terms.
>
> **(The Holy Qur'an, 75)**

Based on the **Qur'an**, several **hadiths** and writings of the Sunni *ulama*, Abd al-Rahman Azzam devotes considerable space to describing those people and resources protected from destruction by the **Qur'an** and the **hadiths** of Muhammad:

> One sees in the basic rules in the Message of Muhammad regarding the conduct of war that noble principle forbidding the extension of warfare to the harming of noncombatants. The rules decree against the killing of the aged, the young, women, the handicapped, those who had withdrawn from life to worship or meditate, those who have refrained from participating in battle, the mass of workers, farmers, and tradesmen--in other words, those today who are called civilians. . . .[83]

. . . .

---

experienced and continues to experience such distortions of its **New Testament** message of peace as well and has often pitted Christian brother against Christian brother in violent conflict.

83

    These prohibitions represent a considerable contrast to the blood-chilling command of *Yahweh* for the ban, that is, the command to kill every man, woman and child.

Modern warfare has become so ruthless that armies in retreat resort to a scorched-earth policy, even if it means death for their compatriots as well as their enemies. Such a practice is not sanctioned under any circumstance by the Shari'ah.[84] Attacks on the possessions of inhabitants left behind by advancing or retreating Islamic armies would be inconceivable. Muslims are strictly forbidden by their religion to burn plants, cut down trees, and deprive resident civilians of their means of livelihood in land that lies in the path of advancing and withdrawing armies.[85]

. . . .

Such examples are clear testimony of the justice that does not permit the slaying of civilians or prisoners or those who incline to space.

84

The *Shari'a* is a general term for the Muslim way of life as codified in Muslim practice and law. Its foundations are basically three: the **Qur'an**, the **hadiths** of Muhammad and the extension of these two as developed by the Muslim *ulama*. In other words, the *Shari'a* comprises the beliefs, values, etiquette, practices, laws, etc. which circumscribed the life of a Muslim. In this sense, it is analogous to the great Jewish *Talmud*. Etymologically, its meaning is most appropriate: it means "a clear path to water." In this sense, then, the *Shari'a* is the "clear path to righteousness."

85

A recent example of a Muslim leader violating this prohibition with a vengeance was seen in Hussein's efforts to make Kuwait unlivable after the Iraqi retreat. Unfortunately, there have been many Muslim leaders who have violated these prohibitions in their conflicts with the Israelis, who have more than reciprocated. One of the most infamous of the Israeli actions was the wanton destruction of the beautiful provincial capital of the Golan, La-Quenitra. Before withdrawing in 1973, they bulldozed or used dynamite to destroy over 90% of the buildings in the town, including the hospital along with stripping the Greek Orthodox Church of its marble interior and destroying its religious icons. Tragically, modern warfare is often pursued with a vengeance and violence that would bring many of the great Hebrew prophets, Jesus and Muhammad to tears.

The prophet was informed after one of the battles that youngsters had been caught between the ranks and killed. He was seized by a deep sorrow and some said to him: "Why do you grieve? Are they not the children of polytheists?" The Prophet became very annoyed and replied, "They are more worthy than you, for they are innocent; are you not sons of polytheists? Beware of killing children! beware of killing children!"[86]

Bukhari related that a funeral procession once passed by. The Prophet stood up out of reverence, and his Companions followed suit, though saying to him, "It is the funeral of a Jew." To this he replied, "Is it not that of a soul! if you behold a funeral, then stand."

This respect for the human being is general, and allows for no exceptions. The slaying of noncombatants or prisoners for unbelief alone cannot be permitted.

. . . .

Tradition (*sunnah*) and common law (*'urf*) provide ample rules for proper conduct in war, such as respect for the enemies emissaries and their safe conduct and kindness to captives, insofar as they are entitled to such benevolence, become equal in this respect with the orphans and the poor of Islam: "And feed with food the needy wretch, the orphan, and the prisoner, for love of Him [saying]: We feed you, for the sake of Allah only. We wish no reward nor thanks from you." (**The Eternal Message of Muhammad**, 144, 146, 149)

These extensive citations should suffice to describe the moral limitations placed on the practice of warfare by the beliefs and values of Islam. They are impressive moral

---

86

One cannot help but wonder how the members of groups such as Hamas and Hizbollah would respond to such a conversation with the Prophet!

prohibitions for any period of human history, but for the Middle Ages they are an astounding moral advance.[87]

Because of such events as the American hostage crisis in Iran during the presidency of Jimmy Carter, the fourth limitation placed on war by the **Qur'an** is quite a surprise to most Americans: the limitations concerning the taking of hostages. *Suras* VIII and XLVII contain pivotal passages concerning the issues of hostages and captives:

> It is not fitting / For an Apostle / That he should have / Prisoners of war until / He hath thoroughly subdued / The land . . . .
>
> O Apostle! say to those / Who are captives in your hands: / "If God findeth any good / In your hearts, He will / Give you something better / Than that which has been taken / From you, and He will / Forgive you: for God / Is Oft-forgiving, Most Merciful."
>
> But if they have / Treacherous designs against thee, / (O Apostle), they have already / Been in treason against God, / And so hath he given / (Thee) power over them. / And God is He who hath / (Full) knowledge and wisdom. (VIII:67, 70-71)

Ali's notes on these difficult *ayats* clarify the treatment of captives and hostages:

> . . . if there has been heavy loss of life already, captives may be taken, and it would be for the Imam to exercise his discretion as to the time when it would be safe to release them, and whether the release should be free or on parole or on a fine by way of punishment
>
> . . . .
>
> . . . .
>
> Note how comprehensive is God's care. He encourages and

---

[87]

One cannot help but wonder what the history of the Western world could have been if Christian leaders and nations had paid more attention to the "Sermon on the Mount" and Muslim rulers and nations to the moral aspects of the true *jihad*!

strengthens the Muslims, at the same time condemning any baser motives that may have entered their minds. He consoles the prisoners of war and promises them better things if there is any good in them at all. . . .

If the kindness shown to them is abused by the prisoners of war when they are released, it is not a matter of discouragement to those who have shown them kindness. . . . God knows all, and in His wisdom will order all things for the best. The Believers have done their duty in showing such clemency as they could in the circumstance of war. For them "God sufficeth" (VIII:62). (**The Holy Qur'an**, 432-33)

Sura XLVII recognizes that in war, prisoners may be taken in order to ensure victory, but like the previous *ayats*, it recommends generosity:

Therefore when ye meet / The Unbelievers (in fight), / Smite at their necks; / At length, when ye have / Thoroughly subdued them, / Bind a bond / Firmly (on them) either / Generosity or ransom: / Until the war lays down / Its burdens. Thus (are ye / Commanded): but if it / Had been God's Will, / He could have exacted / Retribution from them (Himself). . . . (XLVII:4)

As before, the prisoners are to be treated with kindness ("Generosity"). While the *ayat* does allow for ransom, it is listed as a secondary priority and, as several other *ayats* make clear, any profit motive for war is a base motive punished by God. The proper religious motive for dealing with prisoners of war (hostages) is release.[88]

---

[88]

It must be noted that the preceding *ayats* do not completely clarify the hostage taking situation since many of the terrorist groups capturing hostages do so in order to have other captives released. This kind of motive, which is not personal gain, muddies the water. What is, however, much clearer are the moral and religious responsibilities of the captors. Abd al-Rahman Azzam concisely states the Qur'anic position:

Further, although there is some ambiguity in the taking of captives the Qur'anic message concerning their treatment is clear: see footnote #88.

A fifth limitation on the practice of war concerns holy places. The **Qur'an** prohibits any kind of violence in places dedicated to God, that is, in *haram* locations. *Sura* II specifically mentions the sacred Mosque in Mecca, *(ayat* 191):

> But fight then not / At the sacred Mosque, / Unless they (first) /
> Fight you there . . . .

A significant number of Muslim *ulama* extend this prohibition to places sacred to Christians as well as Jews based upon XXII:39-40.

The final limitation concerns fighting during the prohibited months. There are *several ayats* which declare the prohibitions against war during four sacred months:

> The number of months / In the sight of God / Is twelve (in a year)--
> / So ordained by Him / The day He created / The heavens and the
> earth; / Of them four are sacred: / That is the straight usage. / So
> wrong not yourselves / Therein, and fight the Pagans / All together
> as they / Fight you all together. / But know that God / Is with
> those who restrain / Themselves. (IX:36)
> The prohibited month / For the prohibited month,-- / And so for all

---

There is not a single decree in the Koran allowing the slaying or enslaving of a prisoner, and it has never been said that the Prophet of God enslaved a captive. The Koran clearly grants the head of a Muslim state one of two choices (no third!)--grace or ransom: ". . . when ye have routed them, then [make] fast [their] bonds; and afterward [give them] either grace or ransom till the war lay down its burdens." [XXXXVII:4] **(The Eternal Message of Muhammad,** 147)

The implication is fairly clear in Azzam and the *ayat* he cites recalls that ransom is acceptable only until the war's end; then, the only alternative is "grace."

To summarize: the message of the **Qur'an** is possibly ambiguous concerning the taking of hostages, but absolutely clear concerning their treatment. Terrorist groups who murder their hostages are in direct violation of their Holy Book.

things prohibited,-- / There is a law of equality. / If then anyone transgresses / The prohibition against you, / Transgress likewise / Against him. / But fear God, and know that God is with those / Who restrain themselves. (II:194)

Although there are four prohibited months, one is more sacred, *haram*, than any other: the month of the *Hajj*, the sacred pilgrimage to Mecca.[89] Ali explains the *haram* months in the following note:

> The month of Pilgrimage (*Zul-hajj*) was a sacred month in which warfare was prohibited by Arab custom. The month preceding (*Zul-qa'd*) and the month following *Muharram*) were included in the prohibition [The reason for this is that spiritual preparations for the *hajj* begin weeks before the actual pilgrimage, and the *hajji* should have a time of peace to reflect on the spiritual lessons learned during the *hajj* itself] and *Muharram* was specially called *al-haram*. . . . [In] *Rajab*, war was also prohibited. . . . [Ali goes on to indicate that if the enemies of Islam break this prohibition, that is, war against Muslims during the prohibited months, they are justified in fighting back as a defensive measure.] (**The Holy Qur'an**, 77)

Discussion of the prohibited months completes this section of the moral and spiritual limitations placed on the *jihad*. Only one item remains before turning to the

---

[89]

Given the history of violence in the Middle East, especially the national and political conflicts between Muslim countries, the period of peace during the month of *shu-la-haj* has seldom been violated. The *Hajj* is not only one of the most sacred religious events celebrated in the world, it is miracle of peace. For several days, Muslims, who may have been at war with one another weeks earlier, maintain a period of peace in Mecca. No wonder *hajjis*, those who have made the *hajj,* speak of their lives having been changed. It changed the life of Malcolm X, who returned with a new non-racist vision of peace: unfortunately, a vision which may have contributed to his murder by those unwilling to hear a message of toleration and peace.

Qur'anic view of spiritual war: a brief listing of other provisions and issues in the **Qur'an** concerning political war (both *jihad* and *harb*).

There are several other issues the **Qur'an** proclaims concerning war which require only a listing of the issues and supporting *ayats*. There is no hierarchial order in the summary list which follows:[90]

(1)   Several *ayats* promise a Gideon-like victory or a Goliath type slaying for those who fight for God, the true *mujihads*: II:249, 251; VIII:65-66.

(2)   Several *ayats* explain the fighting between Jews and Christians and their internal divisions as the consequences of their failures to heed the true messages of the prophets: II:253; V:67.

(3)   Numerous passages make references to the major battles of Muhammad:

      (a)   Badr: III:3, 123; almost the whole of sura VIII.

      (b)   Uhud: III:121-22, 149-180.

      (c)   The Trench: IX:25; XXXIII:9-20.

      (d)   Others: XVII:5; IX:25-26.

(4)   Several *ayats* describe the aid of *Al-Lah* in battle in terms resembling those of the aid of *Yahweh* as described in the **Hebrew Bible**--for example, giving calmness and courage to the *mujihad*, using nature to overcome the enemy, striking terror into the hearts of the enemy, etc.: VIII: 9, 11, 17, 43.

(5)   LXI:4 describes the attributes of the *mujihad* in battle: strength, discipline and courage.

(6)   LXX:30 describes the provisions for marrying women captured in battle. Having examined at some length the Qur'anic theology concerning political war, it is now time to explore an issue of greater religious significance: spiritual war, that is, the *jihad* fought by the heart.

---

[90]

    Only representative *ayats* are listed; there are in most listed categories several additional *ayats* that either directly or indirectly have relevance.

Spiritual War

The greatest religious revolutions in human history have been initiated by spiritual giants such as Amos and Isaiah, Siddartha Gautama (the Buddha), Yeshua ben Yusuf (the Christ) and Muhammad. As the initiators of new spiritual visions, they shared two fundamental insights that helped change the history of the world and our understandings of human nature. First, each existentially experienced and emphasized in their teachings the fundamental human need for transcendence which separates humans from the beasts of the fields. In other words, each knew that for the human spirit to grow and mature, it must go beyond the tiny-selfish world of the individual ego. In the East, this growth was understood in terms of transcending the self by realizing the *maya* (illusion) of individuality, practicing the spiritual techniques of meditation, self-discipline, the renunciation of worldly possessions, and the eventual loss of individuality in an at-oneness with nature (the cosmos). In the West, the growth of the spirit was understood in terms of opening (submitting) the self to the presence and will of God (that is, righteousness) and devoting oneself to the suffering, loving, hoping needs of other human beings through the practice of justice. Further, each great leader knew the path leading to such spiritual transcendence was not found in external ritual and religious legalism; consequently, Amos and Isaiah, the Buddha, the Christ and Muhammad criticized and rejected the reduction of spiritual truth to the ritual and legal formalism dominating the religious practices and institutions of their cultures.

Second, each recognized that the greatest, most difficult and most significant spiritual battle a human being must fight is with himself. While each advocated different paths and weapons for this battle, each intuitively knew from his own spiritual struggles that achieving transcendence required victory over selfishness, self-absorption, temptation, lust, arrogance, greed, anger, envy, physical appetites, possessiveness, etc.. To use the terminology of Islam, each knew as a *mujihad* that the basic spiritual battle is the *jihad* fought by the heart, that is, what is termed *spiritual war* in this study.

358

Before examining the theology of spiritual war in the **Qur'an**, it is helpful to begin with two *mujihads* who fought *jihads* of the heart: Abel and Yitzhak Rabin. In contrast to the Yahwist account of the Cain and Abel story in Genesis[91] (see Chapter Two), the account in the **Qur'an** adds a spiritual and moral highlight: Abel's comments to Cain before he is murdered. They are worth citing again:

> "If thou dost stretch thy hand / Against me, to slay me, / It is not
> for me to stretch / My hand against thee / To slay thee: for I do
> fear / God, the Cherisher of the Worlds. (V:30)

Only a *mujihad* who had truly won his battle against fear and self-centeredness, that is, who had achieved the transcendence of giving his life to God could have given up his life in this way. The Qur'anic story of Cain and Abel is one of the great spiritual lessons in all of religious literature, for it reveals the heart of faith, that is, the experience of a reality **beyond** the self.

A few days after the assassination by Yigil Amir, David Hoffman, who served as the Jerusalem correspondent for the **Washington Post** from 1992 to 1994, wrote an eulogy for Yitshak Rabin that appeared in the November 13-19, 1995 edition of the **Post**. Early in his eulogy, Hoffman wrote:

> This was his last mission--to save the Jewish state from the
> corrosive effects of the colonization of the territories, the occupation
> of another people and the cycle of violence that it unleashed. From
> his election in 1992 until the day of his death, Rabin led a heroic and
> as yet unsuccessful effort to redirect Israel's energy back into the
> original goals of Zionism, the building of a Jewish state, and away
> from the draining effects of occupation.

---

[91]

The reader is reminded that the Cain and Abel narrative should not be understood as a literal account of two historical brothers. Rather, the story belongs to the literary category of myth, which is to say that it reveals important truths concerning human nature and human relationships even though it does not involve persons who actually lived.

Appropriately, Hoffman concludes his eulogy with Rabin's words:

> "I want to tell the truth," Rabin said in a speech last year
> which included a passage many had not heard him speak before. "For
> 27 years, the Palestinians . . . have risen in the morning and cultivated
> a burning hatred for us as Israelis and as Jews[92] Every morning they
> awake to a difficult life, and it is partly our fault. . . . It cannot be
> denied: the continued rule of a foreign people who does not want us
> has a price. There is first of all a painful price, the price of constant
> confrontation between us and them."

This painful awareness was an astounding recognition on the part of a gruff old
warrior who lost dozens of friends and family members in the decades of conflict
between Israelis and Palestinians. Only a *mujihad* who had victoriously struggled
with self-honesty and overcome the internal spiritual costs of war--anger, hatred and
vengeance--could have turned from violence to peace. In the richest spiritual sense
of a *jihad* fought by the heart, Rabin was a *mujihad*, or in Christian terms, a
peacemaker.

Based on the preceding descriptions of *jihads* fought by the heart, the
following **hadith** further reveals the spiritual greatness of Islam: "Every nation has
its monasticism, and the monasticism of Islam is the jihad." (Khadduri, **War and
Peace in the Law of Islam**, 55) Another **hadith** proclaims the same value in slightly
different words: "Jihad is an act of pure devotion." (**The Encyclopedia of Islam**,
vol.II, 539) Utilizing this background, it is now appropriate to explore the words of

---

92

    As indicated in numerous places in this study, it is important to remember
that this "burning hatred" is not centuries old, as far too many American media
commentators tell the American public. It is basically a product of the late 19th and
20th centuries mess that the Europeans, especially the British and the French, created
in the Middle East after two world wars and the U.N. partition in 1947. Throughout
those centuries since the arrival of Islam in the Middle East, Jews and Muslims lived
in relative peace with one another. The "burning hatred" so often referred to by
journalists developed after the partition and the occupations following the 1967 War.

the **Qur'an** which reveal the nature and spiritual significance of spiritual war, that is, the *jihad* fought by the heart. The strategy for examining the Qur'anic theology of spiritual war is to analyze it under five aspects: (1) *ayats* which speak of the importance of the heart; (2) passages which describe the tests, trials and temptations of earthly existence; (3) weapons of the *mujihad* of the heart--faith, repentance, truth, patience and peace; (4) the promised spiritual rewards --mercy, forgiveness and salvation; and (5) the equality of the sexes in the *jihad* fought by the heart.

To begin, several *ayats* reveal the spiritual significance of the **heart**, but VIII:24 stands out:

> O ye who believe! / Give your response to God / And His Apostle, when He / Calleth you to that which / Will give you life; / And know that God / Cometh in between a man / And his heart, and that / It is He to Whom / Ye shall (all) be gathered.

Ali's note in his translation, **The Holy Qur'an**, is especially revealing:

> If the human heart is refractory and refuses to obey the call to God, that is not the end of the matter. God has to be reckoned with. The refusal may be because there was some pet human scheme which the heart of man was not willing to give up for God's Cause. By no means. Man proposes, but God disposes. If the scheme or motive was perfectly secret from men, it was not secret from God. The heart is the innermost seat of man's affections and desires; but between this seat and man himself is the presence of the Omnipresent.[93] (420)

93

There are several lessons in this *ayat*, two are similar to better known lessons in the **Hebrew Bible** and the **New Testament**. First, the declaration that even though men may try to refuse the call of God, His purposes will be fulfilled is similar to the lesson that Jonah learned when he tried to refuse God's call. Second, that one cannot serve two masters, their own "pet human schemes" and that "the call of God" is similar to Jesus' comments about trying to serve God and mammon in the "Sermon on the Mount."

The spiritual significance of Ali's last statement cannot be underestimated: ". . . between this seat [the heart, which in the **Qur'an** has a meaning similar to its use in both the **Hebrew Bible** and the **New Testament**: the heart is a symbol for the whole of one's life] and man himself is the presence of the Omnipresent." From this *ayat*, it should be clear why it is the *jihad* fought by the heart that is most precious to *Al-Lah*.

III:146 uses the example of the prophets, who, even when faced with danger and disaster never lost heart, that is, never let circumstances diminish their faith in the presence and protection of God:

> How many of the Prophets / Fought (in God's way), / . . . / But they never lost heart / If they met with disaster / In God's way, nor did / They weaken (in will) / Nor give in. / And God / Loves those who are / Firm and steadfast.

The promise is clear: when a *mujihad* has overcome those human obstacles that separate him from God, in his battle against evil, both internal and external, he is never alone. This, then, leads to the question: what are these obstacles? Although they have already been briefly mentioned, one of them deserves special attention: selfishness, that is, self-centeredness. In his note concerning II:244, Ali calls attention to two spiritual truths fundamental in the scriptures of the other children of Abraham: (1) selfishness places a fence between the soul and God, and (2) God knows the innermost thoughts, feelings, needs and motives of human beings:

> Then fight in the cause / Of God, and know that God / Heareth and knoweth all things. (II:244)

> For God's cause we must fight, but never to satisfy our own selfish passions or greed, for the warning is repeated: "God heareth and knoweth all things": all deeds, words, and motives are perfectly open before Him, however we might conceal them from men or even from

ourselves. . . .[94] (**The Holy Qur'an**, 97)

As a final example of the enemies that the *mujihad* of the heart must overcome,
consider the diseases of the heart in XLVII:20-21:

> Those who believe say / "Why is not a Sura / Sent down (for us)?"
> / But when a Sura / Of basic and categorical / Meaning is revealed,
> / And fighting is mentioned / Therein, thou wilt see those / In
> whose hearts is a disease / Looking at thee with a look / Of one in
> swoon at / The approach of death. / But more fitting for them--
> Were it to obey / And say what is just, / And when a matter / Is
> resolved on, it were / Best for them if they / Were true to God.

In his note on these diseases of the heart, Ali mentions: ". . . hypocrisy [one of the
fundamental forms of bad faith or self-deception, see footnote #94], want of courage
[few things require more courage than self-honesty], [want of] self-sacrifice, want of
true understanding." (**The Holy Qur'an**, 1384)

Second, what is the function of **trials, tests** and **temptations** in the spiritual
war of the soul? There are many passages that speak of the tests, trials and
temptations the true *mujihad* must overcome. Consider the following passages, the
last which contains an incisive insight concerning a most dangerous, seductive
temptation for faith. II:214 provides an honest and clear statement that the life of
faith is not one free of trials, testing and suffering:

> Or do ye think / That ye shall enter / The Garden of (Bliss) /
> Without such (trials) / As came to those / Who passed away /
> Before you? / They encountered Suffering and adversity, / And

---

94

One of Ali's more interesting insights in this note is his statement about
concealing our motives and feelings "even from ourselves." The existentialists refer
to this unhealthy spiritual state as bad faith or self-deception. Its opposite is good
faith or self-honesty. The spiritual significance of this insight can be clarified by the
following question: "Can a person be honest with either God or another human being
unless he can be honest with himself?" The answer is obvious!

were so shaken in spirit / That even the Apostle / And those who
were with him / Cried: "When (will come) / The Help of God?"
/ Ah! Verily, the help of God / Is (always) near!

While the honest declaration that the *mujihad's* faith does not remove him from the
realities of life is admirable, most spiritually significant is this *ayat's* promise to the
one who submits his life to God: "Verily, the help of God   Is (always) near!"
III:142 reaffirms the same message and promise for those who remain steadfast in
faith and fidelity to *Al-Lah*:

Did ye think that ye / Would enter Heaven / Without God testing
/ Those of you who fought hard / (In His Cause) and / Remained
steadfast?

In III:154 the same message is combined with a warning (see footnotes #94 and #95):

But (all this) / That God might test / What is in your breasts / And
purge what is / In your hearts / For God knoweth well / The
secrets of your hearts.

It is important to note that the testing is not for the benefit of God's knowing what is
in one's heart, but for the *mujihad* to know what is in his own heart; a point Ali
stresses in his note in **The Holy Qur'an** on this *ayat*:

That testing by God is not in order that it may add to His
knowledge, for he knows all. It is in order to help us subjectively, to
mould our will, and purge us of any grosser motives, that will be
searched out by calamity. If it is a hardened sinner [unrepentant
sinner], the test brings conviction out of his own self.[95] (163)

95

This *ayat* contains a fundamental insight concerning the building of character
and the dangers of self-deception. (See footnote #94.) For example, it is exceedingly
easy for a person to tell himself that he is an honest and charitable person, but the
danger here is self-deception. The only reliable way for anyone to know if he is
indeed honest and charitable is the test of actual experience. If one finds that he lies
in order to escape from a difficult situation, the truth is that honesty is not a personal

Later in *sura* III there are two *ayats* responding to one of the two most common questions asked by all of Abraham's children: Since God is just, then "why do good things happen to evil people?" and "why do bad things happen to good people?":

> Let not the Unbelievers / Think that Our respite / To them is good for themselves: / We grant them respite / That they may grow / In their iniquity: / But they will have / A shameful punishment. God will not leave / The Believers in the state / To which ye are now / Until He separates / What is evil / From what is good. / Nor will he disclose / To you the secrets of the Unseen, / But he chooses / Of His Apostles / (For the purpose) / Whom He pleases. / So believe in God / And His Apostles: / And if ye believe / And do right, / Ye have a reward / Without measure. (III:178-79)

Ali's notes on these two *ayats* are most illuminating:

> That the cup of their iniquity may be full. The appetite for sin grows with what it feeds on. The natural result is that the sinner sinks deeper into sin. If there is any freedom of will, this naturally follows, through God's Grace is always ready for the repentant. If the Grace is rejected, the increase of iniquity makes the nature of iniquity plainer to those who otherwise might be attracted by its glitter. . . .
>
> The testing of good men by calamities and evil men by leaving them in the enjoyment of good things is part of the Universal Plan, in which some freedom of choice is left to man. The psychological and subjective test is unfailing, and the separation is effected partly by the operation of the human wills. . . .
>
> **(The Holy Qur'an**, 169)

On the spiritual level, the insights in these two *ayats* concerning "good and bad

---

value. Only the trials, temptations and sufferings of life can adequately reveal a person's true character or his self-deception. (See footnote #4 in the "Prologue" for a more developed discussion of the nature of values, beliefs and self-honesty.)

things" and "good and evil persons" are immense. First, trials, temptations, calamities and sufferings not only test the psychological character of a person but the honesty of their faith. This test does not mean that good things do not happen to good people, but in the spiritual struggle with the calamities and sufferings of life, one comes to know the nature and depth of his beliefs and values. Second, the good things that happen to bad people function spiritually in two ways: (a) as a continuing test for the believer of the justice of God's Plan; and (b) as a deepening seduction for the sinner to remain in the enjoyment of sin. However, since believers also experience good things such as success and wealth, even the good things that happen to believers can provide tests of faith for the *jihad* by the heart--perhaps an even more dangerous test than calamity and suffering.

VIII:28 describes the test and temptation of success by using the metaphor of a big family:

> And know ye / That your possession[96] / And your progeny / Are but a trial; / And that it is God / With whom lies / Your highest reward.

Ali's note decisively describes the seductive danger of success:

> A big family--many sons--was considered a source of power and strength. . . . So in English, a man with many children is said to have his "quiver full" [see Psalms CXXVII:4-5]. . . . So with property and possessions: they add to a man's dignity, power, and influence. But both possessions and a large family are temptation and a trial. They may turn out to be a source of spiritual downfall, if they are mishandled, or if the love of them excludes the love of God.
> **(The Holy Qur'an**, 422)

96

The 20th century French existential philosopher Gabriel Marcel describes the dangers of success and possessions in a concise, insightful way when he states that **to possess is to be possessed!**

Success, power, possessions and many other "good things" are spiritual dangers that *mujihads* by the heart must always struggle to overcome because they can lead to comfort, complacency and often arrogance.[97]

As the preceding indicates, the **Qur'an** aptly describes both the nature and the dangers of the trials, temptations and sufferings which inevitably occur in the life of every human being. However, it also makes a promise to the believer that is reassuring as well as hopeful:

> On no soul doth God / Place a burden greater / Than it can bear. / It gets every good that it earns, / And it suffers every ill that it earns. / (Pray:) "Our Lord! Condemn us not / If we forget or fall / Into error; Our Lord! / Lay not on us a burden / Like that which Thou / Didst lay on those before us; / Our Lord! lay not on us / A burden greater than we / Have strength to bear. / Blot out our sins, / And grant us forgiveness. / Have mercy on us. / Thou art our Protector; / Help us stand against those / Who stand against Faith."[[98]] (II:186)

---

[97]

The dangers of success, power, possessions, etc. for those who believe in God has been a constant theme in Christian theology over the past few centuries. In the 19th century, the Danish Christian Soren Kierkegaard wrote extensively of the danger of what he termed Worldly (or Comfortable) Christianity, that is, a Christianity which did not require the tests, trials and sufferings of sacrifice. Shortly after the Second World War, Franklin Littel, author of the **German Phoenix**, a story of the rebirth of Christianity in Germany after the Nazis, described a discussion he had with a German exchange student at the University of Michigan. In the midst of their conversation about American Christianity, Littel asked him what he found most surprising or unusual about the churches in American. After pausing for a moment, the young man replied that the biggest surprise for him was that all the churches had cushions in their pews; then he smiled and said: "But all the sermons had cushions in them too!" Comfortable Christianity or comfortable Islam is perhaps the most subtle of all the spiritual wars a *mujihad* must fight.

[98]

This *ayat* and its prayer expresses many of the same hopes and needs as those

While *mujihads* by the heart must struggle with the various tests and burdens of life, the **Qur'an** makes two promises to those who submit their lives to God, that is, to *Muslims*: In your struggle you are never alone, for God is always present, and God will not place a burden on the *mujihad* which is beyond his spiritual endurance.

Third, what are the **weapons** that *Al-Lah* gives to the *mujihad* for his spiritual wars? CIII: 2-3 together with Ali's notes reveal eight of the most important God given resources (weapons) for the *mujihad*'s struggle against evil:

> Verily Man / Is in loss,
>
> Except such as have Faith, / And do righteous deeds, / And (join together) / In the mutual teaching / Of Truth, and of / Patience and Constancy. (CIII:2-3)
>
> Faith is his armour, which wards off the wounds of the material world; and his righteous life is his positive contribution to spiritual ascent. . . .
>
> If he [the *mujihad*] lived only for himself, he would not fulfill his whole duty. Whatever good he has, especially in spiritual and moral life, he must spread among his brethren, so that they may see the Truth and stand by it in patient hope and unshakable constancy amidst all the storms and stress of outer life. For he and they will then have attained Peace within. (**The Holy Qur'an**, 1783)

The spiritual weapons of the *mujihad*, then, are: faith, righteousness, community ("join together"), truth and teachers of truth, patience, "unshakable constancy," "patient hope," and "Peace within." With these weapons, the *mujihad* of the heart overcomes the trials and tribulations of life because he has submitted his life to the Will of *Al-Lah*. Fundamental to this submission is a spiritual act which is also at the

---

expressed in two of the most cherished passages in the **Hebrew Bible**--Psalm 23, David's Shepherd Psalm--and in the **New Testament**, the Lord's Prayer from the "Sermon on the Mount."

heart of the Jewish and Christian understandings of man's relationship to God--repentance:

> When those come to thee / Who believe . . . / Say: "Peace be on you: / Your Lord hath inscribed / For Himself (the rule / Of) Mercy: verily / If any of you did evil / In ignorance, and thereafter repented, and amended / (His conduct), lo! He is / Oft-forgiving, Most Merciful. (VI:54)

What an astounding *ayat*! For the Muslim who has done evil but has also fought the *jihad* by the heart, that is, who has honestly admitted his sin, repented for his sin and changed his conduct, the rewards of God are mercy, forgiveness and peace (that is, salvation). This repentance leads to the fourth aspect of spiritual war.

What are the **rewards** (promises) of *Al-Lah* for *mujihads* of the heart? To begin with, those *mujihads* who have suffered, been injured in their striving and struggled against evil are promised the mercy and forgiveness of *Al-Lah*, that is, they receive hope:

> Those who believed / And those who suffered exile / And fought (and strove and struggled) / In the path of God-- / They have the hope / Of the Mercy of God: / And God is Oft-forgiving, / Most merciful. (II:218)

The hope and the promise of God's mercy and forgiveness is especially emphasized for those whose *jihads* by heart, mouth, hand or sword result in the loss of their lives, that is, those who become martyrs to the Cause of God:

> And if ye are slain, or die, / In the way of God, / Forgiveness and mercy / From God are far better / Than all they could amass. (III:157)

Several *ayats* later, III:169-70, this same "crown of immortality," is again promised to the *mujihad* who has been slain in the Cause of God. IX:20 and Ali's accompanying note emphasize that salvation is the eternal destiny for those who fight with their hearts, mouths and hands, that is, in non-violent ways to overcome evil:

Those who believe and suffer / Exile and strive with might / And main, in God's cause, / With their goods and persons, / Have the highest rank / In the sight of God: / They are the people / Who will achieve (salvation). (IX:20)

Here is a good description of Jihad. It may require fighting in God's cause as a form of self-sacrifice. But its essence consists in (1) a true and sincere faith, which so fixes its gaze on God, that all selfish or worldly motives seem paltry and fade away, and (2) an earnest and ceaseless activity, involving the sacrifice (if it need be) of life, person, or property, in the service of God. Mere brutal fighting is opposed to the whole spirit of Jihad, while the sincere scholar's pen or preacher's voice or wealthy man's contributions may be the most valuable forms of Jihad. (**The Holy Qur'an**, 444)

This passage and Ali's commentary cannot be underestimated, for both clearly affirm that the *jihad* which has "the highest rank / In the sight of God" is the spiritual *jihad* by the heart, that is, the striving with ". . . might / And main, in God's cause, / With . . . goods and . . . persons." In the sense of the spiritual *jihad* fought by the heart, several **hadiths** proclaim that *jihad* is the "monasticism of Islam" and an "act of pure devotion." The scholar, the preacher, the social worker, the nurse or doctor, the farmer who helps a neighbor with his field, the mediator who struggles to bring peace to warring factions and any human being--Muslim, Jew or Christian--who says **NO** to those forces which dehumanize and destroy human life and dignity and who strives in positive, non-violent ways to build respect and understanding among God's many children are *mujihad*s with ". . . the highest rank / In the Sight of God." In this recognition, the **Qur'an** reaches its spiritual-moral summit.

Remembering that the *jihad* by the sword is last in merit, and that the **Qur'an** limits the participation of women in political *jihad* by the sword to indirect support for the troops,[99] the following *ayat* and Ali's commentary help correct another stereotype of Islam:

> And their Lord hath accepted / Of them, and answered them: / "Never will I suffer to be lost / The Work of any of you, / Be he male of female: / Ye are members, one of another: / Those who have left their homes, / Or been driven out therefrom, / Or suffered harm in My cause, / Or fought or been slain,-- / Verily, I will blot out / From them their iniquities, / And admit them into Gardens / With rivers flowing beneath;-- / A reward from the Presence / Of God, and from His Presence / Is the best of rewards." (III:195)

In Islam the equal status [before God] of the sexes is not only recognized but insisted on.[100] If sex distinction, which is a

---

99

Given the methods and the weapons of 7th century warfare, this limitation was essentially a consequence of biology. Muhammad certainly knew nothing of modern means of warfare which have changed the physical requirements for battle. What the Prophet would say today about women in battle must, then, remain open.

100

There is concern and criticism from many Western nations about the treatment of women in many Muslim countries. Much of this criticism is morally appropriate, for women's rights and needs do lag far behind in many third world environments where Islam is the majority religion. However, to be fair, some of the criticisms are both chauvinistically hypocritical and historically-environmentally ignorant. First, many of those nations who are quick to criticize still need to "clean their own houses." Unquestionably, the rights of women in the U.S. are far above that of the majority of the world, Islam included, but we still have a long way to go in order to state with non-hypocritical honesty that women have equal status with men. Further, far too many criticisms from the U.S. assume that American democracy can be transmitted into any environment and is a necessary condition for human rights. Both assumptions not only beg the question, they ignore the internal problems democracy always creates in any political situation. Second, such criticisms are usually based on an ignorance of history and environment. In many third world environments, the primary struggle is survival against a hostile or inadequate environment; issues of sexual equality necessarily take a back seat to those of survival. For the 7th century C.E. the **Qur'an** provided women with rights

distinction in nature, does not count in spiritual matters, still less of course would count artificial distinctions such as rank, wealth, position, race, colour,[101] birth, etc. (**The Holy Qur'an**, 175)

This affirmation of the equality of the sexes--and by extension the races--is an appropriate note on which to conclude the exploration of spiritual war, the *jihad* by the heart, in the **Qur'an**. Before examining the theology of eschatological war, however, a corrective perspective is needed. Because this study devotes forty pages to political war and less than half as many to spiritual war does not lead to a conclusion that the political *jihad* is more important than the spiritual one. In fact,

---

of inheritance, divorce and religious status unparalleled anywhere in the Christian world. Tragically, as Islam was experiencing its age of enlightenment (9th-12th centuries), the destructions of the Mongol hordes drove it back into a dark age. After the Mongols, centuries of control by Turks and then Europeans kept Islam from experiencing the kind of renaissance that changed Europe. Even with the benefits of the renaissance, modern science and the development of constitutional states, it has taken over four hundred years for any serious actions improving women's rights and status to occur. Criticisms of the status of women in Islam cannot realistically expect most of the Muslim world, which does not have the considerable environmental, economic and political advantages as most of the industrialized West, to achieve in a few decades what required centuries in Europe and the United States. This does not mean that the criticisms should stop, only that they should rid themselves of their patronizing chauvinism and pay attention to the historical and environmental background within which any progress on the rights of women must advance in the Muslim world.

101

A question many Americans often ask about Islam is: what is the relationship between Black (variously called American and African-American) Islam and Islam? It is a difficult question to answer. In some way it is like asking the question: are Mormons Christians? The answer differs depending on the person responding: a Mormon says "Yes," while the average Baptist says "No." Based on the message of the **Qur'an**, not only in III:195 but in many *ayats*, the **Qur'an** rejects racism. Perhaps, then, the best response to the initial question is: "Any Muslim group, or Christian as well, that practices racism is distorting one of the fundamental truths of monotheism--"**ALL** humans beings are the created children of God." Since both Islam and Christianity are universal monotheisms, then, any Christian or Muslim group which advocates racism distorts the holy revelations of God in both the **New Testament** and the **Qur'an**. The final chapter returns to this truth.

the reverse is true; the spiritual *jihad* becomes fundamental in the **Qur'an** and the one most precious in the sight of *Al-Lah*. This understanding places the **Qur'an** among the greatest spiritual revelations in human history.

Eschatological War

Before exploring the theology of cosmic war in the **Qur'an**, it is helpful to examine the apocalyptic traditions that formed part of the religious environment of pre-Islamic Arabia. Apocalyptic eschatology was no stranger to the Arabs of Muhammad's day or the Byzantine Empire. By the time of Muhammad, such end of time views had a history exceeding a millennium. While it is a matter of some scholarly debate, every year the evidence mounts that the emergence of the first systematic apocalyptic eschatology was among the Zoroastrians of ancient Persia. This should not be surprising since the development of cosmic eschatologies, that is views about the end of the created universe, require the theological foundation of monotheism. The animistic polytheism of the Arabs provided no foundation for eschatological views but their historical and geographical situation provided many opportunities for their commercial interaction with the three monotheisms of the Middle East: Zoroastrianism, Judaism and Christianity. As the Arabs of Muhammad's time were ripe for the appearance of an Arab monotheism so they were ripe for the accompanying eschatology.

Since various disasters were an integral part of Jewish and Christian eschatologies--for example, the Four Horseman of the Apocalypse: War, Famine, Pestilence and Death--the history of the Middle East provided a fertile seedbed for eschatological speculations. In other words, it is difficult to find significant periods of time or generations that did not witness the terrible destructions of these Four Horseman. Wars, famines, disease, earthquakes and various other kinds of calamities were constant features of the history and environment of the Middle East. The common occurrence of these signs of the coming apocalypse provides for the flexibility of eschatological thought and the easy manner of its movement from one religious perspective to another. Most especially, times of conflict, periods of chaotic change and eruptions of natural disasters evidence passionate attachment to eschatological views.[102]

The political chaos following the death of Alexander the Great combined with the violent conflicts for power among his survivors encouraged the growth of apocalypses. By the time of the dissolution of the Roman Empire in the fourth and fifth centuries, eschatological thought had a new and more powerful religious vehicle for encouraging end of time fears and hopes than ever before: Christianity. In the Christian dualism between good and evil, eschatology reached a flowering far beyond Judaism. The Zoroastrian eschatological elements of a Final Conflict between the Sons of Light and the Sons of Darkness led by a savior figure born of a virgin sent by God to lead the Sons of Light were powerfully syncretized in the person of the returning Christ. In other words, apocalyptic eschatology was a powerful element of popular religious thought in these pre-Muhammad decades of the Byzantine Empire. In Arabia, it awaited a prophet with a monotheistic vision to give it both focus and force.

Given the intense apocalyptic background of the Byzantine empire and its influence on pre-Islamic Arabia, there are over 400 *ayats* referenced in Ali's index to his translation and commentary, **The Holy Qur'an**, which concern the Day of Judgment. This number is second in the index only to those *ayats* which speak of *Al-Lah*. Almost every page of the **Qur'an** reminds the reader of the Day of Judgment. In those passages proclaiming the end of time and the Day of Judgment, Qur'anic

---

[102]

This feature of interpretative flexibility is important, for it allows cosmic eschatology to be transmitted from one environment to another and from one time period to another. The disastrous nature of the signs also helps, for wars, famines, earthquakes, etc. are common occurrences throughout world history. Further, once the vision of the end of time is accepted, the flexible metaphorical nature of the signs allows for almost any occurrence to count as a sign for the believer. In logic this is called begging the question, but the popular term for it is a "self-fulfilling prophecy."

emphases are on the apocalyptic signs, the initiation of a world of peace and justice, the resurrection of the dead and their judgment to either Paradise or to Hell. Many of the signs mentioned would be familiar to post-exhilic Jews and Christians: the "heavens are rent asunder," the "sky is cleft asunder," the "sky turns into molten brass," the "stars and the oceans are scattered," the "trumpet sounds," and so on. While there is violence in these metaphors, the emphasis is on the miraculous nature of the events not the violence. Concerning the resurrection of the dead and their judgment, again, the emphasis is on the miraculous power of God to bring forth new life from the dust of the grave and the justice, mercy and forgiveness of God on the Day of Judgment. The **Qur'an** employs several metaphorical nouns to refer to this Day: "Day of Sorting," "Day of Distress," "Day of Separation," "Day of Reckoning," and "Day of Accountability." The major passages proclaiming the resurrection of the dead[103] have two major emphases: first, to serve as an apology against those--often Jews and Christians--who scoffed at a resurrection from the dust (that is, the decomposed body) in the grave; and, second, to affirm the bliss of Paradise for the *mujihad* and the terrors of Hell for the unrepentant.[104]

Although the **Qur'an** shares an apocalyptic cosmic vision with post-exhilic cosmic eschatological writings in the **Hebrew Bible** and the **New Testament**, the emphasis in early Islam, unlike both post-exhilic Judaism and first century Christianity, decisively is a **This-Worldness** rather than an **Other-Worldness**. For this reason, the few references in the **Qur'an** to eschatological *jihad* center on a future historical war which will create a historical world of justice and peace as prerequisite for the Final Judgment. The cosmic war between the Sons of Light and

---

[103]

Among the most important are: XVI:38-40; XVII:49-52; XIX:66-72; XXII:5; XLVI:33-34; L:3, 20-29, 40-44; LXXV:1-15; and LXXXVI:5-8.

[104]

Later Muslim tradition greatly enhanced the specifics of the Day of Judgment by incorporating additional **hadiths** and considerable Christian cosmic eschatology.

the Sons of Darkness that mesmerized so many Jews and Christians is given little notice in Islam, especially Sunni Islam. In other words, Qur'anic eschatological emphasis centers more on justice and peace than war, although it realizes that a *jihad* will be fought to create the *dar al-Islam*, the world of peace and justice in submission to God. In this sense, the Divine Purpose for the future historical *jihad* will create the historical existence the kingdom of God and return the sons of Adam to their original condition of peace--a point that Richard Martin clarifies in the following:

> Islam is self-consciously a universal missionary religion that seeks to restore humankind to its original condition in the seed of Adam [submission to God]. . . . To achieve this goal a political entity governed by the Guidance must be established. . . . [105] Until the final condition has been restored, Muslims must struggle, make effort (*jihad*) in the Path of God against the forces of deception and unbelief. In this framework, the "other"[106] presents a condition of conflict in the world, one that is potentially violent. The end or final return to God (*akhira*), however, is peace, peace for all humankind. ("The Religious Foundations of War, Peace, and Statecraft in Islam,"

105

This belief in creating a political entity submissive to the laws and the will of God is also shared by many Jewish and Christian groups, especially the more extremist groups. While the First Amendment has significantly limited the political power of such groups in the United States, such is not the case in Israel where the growth in religious extremism has led to deep fractures in Israeli society. As a result, a new feature has entered the peace process: the potentiality for Israeli violence against other Israelis. The growth of this extremism has also increased pressure to make Jerusalem the capital of Israel, that is, to "ethnically cleanse" Jerusalem so that it is entirely Jewish. Such views can only destroy the peace process and set into motion a cycle of renewed violence.

106

For some Islamic *ulama*, the other represents all non-Muslims in the strict sense of the term *Muslim*; for others, however, the other does not include Jews, Christians and other monotheists, for they are Peoples of the Book.

in Kelsay and Johnson, **Just War and Jihad: Historical and Theoretical Perspectives on War and Peace in Western and Islamic Tradition**, 96-7)

Because there are so few passages in the **Qur'an** directly concerning eschatological *jihad* at the end of time, the strategy for examining eschatological war in Islam differs from the two preceding chapters which extensively cited scriptural verses. Instead, an outline of the basic features of Muslim eschatology provides background for the central feature of the *jihad* at the end of time: the appearance of the *Mahdi*. In general, the Islamic theology of eschatology is as follows:

(1)   As human history moves forward, there will be an increase in unbelief, but there will also remain cores of believers who continue to show the increasingly unspiritual world the power of God in their lives through the various kinds of *jihad* discussed earlier.

(2)   As the time approaches for the Final Judgment, the *Mahdi*, the "Guided One" from the family of the Prophet Muhammad will appear.[107] It is the *Mahdi* who initiates the eschatological *jihad* which creates the universal world of peace and justice; however, because the world has become increasingly unrighteous, it may require a political *jihad* to create righteousness, justice and peace.

---

[107]

For the minority Shi'a the appearance of *the Mahdi* is really a reappearance of Muhammad ibn Hasan (872-939? C.E.), the Twelfth Imam after Muhammad, who did not die, but was taken to Heaven by *Al-Lah* to prevent his murder. His return will mark the initiation of the eschatological world of peace and justice promised in several **hadiths**. Mahdism became much more important among minority groups like the Shi'a because of their persecution by the majority Sunni. This same pattern is also found in Judaism and Christianity: for the oppressed, beliefs in a future world of righteousness and justice become much more important than for unoppressed majority groups. Such eschatological beliefs provide comfort, endurance and, most importantly, hope for the future, and these are critical spiritual needs for any religious group experiencing oppression.

(3)   After the appearance of the *Mahdi*, the Antichrist will appear.[108]

(4)   With the appearance of the Antichrist, Jesus will descend in his Second Coming and join forces with the *Mahdi*.[109]

(5)   Jesus and the *Mahdi* after executing the Antichrist will create a world of universal justice and peace lasting forty years. Jesus will live as a beneficiary of this peace and then peacefully die. He will be buried at Medina beside the caliph Uthman.

(6)   After forty years of peace and justice, the angel *Israfil* will blow the Trumpet signaling the immanence of the day of Judgment.[110]

(7)   Later **hadiths** emphasize the appearance of the angels *Munkar* and *Nakir* on the Day of Judgment. Their function is questioning each resurrected body-soul for eternal disposition to Heaven or Hell, and then the angel of Death assumes

---

108

Both the identity and the nature of this Antichrist are unclear. Islamic eschatological tradition seems to make him more than human, and traditions developed that linked him with *Iblis* (Satan) as co-conspirators in the eschatological *jihad*, but the **Qur'an**, just like the **New Testament** does little to provide clarity concerning either the identity or the nature of this character in the eschatological drama.

109

The Qur'anic position on the crucifixion considerably differs from of the **New Testament**. According to the **Qur'an**, Jesus did not die on the cross. This is why he was able to appear to the disciples after the crucifixion and before he was taken to Heaven by God, like the Twelfth Imam, without having "tasted death." Like the Twelfth Imam, the *Mahdi*, God will send him back to earth when the time is right for overcoming evil and creating universal peace. Some later Islamic traditions claimed that Jesus would descend from Heaven during the afternoon prayer at the white minaret east of Damascus (see Peters, **Judaism, Christianity, and Islam**, vol.3, 352).

110

While there are many passages in the **Qur'an** concerning the Day of Judgment, among the most important are: LXXXII:1-19; LXXXIII:10-20; and LXXXVIII:1-16.

responsibility for those bound for Hell.[111]

A most interesting controversy developed in Islam concerning the eternity of Hell which was not unlike the controversy that Origen of Alexandria (185-255 C.E.) raised in Christianity when he argued that the punishments in Hell were remedial rather than eternal, and that at the end of time God's love would save all the lost soul's in Hell. Origen even carried the logic of his argument , which was based on the infinite power of God's love and forgiveness to save all of His creation, to conclude that at the end of time even Satan would be forgiven and saved. Some Muslim *ulama* have concurred with Origen and interpreted the **Qur'an** as predicting the eventual return of *Iblis* (Satan) to the Garden of Bliss from which he was originally expelled. (See II:34.) In Islam the controversy arose mostly because of a passage in sura XI:

> In that is a Sign / For those who fear / The Penalty of the Hereafter: / / That is a Day for which mankind / Will be gathered together: / That will be a day / Of testimony. / Nor shall we delay it / But for a term appointed.
>
> The day it arrives, / No soul shall speak / Except by His leave: / Of those (gathered) some / Will be wretched and some / Will be blessed.
>
> Those who are wretched / Shall be in the Fire: / There will be for them \ Therein (nothing but) the heaving / Of sighs and sobs:
>
> They will dwell therein / For all the time that / The heavens and the earth / Endure, except as thy Lord / Willeth: for thy Lord / Is the (sure) Accomplisher / Of what he planneth.
>
> And those who are blessed / Shall be in the Garden: / They will dwell therein / For all the time that / The heavens and the earth / Endure, except as thy Lord / Willeth: a gift without break. (XI:103-108)

The key *ayat* in this controversy about the eternality of hell is 107: "They will dwell therein [Hell] / For all the time that / The heavens and the earth / Endure. . . ." Ali clarifies the theological debate over Hell in the following terms:

> *Khalidin*: This is the word which is normally translated "dwell for ever" or "dwell for aye". Here it is definitely connected with two conditions. . . . (1) as long as the heavens and the earth endure, and (2) except as God wills. Some Muslim theologians deduce from this the conclusion that the penalties referred to are not eternal, because the heavens and the earth as we see them are not eternal, and the punishments for the deeds of a life that will end should not be such as will never end. The majority of Muslim theologians reject this view. They hold that the heavens and the earth here referred to are

As is the case with all religious eschatologies, the meaning of signs such as "wars and rumors of wars" lies in the interpretative eye of the believer. Consequently, little more needs to be discussed concerning eschatological war *(jihad)* at this point. As an appropriate transition to exploring the theologies of peace in the **Qur'an**, the following **hadith** is pivotal concerning the hope of the *Mahdi*, concludes this section on theologies of war with a spiritual hope for a future world of justice, which is the foundation for world peace:

> . . . on the authority of Abu al-Tufayl, on the authority of Ali, on the authority of the Prophet, who said: "If only one day in the whole duration of the world remained, God would send a man of my family who would fill the world with justice, as it has been filled with injustice." (F.E. Peters, **Judaism, Christianity, and Islam**, vol.3, 353)[112]

Theologies of Peace

All three Holy Books affirm that peace is the originally created condition of humankind, that humans have fallen from the state of grace and peace into the spiritual illness of conflict and that God moves human history toward a re-created fulfillment of the original purpose of creation: universal peace and justice. The

---

not those we now see, but others that will be eternal. They agree that God's Will is unlimited in scope and power, but that It has willed that the rewards and punishments of the Day of Judgment will be eternal. This is not the place to enter into this tremendous controversy. (**The Holy Qur'an**, 543.)

With only a few changes in Ali's statement, it could have been written about the Christian controversy concerning the eternality of Hell, originally raised by Origen.

112

This man of the family of Muhammad is the long-awaited and passionately hoped-for *Mahdi*, the "Guided One" from *Al-Lah*. This is an expectation and a hope shared by Jews who await God's *Mesiah* and Christians who await the return of the *Christos*.

major difference between the Qur'anic approach to this universal state and the approaches of Christianity and post-exhilic Judaism is found in the **This-World** practical orientation of the **Qur'an** and the **Other-World** eschatologies of post-exhilic Jewish Biblical writings and the **New Testament.** Nonetheless, all three of Abraham's children share a common vision of peace and hope in the providence of God for a universal world of justice.

Arabic Terms For Peace

Although the term *salaam*[113] is the most important Arabic term for peace in the **Qur'an**, the Holy Book also includes other cognates of the Semitic root *SLM* as well as several other terms. The non-cognate terms indicating various kinds of peace are: *amn* means "peace, security"; *sakina* means "peace, calm, confidence, tranquility"; *raaha* means "peace, rest"; *huduwu* means "peace, quietness"; *sulh* means "peace, cessation of war or conflict"; and *silm* means "time of peace." The dominant noun, however, is *salaam*; a verbal noun constructed from *salima*, which means "to be well, to be uninjured." As with the Hebrew term *shalom*, *salaam* can mean many different but related things: peace, health, prosperity, security, permanence, fulfillment, and as with *shalom*, a salutation used upon greeting and departing.[114] There are two cognates of *SLM* that are important: *salim* meaning "soundness, perfection" and *sallama* meaning "preservation, salvation, deliverance."[115]

113

The Arabic term is also transliterated as *salam.*

114

See footnote #66 in Chapter Two concerning the greetings, *Assalamu 'alaykum* (Peace be upon you.) and *Wa'alaykum assalam* (And upon you peace.) and the departing salutations, *Ma'a salama* (Go with peace, safety.) and *Allah yisallimak* (May God make you safe.).

115

Given the Qur'anic affirmation that peace is the state of the original creation and that humans have fallen from the peace (bliss) of the Garden into a state of

While all of these terms and cognates are important, *salaam* dominates the theology of the **Qur'an**. It is important to remember that the noun *salaam* means much more than just peace in the world but also the fundamental condition and experience in the next world, and the *dar al-Salaam* (House of Peace) is another term for Paradise. LIX:23 lists *Al-Salaam* as one of the Names of *Al-Lah*: that is, God of Peace. XXXIII:56 recommends saying both *salat* (prayer) and *salaam* whenever the name of the Prophet is mentioned: Muhammad, "May the blessing and peace of God be upon him." This common ascription is in itself a prayer of peace for Muhammad. Further, several passages recommend saying *salaam* before entering a dwelling.[116]

As a salutation upon greeting or departing (footnotes #64 and #65 in Chapter Two), *salaam* has almost all of the same connotations and uses as the Hebrew *shalom* and the Greek *eirene* as well as several other important religious uses in Islam. In the daily ritual of *salat* (prayer), the *"Salaam [Assalamu] 'alaykum"* precedes the *Shahadah*: the affirmation that "There is no God but God, and Muhammad is his Prophet." There are several Muslim mystical groups which make a ritual of saying the seven *salaams* daily. These are the *salaams* found in XXXVI:58 ("Peace! --a Word / Of salutation from a Lord / Most Merciful!); XXXVII:79 (Peace on Noah); XXXVII:109 (Peace on Abraham); XXXVII:120 (Peace on Moses and Aaron); XXXVII:130 (Peace on Elias); XXXIX:73 (Peace on entering the Garden of Bliss); and XCVII:5 (Peace until the rising of the morning). As noted in XXXIX:73 and examined in the final section on eschatological peace, the **Qur'an** describes the greeting given by the angels for those entering the Garden of Peace as:

---

conflict (sin), it is neither surprising nor accidental that one of the terms for salvation (or deliverance) is formed from the root *SLM* meaning "peace." In other words, salvation is to be found in experiencing the peace of submitting one's life to *Al-Lah*, a peace eschatologically fulfilled in the Garden of Bliss, that is, the Garden of Wholeness, Health, Perfection, Fulfillment, Security and Justice.

116

Compare XXIV:61 with Matthew 10:12 and Luke 10:5.

"Assalamu 'alaykum!"

As is evident from the preceding, the term *salaam* is as rich in spiritual meaning as *shalom* and *eirene*. Also, the **Qur'an**, like the **Hebrew Bible** and the **New Testament**, unequivocally affirms that *Al-Lah* is the source of *salaam*:

> God is He, than Whom / There is no other god;-- / The Sovereign, the Holy One, / The Source of Peace (and Perfection), / The Guardian of Faith, / The Preserver of Safety, / The Exalted in Might, / The Irresistible, the Supreme: / Glory to God! (LIX:23)

Ali's note faithfully recognizes the inadequacy of translated words for describing the indescribable, transcendent Source of the peace of creation:

> How can a translator reproduce the sublimity and the comprehensiveness of the magnificent Arabic words, which mean so much in a single symbol? (1) "The Sovereign" in our human language implies the one undisputed authority which is entitled to give commands and to receive obedience, and which in fact receives obedience; the power which enforces law and justice. (2) Human authority may be misused, but in the title "the Holy One", we postulate a Being free from all stain or evil, and replete with the highest Purity. (3) "*Salam*" has not only the idea of Peace as opposed to Conflict, but wholeness as opposed to defects: hence our paraphrase "Source of Peace and Perfection". (4) *Mu-min*, one who entertains Faith, who gives faith to others, who is never false to the faith that others place in him: hence our paraphrase "Guardian of Faith". (5) "Preserver of Safety": guarding all from danger, corruption, loss, etc. . . . These are the attributes of kindness and benevolence. . . . **(The Holy Qur'an**, 1528)

Cognizant of the inadequacy of translating *salaam* as peace, it is now appropriate to examine the three dimensions (theologies) of peace in the **Qur'an**: political peace, spiritual peace and eschatological peace.

Political Peace

The place to begin the study of political peace is with the **Qur'an**'s judgment that war is a defect, that is, a spiritual illness. The recognition that violence is a spiritual illness is affirmed in many passages, but few do so with the spiritual pathos of the Cain and Abel story when Abel refuses to lift his hand in violence against his murderous brother: "It is not for me to stretch / My hand against thee / To slay thee: / For I do fear / God, the Cherisher of the Worlds." Sura V continues to affirm the spiritual merit of peace and charity over violence and vengeance in an *ayat* resembles a most important part of the **New Testament**, the "Sermon on the Mount"[117]:

> We ordained therein for them [the Jews]: / "Life for life, eye for eye, / Nose for nose, ear for ear, / Tooth for tooth, and wounds / Equal for equal." But if / Any one remits the retaliation / By way of charity, it is / An act of atonement for himself. (V:48)

The fundamental emphasis in **the Qur'an** on peace as the state of both political and spiritual health is beautifully illustrated in the two passages which mention Abraham's prayer for the most sacred of all cities, Mecca:

> And remember Abraham said: / "My Lord, make this a City / Of Peace   And feed its People / With fruits,--such of them / As believe in God and the Last day." (II:126)
>
> Remember Abraham said: / "O my Lord! make this city / One of peace and security; / And preserve me and my sons / From worshipping idols." (XIV:35)

Ali's notes on these ayats indicate the eschatological aspects of Abraham's petition

---

[117]

While there are many passages in Matthew 5-7, the "Sermon on the Mount," which affirm the same values as those in V:48, see for comparison especially the "You have heard it said to the people in olden times [the Jews], you shall not . . . " teachings and the "love your enemies" teaching in Matthew 5.

384

as well as the political and spiritual significance:

> The root *salama* in the word Islam implies (among other
> ideas) the idea of Peace, and therefore when Mecca is the city of
> Islam, it is also the city of Peace. The same root occurs in the latter
> part of the name Jerusalem, the Jewish City of Peace. When the day
> of Jerusalem passed . . . Mecca became the "New Jerusalem"[118]--or

---

118

Remember that in both the **Hebrew Bible** and the **New Testament**, the "New Jerusalem" is the eschatological "City of Peace" created when the Sons of Light destroy the Sons of Darkness and the Kingdom of God commences on the earth. Although there are disagreements between Jews and Christians **and** Muslims concerning the location of the City of Peace, Jerusalem or Mecca, this disagreement should be of less significance than their shared vision of peace and justice. As Karen Armstrong argues in her new book, **Jerusalem: One City, Three Faiths**, the true holiness of the City of Peace, whether it be Jerusalem or Mecca, depends on how successfully it lives up to the spiritual values of justice, harmony, tolerance, charity, and holiness.

Even though Muslims believe references to the "City of Peace" in the **Qur'an** mean Mecca, Jerusalem as a holy city has a most significant place in the cosmic eschatology of the Day of Judgment. In their stunning visual and religious exploration of the Dome of the Rock Mosque, Said Nuseibeh and Oleg Grabar describe the eschatological significance of this third most sacred place in the world for Muslims:

> On the east gate [entrance into the Mosque], the message is
> quite different [than on the north gate]. It proclaims God's power:
> "Lord of power, You give power to whom You please and You take
> power from whomever You please." It ends with a long prayer
> asking God to bless Muhammad, His prophet and His servant, and to
> accept Muhammad's intercession for the faithful: "We ask you, our
> God, by Your mercy, by Your beautiful names, by Your noble face,
> by Your immense power, by Your perfect word by which heaven and
> earth stand together, and with Your mercy we are preserved from the
> devil and we are all saved from Your punishment on the Day of
> Resurrection, by Your abundant grace, by Your great nobility, by
> Your clemency, Your power, Your forgiveness, and Your kindness,
> that You bless Muhammad, Your servant and Your prophet, and that
> You accept his intercession for his community." This eschatological
> expectation of divine mercy is set on the side of the building facing
> the valley that contained the entrances to both hell and paradise,

rather the old and original "City of Peace" restored and made universal. (53)

This prayer of Abraham, the True in faith, the progenitor of the Semitic peoples and the Prototype of their Religion, is introduced . . . to illustrate . . . how the new revelation through the Ka'ba bears out the universal Revelation of Prayer and charity, Love of God and man, recognition of God's handiwork in nature, and Insistence on turning man always from false worship and ingratitude to God. . . . Jerusalem for the Mosaic Law and the Gospel of Jesus, was the center and symbol for the Jewish race, thought all of God's truth is universal; Mecca, the center of the Arab race, was to throw of its tribal character and become universal. . . . (**The Holy Qur'an**, 630)

Whether Jerusalem or Mecca, the spiritual vocation of the citizen of the City of Peace is to become a *mujihad* of the heart, mouth and hand, that is, using **New Testament** terminology, to become a "peacemaker":

Wherewith God guideth all / Who seek His good pleasure / To ways of peace and safety, / And leadeth them out / Of darkness, by his Will, / Unto the light,--guideth them / To a Path that is Straight. (V:18)

From the account of Cain and Abel to Abraham's Prayer to the creation of the New

---

where the believers will gather on the Last day, and beyond it the Mount of Olives, already identified by Christians as the place of Christ's return at the end of time. Over the centuries, nearly all buildings and associations in the eastern half of the Haram were associated with the Last Judgment, God's forgiveness, and comparable themes. For example, the Golden gate is known in Muslim sources as the gate of Mercy and Repentance; the small Dome of the Chain is the place where the just and the damned will be separated; the *Sirat* bridge, which leads to eternal life, crosses from the Haram to the Mount of Olives. . . . (**The Dome of the Rock**, 49,51)

City of Peace, the spiritual health of peace is clearly affirmed over the spiritual illness of war. For this reason, on the political level, the **Qur'an** places considerable emphases on treaties of peace.

The **Qur'an** also emphasizes family justice (peace within the family), seeking peace with enemies, peace with the other Peoples of the Book, the sacred obligation to keep treaties and even a prohibition against misusing the name of *Al-Lah* in a hypocritical manner as a bind of one's honesty in making an oath of peace.[119] The **Qur'an** proclaims that more than charity begins at home but peace and justice as well:

> But if anyone fears / Partiality or wrong-doing / On the part of the testator, / \ And makes peace between / (The parties concerned), / There is no wrong in him: / For God is Oft-forgiving, / Most Merciful. (II:182)
>
> If ye fear a breach / Between them twain, / Appoint (two) arbiters, / One from his family, / And one from hers; / If they wish for peace, / God will cause Their reconciliation: / For God hath full knowledge, / And is acquainted / With all things. (IV:35)

Both of these passages concern two common experiences which can and often do produce conflict, sometimes even violence, among families: inheritance and divorce. The Qur'anic position is both moral and practical. In those family disputes that cannot be settled from within, a fair and impartial arbiter searches for ways to make peace between those at war with one another. Both of these passages explicitly indicate that a peaceful dispute must be a just one, that is, without "partiality or wrong-doing." It is sound advice, for if one cannot achieve peace at home, what hope is there for peace among strangers much less familiar enemies.

In a manner similar to the **New Testament**, the **Qur'an** commands the

---

119

There are many other aspects of oaths, treaties and alliances mentioned in the **Qur'an**, but the ones mentioned above are the elements most important to the theology of political peace.

seeking of peace among one's enemies, even when doing so may produce risks:

> But if the enemy / Incline towards peace, / Do thou (also) incline / Towards peace, and trust / In God: for he is the One / That heareth and knoweth / (All things).
>
> Should they intend / To deceive thee,--verily God / Sufficeth thee: He it is / That hath strengthened thee / With his aid and / With (the company of) the Believers;
>
> And (moreover) He hath put / Affection between their hearts: / Not if thou hasdst spent / All that is in the earth, / Couldst thou have produced / That affection, but God hath done it: for He / Is Exalted in might, Wise. (VIII:61-3)

Ali's note on these *ayats* is most illuminating:

> While we must always be ready [prepared] for the good fight [*jihad* by the sword] lest it be forced on us, even in the midst of the fight we must be always ready for peace, if there is any inclination towards peace on the other side. There is no merit merely in the fight by itself. It should be a joyful duty not for itself, but to establish the reign of peace and righteousness and God's law.
>
> In working for peace there may be a certain risk of treachery on the other side. We must take that risk: because the man of God has God's aid to count upon. . . . On the immediate occasion [of these *ayats*], the greatest miracle and most wonderful working of God's grace was the union of hearts produced among the jarring, war-like, excitable elements of Arabia under the gentle, firm guidance of Muhammad, the Apostle of god. At all times we must pray to God for this gift above all--union, understanding, and sincere and pure affection among those who take God's name. With it there is strength and success. (**The Holy Qur'an**, 430-31)

The spiritual merit of seeking peace further emphasizes the strong prohibitions in the **Qur'an** on violating oaths and alliances of peace, (see VIII:72 and IX:4), unless the other party in the treaty violates the oath of peace, (see IV:90). Further, the **Qur'an** warns against the misuse of God's name in binding false oaths of peace:

> And make not / God's (name) an excuse[120] / In your oaths against / Doing good, or acting rightly, / Or making peace / Between persons; / For God is One / Who heareth and knoweth / All things. (II:224)

Ali's note clarifies the meaning of this interesting ayat:

> The Arabs had many special kinds of oaths, for each of which they had a special name. . . . In II:224 we are first of all told in perfectly general terms that we are not to make an oath in the name of God an excuse for not doing the right thing . . . or from refraining from doing something which will bring people together. If we are swayed by anger or passion or mere caprice, God knows our inmost hearts, and right . . . conduct is what He demands from us. (**The Holy Qur'an**, 89)

While the **Qur'an** commands the honest seeking and keeping of treaties of peace among even Pagans and enemies, it emphasizes even more strongly the forming of alliances with the other Peoples of the Book.

As prerequisite for exploring those Qur'anic passages speaking of peace with Jews and Christians, it is informative to examine a specific example of treaties of peace with each. The alliance of peace with the Jews of Medina was written into the Constitution of Medina: "Believers are friends one to the other to the exclusion of outsiders. To the Jew who follows us belong help and equality. He shall not be

---

120

Compare this *ayat* with the second commandment: "You shall not take the name of the Lord your God in vain." (See Exodus 20 or Deuteronomy 5.)

wronged nor his enemies aided. The peace of believers is indivisible."[121] The first
official treaty with Christians was that of Umar with the Christians of Syria and Iraq:

> I [the ambassador sent by Umar] have finally arrived at Hira
> and met . . . with a few of the leaders of the city. I invited them to
> believe in Allah and his apostle, but they refused. I have therefore
> offered them either to accept the *jizza[122]* or fighting . . . . [They
> accepted the *jizza*]

> It was therefore agreed that [the Christians of Hira] will not
> violate their compact [treaty]. They shall not support an unbeliever
> against . . . a Muslim. . . . If any of their men become weak or old,
> or afflicted with disease, or was rich and became poor, the *jizza* shall
> be lifted from him and he and his family will be supported by the
> Public treasury. . . . [123] They shall have the right to wear any kind

---

121

See W. Montgomery Watt's **Muhammad: Prophet and Statesman** for an
unbiased discussion of the tragic consequences that occurred when this treaty was
violated by the Jewish Quraiza.

122

The *jizza* was a collective tax rather than an individual one that was required
of all non-Muslim groups living in Muslim lands. Although it was sometimes
abused by Muslim leaders just like a significant majority of Christian rulers in
Europe oppressed their fellow Christians with burdensome taxes to pay for their
courts and wars, the tax itself was in most instances neither oppressive nor abusively
applied. The claim that an oppressive *jizza* was used to convert Christians to Islam
is mostly a bogus claim, although it was sometimes abused in this way. Perhaps in
this manner, it resembles the abuse of indulgences by the Church in Europe.
Fundamentally the *jizza* was a reasonable expectation, for Christians as well as
Muslims should be expected to provide financial support for the running of political
municipalities. Muslims paid their own taxes, the fundamental one being the *zakat*,
which was individual. One of the moral advantages of the *jizza* was that it was
collective rather than individual; thus, the Christian leaders who assumed control of
collecting and paying it always had the option of a graduated tax on individuals
according to their means. (See also footnote #123.)

123

See the previous footnote. The **Qur'an** stresses just and charitable treatment

of clothes save military uniforms, provided the clothes be not similar to the Muslims . . . . (Majid Khadduri, **War and Peace in the Law of Islam**, 183-4)

Later treaties, unfortunately, often included a prohibition against building new churches or synagogues, but Christians and Jews were allowed to maintain their existing places of worship.[124]

Even though later treaties with Jews and Christians were more restrictive, the most limiting never forbid Jewish and Christian worship because they were also monotheistic Peoples of the Book and because of a most important and enlightened passage in the **Qur'an** concerning religious conversion:

Let there be no compulsion / In religion: Truth stands out / Clear from Error: whoever / Rejects Evil and believes / In God hath grasped / The most trustworthy / Hand-hold, that never breaks. / And God heareth / And knoweth all things. (II:256)

In this *ayat,* the **Qur'an** reveals a truth about the nature of faith too often abused:

---

of all human beings and especially of the young, old, sick, poor, orphans and widows. Notice the directions in the treaty to the Christian leaders of Hira that all their citizens are to be treated according to the moral injunctions in the **Qur'an**. Such exemplary values were, needless to say, often forgotten and abused by Muslim and Christian leaders in the *dar al-Islam*, but when this occurred it was a violation of the holy revelation. Abuse of the poor, sick, old, etc. in Christian Europe was much more extensive than in Muslim controlled countries during the 8th to 12th centuries.

[124]

See XXII:39-40 which speaks of churches and synagogues as places in which the "name of God is commemorated. . . ." Although the prohibition against building new churches and synagogues is unfortunate, the passage in XXII prohibited the tearing down of Jewish and Christian places of worship. This was a courtesy seldom returned by either Jews or Christians when they had the power to engage in such destructions. However, there were also Muslim leaders who violated this Qur'anic prohibition. Again, it is most important to separate the beliefs, values and truths that a religion teaches from the distortions of these beliefs, values and truths by individuals and groups for their own chauvinistic and political purposes.

faith cannot be forced either by physical threat or intellectual argument. To summarize, the **Qur'an** emphasizes peace among the children of Abraham for three fundamental reasons: (1) they are all monotheists who worship the One true God; (2) faith cannot be compelled; and, (3) God knows the heart (faith) of a person, and only God can justly determine his eternal destination.[125]

While faith and the spiritual commitment to peace cannot be compelled since both come from the hearts of humans, the **Qur'an** recognizes the divisive power of quarrels and speaks to arguments among believers (Muslims) in many passages. *Sura* XLIX advises practical procedures to keep arguments among believers from leading to discord:

> If two parties among / The Believers fall into / A quarrel, make ye peace / Between them: but if / One of them transgresses / Beyond bounds against the other, / Then fight ye (all) against / The one that transgresses / Until it complies with / The command of God; / But if it complies, then / Make peace between them / With justice, and be fair: / For God loves those / Who are fair (and just).
>
> The Believers are but / A single Brotherhood; / So make peace and / Reconciliation between your / Two (contending) brothers; / And fear God, that ye / May receive Mercy. (XLIX:9-10)

Few *ayats* could be clearer concerning the command of God for peace based on justice, fairness and reconciliation. As noted in other *ayats*, the **Qur'an** emphasizes

---

[125]

    One cannot help but wonder how different the history of the relationships among Abraham's children could have been if each had taken these lessons of the **Qur'an** to heart, lessons which are found in all three Holy Books. Both in their external relationships with the other two and their internal relationships with diverse groups within, many Jews, Christians and Muslims have been arrogantly quick to condemn God's children to eternal hell because they differed in their understandings of God's truth. Fortunately, God's love is much more forgiving than the synagogue, church or mosque have historically proclaimed.

the spiritual merit of forgiveness and rejects anger and vengeance. (See V:48, XXXIX:53, XLII:37, XLII:40 and LVII:21.)

Arguments and disputes with non-Muslims, which can be over political, personal or religious differences, are divided into two categories: arguments with those ignorant of *Al-Lah* and arguments with the Peoples of the Book, that is, Jews and Christians. Concerning the former category, the two following *ayats* are representative:

> And the servants of (God) / Most Gracious are those / Who walk on the earth / In humility, and when the ignorant / Address them, they say, / "Peace!" (XXV:63)
>
> And when they hear vain talk, / They turn away therefrom / And say: "To us our deeds, / And to you yours; / Peace be to you: we / Seek not the ignorant." (XXXVIII:55)

Ali's notes on these two *ayats* recommend the spiritual values of humility and toleration:

> *Ignorant*: in a spiritual sense. *Address*: in the aggressive sense. Their [Muslims'] humility is shown in two ways: (1) to those in the real search for knowledge, they give such knowledge as they have and as the recipients can assimilate; (2) to those who merely dispute, they do not speak harshly, but say "Peace!", as much as to say, "May it be well with you, may you repent and be better"; or "May God give me peace from such wrangling". . . . (941)
>
> The righteous do not encourage idle talk or foolish arguments about things sacred. If they find themselves in company in which such things are fashionable, they leave politely. Their only rejoinder is: "We are responsible for our deeds, and you for yours; we have no ill will against you; we wish you well, and that is why we wish you to know of the knowledge we have received. . . . **(The Holy Qur'an,** 1017)

Consistent with its view of arguments among believers, the **Qur'an** emphasizes the Muslim's responsibility to either directly avoid conflict or indirectly to seek peace even in disputes with non-Muslims. Thus, same moral principles apply to conflicts with other Peoples of the Book:

> Quite a number of the People / Of the Book wish they could / Turn you (people) back / To infidelity after ye have believed, / From selfish envy, / After the truth hath become / Manifest unto them: / But forgive and overlook, / Till God accomplish / His purpose; for God / Hath power over all things. (II:109)

Ali's commentary on this *ayat* stresses the depth of forgiveness and toleration ("overlooking") required of Muslims in religious conflicts with the other Peoples of the Book:

> Three words are used in the Qur'an, with a meaning akin to "forgive", but each with a different shade of meaning. *'Afa* (here translated "forgive") means to forget, to obliterate from one's mind. *Safaha* (here translated "overlook") means to turn away from, to ignore, to treat a matter as if it did not affect one. *Gafara* (which does not occur in this verse) means to cover up something, as God does to our sins with His grace: this word is particularly appropriate in God's attribute of *Gaffar*, the One who forgives again and again.
>
> **(The Holy Qur'an**, 47)

Whether within the community of faith or in its relations with those outside, the Qur'anic emphasis on peace based on justice rather than war is a message that is spiritually universal and transcends any specific Muslim state or period of time. The Qur'an's theology of political peace is one founded on the value of justice, the righteousness of submitting one's life to God and the awareness that political peace is the externalization of that internal state for which God created human beings: spiritual peace. Thus, as a transition to the next section on spiritual peace, consider the following insightful passage from Abd al-Rahman Azzam:

According to Sir Thomas Arnold [his book, **The Preaching of Islam: A History of the Propagation of the Muslim Faith**], the spiritual conquests of Islam were not affected by the decline of the Islamic state or the decrease in its political power. Sir Thomas maintains that in the days of its political defeats Islam achieved its greatest spiritual victories.

In the annals of Islam, there are two important events which testify to this. First, when the Mongols and the Seljuk Turks trod on the necks of the Muslims, Islam conquered their hearts, for although they were the conquerors, they adopted the religion of the conquered. In this transformation Islam was assisted by neither sword nor authority. Second, if we turn . . . to the Truce of al-Hudaybiyah [the treaty of peace between Muhammad and the Meccans], which distressed some Muslims because the truce called for the sheathing of the sword for ten years, we discover that it was in this period that Islam achieved its greatest spiritual victory. The peaceful conquests of the faith ensuing from the Truce of al-Hudaybiyah paved the way for the conquest of the Meccans' hearts and the conversion of all Arabia. (**The Eternal Message of Muhammad**, 153)

Since the foundation for political peace is spiritual peace, and the source of both is *Al-Lah*, it is now time to explore the **Qur'an**'s theology of spiritual peace.

Spiritual Peace

As suggested by the section on spiritual war (see pages 357-72), spiritual peace requires the *jihad* fought by the heart. The reason spiritual peace can only be found by the *mujihad* of the heart is clarified in XXX:30 and Ali's insightful commentary on this *ayat*; the reason is the **"crookedness"** of human beings:[126]

> So set thou thy face / Steadily and truly to the faith: / (Establish)
> God's handiwork according / To the patterns on which / He has
> made mankind: / No change (let there be) / In the work (wrought)
> / By God. . . . (XXX:30)
>
> As turned out from the creative hand of God, man is innocent,
> pure, true, free, inclined to right and virtue, and endued with true
> understanding about his own position in the Universe and about God's
> goodness, wisdom, and power. That is his true nature, just as the
> nature of the lamb is to be gentle and of the horse to be swift. But
> man is caught in the meshes of customs, superstitions, selfish desires,
> and false teaching. This may make him pugnacious, unclean, false,
> slavish, hankering after what is wrong or forbidden, and deflected
> from the love of his fellow-men and the pure worship of the One True
> God. The problem before spiritual Teachers is to cure this
> crookedness, and to restore human nature to what it should be under
> the Will of God. (**The Holy Qur'an**, 1059)

Because of humans' crookedness and inability to overcome the power of sin
and evil without Divine help, the first step for the *mujihad* of the heart is submission
to the Will of *Al-Lah*, that is, becoming a Muslim, in the words of the **Qur'an:**

126

What Ali aptly describes as "crookedness" has been described by the term
"original sin" in much Christian theology. Further, the **Qur'an,** like the **New
Testament,** finds this crookedness (sin) so powerful that it can only be overcome
with the help of God. Muslims do, however, disagree with Christians concerning the
nature of the help needed: for Muslims it is submission to the will of God while for
Christians sin is so overwhelmingly powerful that it requires the sending of the
Christ, his sacrifice and resurrection. Both monotheisms, however, agree that
humankind as originally created was characterized by goodness, innocence and
peace, but because of disobedience, humans have fallen into a state of chaos and
conflict, that is, sin and crookedness.

> O ye who believe! / Enter into Islam[127] / Whole-heartedly; / And follow not / The footsteps / Of the Evil One; / For he is to you / An avowed enemy. (II:208)

This submission is far from easy, for it requires putting aside selfishness, arrogance, anger, lust, ignorance, etc.. Further, it requires sacrifice and discipline, but the reward is great: spiritual peace from God. Like Judaism and Christianity, spiritual peace is a gift because God is its source:

> God is he, than Whom / There is no other god;-- / The Sovereign, the Holy One, / The Source of Peace (and Perfection) / . . . . (LIX:23)[128]

The promise of the **Qur'an** for the *mujihad* of the heart is clear and certain:

> Wherewith God guideth all / Who seek His good pleasure / To ways of peace and safety, / And leadeth them out / Of darkness, by His Will, / Unto the light,--guideth them / To a Path that is Straight. (V:18)

As is true for Jews and Christians, the darkness of the world (external evil) and the darkness of the human soul (sin and temptation) can only be overcome with the help of God; in other words, to use the beautiful metaphor in V:18, only God has the power and wisdom to lead His created children from the darkness of the world to the light of His path.

Since spiritual peace can be accomplished only through submission to *Al-Lah*, that is, through the practices of righteousness and justice, the **Qur'an** provides guidance on how to fight the *jihad* by the heart. To begin with, attentive, disciplined, thoughtful, humble, peaceful (that is, without anger or other kinds of internal chaos)

127

See the previous section, "The Peace--Surrender of Islam and the Muslim" for an etymology and interpretation of the sacred terms *Islam* and *Muslim*.

128

See pages 381-82.

and reverent reading and reciting of the **Qur'an** is essential:[129]

> When the Qur'an is read, / Listen to it with attention, / And hold
> your peace: / That ye may receive Mercy.
>
> And do thou (O reader!) / Bring thy Lord to remembrance / In thy
> (very) soul, / With humility and reverence, / Without loudness in
> words, / In the mornings and evenings; / And be not thou / Of
> those who are unheedful. (VII:204-5)

In addition to reverent and regular reading and reciting of the **Qur'an**,
Muslims are to remember the gifts of safety and peace that God gave to the great
prophets and to pray the blessings of God's peace on them.[130] Among the many
prophets the **Qur'an** mentions in this context, the following are representative:
Noah, Yahya (John the baptizer) and Muhammad.

> The word came: "O Noah! / Come down (from the Ark) / With
> Peace from Us, / And Blessings on thee / And on some of the
> Peoples / (Who will spring) from those / With thee. . . . (XI:48)

Ali's note stresses the peace that flows from God into the souls of those who obey:

> Those who truly seek God's light and guidance and sincerely
> bend their will to His Will are freely admitted to God's grace.
> Notwithstanding any human weakness in them, they are advanced
> higher in the spiritual stage on account of their Faith, Trust, and
> Striving after Right. They are given God's Peace, which gives the

---

129

  Islam places great emphasis on reading and reciting the **Qur'an**. Throughout
the history of Islam, there have been many spiritual leaders who have memorized the
whole of the **Qur'an**, an accomplishment highly revered by their peers and later
generations. For those who do not memorize the **Qur'an**, there is an expectation
among many Muslims that one/seventh of the Holy Book is to be read or recited
daily so that the whole is read or recited each week.

130

  See the previous discussion of the seven *salaams*.

soul true calmness and strength, and all the blessing that flow from the spiritual life. This was given not only to Noah and his family but to all the righteous people who were saved with him. And their descendants were also promised those blessings on condition of righteousness. **(The Holy Qur'an**, 526)

Sura XIX includes four *ayats* concerning *Yahya* which mention God's blessings of peace in words that have been variously interpreted concerning the nature of John's death:[131]

(To his son came the command): / "O Yahya! take hold / Of the Book with might": / And We gave him Wisdom / Even as a youth, And pity (for all creatures) / As from Us, and purity: / He was devout, / And kind to his parents, / And he was not overbearing / Or rebellious.

So Peace on him / The day he was born, / The day that he dies, / And the day that he / Will be raised up / To life (again)! (XIX:12-15)

Ali's commentary on this passage agrees with the Christian tradition concerning John's death (see footnote #131), but more importantly stresses the peace that comes as a gift from God to John because of his spiritual attributes:

John the baptist did not live long. He was imprisoned by Herod . . . whom he had reproved for his sins, and eventually beheaded at the instigation of the woman with whom Herod was

---

131

As indicated footnote #6 in Chapter Two, the major Muslim tradition concerning the death of John the baptizer differs from that of Christianity, which has John beheaded by Herod. This tradition has John dying peacefully in old age and eventually being enshrined in a tomb in the Umayyad Mosque at Damascus. Ali, see his note which follows XIX:12-15 above, interprets these *ayats* in a manner that agrees with the Christian tradition. In point of fact, the *ayats* themselves do not specify the nature of John's death, only the blessing of *Al-Lah* on him because of his righteousness.

infatuated. But even in his young life, he was granted (1) wisdom by God, for he boldly denounced sin; (2) gentle pity and love for all God's creatures,[132] for he moved among the humble and the lowly, and despised "soft raiment"; and (3) purity of life, for he renounced the world and lived in the wilderness. All his work he did in his youth. These things showed themselves in his conduct, for he was devout, showing love to God and to God's creatures, and more particularly to his parents . . . this was also shown by the fact that he never used violence, from an attitude of arrogance, nor entertained a spirit of rebellion against human or divine Law. (**The Holy Qur'an**, 770)

The final example recalls for the reader a most important event in the life of Muhammad and his dear friend Abu Bakr, the *Hijrah*, the flight from Mecca to Medina:

> If ye help not (your Leader), / (It is no matter): for God / Did indeed help him, / When the Unbelievers [Meccans] / Drove him out: he had / No more than one companion [Abu Bakr] / They two were in the cave, / And he said to his companion, / "Have no fear, for God / Is with us": then God / Sent down His Peace upon him, / And strengthened him with forces / Which he saw not, and humbled / To the depths the word / Of the Unbelievers. / But the Word of God is exalted to the heights: / For God is Exalted in Might. . . . (IX:40)

132

    One of the attributes for which Muhammad is admired in Muslim tradition is his uncommon gentleness with children and kindness with animals. While the former was a common Arabic attribute, the latter was exceedingly rare in the harsh environment of Arabia. Wonderful stories are told about his protection and love of animals.

Ali's note again stresses the spiritual peace that comes from trusting one's life to God:

> ... the Apostle was hunted out of Mecca and performed his famous
> *Hijrat.* His enemies plotted for his life. He had already sent his
> followers on to Medina. Ali had volunteered to face his enemies in
> his house. His single companion was Abu Bakr. They two concealed
> themselves in the cave of Thaur, three miles from Mecca, for three
> nights, with the enemy prowling around in great numbers in fruitless
> search for them. "We are but two," said Abu Bakr. "Nay," said
> Muhammad, "for God is with us." Faith gave their minds peace, and
> God gave them safety. They reached Medina, and a glorious chapter
> opened for Islam. (**The Holy Qur'an**, 452)

For Muslims, this passage is especially precious for several reasons: (1) it proclaims God's protection of Muhammad at a terrible and frightening time in his life; (2) it affirms the spiritual peace that comes from trust and faith in God even during the worst of times; and (3) by extension, it promises this same spiritual peace to all who remain faithful and trust their lives to the Will of *Al-Lah.*

Because religions often speak of things--truths, realities, beliefs, presences-- which cannot be seen, believers must have concrete affirmations of the truths of faith. One of the most important of all concrete evidences for the truths of faith is found in the lives of human beings who have experienced the safety, protection and peace of God. Human beings who experience and testify to the presence of the Unseen God in their lives are of utmost importance in religion.[133] Thus, recalling the lives of

---

133

The three most successful missionary religions in human history are Buddhism (over 400 million), Christianity (over a billion) and Islam (over a billion). While these three giants share several common values as well as profess many different beliefs, one of the most significant features they have in common is that each has an individual founder. Whatever is seen by the eye of faith of the believer in the lives of the Buddha, the Christ and the Prophet, each one of these men was one of the most exceptional human spirits who ever lived. Just the example of their lives has filled millions of human beings with admiration and reverence for centuries.

prophets, saints, mystics, and other holy persons provides more than just inspiration but exemplary role models.

Before moving to the final section of this chapter on eschatological peace, it is revealing to explore five additional passages in the **Qur'an** that describe the spiritual characteristics of and the promise of God's peace to *mujihads* of the heart; characteristics which, like the peace that reinforces them, come as gifts from God.[134] These five should suffice, when combined with the preceding ones describing the peace of God given to the prophets, to illustrate both the characteristics of and the promises to *mujihads* of the heart.

Sura XIX includes an important conversation between Abraham and his father that stresses the spiritual attribute of forgiveness:

> (The father) replied / "Dost thou / Hate my gods, O Abraham? / If thou forbear not, I will / Indeed stone thee: / Now get away from me / For a good long while!"
>
> Abraham said: "Peace be / On thee: I will pray / To my Lord for they forgiveness: / For He is to me / Most gracious. (XIX:46-7)

Ali identifies love and forgiveness as the fundamental spiritual lesson in this astounding conversation, similar to the conversation between Cain and Abel:

> Note the gentle persuasive tone of Abraham in his speeches
> ... contrasted with the brusque and repellent tone of the father's reply
> in this verse. The one was the outcome of the True Light which had
> come to Abraham from God, as the other was the outcome of Pagan
> arrogance and worship of brute force. The spiritual lesson from this

---

Combined with their teachings, they have provided their followers with both universal truths and the concrete examples of lives lived in spiritual depth and richness.

134

For those familiar with the "Beatitudes" which begin the "Sermon on the Mount" in Matthew 5-7, the five passages that follow allow for several interesting comparisons regarding the spiritual qualities most revered by Christianity and Islam.

episode of Abraham's life may be stated in four propositions: (1) the pious son is dutiful to the father and wishes him well in all things, material and spiritual; (2) if the father refuses God's Light, the son will do his utmost to bring such Light to the father; (3) having received the Light, the son will never renounce the Light, even if he has to forfeit his father's love and renounce his home; (4) even if the father repels him and turns him out, his answer will be a soft answer, full of love and forgiveness. . . .   (**The Holy Qur'an**, 777)

Sura L adds the attributes of repentance and whole-hearted devotion to those of love, forgiveness, trust, humility, gentleness, faith and submission evidenced in preceding *ayats*:

(A voice will say:) / "This is what was / Promised for you,-- / For everyone who turned / (To God) in sincere repentance, / Who kept (His Law),   "Who feared (God) / Most Gracious unseen, / And brought a heart / Turned in devotion (to Him). . . .   (L:32-33)

Ali's commentary identifies four attributes of the *mujihad* of the heart, attributes which are the very meaning of being a Muslim:

The description of the Righteous is given in four masterly clauses: (1) those who turned away from Evil in sincere repentance; (2) those whose new life was good and righteous; (3) those who in their innermost hearts and in their secret doings were actuated by God-fearing love . . . and (4) those who give up their whole heart and being to Him.

. . . .

The true meaning of Islam: peace, security, salutation, and accord with God's plan in all Eternity. (**The Holy Qur'an**, 1416)

Ali's note accompanying XXV:74 provides an even more comprehensive list of the spiritual attributes of *mujihads* of the heart:

Those are the ones who / Will be rewarded with / The highest place in heaven, / Because of their patient constancy: / Therein shall they be met / With salutations and peace. (XXV:75)

Let us recapitulate the virtues of the true servants of God: (1) they are humble and forebearing to those below them in spiritual worth; (2) they are constantly, by adoration in touch with God; (3) they always remember the Judgment in the Hereafter; (4) they are moderate in all things; (5) they avoid treason to God, to their fellow creatures, and to themselves; (6) they give a wide berth not only to falsehood but to futility; (7) they pay attention, both in mind and manner, to the Signs of their Lord; (8) their ambition is to bring up their families in righteousness and to lead in all good. (**The Holy Qur'an**, 944)

For *mujihads* of the heart, whose weapons are repentance, forgiveness, love, gentleness, trust in and fear of God, righteousness, justice, faith and submission, the promise of peace is secure; consider the two following passages:

(To the righteous soul! / Will be said:) / "O (thou) soul, / In (complete) rest / And satisfaction!

"Come back thou / To thy Lord,-- / Well pleased (thyself), / And well-pleasing / Unto Him! (LXXXIX:27-8)

Except such as have Faith, / And do righteous deeds, / And (join together) In the mutual teaching / Of Truth, and of / Patience and Constancy. (CIII:3)

In his commentaries on these two passages Ali stresses the "Peace within" and the "patient hope and unshaken constancy admist all the storm and stress of outer life" that awaits *mujihads* of the heart. (**The Holy Qur'an**, 1783) While the spiritual peace which awaits *mujihads* of the heart in this world is immense, the eschatological peace awaiting them is infinitely and eternally immeasurable.

Eschatological Peace

The Qur'anic theology of eschatological peace has already been indirectly described in the section on eschatological war. Fundamental to the view in the **Qur'an** concerning the eschatological actualization of a world of peace is a historical eschatological war against evil fought by both the *Mahdi* and the returning *Christos*. Also basic to the Qur'anic view of the historical period of justice and peace before the final Day of Judgement is a focus on Mecca as the eschatological City of Peace, that is, the New Jerusalem, (see footnote #118). *Sura* XXIV contains a lengthy *ayat* which proclaims the eventual victory of justice and peace and the blessedness of those who are God's *mujihads*:

> God has promised, to those / Among you who believe / And work righteous deeds, that He / Will, of a surety, grant them / In the land, inheritance / (Of power), as He granted it / To those before them; that / He will establish in authority / Their religion--the one / Which He has chose for them; / And that He will change / (Their state), after the fear / In which they once (lived), to one / Of security and peace: (XXIV:55)

This comprehensive *ayat* reminds Muslims of God's protection of the faithful in the past, promises future peace and security for the righteous in this world and proclaims the eventual creation of a world of peace and justice under the guidance of God before the Day of Judgment. However, as noted in the section on eschatological war, the **Qur'an** says little concerning the specifics of these eschatological events. Instead, it emphasizes the blessings of Paradise,[135] the salutations of "Peace" upon those who enter and descriptions of the occupants of the Garden of Bliss.

Among the many passages which describe the bliss of Paradise, the six following are representative. *Suras* VI and X wonderfully describe Paradise as the

---

[135]

See footnote #75 for Ali's description of Paradise and footnote #111 for a discussion of the eternality of Hell.

eternal Home of Peace:

> For them will be a Home / Of Peace in the presence / Of their Lord:
> He will be / Their Friend, because / They practiced (righteousness).
> (VI:127)
>
> But God doth call / To the Home of Peace: / He doth guide whom
> he pleaseth / To a Way that is straight. (X:25)

Ali's commentary finds the descriptive phrase *Home of Peace* most apt because in Paradise "there is no fear, nor disappointment, nor sorrow. . . ." (**The Holy Qur'an**, 491) *Sura* XIII continues the description of Paradise in a manner making the term *Home* even more appropriate and appealing:

> Gardens of perpetual bliss: / They shall enter there, / As well as the
> righteous / Among their fathers, their spouses, / And their
> offspring: / And angels shall enter into them / From every gate
> (with the salutation):
>
> "Peace unto you for that ye / Persevered in patience! Now / How
> excellent is thy final Home!"

Ali's commentary emphasizes the spiritual nature of family relationships in Paradise:

> The relationships of this life are temporal, but love in
> righteousness is eternal. In the eternal Gardens of Bliss the righteous
> will be re-united with all of those near and dear ones whom they have
> loved, provided only that they were righteous also; for in eternity
> nothing else counts. Blood-relationships and marriage relationships
> create certain physical bonds in this life, which may lead to much
> good, and possibly also to evil. All that is physical or evil will go.
> But the good will come forth with a new meaning in the final
> Reckoning. Thus ancestors and descendants, husbands, wives,
> brothers, and sisters . . . whose love was pure and sanctified, will find
> new bliss in perfecting their love and will see a new and mystic
> meaning in the old and ephemeral bonds. (**The Holy Qur'an**, 611)

406

Sura XXXVI contains an extensive, symbolic description of the final Home of Peace for the righteous:

> Verily the Companions / Of the Garden shall / That Day have joy
> / In all that they do; / They and their associates / Will be in groves
> / Of (cool) shade, reclining / On Thrones (of dignity);
> (Every) fruit (enjoyment) / Will be there for them; / They shall
> have whatever / They call for;[136]
> "Peace!"--a Word / (Of salutation) from a Lord / Most Merciful!
> (XXXVI:55-58)

Ali's notes on these *ayats* stress their symbolic character; for example, he interprets the term "fruit" as follows:

> . . . the Bliss in the Hereafter has an inner quality, expressed
> by the word *fakinatun*. The root *fakihat* is derived from the idea that
> the flavour of choice, ripe fruit, delights the heart of man . . . so
> *fakihat*, 'fruit', stands here for that special choice enjoyment, which
> goes with . . . well-cultivated taste. In other words, it suggests the
> highest kind of joy which depends upon the inner faculty rather than
> any outward circumstance. This is again emphasized by the second
> clause, "they shall have whatever they call for". Again using the
> language of this life, the musician's heaven will be full of music; the
> mathematicians will be full of mathematical symmetry and
> perfection; the artist's will be full of the beauty of form, and so on.
> **(The Holy Qur'an**, 1183)

As a final descriptive passage concerning Paradise, consider *sura* XIX which promises a Garden free of "vain discourse" and Peace:

> Gardens of Eternity, those / Which (God) Most gracious / Has

---

136

It is important to remember Ali's warning about taking symbolic (metaphorical) descriptions as literal. (See footnote #75.)

promised His servants / In the Unseen; for His promise / Must (necessarily) come to pass.

They will not there hear / Any vain discourse[137], but / Only salutations of Peace: / And they will have therein / Their sustenance, morning / And evening. (XIX:61-2)

Ali's commentary emphasizes that Heaven is the "perfection of Islam":

> *Salam*, translated "Peace", has a much wider signification. It includes (1) a sense of security and permanence, which is unknown in this life; (2) soundness, freedom from defeats, perfection as in the word *salim*; (3) preservation, salvation, deliverance, as in the word *sallama*; (4) salutation, accord with those around us; (5) resignation, in the sense that we are satisfied and not discontented; besides (6) the ordinary meaning of Peace, *i.e.*, freedom from any jarring element. All these shades of meaning are implied in the word *Islam*. Heaven therefore is the perfection of Islam. (**The Holy Qur'an**, 780)

Given that the most extensively used term to describe Paradise is *salaam*, it is not surprising that there are dozens of passages which describe "Peace" as the salutation given to those who enter the eternal Home of Peace. Consider XIV:23 as

---

137

Since I am a philosopher by professional training and vocation, perhaps the following comment is forgivably acceptable: I never read this *ayat* without the thought passing my mind that the elimination of "vain discourse" frees Paradise of the dangers of professional academic meetings and conferences, especially those dominated by professional philosophers. Abraham Kaplan, in an interview in **Time** magazine over two decades ago, concluded an interview on the status of professional philosophy in the United States with the following insightful observation: "The word *philosophy* means the "love of wisdom," and the love of wisdom is, I suppose, like any other sort of love, so often the professional knows the least about it." Surely, for Paradise to be paradise, it must be free of the kind of "vain discourse" that forgets the fundamental value of love.

a typical example:[138]

> But those who believe / And work righteousness / Will be admitted
>
> to Gardens / Beneath which rivers flow, / To dwell therein for aye
>
> / With the leave of their Lord. / Their greeting / Will be: "Peace!"

In addition to the salutation of "Peace" for those entering Paradise, there are passages which speak of the special blessings of Peace upon specific individuals as they enter the Home of Peace.[139] Of special interest to Christians is the Peace given to Jesus in *sura* XIX:33:

> 'So Peace is upon me [Jesus] / The day I was born, / The day that
>
> I die, / And the day that I / Shall be raised up / To life (again).[[140]]

138

See also XV:46, XXXIX:73, LVI:90-91 and XLIV:55 for other examples of the salutation of "Peace" upon entering the Home of Peace.

139

See footnote #131 concerning the special Peace given to *Yahya* (John the Baptizer).

140

In translation, it is easy for Christians to misunderstand this *ayat*'s reference to the ". . . day that I / Shall be raised up /To life (again)." For Muslims this does not refer to the resurrection three days after the crucifixion because the Qur'anic position on the crucifixion is that Jesus did not die on the cross. The key *ayat* is the enigmatic *ayat* IV:157:

> That they [the Jews] said (in boast), / "We killed Christ Jesus / The
> son of Mary, / The Apostle of God";-- / But they killed him not,
> / Nor crucified him, / But so it was made / To appear to them, /
> And those who differ / Therein are full of doubts, / With no
> (certain) knowledge, / But only conjecture to follow, / For a surety
> / They killed him not;--

Ali explains the Muslim position on the crucifixion in his commentary on this *ayat*:

> The end of the life of Jesus on earth is as much involved in
> mystery as his birth, and indeed the greater part of his private life,
> except for the three years of his ministry. It is not profitable to
> discuss the many doubts and conjectures among early Christian sects
> and among Muslim theologians. The Orthodox Christian Churches
> make it a cardinal point of their doctrine that his life was taken on the
> cross, that he died and was buried, that on the third day he rose in the

Although they have been identified in many previous citations, it is appropriate to conclude this chapter on theologies of war and peace in the **Qur'an** with two *ayats* which identify the residents of the eternal Home of Peace, for they are the true Muslims.

> But the Apostle, and those / Who believe with him, / Strive and fight with their wealth / And their persons: for them / Are (all) good things: / And it is they / Who will prosper.
>
> God has prepared for them / Gardens under which rivers flow, / To dwell therein: / That is the supreme felicity [blessedness]. (IX:88-89)

Who are the residents of Paradise? Those who "strive" in God's cause! XVI:31-2 describes them in a manner that is similar to one of the beatitudes:[141]

> Gardens of Eternity which they / Will enter: beneath them / Flow (pleasant) rivers: they / Will have therein all / That they wish: thus doth / God reward the righteous,--

---

body with his wounds intact, and walked about and conversed, and ate with his disciples, and was afterwards taken up bodily to heaven. This is necessary for the theological doctrine of the blood sacrifice and vicarious atonement for sins, which is rejected by Islam. . . . [Ali then describes the many sectarian disputes in early Christianity over the crucifixion, resurrection and divine nature of the Christ.] The Qur'anic teaching is that Christ was not crucified nor killed by the Jews, not withstanding certain apparent circumstances which produced the illusion in the minds of some of his enemies; that disputations, doubts, and conjectures on such matters are vain; and that he was taken up to God. . . . (**The Holy Qur'an**, 230)

The enigmatic phrase, "But so it was made / To appear to them," is the source of considerable theological argument and interpretation by Muslim *ulama*. One of the most intriguing is as follows: because Judas was the betrayer, when the soldiers came to arrest Jesus, *Al-Lah* changed his physical appearance to resemble Jesus; thus, it was Judas who was crucified as punishment for his betrayal, not Jesus. See the eschatological role of Jesus in the section on "Eschatological War."

141

See Matthew 5:8: "Blessed are the pure in heart, for they shall see God."

> (Namely) those whose lives / The angels take in a state /Of purity,
> saying (to them), / "Peace be on you; enter ye / The Garden,
> because of (the good) / Which ye did (in the world)."

Who are the citizens of Paradise? The "pure in heart," that is, *mujihads* of the heart first; second, *mujihads* of the tongue and hand; and last and least, *mujihads* of the sword.

Having examined their shared traditions of beliefs and values as well as the theologies of war and peace in their Holy Books, only one task remains: an apology for peace among these too often quarrelsome children of Abraham, or, in other words, a scriptural-theological plea for humility, toleration, respect and PEACE!

CHAPTER FIVE

REFLECTIONS ON THE TRUE SPIRITUAL JIHAD:
AN APOLOGY FOR PEACE AMONG JEWS, CHRISTIANS AND MUSLIMS

As Americans were sleeping late because of celebrations the previous evening, making new year's resolutions, watching football bowl games and hoping that 1997 would be a year of peace and prosperity, those living in the Middle East witnessed the continuing cycle of hatred and violence that has spiritually, politically and economically devastated this small part of the world for decades. A bomb was set off in a crowded bus in Damascus resulting in at least 40 injuries and deaths[1] and a Private in the Israeli army, Noam Friedman, opened fire in a crowded Palestinian market wounding five civilians. When asked why he shot at innocent Palestinians, his response as recorded by the AP was: "They're not innocent. They hate the Jews." While Friedman's words do not mention God or Holy War, they nonetheless echo an emotional and ideological attitude that also motivated Goldman's massacre of Muslims praying in Hebron and Amir's assassination of Rabin as well as hundreds of Arabs throughout the past five decades who have joined such groups as Hamas and Hizbollah. This distorted intellectual, emotional and spiritual attitude has its

---

[1]

     At present, although the Syrian government blames the state of Israel for the act of terrorism, there is no definitive evidence that identifies those who committed this crime.

origins in the unholy merging of several dimensions of human existence: ethnicity, politics, oppression and religion. In religion it originally took the form of the ban (*herem*) in pre-exhilic Judaism and, unfortunately, from Judaism was passed into both Christianity and Islam. In other words, this kind of attitude reflects a spiritual illness plaguing the children of Abraham at different times throughout history in their relations with each other. Because Susan Niditch's statement of the nature of this kind of spiritual illness reveals so much, it is worth re-citing in part:[2] (Words in bold are inserted for emphasis)

> It is not easy for humans to kill others. To participate in mass killing in war is destructive of **individual psyches** and of the larger **community's mental health**. . . . The ban-as-God's-justice ideology actually motivates and encourages war, implying that **wars of extermination** are desirable in order to **purify the body politic** of one's own group, to eradicate evil in the world beyond one's own group. . . . In the ban-as-God's-justice a **sharp line is drawn between them and us, between clean and unclean, between those worthy of salvation and those deserving elimination.** The **enemy** is thus . . . a **monster, unclean and diseased.** The ban-as-God's-justice thus allows people to accept the notion of **killing other humans by dehumanizing them** and the process of dehumanization can take place even within one's group during times of stress, distrust, and anomie.[3] (**War in the Hebrew Bible**, 77)

2

See Chapter Two for the complete citing of this important paragraph.

3

Niditch's recognition that times of stress and distress can turn *herem* theology from the external enemy inward to acts of violence against the unclean within the community is distressingly applicable to Israel today. One of the new kinds of violence that is increasingly probable is Israeli violence against other Israelis. Given the considerable threat to national security posed by her Arab neighbors, this new internal threat to security is a most ominous sign for the peace process.

Recalling the two kinds of anti-Semitism, Jewish anti-Semitism and Arab anti-Semitism, which complicate real progress for any lasting peace, there is another way to describe the spiritual irony and illness in Friedman's ideology. His reason for firing on "innocent Palestinians" was that none of them were innocent because they hated the Jews, that is, they were anti-Semites (Jewish anti-Semitism), but Friedman's view reflects the second kind of anti-Semitism in the area (Arab anti-Semitism),[4] that is, he is also an anti-Semite. The vicious circle of destruction and violence this kind of attitude unleashes is far too evident, not only in the Middle East but throughout the world.

As stated in the "Prologue," and revealed in the title of this study, its major purpose is providing an understanding of the shared traditions and the theologies of war and peace among Abraham's children in order to offer a scriptural-theological apology for peace. As preparation for that apology three tasks help provide background: (1) a definition of the term *apology* as used in this context; (2) several preliminary comments on the distortion of *holy war, or* what could be more appropriately termed *unholy war*, before contrasting its appropriate role in henotheism with its inappropriate use in moral monotheism ; and (3) a brief reflection on the sacredness of peace.

As used in this chapter, presenting an "Apology for Peace Among Jews, Christians and Muslims" has little to do with the modern use of the term *apology* as an expression of regret for an injury or state of affairs; rather, the term is used in its classical sense as a "speech of defense." Etymologically the term derives from a Greek verb, *apologeomai*, which means "to speak in one's own defense"; hence, *apologia* means "a speech of defense." Because much of the first four centuries of Christian history were filled with conflicts, both externally with other religions and internally among competing interpretations of the accounts and teachings that

---

4

      As defined earlier, Jewish anti-Semitism refers to bigotry against Jews and Arab anti-Semitism to bigotry against Arabs.

became the **New Testament**, the discipline of *apologetics* came to mean a written defense or justification of theological positions. The sense of apologetics in the "Apology for Peace . . . " used in this chapter reflects a written theological position which presents a scriptural interpretation of peace based on a critical (higher and lower criticism)[5] study of all three Holy Books.[6] The first two steps in this apology, then, are preparatory comments concerning unholy war and preliminary reflections regarding the sacredness of peace.

Unholy War

As understood in the sense of "popular religion," that is, those religious beliefs, values and practices that became accepted as orthodox by the masses of believers,[7] this apology begins, then, with the assertion that in a moral monotheism there are **NO HOLY WARS**. In other words, although popular religion may believe in holy wars, from the moral perspective of monotheism, these can only be **UNHOLY WARS**. This judgment, however, does not exclude the possibility for

---

[5]

See the description of these methods in the Prologue..

[6]

I am aware that the apology (theological-ethical argument) that follows is not only subject to dispute, but that it is likely to be most persuasive to those who least need to hear it because their minds are already open to accepting God's revelations as extending beyond any single Book. In other words, I am aware that the apology which follows is akin to "Preaching to the Choir," but surely the message of peace is of such psychological and moral need in today's world and of such spiritual significance for true holiness, that any preaching, no matter how poorly done or to how many choirs, is of some value. I can only hope that this is so!

[7]

As should be evident, changing historical circumstances bring about considerable re-interpretations of orthodoxy, especially as understood by the masses of believers. Because "popular religion" is prone to syncretism, that is, incorporating popular and common beliefs and practices into religion, it much too easily and often incorporates the kinds of ethnic and national chauvinisms mentioned in several previous sections of this study into its interpretations of sacred revelation.

honorable wars.[8] This judgment requires clarification.

There are no political holy wars such as Jewish **herems**, Christian **crusades** or Muslim offensive **jihads by the sword** and consequently no political holy warriors such as **crusaders** or **mujihads**) in a moral monotheism, for all human beings are the created children of God.[9] This truth, however, has been a hard one for monotheists to learn throughout Western history. One great human spirit who learned this truth the hard way was Martin Niemoller, the German U-Boat captain and decorated war hero who left his Naval commission and became a Christian minister during the Nazi regime. Because of his opposition to Hitler and his resistance to the Nazification of the German Church, his family was constantly threatened, his home bombed and, eventually, he was arrested and spent several years in prison where he was known as Hitler's "personal inmate." After the war when he was released, in only two short sentences, Niemoller reminded us all that there are no political holy wars or warriors: "It has taken me many years of my life to realize that God is not the enemy of my enemies. . . . He is never the enemy of His enemies." (Translation by Charles Littell in his book, **The German Phoenix**.)

While there are no holy wars or holy warriors, there are honorable wars and honorable warriors as well as dishonorable ones. The dishonorable warrior, at best, fights for personal glory, or at worst, kills for the traditional spoils of victory[10] or the

---

8

As used in this context, an honorable war is usually termed in Western religious tradition as a just war. Since Constantine, arguments both for and against just war have occupied some of the best Christian thinkers and leaders in their efforts to relate Christian beliefs and values to changing historical situations and events.

9

This religious assertion provides the basis for the "Apology for Peace" which concludes this study. It is examined in the two major sections of this chapter which examine the differences between henotheism and monotheism and the moral nature of chosenness in a monotheism.

10

Of all the spoils of victory, the one that is most important is land. Human beings kill one another over many things, but at the top of the list, especially as

love of power. In a similar manner, the dishonorable war is an offensive war which results from human greed, the lust for power and the sadism of control.

The honorable warrior fights for one purpose and one alone--an honorable peace--because he (or she) knows the terrible human costs and destructiveness of war: costs and destructiveness that go far beyond political slogans and rhetoric, flag waving, false patriotism and distorted religious emotions. The Greek historian Herodotus stated the human tragedy and despair of war as clearly as it has ever been communicated: "In times of peace, sons bury their fathers; in times of war, fathers bury their sons." Today, this horrible truth extends to both daughters and mothers. The honorable warrior battles for life, not death; and thus, the honorable war is fought for one or more of the following reasons: to stop the advance of tyranny, to defend those who cannot protect themselves or to defend one's home.[11] Only in these three cases is the choice for war a decision founded upon the value of life rather than the passion for destruction. The Frenchman Albert Camus reminded us of this over 40 years ago:

> Europe (and France) has not yet emerged from fifty years of nihilism,[12] but the moment people begin rejecting the mystifications on which that nihilism is based then hope is possible. The whole question is to know whether or not we shall develop faster

---

regards wars, is land. Many previous sections of this study speak of the importance of land in theologies war, especially political war.

[11]

As examined in Chapter Two, the **Qur'an** addresses the issue of honorable war in a more adequate and explicit manner than either the **Hebrew Bible** or the **New Testament**. This is most clearly seen in the understanding of justified political war as defensive and in the limitations on political war imposed by the **Qur'an**.

[12]

The same sentence just as accurately describes the situation between Israel and her neighbors during the last fifty years since the partition. Camus' hope for Europe is as important and needed in the Middle East today as it was for Europe at the end of World War II.

[emotionally, intellectually and spiritually] than the rocket with a
nuclear warhead. . . . This is the wager of our generation. If we are
to fail, it is better, in any case to have stood on the side of those who
choose life than on the side of those who are destroying [choose
death]. ("The Wages of Our Generation," **Resistance, Rebellion and
Death**, 187-88)

The honorable war affirms the values of life and justice; the honorable warrior fights
believing in the sacredness of and hoping for the actualization of peace.

The Sacredness of Peace[13]

13

The reflections on the "Sacredness of Peace" that follow were originally
prepared as the concluding meditation for a "Conference on the Holocaust: Fifty
years After" held at Austin Peay State University during spring 1995. The
incongruity of including them in this section of the final chapter is only an apparent
one for two reasons. First, it was during the Nazi era that another *herem* theology of
eliminating the enemy within, the internally impure, resulted in one of the worst
atrocities in human history: the Final Solution. Chauvinistically, most Holocaust
conferences and courses claim that there is no other comparable atrocity in the whole
of human history, but, tragically, this is not the case. While the Holocaust was
unique, (all historical events are unique, that is, no two are exactly alike), the claim
that it was **singular** (that is, it was so unlike any other atrocity in human history that
it denies comparisons and must always be given a priority and consideration above
all other acts of human genocide) is significantly questionable. History, both
Western and Eastern, has been plagued with far too many Final Solutions, and in the
West they are usually justified in terms of a *herem* ideology. Second, there is a
relevance for including reflections from a Holocaust conference in this study because
of a concern that has emerged regarding its political uses in arguments by a minority
of Jewish and Christian groups (mostly in the U.S.). Unfortunately there are those
who use the Holocaust as a reason for retaining the boundaries of "Greater Israel"
(that is, the occupied territories as belonging to Israel) and as a reason for the
necessity of the eventual purification of Jerusalem as the capital and center of the
Israeli state by slowly evicting its Palestinian population through political and
economic strategies. These are troubling issues that concern Jews and Christians in
the United as well as Israelis and Palestinians in the Middle East. Lest this concern
be misunderstood, I conclude this footnote with the following statement: Nothing
should ever be done to minimize the atrocity of the Holocaust in terms of its

This study of war and peace has centered on the beliefs and values of a revelation that began in the desert of Sinai and eventually provided the prophetic traditions which produced three of the West's great monotheisms: Judaism, Christianity and Islam. Examining these prophetic traditions has partially revealed both the grandeur and the destructiveness of the human spirit: that is, the capacity of the human being to distort truth into lies, beauty into ugliness, kindness into cruelty, justice into oppression, creativity into chaos and goodness into various kinds of evil. While such spiritual distortions and maladies are not uncommon, at certain historical times they have erupted into the most evil-destructive spiritual plague imaginable: genocide, ethnic cleansing, holy wars of extermination and holocausts. Consequently, moral and spiritual studies of and reflections on such atrocities provide opportunities for understanding the human capacities for both goodness and evil as well as the sacredness of justice and peace.

The sacred reveals itself in many ways. One of them is found in the witnesses and the survivors of such genocidal atrocities as the Holocaust who testify to the survival of the human spirit through times of unspeakable cruelty, dehumanization and death. Listening to their testimonies is learning about more than just the horrors of human cruelty and destructiveness but also experiencing the sacredness of life. In the presence of such witnesses and survivors and their memories, words fail and thoughts inadequately distort both the horror and the sacredness they reveal. The

---

historical, political, moral and spiritual costs, but it is also the case that any intrusion of a political agenda into the study of the Holocaust compromises its spiritual and moral considerations, which are of utmost importance for the growth of justice and compassion among human communities. In other words, freed from any political agenda, yearly conferences and courses on the Holocaust can provide two important awarenesses necessary for the moral development of the human spirit: (1) an awareness of the destructiveness of the human spirit when it loses its soul in the distortions of religious, political and ethnic bigotry; and (2) a passionate reminder of our shared responsibilities to affirm the dignity of human life and the sacredness of justice and peace by committing our selves to struggle (to be *mujihads* of the heart, mouth and hand) against those forces which "choose death."

sacred, as all great religions affirm, calls for silence, prayer, hope and peace. Indeed, if a significant part of the human malady that brings forth a holocaust is a spiritual one, then one of the greatest values of remembering and struggling with such atrocities is to move beyond violence, cruelty, war and death to compassion, hope and peace. As a first small step in such an effort, consider the following reflections concerning the sacredness of peace.

While there are two dimensions of peace, the external (that is, political--lack of conflict among peoples) and the internal (that is, the spiritual, mental and emotional), it is internal peace that is prior because it provides the foundation for external peace--a truth which is central to the three revelations of this study. Consider the following sacred passages, offered in chronological order:

> The Prophecy of Micah (Jewish, ca. 7th B.C.E.):
>
> "He has showed you, O man, what is good. And what does the Lord require of you, but to do goodness, to love kindness, and to walk peacefully with God."
>
> The Sermon on the Mount (Christian, 1st C.E.):
>
> "Happy are the peace-makers, for they shall be known as the sons of God."
>
> The **Qur'an** (Muslim, 7th C.E.):
>
> This will be their cry therein: / "Glory to Thee, O God!" / And peace will be their greeting therein! / And the close of their cry / Will be: "Praise be to God / The Cherisher and Sustainer / Of the worlds!"
>
> "Peace! a Word / (Of salutation) from a Lord / Most Merciful.

These passages speak of the most sacred dimension of peace: the internal. Most philosophies and psychologies propound paths for achieving such peace that range from stoic self-discipline to various kinds of new age meditations. For those who do not believe in spiritual transcendence, perhaps one of these methodologies will help them achieve the elusive internal peace that is necessary for external peace.

420

For those who believe that internal spiritual peace requires transcendent help, perhaps our first step in the pilgrimage leading towards peace of spirit is the petitionary prayer of the Psalmist:

> Search me, O God, and know my heart! / Try me and know my thoughts! / And see if there be any wicked way in me, / and lead me in the way of peace.

Such a plea for transcendent help could be the first step that turns the arrows and spears of war into plows for growing and nails for building. In memory, then, of the martyrs, witnesses and survivors of histories worst atrocities, and as a promise to our children and grandchildren, we must commit ourselves to the search for spiritual peace,[14] that is, the sacred peace which can overcome the destructive capacities of human nature. Only then can there be realistic hopes for peace among humans. As an *ayat* in the **Qur'an** proclaims: "God will not alter what is in people until they alter what is in themselves." While we have the capacities for darkness, chaos and destruction within us, we also have the capabilities to create beauty, goodness, truth and peace. In the words of all three great revelations, with God's help, we have the capabilities to return to the original state and purpose of human life: **PEACE!**

God's Jihad: a Henotheistic Jihad by the Sword OR a Monotheistice Jihad by the Heart?

Crucial to this part of the "Apology for Peace" are the analyses in the second chapter which examine the historical development of the theology of God in the **Hebrew Bible** through four stages: (1) *Yahweh* polytheism (pre-13th to 11th

---

14

As evidenced in the three preceding chapters, while all three Holy Books proclaim theologies of political and eschatological peace, their richest and most important insights concern the relationship between God and the human search for spiritual peace.

centuries B.C.E., Moses to David); (2) *Yahweh* henotheism[15] (early monarchy, 10th to 9th centuries, David to the Assyrian destruction of Israel); (3) Mono-Yahwism (late monarchy, 8th century to the 6th century Babylonian destruction of Jerusalem); and (4) *Eloh-im* Monotheism (exhilic and post-exhilic period, 6th to 3rd centuries). As described in the second chapter, it was during the henotheistic period (roughly from Moses to the Exile) that the theology of the ban (*herem*) developed. The theological connections between henotheism and the *herem* (holy war of extinction) are so important they require reiterating.

Beginning from the henotheistic foundation of believers affirming a special relationship with one god placed above all others leads to the central belief in a henotheism: the chosen relationship between the god and his people, that is, the chosen people. The emotional power of this belief in all three of the monotheisms of this study is evidenced throughout the whole of their histories. Believing that one belongs to the divinely chosen becomes one of the most passionately powerful beliefs in Western religion. Once the relationship of chosenness is firmly established, it is usually understood as a covenant relationship, that is, a relationship from which both sides, the chosen ones and their god, benefit. Since a henotheism does not deny the existence of other gods, it opens the theological door for relationships to exist between other peoples and their gods. From this bifurcation of the gods and their peoples, several theological consequences follow: consequences whose emotional, political, spiritual and moral ramifications still influence the modern world today, especially in the Middle East.

First, the covenant relationship of chosenness includes both responsibility and privilege. Given the nature of henotheism, responsibility is usually understood as fidelity to the laws and commands of the deity while privilege usually includes protection from enemies, victory in war and, the greatest prize of all, land promised

---

15

See footnote #4 in Chapter Two for a definition of the term *henotheism*; this definition is central to the apologetic argument which follows.

422

and given to the chosen ones. Indeed, regarding land, the theology of the *herem* accomplished two purposes during this time of Hebrew henotheism: a religious justification for the seizing of land and one for the occupying and possessing of promised land.[16]

---

[16]

As this section of the chapter continues, it argues that the theology of chosenness to **HAVE**, for example, land, is a distortion in a monotheism but natural in a henotheism. This, however, has not kept the belief in being chosen to **HAVE** land from continuing to be a cherished belief today even in the monotheisms, especially among Israelis. The continuance of the belief in promised land is one of the greatest hurdles to any just peace between Israelis and Palestinians. Consider the following examples of the conflict over land in Israel: "The Guidelines of the Government of Israel--June 1966," which were approved by all of the constituent parties in Netanyahu's Cabinet, excerpts from an editorial by Georgie Anne Geyer and a **Time** magazine report on Hebron titled, "Over Their Dead Bodies."
The government presented to the Knesset will act on the promise that the right of the Jewish people to the Land of Israel is eternal and indisputable, that the State of Israel is the State of the Jewish people . . . and whose main goal is the ingathering and integration of the Jewish people.
The government will work to achieve the following goals:
    (1)   Achieving peace with all our neighbors, while safeguarding national and personal security.
    (2)   Reinforcing the status of Jerusalem as the eternal capital of the Jewish people. . . .

    I.   PEACE, SECURITY AND FOREIGN RELATIONS
      (1) . . . .
      (2)   The government of Israel will propose to the Palestinians an arrangement whereby they will be able to conduct their lives freely within the framework of self-government. The Government will oppose the establishment of a Palestinian state or any foreign sovereignty west of the Jordan River, and will oppose "the right of return" of Arab populations to any part of the Land of Israel west of the Jordan River. . . .
      (9)   The Government views the Golan Heights as essential to the security of the state and its water resources. Retaining Israeli sovereignty over the Golan will be the basis for an arrangement with Syria.
    II.   JERUSALEM

(1)   Jerusalem, the capital of Israel, is one city, whole and undivided, and will remain forever under Israel's sovereignty.
(2)   Freedom of worship and access to the holy places will be guaranteed to members of all faiths.
(3)   The Government will thwart any attempt to undermine the unity of Jerusalem, and will counter any action which is counter to Israel's sovereignty over the city. . . .

IV.   SETTLEMENT
(1)   Settlement in the Negev, the Galilee, the Golan Heights, the Jordan Valley, and in Judea, Samaria and Gaza is of national importance, to Israel's defense and an expression of Zionist fulfillment. The Government will alter the settlement policy, act to consolidate and develop the settlement enterprise in these areas, and allocate the resources necessary for this. . . .   ("Netanyahu Promises a New Look for Israeli Policies," **Report on Israeli Settlement in the Occupied Territories,** vol.6, no.4, July 1996, 1,7)

That this policy is a disaster for the peace process is recognized by most observers of the Middle East. Consider the following comment by Georgie Anne Geyer written during the holiday season 1996:

The Jewish settlements in what are internationally recognized [even occasionally and reluctantly by the United States] as Palestinian lands are not only an "obstacle to peace," as the legalistic like to say; they are profoundly immoral. They are designed to humiliate the Palestinians--and ultimately to move them out and destroy the idea of a Palestinian homeland. [A dream for well over two and one-half million Palestinians living in either refugee camps or ethnic ghettos in the Occupied Territories.] **(The Leaf-Chronicle,** December 20, 1966)

While conflict over who is chosen to have Jerusalem continues as a major peace barrier between Israel and the Palestinians, it is Hebron that has been most in the news. In a report on Hebron in **Time,** December 4, 1996, Johanna McGeary cogently describes the explosive potential for violence that can result from beliefs about promised land:

Leah Hochbaum giggles a lot for a radical fanatic. But the 26-year-old mother of two from New York possesses a will of steel and a boundless faith that she is obeying God's commandment. When she heard Manhattan Rabbi Shlomo Carlebach say it was a Jews duty to reclaim all the land of ancient Israel, she believed, and she came, not just to the Holy Land but to the very heart of the struggle, to the West bank city of Hebron. After a year in the confines of the

Second, henotheistic theology of chosenness naturally implies a division of

---

> Avraham Avinu quarter, one of six minuscule enclaves inhabited by some 400 Jews amid the city's 100,000 Palestinians, she has no doubts and no regrets. . . .
>
> . . . .
>
> Thanks to the immense difficulty of safeguarding the lives of 400 Jews like Hochbaum who refuse to leave, Hebron has emerged as the thorniest issue in the peace process so far. . . . Even if Israeli forces in the city move back soon, the settler's uncompromising zeal could touch off confrontations that might consume any hope of permanent peace.
>
> . . . .
>
> Among the settlers, Baruch Ms'zel is one of the most Messianic. Born in the U.S., the disciple of murdered ultranationalist Rabbi Meir Kahane discarded his U.S. passport years ago. . . . [He] . . . says uncompromisingly, "It is only a matter of time until there is war between the Jews and Arabs, and it will start from here." He believes that redeployment will wreck the peace accords, and he is glad. "The Arabs have to understand that this is a Jewish state, and they have got to leave. Peacefully if they want; if not, we will make them. Just let me rule Hebron for 24 hours, and they would leave."
>
> Muted or assertive . . . the arguments are the same in every household. Many settlers came from America, believing they were ordained by God to take back the whole of the Biblical land, and if they cede ground in Hebron, then Jews could lose all of Israel. . . .
>
> . . . .
>
> Whether or not there is an agreement on Hebron, the Jews there already reject any new arrangements for their community. When the army goes . . . the settlers will rely on their own armed civil defense. "We aren't going to wait in our homes," he [Noam Arnon, spokesman for the Hebron Jewish community] explains, "but are going to go out and prevent them from approaching." Hebron's Palestinians will not tolerate that. Warns a militant local leader, called Nadir, with ties to the violent Islamist group Hamas: "Neither the Palestinian police nor the Israeli army will be able to protect the settlers. They are an alien body, and the only way to achieve their security is to carry their bodies out of here." If peace must come through Hebron, it will be traversing a war zone. (pp.53-54)

These comments echo the pre-exhilic theology of the *herem*, a theology that can lead only to more bloodshed. Fortunately, there are many Jews and Palestinians who reject this ancient henotheistic chauvinism, but the danger of violence from extremist groups on both sides is explosive.

peoples into one of two camps: friends or enemies. However, it doesn't stop there, for it leads to a more destructive division: God's enemies and God's friends. Not surprisingly, combined, these two divisions result in a formula that can be, and has been, used to justify genocide: "The People's Enemies are God's Enemies." At this point, the theology of the henotheistic holy war (*herem*) is completed. While beliefs in chosenness, promised land, God's enemies, the People's enemies and divine help in holy war are natural extensions of henotheism, such is not the case for monotheism. To re-use an earlier metaphor, to add these henotheistic beliefs to the "hand of monotheism," can only be done by cutting off its "moral finger." This requires development.

As the term *monos*, meaning "alone" or "only one," indicates, a monotheism is the claim that there is **One and Only One** God. From this theological position, then, Judaism, Christianity and Islam proceed to affirm that the whole of existence is the creation of the one God. In other words, monotheism provides the theological and logical basis for one of the most precious beliefs held in common among the children of Abraham: the belief in the creation of the entire cosmos.[17] Although there are dozens of creation accounts that emerge from the various religions of the Middle East, the Priestly account[18] in Genesis Chapter One sets the foundation for Jewish, Christian and Muslim understandings of creation. While this account shared several similarities with other creation myths, especially the Mesopotamian *Enuma Elis*, the Priestly creation theology included two elements which made it unique: (1) the blessing of God upon all of creation and His declaration that the created world is good, and (2) claims about the nature of human beings. It is verses 26-7 which

---

[17]

See footnote #11 in Chapter Two for a brief description of the monotheistic foundation for the doctrines of creation and eschatology.

[18]

See footnote #1 in Chapter Four for a description of the modern Documentary Hypothesis, which also lists the four major sources of the *Torah* (*Pentateuch*), the latest being the Priestly source.

became pivotal for all three monotheisms and are central for the apology presented in this chapter:

> God said, 'Let us make man in our own image [Hebrew *selem*], in the likeness of ourselves, and let them be masters of the fish of the sea, the birds of heaven, the cattle, all the wild beasts and all the reptiles that crawl upon the earth'.
>
> God created man in the image of himself, in the image of God he created him, male and female he created them.

It is almost impossible to over-estimate the importance of this claim that humans are created in the image of God, for not only does it affirm that there is a radical difference between human life and all other living creatures, it claims that there is something in human creatures which makes possible a special relationship with the God of creation: His image.[19] As footnote #19 indicates, the depth of a relationship is determined by the richness of the features shared in common. The same is true of communication. A dialogue between human beings and simple physical objects such as rocks and trees is not possible while communication between humans and animals is possible but limited. However, communication among humans is not only possible but one of the richest and most significant features of human existence. It follows from these reflections that the foundation for communications between God and human beings is the claim in Genesis 1:26-27. In other words, discussions between humans and the Divine is possible because of something shared in common: the

---

19

    Any kind of relationship requires something in common. The richer this element of commonness is, the deeper the relationship. I can have a relationship with a rock if someone hits me in the head with one, but this is a relationship limited to physical proximity. I can have a more extensive relationship with the family dog because of physical proximity but more importantly because of the capabilities for limited communication between the two of us. However, the relationship I can have with another human being is deeper and richer that either of the previous two because of the many features we share in common, especially the potentialities for communication.

image. All three religions maintain that communications occur in two ways: (1) from God to humans, that is, through such mediums as dreams, voices, visions, and, most importantly, revelations given to prophets; and (2) from human beings to God, that is through such practices as sacrifice, worship, devotion and, most importantly, prayer.

The affirmation, then, that humans contain the image of God within them is most likely the most important of all the aspects of creation. Its significance is proclaimed over and again in all three Holy Books. For example, compare the following words of the Psalmist with an *ayat* in the **Qur'an**:

> *Yahweh* our Lord, /   how great is your name throughout all the earth!
>
> I look up at your heavens, made by your fingers, / at the moon and the stars you set in place-- / ah, what is man that you should spare a thought for him, / the son of man that you should care for him? Yet you have made him little less than god, / You have crowned him with glory and splendor, / made him lord over the work of your hands, . . .   (Psalm 8:1, 3-5)
>
> What! Are ye [man] the more / Difficult to create / Or the heaven (above)? / (God) hath constructed it:
>
> On high hath He raised / Its canopy, and he hath / Given it order and perfection. / Its night doeth He / Endow with darkness, / And its splendor doth He / Bring out (with light).
>
> And the earth, moreover, / Hath He extended / (To a wide expanse); / He doth draw out / Therefore its moisture / And its pasture; / And the mountains / Hath He firmly fixed; / For use and convenience / To you and your cattle. (LXXIX:27-33)

Ali's commentary on these *ayats* remind human beings of both their insignificance in comparison to God and their grandeur as His creation:

> If man grows arrogant or forgets his accountability to God, in

his ignorance or thoughtlessness, he is reminded that he is only an insignificant speck in God's spacious Creation. All the excellence that man acquires is the gift of God, who has bestowed on him a high destiny if he fulfills the purpose of his creation: II:30-39 [these *ayats* proclaim that the purpose of man's creation is to have power and responsibility over the created world and to obey, worship and glorify God]. . . . [The *ayats* which follow point] . . . to the glory of the heavens and the earth, and how they are both made to subserve the life of man. (**The Holy Qur'an**, 1682)

Thus, in Genesis of the **Hebrew Bible** and Christian **Old Testament** and the **Qur'an**, both the nature and the status of humans beings differs from that of all the rest of creation. In other words, between humans and God exists a special relationship unlike any other in the created universe.

Based on the preceding sacred texts and their affirmations of a special relationship between human beings and God, which in Genesis is described by the term *selem* (usually translated as "image" or "likeness"), the following represents the first part of this apology. Since **ALL**[20] human beings are created in the image of

---

[20]

The text of Genesis is explicitly clear: "God said, 'Let us make man in our image, in the likeness of ourselves. . . . God created man in the image of himself, in the image of God he created him, male and female he created them." While it should be clear from the text that it is **ALL** human beings who are created in the image of God, almost every generation of Jews, Christians and Muslims has included groups which have syncretized their own prejudices (their own image) into the Genesis account. When this happens, the Genesis affirmation is reversed, for God is remade in the image of man. Briefly, two examples should make this clear. Several decades past the Klu Klux Klan began re-translating the Bible. As a result, today the Klan Bible reads: "And God said, 'Let us create the **white** man in our image, so. . . ." It should be evident that the Klan is re-creating God in their image as a religious support for their racial arrogance, which also is found in the Arianization of German Christianity under the Nazis. The German Institute into Jewish Influence on German Church Life declared the Aryan ancestry of Jesus, thus, in a certain sense making God into an Aryan. They also declared the Aryan people the chosen ones of God, the

God, it follows that **ALL are the CHOSEN**[21] **CHILDREN of God**. Because we are all the children of God, though some of His children get lost in chaos, evil, destruction, violence and sin, even those most lost in sin and destruction are still loved by God as the prodigal son was loved in his absence by the father.[22] If there are no unloved children, then it follows that while human beings may have enemies, God has no enemies.[23] If God has no enemies, then the Hebrew *herem*, the Christian crusade and the Muslim *jihad* by the sword (which violates the Qur'anic theology of political *jihad*) are human distortions that violate the most fundamental belief and value in monotheism: **ALL HUMAN BEINGS ARE THE CREATED AND LOVED CHILDREN OF GOD!**

The preceding apologetic argument does not deny the possibility and need for **honorable** war, that is, in Muslim terms, a **defensive** *jihad* by the sword: a war fought to affirm human life and establish justice and peace.[24] However, it does affirm that the true spiritual *jihad* is the one that is fought by the heart, mouth and

---

Jews as God's enemies and their Final Solution a *herem* of purification.

21

The next section of this chapter develops the nature of chosenness that is morally consistent with monotheism and contrasts it with the kind of chosenness that develops within henotheism. This is a critical part of the apology for peace.

22

See footnote #111 in Chapter Four which explores the controversial issue about the eternality of Hell. For a few Muslim *ulama*, as for the Christian Church father Origen, God's love is so infinitely powerful and forgiving that there is no eternal Hell. To use the metaphorical language in the paragraph above, although there are many lost children who will suffer for their sins and crimes, there are none beyond the infinite forgiving and saving love of God: that is, Hell is only a temporary state before the final return to the presence of God.

23

See page 415 for the magnificent spiritual insight of Martin Niemoller concerning God's enemies at the beginning of this chapter.

24

See the previous discussion concerning the difference between **honorable** and **dishonorable (unholy)** war.

hand; in other words, true spiritual *mujihads* fight to create justice and peace. To aid spiritual *mujihads* in their struggles, God has granted several weapons: faith, courage, endurance, fellowship, hope and most importantly prayer.[25] Indeed, while there are many differences in beliefs and practices among Abraham's children, the spiritual experience which binds them most closely together is their affirmation of and need for prayer. In an article in **The Muslim World**, J.N.M. Wyngaard affirms prayer as the spiritual medium for bringing Jews, Christians and Muslims together in peace:

> The [prayer] for guidance on the straight path [Ezra 8:21-23]--so well known to the Prophet Muhammad's contemporaries . . . was . . . precisely as in the Old Testament and Christian prayer, applied more broadly to include the spiritual realm . . . [of] man's journey through the vicissitudes of this life toward heaven. . . .
>
> While there are big differences between the three over beliefs, the prayer for guidance offers a possible point in common--i.e., a shared belief in God's guidance. Since we all belong to the same human family, can we not pray together. . . . Prayers of Muslim and Christian mystics are so similar they can be interchanged. . . . If in true humility we ask God to guide us, to take over in us, to live in us, Muslims and Christians [and Jews] will find one another in prayer. ("Prayer for Guidance: Origins, Historical Background and Meaning," 8, 10)

For all three of Abraham's children, the experience of prayer is at the center of faith. The more assiduously, then, that Jews, Christians and Muslims attend to prayer, the more likely they are to discover the truths and realities that bind them together as God's children in faith rather than get lost in the conflicts which

---

[25]

See footnote #17 in Chapter One for a discussion of the difference between prayer and magic.

inevitably occur when faith is confused with creedal belief. In an address given at the Islamic Center of the Washington Mosque in 1964, Erich Bethmann warned of the danger when faith is confused with belief (creed) and issued a call for all of Abraham's children to return to the common faith which heals and binds, which leads to peace:

> We both, Muslims and Christians [Jews as well], believe in God, God the creator of the universe and of mankind, God the preserver of the universe, and God the final judge of mankind. We believe in an omniscient, omnipotent, eternal God, God everlasting.
>
> . . . .
>
> And God made Himself known; that is the message of true religion. That is the message of Judaism, that is the message of Christianity, that is the message of Islam. . . .
>
> . . . .
>
> . . . . While the Christian looks to a person, to Jesus Christ, as his contact point with God, the Muslim looks to the Holy Qur'an as his contact with God.
>
> . . . . We exist for God's sake and not for our own. Our life should not turn around ourselves but around God. . . . He is the center, not we. And that is exactly what Christ proclaimed when he taught us to pray "Thy will be done."
>
> And that is exactly what Islam means and requires, namely to submit to God, to place your will . . . under God's will. . . .
>
> . . . . But why, then . . . have Muslims and Christians never come together and often opposed one another? . . . . It is mainly due to the fact that we have confused faith with belief. Faith is our basic capability of discerning spiritual things while belief is the acceptance of a set of statements or theories [that is, creeds] about spiritual things. . . .

.... Today we all, whether we be Christian or Muslim [or Jew], have to do all in our power to revive faith among men. We may use different methods, but God is our center, and the closer we come to God, the closer we come to each other. . . . May God bless us in this endeavor. ("Muslim-Christian Relationships," **The Muslim World**, vol.LI, #4, October 1961, 259-64)

Appropriately, Bethmann's talk ends with a prayer of petition: "May God bless us in this endeavor."

Since prayer is at the center of faith rather than intellectual assents to creedal collections of beliefs, three spiritual insights concerning the nature of prayer by the French philosopher Gabriel Marcel provide an appropriate transition to the second part of this apology for peace: an apology for the chosenness which is morally and theologically consistent with monotheism:

The purest form of invocation--prayer--embodies imperfectly in the uttered word, is a certain kind of inner transformation, a mysterious influx, an ineffable peace. **(Creative Fidelity**, 32)

. . . there is another plane, that of faith, of hope, of charity, that of prayer, which is perhaps the only one on which one can serve peace by establishing it first of all in oneself . . . , on this plane, uneasiness cannot be eluded, but only overcome. **(Problematic Man**, 142)

[I] can pray to <u>be</u> more but not to <u>have</u> more. . . . **(Being and Having**, 74)

As evidenced in previous sections of this study, each of the three Holy Books reaches its spiritual height in its theology of spiritual peace; a peace that comes when one opens and submits his life to God. This is why Marcel writes that one may pray to **be more** but not to **have more**. Such a recognition provides a pivotal insight for examining one of the most controversial and divisive beliefs in all three monotheisms: chosenness.

Chosenness TO HAVE or Chosenness TO BE?

There are few beliefs in the history of Western religion that have aroused more passion and generated more conflict than the belief in being the chosen ones of God. Externally, this belief has promoted suspicion and anger between Jews and Christians, Christians and Muslims, and Jews and Muslims. Internally, the belief has been divisive as Sadducees condemned Pharisees, Catholics fought Protestants and Sunnis oppressed and persecuted Shi'ites. In spite of all these conflicts and their consequent destructions, the belief in chosenness continues almost unabated today; a fact which testifies to its religious significance and emotional intensity. Consequently any apology for peace among Abraham's quarrelsome children must address the issue of chosenness.

The place to begin this task is to return to the pre-exhilic origins of chosenness in Hebrew henotheism. As described in Chapter Two, the doctrine of chosenness is fundamental in henotheism. Further, the central importance of this belief in henotheism sets in motion a passionately integrated theology of chosenness, identification of the People's enemies as God's enemies, divinely promised victory in the *herem* (holy war against the enemies of God), requirements for human fidelity to the laws and commands of God and the critical promise of sacred land. In other words, within the context of henotheism, while chosenness means responsibility (righteousness and fidelity), it more importantly means **Having** privileges, status and things not granted to the unchosen ones: such as protection and blessings from God, victory in holy war and, most importantly, **Land**. On the hand of henotheism, these inseparably connected beliefs and privileges fit like a custom-made glove.

For monotheism, however, the fundamental nature of chosenness must be understood in radically different spiritual and moral terms if it is not to violate the theology of monotheistic creation explored in the preceding section. In other words, while chosenness **TO HAVE** is theologically and morally consistent with henotheism, it is a theological distortion and spiritual illness in monotheism. Basic to the theology of creation in monotheism is the affirmation that **ALL HUMANS**

ARE THE CREATED CHILDREN OF GOD, that is, **ALL ARE CHOSEN**. It is important to understand, however, that they are chosen **TO BE** rather than **TO HAVE**. This requires elucidation.

First, it is most illuminating to examine the spiritual dangers of having. Few religious thinkers of the 20th century have described these dangers as insightfully as Gabriel Marcel. One of the dangers in a theology of chosenness **TO HAVE** is its origins in the psychology of covetousness, in Marcel's terms:

> . . . having already exists, in a most profound sense, in desire or covetousness. To desire is in a manner to have without having. This is why there is a kind of suffering or burning which is an essential part of desire. . . . There is also an absolute balance between covetousness and the pain I feel at the idea that I am going to lose what I have. . . .[26] (**Being and Having**, 162)

The covetousness of having, not surprisingly, leads to a further spiritual illness, one which reduces persons to things that can be disposed of, especially when they interfere with the having of those chosen **TO HAVE**. In **Man Against Mass Society**, Marcel describes this illness as eventually resulting in "techniques of

---

26

Marcel's statement reminds one of the last commandment: "You shall not covet your neighbor's house. You shall not covet your neighbor's wife, or his servant, man or woman, or his ox, or his donkey, or anything that is his." A significant part of the moral meaning of this commandment depends on the interpretation of "neighbor." In the black and white bifurcation of either friends or enemies that is fundamental to henotheistic theology, this commandment applies only to friends and most definitely not to enemies. In fact, because the enemy is also the enemy of God, a henotheism theologically and morally justifies the taking of the enemies house, land, oxen and so on. However, in a monotheism, since all humans are the children of God, it follows that the meaning of neighbor must be significantly extended. If we accept the interpretation of neighbor as presented by Jesus in the Sermon on the Mount and that of the **hadith** which concludes this last chapter. It should be clear that neighbor applies to all God's children. Unfortunately, this understanding of neighbor is suffering considerable and understandable erosion in the Middle East as a result of fifty years of conflict and violence.

degradation":[27]

> ... I understand by "techniques of degradation" a whole body of
> methods deliberately put into operation in order to attack and destroy
> in human persons ... their self-respect, and ... to transform them
> little by little into mere human waste products, conscious of
> themselves as such, and in the end forced to despair of themselves in
> the very depths of their souls. (42)

Another common danger that results from a theology of chosenness **TO HAVE**, fanaticism, is uncovered by Marcel in the following paragraph:

> I am thinking in particular of such pseudo-possessions as <u>my ideas
> and opinions</u>. In this case, the word 'have' takes on a meaning which
> is ... threatening. The more I treat my own ideas ... as something
> <u>belonging</u> to me--and so as something I am proud of ... the more
> surely will these ideas ... tend, by their very inertia ... to exercise
> a tyrannical power over me; that is the principle of fanaticism[[28]] in
> all its shapes. (**Being and Having**, 166)

Finally, the danger of having is most clearly revealed when related to the illness of possessing:

27

    It is both frightening and despairing to notice the various ways in which such techniques have become a part of the extremists on both sides in the Middle East conflict. The very identification of peoples as the enemies of God--as is essential to the *herem*, the offensive *jihad* by the sword and the crusades--is a most effective "technique of degradation."

28

    While there are different kinds of fanaticism, it is religious, racial and political fanaticism, often combined, that have contributed to many of the worst calamities in history. It has been recognized by many spiritual leaders that religious fanaticism is just another form of arrogance. The religious fanatic, in one sense, claims to possess God, or at least to have a monopoly on the truth of God. In fanaticism, the spiritual virtue of humility is lost, and the results are destructive for both the spiritual health of the fanatic and those around him.

Here we find again our previous reflections on having--at least where having is, properly speaking, possession. I would note in passing that in French and also, it seems, in English, this word can be both active and passive, and this seems to me to be very revealing. In a sense it is true to say that to possess is to be possessed, precisely because possessing is not free from a secret anxiety. . . . **(The Existential Background of Human Dignity,** 103)

Chosenness **TO HAVE** is essentially chosenness **TO POSSESS.**

BUT righteous believers, true *mujihads* of the heart, cannot have God any more than they can morally pray **TO HAVE** more. Rather, at the heart of faith, as recognized by all three monotheisms, is not the claim that God belongs to a special people, but that all peoples belong to God. Understood in terms of prayer, the fundamental act of belonging to God is not found in the petition **TO HAVE** but in the struggle **TO BE** open to the presence of God, in Muslim terms, submiting to God. Consequently, the only kind of chosenness that is both morally and theologically consistent with monotheism is chosenness **TO BE**; but **TO BE** what? Fortunately, the answer to this question emerges over and again throughout the revelations of all three Holy Books: to be *mujihads* of the heart, mouth and hand; that is, struggling to love kindness, to practice justice, to walk humbly with God, to experience and give forgiveness, to love and be loved, to let the light of God's image shine through one's life, to struggle against evil and in the cause of good, to reject ugliness and create beauty, to deny violence and become a peacemaker, and to participate in the promises of God for eternal peace. To be chosen of God is a chosenness **TO BE**, not **TO HAVE.**

Since the struggles of *mujihads* of the heart are *jihads* **TO BE** righteous and just, and, thus, to contribute to the creation of peace among humans, it is appropriate to conclude this apology for peace among Abraham's children--an apology built on two foundations, "All humans are created in the image of God" and "The chosen of God are chosen **TO BE**"--by returning to the Holy Books themselves. Consider the following revelations from the **New Testament** and the **Qur'an**:

> 'You have learnt how it was said: *You must love your neighbor* and hate your enemy." But I say this to you: love your enemies and pray for those who persecute you; in this way you will be sons of your Father in heaven. . . .' (Matthew 5:43-44)
> Repel evil with that / Which is best: / We are / Well acquainted with / The things they say. (XXIII:96)

Ali's note on this *ayat*, while not explicitly counseling the love of one's enemies, does nonetheless indicate that Muslims are to return good for evil:

> Whether people speak evil of you, in your presence or behind your back, or they do evil to you in either of those ways, all is know to God. It is not for you to punish. Your best course is not to do evil in your turn, but to do what will best repel evil. Two evils do not make a good. (**The Holy Qur'an**, 890)

As a final example of chosenness **TO BE**, contemplate the following spiritual lessons from the **New Testament** and a cherished **hadith**:

> Then the King will say to those on his right hand, "Come, you who my Father has blessed, take for your heritage the kingdom prepared for you since the foundation of the world. For I was hungry and you gave me food; I was thirsty and you gave me drink; I was a stranger and you made me welcome; naked and you clothed me; sick and you visited me. . . . Next he will say to those on his left hand, "Go away from me, with your curse upon you. . . . For I was hungry and you never gave me food; I was thirsty and you never gave me water. . . sick and you never visited me. . . . " Then it will be their turn to ask, "Lord, when did we see you hungry or thirsty . . . or sick . . . and did not come to your help?" Then he will answer, "I tell you solemnly, in so far as you neglected to do this to one of the least of these, you neglected to do it to me." (Matthew 25:34-45)

O Son of Adam, I fell ill and you visited me not. He will say: O Lord, how should I visit You when You are the Lord of the worlds? He will say: Did you not know that my servant So-and-so had fallen ill and you visited him not? Did you not know that had you visited him you would have found Me with him? O Son of Adam, I asked you for food and you fed Me not. He will say, O Lord, and how should I feed you when You are the Lord of the worlds? He will say: Did you not know that my servant So-and-so asked you for food and you fed him not? Did you not know that had you fed him you would surely have found . . . [Me with him]. O Son of Adam, I asked you to give Me to drink and you gave me not to drink. He will say: O Lord, how should I give you to drink when you are the Lord of the worlds? He will say: My servant So-and-so asked you to give him to drink and you gave him not to drink. Had you given him to drink you would have surely found . . . [Me with him]. (Sacred Hadith #14, from **Forty Sacred Hadiths**, 88-91)

To be *mujihads* of the heart is to center life in the struggles for righteousness and justice and to experience the presence of God in love, hope and prayer. For those who truly love God center their lives in prayer, and even though their voices may differ, surely they pray with the same heart, for we are **ALL THE CHOSEN CHILDREN OF GOD!**

EPILOGUE: MANY VOICES AND PRAYERS, BUT ONE HEART

One day in late May 1993, just as the sun was setting, I stepped onto a small outdoor balcony attached to a room on the eleventh floor of the El Ferradis Hotel in Damascus, Syria. As the last rays of the sun began to fade, the evening air was filled with the antiphonal music of dozens of mosques calling Muslims to the sunset prayer. From all four corners of the city (it seemed like the four corners of the world), the emotional and powerful call to prayer filled the sky as faint stars became visible: "God is most great. . . . There is no God but God. . . . Muhammad is His prophet. . . . Come to prayer. . . . Come to fulfillment. . . . There is no God but God. . . . God is most great. . . ." Even without knowing the Arabic, the music of the words and the powerful, simple assertion of the Oneness and majesty of God in the call to prayer provided one of those moments essential to religious consciousness: the awareness of the ineffable, that is, the awareness and experience of a Truth and a Reality beyond the tiny world of self and the empirical world. Arabic or English, "We worship God with different voices but One heart."

Three days later, in the remote and ancient Christian village of Maloula, Syria--the only place left in the Middle East where the Aramaic that Jesus used is still spoken--I visited the oldest convent in Christendom. The Convent of Tekla was founded by Tekla, a disciple of the Apostle Paul, who was driven into northern Syria by persecution. As the Mother Superior of the Convent told the story of Tekla (she spoke in Arabic which was translated by a friend) and the miracle of the mountain splitting in half and a fresh spring flowing from its rupture, her eyes literally filled with tears of joy and wonder. The skeptical questions that her story might raise in many minds were irrelevant and meaningless to her. As she told the story, it was a narrative which revealed the wonderful power and grace of God. Although we may have different understandings of events, "We worship God in One spirit."

One day later I visited the Shrine of Zeynab (Muhammad's granddaughter through Fatima and Ali), which is a thirty minute drive from Damascus. It is mostly a woman's shrine although many men were present. The shrine and its minaret are layered in a bright blue mosaic. Inside the shrine, the rays of the sun, gleaming through the immense windows, reflecting off the blue mosaic, and passing through a large chandelier, created a natural laser effect. Zeynab's tomb remains one of the most beautiful and stunning religious shrines I have ever visited. However, far beyond its physical beauty was a religious beauty in a conjunction of immense significance. As women engaged in their religious devotionals at Zeynab's tomb, their children ran, played, and laughed: worship and laughter--what a joyous spiritual experience to share together. "We worship God in different ways, but with One heart."

On the Sunday before Christmas 1994 feeling lonely for my wife and daughters, I wandered into a Greek Orthodox Church in Amman, Jordan. It is located across the street from the stunning Al-Abdullah Mosque where King Hussein attends Friday prayer and one block from a Coptic Christian Church. Sunday worship was just beginning, and I was welcomed to participate. Even though the entire service was conducted in Arabic, which I do not know, the musical quality of the liturgy and congregational responses and the visual beauty of the sanctuary and rituals made the service a moving spiritual time of worship. During the first part of the liturgy as the cross and the **New Testament** were walked through the congregation, many worshippers touched or kissed each as well as lit candles and kissed several icons around the sanctuary. The period of worship lasted over two hours, most of the time spent standing; however, this was much less than the three hour Coptic service I attended the next Sunday where most people stood for over two and one-half hours. The Coptic liturgy concluded with a sharing of the bread and the cup. Both services were experiences of spiritual beauty, for whether in Arabic or English, Egyptian Coptic or Latin, "We worship God with different voices but with One heart."

On the day before Christmas eve 1994, I stood in reverent awe before the massive Wailing Wall,[1] listening to the Hebrew devotions of dozens of devout Jews. It was a moment of ineffable silence as hundreds of years of tradition, suffering, expectation and hope merged in their prayers. Less than 36 hours later, I attended the Mass of the Nativity in Saint Cahterine's Church adjoining the Church of the Nativity[2] in Bethlehem. The Mass began at midnight and concluded nearly fours later. Various parts of this ancient, rich and visually beautiful liturgy were conducted in Arabic, Latin, French, German and English. Whether in Hebrew, Arabic, Latin, French, German, English or any other language, **"THOSE WHO PRAY TO GOD PRAY WITH ONE HEART!"**

---

[1]

A part of the Western Wall that remained standing after the 70 C.E. destruction by the Romans of the Temple rebuilt after the Babylonian Exile (after 539 B.C.E.) and greatly expanded by Herod the great during the early part of the 1st century C.E..

[2]

The Church of the Nativity claims to be the built over the original site of the Manger. To enter the Manger, one must enter the basement of the Church of the Nativity.

APPENDIX A

INDEX TO MAJOR PASSAGES CONCERNING WAR (BATTLE)
IN THE HEBREW BIBLE

The following index is divided into four categories: political war, spiritual war, historical eschatological war, and cosmic eschatological war. A brief description is needed for each. The category of political war includes references to such terms as *war, battle, killing enemies, warfare, warrior(s), and the ban (holy war)* as they pertain to present or past historical conflicts described in the **Hebrew Bible**. Spiritual war includes references to internal conflict in a person, often described as "I have no peace." Historical eschatological war includes references to prophecies of future, but not end of time, historical wars, often involving the promise of God's help and protection for the Chosen Ones. Cosmic eschatological war includes references to war and destruction at the end of time. For this last category, the more metaphorically symbolic passages, such as the "moon turning to blood," have been omitted. Note that several passages are listed under more than one category since those passages can be interpreted in more than one way. In some instances, where the term *war* dominates a whole chapter, the chapter is listed rather than individual verses. The books are separated and listed as in the standard Christian Bible whose **Old Testament** is arranged according to the **Septuagint** translation of the **Hebrew Bible**. If a book is not listed, then it contains no significant references to any of the four kinds of war. Further, the index does not list every single use of the included terms, only the most important ones.

A brief glance at the number of references is informative: political war (over 190), spiritual war (over 6), historical eschatological war (over 70), and cosmic eschatological war (over 30). These numbers are given using the general approximation "over" because several passages use the term more than once. This list indicates a concentration in the **Hebrew Bible** on historical wars (past, present and future, at least as understood by the writers at the times they wrote) rather than spiritual war. Further, with a very few exceptions, the references to cosmic eschatological war are clearly post-exhilic. One last note: of special importance in the theology of war in the **Hebrew Bible** are Deuteronomy 20:10-17, which provides a distinction between war and the ban (holy war), and Judges 5:2-31, which is Deborah's Song of Victory, perhaps the oldest writing in the **Hebrew Bible**.

Political War

Genesis 14:1, 19; 16:11; 35:25-29; 49:5-7.

Exodus 1:8-10; 13:17; 14:13-14; 18; 15:3-16; 17:14-15; 23:22-27.

Leviticus 26:6-8; 26:14-46.

Numbers 10:8-9; 10:35; 13:9; 14:41; 21:1, 14, 34; 25:16-18; 31:1-7.

Deuteronomy 1:20-21, 30; 2:1, 32; 3:3, 21-22; 4:1, 34; 7:1-12, 17-24; 9:2-3; 10:29-30; 11:24-5;   20:1-4, 10-17; 21:10-11; 25:17-19; 28:25-68; 31:6-8, 28; 32:29-30.

Joshua 2:24; 3:9-11; 5:13; 6:2-21; Ch.8; 9:1; 10:1-40; 11:18-20; Chs. 12--21 summarize lands conquered; Chs.23-4, Joshua's farewell address.

Judges Ch.1, summary of wars; 3:1, 10, 15, 28, 31; 4:4-7, 14-15; 5:2-31, Deborah's Song of Victory; Ch.6-7, Gideon's miraculous victory; Ch.9, Abimelich; 10:6-- 12:60, Jephthah; Chs. 13--17, Samson; 18:16.

I Samuel 4:1, 7; 5:6-12, 24; 7:8-14; 10:1; Ch.11; 14:6, 15; 15:2-3; 16:14, 18; 17:1-9, 41-47; 19:1-5; 21:14; 23:4; 25:28; 28:16; 30: 6-8, 22.

II Samuel 5:19, 22-25; 11:11; 22:15-51.

I Kings 8:44-45; 14:19, 30; 15:7, 15-19, 37; 16:20; 18:20; 20:28; 22:4, 13-17.

II Kings 3:21-27; 6:8; Chs. 18-19, destruction of an Assyrian army.

I Chronicles 5:22, 26; Chs 18-19; 20:4; 21:12; 28:3.

II Chronicles 12:1-12, 15; 13:2; 15:6; 16:7-9; 24:23-4; 28:10-11; 32:7-8; 33:11

Nehemiah 4:19.

Psalm 24:8; 120.

Ecclesiastes 3:8

Isaiah 8:9; 12:4-5; 13:3; Ch.31; 34:2; 37:5-7; 42:25.

Jeremiah 8:15; 21:3-4; 23:17; 28:8-9; 46:25; 50:20.

Ezekiel 13:10-19.

Jonah Ch.3.

Micah 3:5.

Nahum 1:15.

Spiritual War

Job 3:26.

Psalm 120.

Isaiah 57:21; 59:8.

Lamentations 3:16-18.

Historical Eschatological War

Exodus 17:14-15; 23:22-27.

Numbers 10:8-9; 10:35; 13:29-33; 14:41; 32:20-23.
Deuteronomy 9:23; 20:1-4; 21:10-11; 25:17-19; 32:43; 33:29.
Joshua 3:9-11.
I Kings 8:44-45; 20:22-25, 28; 22: 13, 17, 44.
II Kings 3:13-20; 6:11-12.
Nehemiah 4:19.
Isaiah 5:26-30; 8:9; Chapters 13-21; 29:7; Ch.31; 34:2; 37:5-7.
Jeremiah 5:21-31; 46:25.
Ezekiel 13:10-19; 23:22-25.
Hosea 10:7-10; 14:3.
Amos 2:14-16; 3:6-12; 4:11; 5:8-9.
Micah 1:10-16; 4:11.
Jonah Ch.3.
Habakkuk 1:5-17.
Nahum 1:15.

Cosmic Eschatological War

Psalm 102:25.
Isaiah 44:6; 45:13; 47:4; 48:20; 51:15; 54:5; 59:15-20.
Jeremiah 5:12, 19; 10:12.
Ezekiel 39:17-20.
Daniel 7:21; 9:26; 11:10.
Joel 1:15; 2:1-2, 10-11; 4:9-14.
Amos 5:18-20; 9:5
Micah 4:11-12.
Zephaniah 1:7-18; 2:14; 3:9.
Zechariah 8:10; 10:5; 14:2.

APPENDIX B

INDEX TO MAJOR PASSAGES CONCERNING PEACE IN
THE HEBREW BIBLE

The following table is divided into four categories: uses of peace as a greeting or a blessing, political peace, spiritual peace and eschatological peace. Because the references to peace are considerably less than those to war, the last category includes references to both historical eschatological and cosmic eschatological peace. The numbers provide an interesting contrast to those for war in Appendix A: Political War (over 190)--Political Peace (over 80); Spiritual War (over 6)--Spiritual Peace (over 50); and Eschatological War (over 100)--eschatological Peace (over 40). In other words, there are about twice as many major passages concerning war as peace. Unquestionably, for the violent times of the formation of the **Hebrew Bible**, war and conflict were the common experiences, but this 2 to 1 ratio is deceptive as the last section of Chapter Two indicates.

Peace as a Greeting (Blessing)
(Representative passages)
Numbers 6:22-26.
Judges 6:23; 18:6.
I Samuel 16:4-5; 20:42; 25:35; 29:7.
II Samuel 15:9.
II Kings 5:19.
Psalms 122:6-9; 125:5.
Jeremiah 6:13-14.

Political Peace
Genesis 15:13-15; 26:29-31, 38; 37:4.
Exodus 18:23.
Leviticus 26:3-8.
Deuteronomy 2:26.

Joshua 9:14; 11:23; 18:16.
Judges 8:9; 11:13; 21:13.
I Samuel 3:21-23; 7:14; 16:4-5; 29:7.
II Samuel 10:19; 19:24, 30; 20:19.
I Kings 2:5; 5:4-5, 12, 26; 20:18; 22:1.
II Kings 20:19; 23:19-20.
I Chronicles 4:40; 22:8-9, 18.
II Chronicles 4:40; 14:6; 19:1; 22:9.
Psalms 3:8; 7:4; 55:18, 21; 120; 122:6-9; 125:5: 147:7, 14.
Proverbs 10:7.
Ecclesiastes 3:8.
Isaiah 9:6; 14:7; 27:5 32:16-18; 33:20; 36:16; 48:18; 52:2, 7; 53:5; 54:13; 59:8; 60:17.
Jeremiah 8:15; 12:5; 14:13; 23:17; 28:8-9; 29:5-8; 34:4-5; 46:27.
Daniel 11:6.
Micah 5:5.
Nahum 1:15.
Haggai 2:9.
Zechariah 6:13; 8:10, 12.

Spiritual Peace

Genesis 15:13-15; 29:5-6.
Exodus 18:6.
Numbers 6:22-26.
Judges 6:23; 18:6.
II Samuel 20:19.
I Kings 2:23.
II Kings 22:20; 23:19-20.
I Chronicles 22:8-9.
Job 21:13, 21.
Psalms 3:2-8; 37:37; 72:7; 120; 122:6-9.
Isaiah 9:6; 26:2-3; 27:5; 29:5-8; 32:16-17; 33:20; 38:17; 48:18, 22; 52:7; 53:5; 52:12; 54:10, 13; 57:2, 19; 60:12; 66:12.
Jeremiah 12:5.
Ezekiel 34:20; 37:26.
Zechariah 8:10-19; 9:9-10.
Malachi 2:6.

Eschatological Peace

I Kings 2:23.
Psalms 37:37; 46:8-10; 85:8.
Isaiah 9:6-9; 14:7; 26:2-3; 27:5; 33:20; 49:1-6; 50:4-11; 52:7, 12; 53:5; 54:10-17; 57:2, 10; 59:8; 60:17; 65:66 66:12.

Jeremiah 2:4; 28:8-9; 29:5-8; 34:4-5; 37:36.
Ezekiel 34:20-25; 37:26, 36.
Daniel 10:8.
Micah 4:3.
Nahum 1:15.
Haggai 2:9
Zechariah 1:11; 8:16-19; 9:9-10.
Malachi 2:5.

As in Appendix A on War, passages that are listed in more than one category can be interpreted in various ways.

APPENDIX C

INDEX TO MAJOR PASSAGES CONCERNING WAR (BATTLE)

IN THE NEW TESTAMENT

References to war (battle, fight) in the **New Testament** are meager, overall less than four dozen. This is a striking contrast to the **Hebrew Bible** which includes over 300 references to war. While political war occupies an important place in the **Hebrew Bible** (over 190 references) there are less than half a dozen references to political war in the **New Testament**. As the following index establishes, the majority of references to war in the **New Testament** are references to cosmic eschatological war (over 20). The following index, follows the pattern in Index A except there is no need to separate historical eschatological war from cosmic eschatological war since the former is basically ignored in the **New Testament** except as a **SIGN** of cosmic eschatology.

Political War

Matthew 10:34-5.
Luke 3:14; 12:51-2; 22:36,38.
Hebrews 11:32-40.
James 4:1-5.

Spiritual War

Matthew 4:8-10.
Luke 4:5-8.
Romans 7:14-25.
I Corinthians 9:7; 14:8.
II Corinthians 10:3-5
I Thessalonians 5:8.
Ephesians 6:17..
I Timothy 1:18-19; 6:12.
Philemon 1:2.

James 4:1-5.
I Peter 2:11.

Eschatological War

Matthew 10:34-35; 22:1-14; 24:4-8.
Mark Ch.13.
Luke 12:51-2; 19:41; Ch.21.
Romans 16:20.
I Corinthians 14:8.
Ephesians 6:10-17.
I Thessalonians 5:1-2.
I Timothy 1:18-19; 6:12.
Revelations 12:7, 17; 9:16; 13:4,7-10; 16:16; 17:14; 19:11-19; 20:7-10.

APPENDIX D

INDEX TO MAJOR PASSAGES CONCERNING PEACE IN THE NEW TESTAMENT

A brief comparison with Appendix B indicates that the number of references to peace in the **New Testament** (approximately 150) are comparable to that in the **Hebrew Bible** (approximately 180). These numbers by themselves are deceptive for two reasons: first, the 27 books of the **New Testament** taken together are less than half the size of the 39 (or 24 arrangement in the Masoretic Text) books of the **Hebrew Bible**. Statistically of more significance are comparisons in specific categories: **Political Peace**--over 90 in the **Hebrew Bible** and less than 30 in the **New Testament**; **Spiritual Peace**--almost the same number of references in both Holy Books; and **Eschatological Peace**--over 40 in the **Hebrew Bible** and over 30 in the **New Testament**. Of even more significance, however, is the ration of references to war and references to peace within each revelation: the **Hebrew Bible** --twice as many passages concerning war as peace and the **New Testament**--five times as many references to peace as to war.

As in Appendix B, the references to peace are divided into four categories: as a salutation, political peace, spiritual peace, and eschatological peace.

Peace as a Salutation

Mark 5:35.
Luke 2:13, 29-32; 7:50; 8:48; 10:5; 24:36.
John 14:27; 20:21, 26.
Acts 15:33; 16:35.
Romans 15:33.
I Corinthians 1:3; 16:11.
II Corinthians 1:2; 13:11.
Galatians 1:3.
Ephesians 1:2; 6:23.
Philippians 1:2; 4:7, 9.

Colossians 1:2.
I Thessalonians 1:1.
II Thessalonians 1:2.
I Timothy 1:2.
II Timothy 1:2.
Titus 1:4.
Philemon 1:3.
I Peter 1:2; 5:14.
II Peter 1:2.
II John 1:3.
III John 1:15.
Jude 1:1.
Revelation 1:4.

Political Peace

Luke 2:13-14; 14:32.
Acts 9:31; 12:20; 14:2; 24:2.
Romans 12:18; 14:17-19.
I Corinthians 7:15; 14:32.
II Corinthians 13:11.
Ephesians 2:14-18; 6:14.
I Thessalonians 5:3, 13.
I Timothy 2:1-2.
II Timothy 2:22.
Titus 3:1.
Hebrews 12:14.
James 3:17.
I Peter 3:10-11.

Spiritual Peace

Mark 5:34-35.
Luke 2:13-14; 2:29-32; 7:50; 8:48; 24:36.
John 14:27; 16:33; 20:21, 26.
Acts 10:34-36.
Romans 2:10; 3:17; 5:1-5; 8:6; 14:17-19; 15:13.
I Corinthians 14:32.
II Corinthians 5:19; 13:11.
Galatians 5:22; 6:15.
Ephesians 2:14-18; 4:3; 6:14.
Philippians 4:7.
Colossians 1:19-20, 22; 3:15.
II Thessalonians 3:16.
II Timothy 2:22.

Hebrews 12:11; 13:20.
I Peter 3:10-11.

Eschatological Peace

Luke 2:13-14, 29-32; 19:41-2.
John 14:27; 16:31-33.
Acts 10:34-36.
Romans 2:9-10; 5:1-5; 14:17-19; 15:13; 16:20.
II Corinthians 13:11.
Ephesians 2:14-18; 6:10-14.
Philippians 4:7.
Colossians 1:19-22.
I Thessalonians 5:23.
Hebrews 12:13-14; 13:20.
Revelations 8:6; 12:10; 14:17.

* Passages which are listed in more than one category can be interpreted in various ways.

APPENDIX E

INDEX TO MAJOR PASSAGES CONCERNING WAR (JIHAD)
IN THE QUR'AN

The following index is divided into three dimensions of war (*jihad*): political war, spiritual war and eschatological war. These terms are used in basically the same way as they are in Appendices A and C. Most of them include the use of the term *jihad* (struggle, battle, fight) or a cognate. As the section on "Theologies of War" in Chapter Four indicates, the term *jihad* is so rich in meaning that the simple translations of "war," "battle," and "fight" do not do it justice. There is the further complication that according to most Muslim commentaries, there are four kinds of *jihad* in the **Qur'an**. Consequently many of the passages listed in the three categories below may involve one or more of the four kinds of *jihad*: the heart, the tongue, the hand and the sword. As before, *ayats* listed in more than one dimension can be interpreted in different ways.

A brief comparison with Appendices A (**Hebrew Bible**) and C (**New Testament**) indicates the following number of references:

Hebrew Bible:
> Political War: 190+
> Spiritual War: 6+
> Eschatological War: 30+

New Testament:
> Political War: 6-
> Spiritual War: 20+
> Eschatological War: 20+

Qur'an
> Political War: 60+

Spiritual War:	20+
Eschatological War	15+

In comparing these tables there are two parameters to keep in mind: (1) in size the **Qur'an** is approximately two-thirds the size of the **New Testament**; and (2) the three dimensions of war listed for the **Qur'an** can be further analyzed in terms of four kinds of *jihad.*

Political War

II: 190-91, 193 216, 217, 218, 244, 246, 249, 251, 253, 279.
III: 13, 121-22, 123, 142, 146, 149-180 (Uhud, especially 157, 166, 167).
IV: 71, 74, 75, 76, 90, 92, 95.
V: 36, 67.
VI: 151.
VIII: Badr (Whole sura, especially 1-19).
IX: 12-13, 25, 36-37.
XVII: 5, 33.
XXII: 39-40.
XXXIII: 9-20.
XLVII: 4.
XLVIII: 16, 22.
LVII: 25.
LXI: 4.
LXX: 28-29.

Spiritual War

II: 214, 216, 218, 244.
III: 146-7, 157, 169, 179 195.
IV: 74, 75, 76, 96.
VIII: 24, 28.
IX: 20.
XVII: 19.
XXIX: 5.
XLVII: 20, 35.
LXI: 4.
LXX: 28.
CIII: 3.

Eschatological War

II: 218.
III: 142, 169, 195.
IV: 74, 92, 96-96.
V: 36.

VIII: 67.
IX: 88-9, 100, 111, 120.
XLVII: 4.
LXI: 10-13.

APPENDIX F

INDEX TO MAJOR PASSAGES CONCERNING PEACE

IN THE QUR'AN

The following index is divided into the same categories as Appendices B (**Hebrew Bible**) and D (**New Testament**): peace as a salutation, political peace, spiritual peace and eschatological peace. Because the Hebrew *shalom* and the Arabic *salaam* etymologically have the same root, *SLM*, there is considerable overlap in the Hebrew conception of peace and the Muslim one.

A brief comparison with Appendices B and D indicates the following number of references concerning political, spiritual and eschatological peace:

Hebrew Bible:
Political Peace:	80+
Spiritual Peace:	50+
Eschatological Peace:	40+

New Testament:
Political Peace:	30+
Spiritual Peace:	50+
Eschatological Peace	30+

Qur'an:
Political Peace	30-
Spiritual Peace:	20+
Eschatological Peace:	25-

For those who think of the **Qur'an** as concentrating on war, a comparison of the tables in Appendices E and F reveals that there are nearly as many references to peace (75) as to war (85). Further, remembering that the **Qur'an** is approximately two-thirds the size of the **New Testament**, the number of references to peace in the **Qur'an** (75) is approximately the same number as those to peace in the **New Testament** (110 times 2/3 = 74).

Peace as a Salutation (representative examples)

VI: 54.
XI: 69.
XIV: 23.
XV: 46, 52.
XXV: 75.
XXXIII:56.
XXXVI:58.
XXXVII: 79, 109, 120, 130, 181.
XXXIX: 73.
LI: 25.
LVI: 90-1.
XCVII:5.

Political Peace

II: 11, 126, 182, 224.
IV: 35, 90.
V: 18, 30-33, 48.
VIII: 61-2, 72.
IX: 4.
XIV: 35.
XX: 47.
XXV: 63.
XXVIII: 55.
XLVIII: 18.
XLIX: 9.
LIX: 23.

Spiritual Peace

II: 208, 126.
V: 18, 30-33.
VI:54.
VII: 204-5.
IX: 40.
XI: 48.
XVII: 95.
XIX: 12-15, 47.
XXIV: 55.
XXV: 63.

XXVIII: 59.
L: 32-34.
LIX: 23.
LXXXIX: 27.
CIII:1-3.

Eschatological Peace

II:126.
VI: 127.
VII: 46.
IX: 88-9.
X: 10, 25.
XIII: 24.
XIV: 23.
XV: 46.
XVI:32.
XIX: 12-15, 33, 61-2.
XXIV: 55.
XXV: 75.
XXXVI: 55-8.
XXXIX: 73.
XLIV: 55.
L: 32-34.
LVI: 90-91.

* Almost without exception, references to eschatological peace are to the Garden, that is, the eternal life of Paradise.

BIBLIOGRAPHY

Albright, William F. **From the Stone Age to Christianity**, Doubleday Anchor Books, Garden City, NY, 1957.

Ali, A. Yusuf. **The Holy Qur'an**, text, translation and commentary by Ali, Amana Corporation, Brentwood, Maryland, 1983. Ali's translation has been re-printed by Tahrike Tarsde Quran, Inc..

The Anchor Bible Dictionary, ed. by David Freedmann, Doubleday, New York, NY, 1992.

Armstrong, Karen. **A History of God**, Ballentine Books, New York, NY, 1993.

_____. **Holy War: The Crusades and Their Impact on Today's World**, Doubleday, New York, NY, 1991.

_____. **Muhammad**, Harper Collins, San Francisco, CA, 1992.

Azzam, Abd-al-Rahman. **The Eternal Message of Muhammad**, trs. by E. Farah, Mentor Books, New York, NY, 1964.

Bainton, Roland H. **Christian Attitudes Toward War and Peace**, Abingdon Press, NY, 1960.

Barclay, William. **Barclay on Peace**, Presbyterian Peace Fellowship, New York, NY, 1983.

Bethmann, Erich W. "Muslim-Christian Relitionships," **The Muslim World**, vol.LI, #4, October 1961, 259-64.

466

Biblical Archeological Review, vol.22, no.4, July/August 1996, BAR Interviews William Dever, "Is This Man a Biblical Archeologist?," 30-64.

Bonhoeffer, Dietrich. **Letters and Papers from Prison**, Collins Fontana Books, London, United Kingdom, 1965.

Boyce, Mary. **Textual Sources for the Study of Zoroastrianism**, The University of Chicago Press, Chicago, IL, 1988.

Bultmann, Rudolph. **Theology of the New Testament**, trs. by Kendrick Grobel, Charles Scribner's Sons, New York, NY, 1955.

Camus, Albert. **Resistance, Rebellion and Death**, The Modern Library, New York, NY, 1963.

Chesnoff, Richard Z. "God's City," **U.S. News and World Report**, December 18, 1995, 60-70.

Cohon, Samuel S. "The Name of God, A Study in Rabbinic Theology, **Hebrew Union College Annual**, vol. XXIII, part 23, 579-604.

Conzelmann, Hans. **An Outline of the Theology of the New Testament**, Harper and Rowe Publishers, New York, NY, 1969.

Cragie, Peter C. **The Problem of War in the Old Testament**, William B. Eerdmans Publishers, Grand Rapids, MI, 1978.

Cross, Crescent, and Sword: The Justification and Limitation of War in Western and Islamic Tradition, ed. by J. Kelsay and J.T. Johnson, Greenwood Press, Westport, CN, 1990.

Dabbous, Maha. "John the Baptist--Part V," **Review of Religions**, vol.91, no.7, July 1996, 34-45.

Donner, Fred M. "The Sources of Islamic Conceptions of War," in Kelsay and Johnson's **Just War and Jihad: Historical and Theoretical Perspectives on War and Peace in Western and Islamic Tradition**, op. cit..

Durant, Will. **The Story of Civilization, vol. 4: The Age of Faith**, Simon and Schuster, New York, NY, 1950.

The Encyclopedia of Islam, vol.II, ed. by Pellat and Schacht, E.J. Bull, London, United Kingdom, 1983.

Ferguson, John. **War and Peace in the World's Religions**, Oxford University Press, New York, NY, 1978.

Forty Hadith Qudsi, trs. by E. Ibrahim and D. Johnson-Davies, Dar Al-Koran Al-Kareem (The Holy Koran Publishing House), Beirut, Lebanon, 1980.

Furnish, Victor Paul. "War and Peace in the New Testament," **Interpretation**, vol.XXXVIII, no.4, 363-79.

Geyer, Georgie Anne. "White House Literally 'For Rent'," **The Clarksville Leaf-Chronicle**, December 20, 1996, editorial page.

Good, Robert M. "The Just War in Ancient Israel," **Journal of Biblical Literature**, vol.104, Spring, 1985, 385-400.

Hammer, Paul H. "The Gift of Peace in the New Testament," **Peace, War and God's Justice**, ed. by T.D. Parker and B.J. Fraser, The United Church Publishing House, Toronto, Canada, 1989.

Hanson, Paul D. "War and Peace in the Hebrew Bible," **Interpretation**, vol.XXXVIII, no.4, 341-62.

Heschel, Abraham. **The Prophets**, Harper Torchbooks, New York, NY, 1962.

Hodgson, Marshall G.S. **The Venture of Islam, vol. 1: The Classical Age of Islam**, The University of Chicago Press, Chicago, IL, 1974.

_____. **The Venture of Islam, vol. 2: The Expansion of Islam in the Middle Periods**, op.cit..

_____. **The Venture of Islam, vol. 3: The Gunpowder Empires and Modern Times**, op.cit..

Hoffman, David. "A Soldier's Vision," **The Washington Post National Weekly Edition**, November 13-19, 1995, 24.

The Interpreter's Dictionary of the Bible, ed. by George Buttrick, Abgindon Press, Nashville, TN, 1962.

The International Standard Bible Encyclopedia, ed. by G.W. Bromiley, Eerdmans Publishing Co., Grand Rapids, MI, 1982.

468

Israel's Prophetic Tradition, ed. by Coggins, Phillips, and Knibb, Cambridge University Press, Cambridge, United Kingdom, 1984.

Jones, W.T. **A History of Western Philosophy: The Medieval Mind**, Harcourt Brace Jovanovich College Publishers, New York, NY, 1980.

Just War and Jihad: Historical and Theoretical Perspectives on War and Peace in Western and Islamic Tradition, ed. by J. Kelsay and J.T. Johnson, Greenwood Press, Westport, CN, 1991.

The Jerusalem Bible, Alexander Jones (general editor), Doubleday and Comany, Inc., Garden City, NY, 1966.

Khadduri, Majid. **War and Peace in the Law of Islam**, The John Hopkins Press, Baltimore, MD, 1955.

Kang, Sa-Moon. **Divine War in the Old Testament and in the Ancient Near East**, Walter de Gruyter, New York, NY, 1989.

Khouri, Rami G. "MacDonalds vs the Islamic holy warriors," **Jordan Times**, December 6, 1994.

Knibb, Michael. "Prophecy and the emergence of the Jewish apocalypses," **Israel's Prophetic Tradition**, ed. by Coggins, Phillips, and Knibb, Cambridge University Press, Cambridge, United Kingdom, 1984.

Lanagan, John. "The Western Moral tradition on War: Christian Theology and Warfare," **Just War and Jihad: Historical and Theoretical Perspectives on War and Peace in Western and Islamic Tradition**, op.cit., pp. 67-89.

Landy, Francis. "The Name of God and the Image of God and Man: A Response to David Clines," **Theology**, vol. LXXXIV, no. 699, May 1981, 164-70.

Lang, Bernhard. **Monotheism and the Prophetic Minority**, The Almond Press, Sheffield, United Kingdom, 1983.

Lasserre, Jean. **War and the Gospel**, trs. by Oliver Coburn, Herald Press, Scottdale, PA, 1962.

Lewis, Bernard. "The Roots of Muslim Rage," **Atlantic Monthly**, September 1990.

Lind, Millard C. **The Theology of Warfare in Ancient Israel**, Herald Press, Kitchener, Ontario, 1980.

Little, David. "'Holy War' Appeals and Western Christianity: A Reconsideration of Bainton's Approach," **Just War and Jihad: Historical and Theoretical Perspectives on War and Peace in Western Tradition and Islam**, op.cit., pp.121-139.

Marcel, Gabriel. **Being and Having**, trs. by K. Farrer, Harper Tourchbooks, New York, NY, 1965.

_____. **Creative Fidelity**, trs. by R. Rosthal, Noonday Press, New York, NY, 1964.

_____. **The Existential Background of Human Dignity**, Harvard University Press, Cambridge, MS, 1963.

_____. **Man Against Mass Society**, trs. by G.S. Fraser, Henry Regnery Co., Chicago, IL, 1967.

_____. **Problematic Man**, trs. by B. Thompson, Herder and Herder, New York, NY, 1967.

Matheson, Peter. **The Third Reich and the Christian Churches: A Documentary Account of Christian Resistance and Complicity During the Nazi Era**, Eerdman's Publishing Co., Grand Rapids, MI, 1981.

Martin, Richard C. "The Religious Foundations of War, Peace, and Statecraft in Islam," **Just War and Jihad: Historical and Theoretical Perspectives on War and Peace in Western and Islamic Tradition**, op. cit..

McGeary, Johanna. "Over Their Dead Bodies, **Time**, November 4, 1996, 53-4.

_____. "Yours, Mine, and Ours," **Time**, June 3, 1996.

Macquarrie, John. **The Concept of Peace**, Harper and Row, Publ., New York, NY, 1973.

Niditch, Susan. **War in the Hebrew Bible**, Oxford University Press, New York, NY, 1993.

Nuseibeh, Said and Grabar, Oleg. **The Dome of the Rock**, Rizzoli International Publishers, New York, NY, 1996.

Nysse, Richard. "Yahweh Is a Warrior," **Word and World**, vol.VII, No.2, Spring 1987, 192-201.

Peters, F.E. **Children of Abraham**, Princeton University Press, Princeton, NJ, 1984.

_____. **Judaism, Christianity, and Islam, volume 1: From Coventant to Community,** Princeton University Press, Princeton, NJ, 1990.

_____. **Judaism, Christianity, and Islam, volume 2: The Word and the Law and the People of God**, op.cit..

_____. **Judaism, Christianity, and Islam, volume 3: The Works of the Spirit**, op.cit..

von Rad, Gerhard. **Genesis**, trs. by John Marks, The Westminster Press, Philadelphia, PN, 1956.

_____. **Holy War in Ancient Israel**, trs. by M. Dawn, Eerdmans Publishers, Grand Rapids, MI, 1971.

Rahman, Fazlur. "Islam's Attitude toward Judaism,: **The MuslimWorld**, vol.LXXII, #1, Jan. 1982, 1-12.

_____. **Major Themes of the Qur'an**, Bibliotheca Islamica, Minneapolis, MN, 1989.

Report on Israeli Settlement in the Occupied Territories, vol.6, no.4, July 1996, "Netanyahu Promises a New Look for Israeli Policies," 1-7.

Rippin, Andrew and Knappert, Jan. **Textual Sources for the Study of Islam**, The University of Chicago Press, Chicago, IL, 1986.

Robson, James. "'Islam as a Term," **The Muslim World**, vol.XLIV, #2, April 1954, 101-09.

Rodinson, Maxime. **The Arabs**, trs. by Arthur Goldhammer, the University of Chicago Press, Chicago, IL, 1981.

Sales, Michael. "Who Can Write the Name of God? --From the Holiness of His Name to the Seriousness of All Words," **Communio (International Catholic Review)**, vol. XX. no. 1, Spring 1993, 26-48.

Schurer, Emil. **A History of the Jewish People in the Time Of Jesus Christ**, Scribner's Publishers, New York, NY, 1891.

Scott-Craig, T.S.K. **Christian Attitudes to War and Peace**, Oliver and Boyd, Edinburg, Scotland, 1938.

Smith, Mark S. **The Early History of God**, Harper and Row, Pub., San Francisco, CA, 1990.

Swain, J. Carter. **War, Peace, and the Bible**, Orbis Books, Maryknoll, N.Y, 1983.

Tabataba'i, Allamah Sayyid Muhammad Husayn. **Shi'ite Islam**, trs, by Seyyed H. Nasr, State University Press of New York, Albany, NY, 1997.

Textual Sources for the Study of Zoroastrianism, ed. by and trs. by Mary Boyce, The University of Chicago Press, Chcago. IL, 1986.

Theological Dictionary of the New Testament, ed. by G. Kittel, trs. by G. W. Bromiley, Eerdmans Publishing Co., Grand Rapids, MI, 1971.

Tillich, Paul. **Theology of Peace**, Westminster--John Knox Press, Louisville, KY, 1990.

UBS Triennial Translation Workshop, The "Names of God" Workshop, Victoria Falls, Zimbabwe, 8-12 May 1991 in **The Bible Translator**, vol. 43, no. 4, October 1992, 403-06.

Walzer, Michael. "The Idea of Holy War in Ancient Israel," **The Journal of Religious Ethics**, vol.20, no.2, Fall 1992, 215-28.

Watt, W. Montgomery. "Belief in a 'High God' in Pre-Islamic Mecca," **Journal of Semitic Studies**, vol. XVI, #1, Spring 1971, 35-40.

_____. **Muhammad: Prophet and Statesman**, Oxford University Press, New York, NY, 1964.

Wyngaard, J.N.M. "Prayer for Guidance: Origins, Historical background and Meaning," **The Muslim World**, vol.LVIII, #1, January 1968, 1-11.

INDEX

Before listing the index, it is important to understand the strategy used in its construction. First, because computer generated indices are mechanically driven and list all occurrences of a term, significant or otherwise, the following index is author generated. Thus, page numbers listed after included terms eliminate all insignificant uses. Second, in a study of war and peace in the **Hebrew Bible**, the **New Testament** and the **Qur'an**, certain terms that might be expected in an index are excluded because they occur hundreds of times throughout the manuscript. Excluded terms are the following: Hebrew, Jew, Judaism, Christian, Christianity, Muslim, Islam, **Hebrew Bible**, **New Testament**, **Qur'an**, **Hadith**, *Eloh-im*, *Yahweh*, *Al-Lah*, war (however, the index includes uses of the Hebrew *herem*, Greek *polemos* and Arabic *jihad*), and peace (the index includes uses of the Hebrew *shalom*, Greek *eirene* and Arabic *salaam*). Third, the index is divided into two sections: (1) Names and Historical Places; and, (2) Theological and Philosophical Concepts. Names of authors cited are not included in the index. Synonymous names--e.g., Jacob (Israel) or Satan (Iblis)--are listed together and synonymous or complimentary theological-philosophical terms--e.g., Heaven (Paradise, The Garden) or *jihad-mujihad*--are listed together. Finally, page numbers in the index reference footnote uses as well as those in the main text.

NAMES AND HISTORICAL PLACES

THEOLOGICAL AND PHILOSOPHICAL CONCEPTS

TORONTO STUDIES IN THEOLOGY